Food · Wine · The Italian Riviera & Genoa

FOOD

WINE

The Italian Riviera & Genoa

{ BY }

DAVID DOWNIE

PHOTOGRAPHS BY ALISON HARRIS

A Terroir Guide

THE LITTLE BOOKROOM

Book design:
Jessica Hische and Andy Evans / Louise Fili Ltd
Maps: Adrian Kitzinger

Library of Congress Cataloging-in-Publication Data

Downie, David.
Food, wine, the Italian Riviera, & Genoa : a terroir guide / by
David Downie ; photographs by Alison Harris.
p. cm.
Includes index.
ISBN 1-892145-64-2 (alk. paper)
1. Terroir—Italy—Riviera.
2. Terroir—Italy—Genoa.
3. Wine—Flavor and odor—Italy—Riviera.
4. Wine—Flavor and odor—Italy—Genoa.
5. Cookery—Italy—Riviera.
6. Cookery—Italy—Genoa. I. Title.
TP559.I8D69 2008
641.2'2094518—dc22
2008009192

Published by The Little Bookroom
435 Hudson Street, 3rd floor
New York NY 10014
editorial@littlebookroom.com
www.littlebookroom.com
Distributed by Random House, Random House International,
and in the UK by Signature Book Services.

ACKNOWLEDGEMENTS

The author and photographer wish to express their sincere thanks to Dr. Virgilio Pronzati, Anne Harris, Arch. Saverio Fera, Vittorio Bozzo, Anssi and Kaisa Blomstedt, and Mauro and Miriam Catalini, for their invaluable assistance and advice.

TABLE OF CONTENTS

· · · · · · · · · · · · · · · ·

INTRODUCTION   10

The Italian Riviera's Food and Wine • Italian Terroir Terminology • Tables with a View • The Numbers • Top Tables not in this Guidebook

PRACTICALITIES 22

CHAPTER 1: FOOD   25

Olive Oil • The Three DOP Classes of Oil • DOP, d'origine protetta • Fugassa/Focaccia • Savory Vegetable Tarts • Farinata • Green Cuisine • Testaroli • Chestnuts • Seafood • Anchovies • Basil and Pesto • Garlic • Cheese • Coffee, Café and Caffè • "Artisanal" Ice Cream

CHAPTER 2: WINE   47

Wines of the Eastern Riviera di Levante: Riviera di Levante Grape Varieties • Wines of the Western Riviera di Ponente: Riviera di Ponente Grape Varieties • *A Grab Bag of Remarkable Riviera Wines* • *Top Winemakers Overall, Riviera di Levante: From Luni to Genoa*

CHAPTER 3:
FROM TUSCANY AND EMILIA
TO LA SPEZIA—LA LUNIGIANA   57

Bocca di Magra • Castelnuovo Magra • Lerici • Montemarcello • Nicola di Ortonovo • Sarzana • *Top Olive Oil Makers of the Eastern Riviera di Levante* • Vincinella and Bolano • *Two Local Indigenous Grape Varieties*

CHAPTER 4: GREATER LA
SPEZIA AND CINQUE TERRE   83

Cinque Terre • Riomaggiore • Manarola • Corniglia • Vernazza • Monterosso • La Spezia • Levanto • Portovenere • *Organic, Shade-Grown Basil* • *Riviera Terraces*

CHAPTER 5:
VARESE LIGURE AND VAL DI VARA · 115

A Road Trip from La Spezia to Varese Ligure • Varese Ligure

CHAPTER 6:
SANTO STEFANO D'AVETO   123

A Road Trip from Chiavari to Santo Stefano d'Aveto • Santo Stefano d'Aveto

CHAPTER 7: SESTRI LEVANTE
TO CHIAVARI—IL CHIAVARESE   131

Carasco • Castiglione Chiavarese • Chiavari • Lavagna • Né and Conscenti di Né • Sestri Levante

CHAPTER 8: RAPALLO TO PORTOFINO
AND CAMOGLI TO SORI   169

Camogli • *Tables with a View and Good Food* • *The Tonnara of Camogli* • Portofino • Rapallo • Recco • Ruta and San Rocco di Camogli • San Massimo di Rapallo • Santa Margherita Ligure • Sori • *Wild Boar*

CHAPTER 9: GREATER GENOA   219

Genoa's Harbor and Medieval City • Genoa's Central Business and Nineteenth-Century Districts • Upper Genoa • *Ravioli and Pansôti* • Eastern Genoa • Western Genoa • *Genoese Pesto Mania and the Basil of Prà* • Suburban/Outlying Genoa • *Easter Savory Tart* • *Genoa's Pandolce Christmas Cake*

CHAPTER 10:
GREATER SAVONA—IL SAVONESE   287

Albissola Marina • Celle Ligure • Quiliano • Sassello • Savona • Stella • *Top Winemakers of Riviera di Ponente, from Savona to France* • *Top Olive Oil Makers of the Western Riviera di Ponente*

CHAPTER 11:
FINALE LIGURE—IL FINALESE 309

Calice Ligure • Calizzano • Finale Ligure and Finalborgo •
Loano • Noli • Varigotti

CHAPTER 12: ALBENGA TO ALASSIO 323

Alassio • Albenga • *The Garlic of Vessalico* • Bastia d'Albenga,
Leca d'Albenga • Villanova d'Albenga • An Olive Oil and Wine
Route: Albenga to Andora • *Top Wineries for Riviera Ligure di
Ponente DOC Pigato* • *Top Wineries for DOC Vermentino*

CHAPTER 13:
GREATER IMPERIA—L'IMPERIESE 351

Cervo-San Bartolomeo al Mare-Villa Faraldi • Diano Arentino-Castello-Gorleri-Marina-San Pietro • Imperia-Oneglia •
*Everything You Ever Wanted to Know about Olives, Oil and
the Mediterranean* • Imperia-Porto Maurizio • An Olive Oil
and Wine (and Gourmet Foods) Route: Imperia Province and
its Extended Hinterland

CHAPTER 14:
SAN REMO TO VENTIMIGLIA
AND THE BORDER WITH FRANCE 375

Bordighera • San Remo • Ventimiglia • *The Rock Villages of
the Western Riviera* • An Olive Oil and Wine (and Gourmet
Foods) Route: The Hinterland of Taggia, San Remo, Bordighera and Ventimiglia

FOOD AND WINE GLOSSARY.............400

INDEX OF PLACE NAMES...................412

INDEX OF VENUES..............................414

INDEX OF VENUES BY TYPE.............428

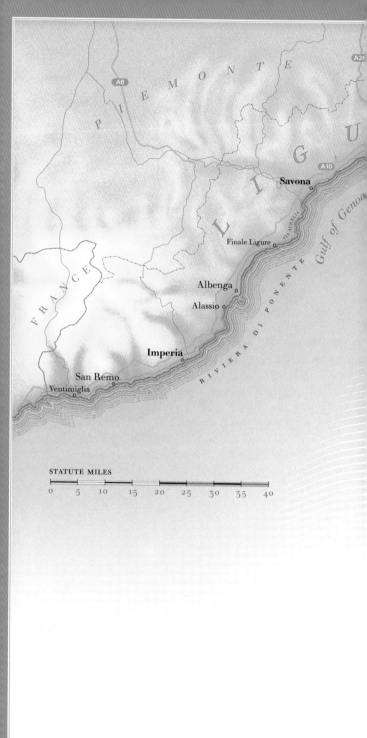

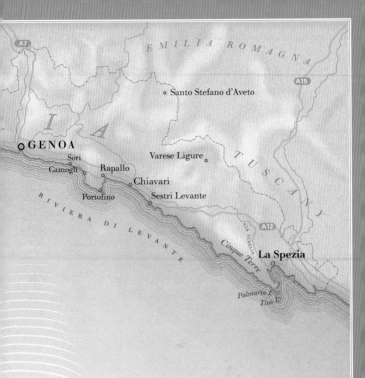

INTRODUCTION

....

*T*O MODEL THE ITALIAN RIVIERA IN THREE DIMENSIONS, TAKE 350 KILOMETERS—OVER 200 miles—of jagged, mountainous Mediterranean coastline, bend it into a boomerang, carve a thousand valleys and as many peaks from it and sprinkle generously with gaily painted villages, vineyards, olive groves and pocket-sized fishing ports. Add a fourth dimension by filling the air with the scent of basil and baking focaccia.

The region's official name is Liguria, because at least some of its 1.6 million inhabitants are descendants of the Ligurian tribes of pre-Roman Antiquity. Certainly, Ligurians are Italian, but regionalism remains strong. As statesman Giovanni Giolitti said when Italy was unified in 1860, "We've made Italy, now we must make the Italians." It's an ongoing process. For the time being, the culture, dialects and above all the food of the Riviera are still distinctly *ligure* or *genovese*. "Ligurian" and "Genoese" are largely interchangeable, broadly meaning "of Genoa and the Italian Riviera." Pesto *alla genovese* is a prime example. It's made everywhere in the region—and around the world—but like many Riviera recipes is identified with the capital city. That's because Genoa adopted the much older way of making pesto—using mixed herbs and nuts, garlic, pine nuts, olive oil and farmstead cheese—and refined it, substituting basil for parsley or marjoram, *parmigiano reggiano* or *pecorino sardo* for rustic, homemade curds and pine nuts for walnuts. Adopt-and-refine has long been Genoa's *modus operandi*, taking roughshod regional bumpkins and turning them into city slickers ready for export.

Genoa may no longer be Italy's powerhouse, but it was among the richest and most influential maritime republics of the western world for many centuries, home to Columbus and the bankers who underwrote the Spanish conquest of the Americas, not to mention many of Italy's richest clans. In a variety of incarnations, including a Dogate, similar to Venice's, the Republic of Genoa lasted for 1,000 years, from the Middle Ages to the early nineteenth century. During that time, Genoa ruled the whole of Liguria, plus Corsica and several Mediterranean colonies. The city's influence is still widely felt, especially in the region's eastern provinces. That's why it's said the Riviera's inhabitants speak "Genoese" dialect and eat "Genoese" food. Happily, it's not that simple.

The Italian Riviera borders on Tuscany, Emilia, Piedmont and France, and is divided into four administrative provinces. Starting from the east, they are La Spezia, Genoa, Savona and Imperia. The eastern Riviera is defined as running from Tuscany to Genoa, and known among locals as the "Riviera di Levante," because *levante* means "rising," as in rising sun. The western Riviera, from Genoa to France, is the "Riviera di Ponente," because *ponente* means "setting." Genoa, crowning and bridging the two, belongs to both and neither. Despite Italy's unification, it remains a distinctive, proud city-state.

Regionalism and particularism enhance the diverse food cultures and cooking of the Riviera. Like the region's dialects, its wines and dishes differ from village to village, valley to valley, from Levante to Ponente and from coast to interior. The unsung and sparsely populated hinterland of Liguria is called *l'entroterra*, and covers nine-tenths of the region's land area. Each regional sub-unit is convinced its products and foodways are authentic, the best of Liguria. You might call this culinary *campanilismo*. The term usually describes the fractious Italian conviction that, centered on the neighborhood *campanile*, "my parish knows best." *Campanilismo* is shared by many parts of Italy, and finds high expression among Liguria's isolated worlds, separated by a few miles of land or sea.

The result is that, strictly speaking, no single Riviera cuisine exists. The region merely shares a number of ingredients, techniques and penchants—the paradoxical veneration for vegetables and herbs, for instance. Liguria is a narrow strip of land, and just about everyone on it stares out to sea, yet residents often shun fresh fish, preferring chard, chestnuts, mushrooms, rabbit and boar—and pesto, vegetables and field greens. Air-dried cod and salted anchovies are the cult fish. Enormous quanitites of sea bass and swordfish are consumed on the Riviera, but the biggest eaters of them are the free-spending Milanese. They consider Liguria their playground and beach resort, conveniently located just ninety minutes by car from landlocked Milan.

The hit-list of regional Riviera foods includes *farinata*, the chickpea-flour tart, focaccia plain or topped with sautéed white onions, rockfish and anchovies in soups, stews and tarts, plus pesto, ravioli, cod, savory vegetable tarts and stuffed vegetables, and, for dessert, *pandolce* cake studded with pine nuts and candied fruit, or simple wine-dipping cookies and lightly sweet dry biscuits.

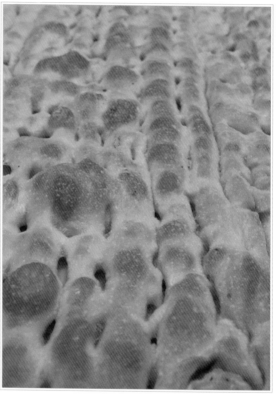

Lightness is the rule in Riviera cooking, reflecting the region's ingredients. The two favorite herbs are basil, which is picked when pale, young, tender and lemony; and marjoram, used fresh and still musky-sweet. Parsley, thyme and rosemary are also popular, and show up in scores of recipes. Herbs are an important component of so many Riviera dishes that it could be said they define Ligurian cooking, distinguishing it from other Italian cuisines. Terms such as "gutsy," "buttery," "meaty" and "rich" rarely apply. "Delicate," "refined," "ethereal" nearly always do. Riviera food distills the essence of the Mediterranean.

By and large, the traditional wines of the Riviera are also light in body, dry and fruity, without being fruit-forward, high in alcohol or redolent of oak. Sea breezes cool the Riviera's terraced vineyards, some of them perched 1,000 vertical feet above the Mediterranean. So while there's no lack of sun or heat to ripen the grapes, they benefit from cool evenings and salty mists, similar to those of California's coastal growing areas.

As with the region's variegated cooking, the watchword with Riviera wines is *tipicità*, meaning trueness to type, an essential component of *terroir*. There is no such thing as Ligurian Chardonnay, and no ho-hum predictability to the grapes grown and wines made (though some Riviera winemakers are now targeting export markets and producing New World-style wines). Most Ligurian grape varieties have been here since the Middle Ages, perhaps earlier. It's widely believed, for instance, that the Vernaccia of San Gimignano in Tuscany actually came from Vernazza, one of the Cinque Terre's five villages. Unexpectedly for a region with refreshingly light wines, the Cinque Terre also produces minute quantities of one of the country's greatest dessert wines, Sciacchetrà.

The Numbers

Surface area: 5,418 square km	*Average size of farm:* 1.46 hectares (3.7 acres)
Population: 1,621,000	
Population density: 299 inhabitants per square km	*Cattle:* 16,468
	Buffaloes: 20
Regional capital: Genoa, pop. 632,000	*Porkers:* 1,477
	Sheep: 17,717
Provincial capitals: Genoa; Imperia: pop. 40,300	*Goats:* 7,672
La Spezia: pop. 95,100 Savona: pop. 61,900	*Horses:* 2,585
Farms: 43,739	*Fowl:* 277,338

Source: Liguria Regional Government, www.regione.liguria.it

ITALIAN *TERROIR* TERMINOLOGY

Where the French say *terroir* to designate authentic, unadulterated foods and wines tied to a region's soil and seasons, the Italians use several terms. *Tipico* identifies something as coming from a specific area; *prodotti tipici* and *piatti tipici* are what we would call local or regional specialty foods and dishes.

Tipicità is a buzz word among wine lovers, especially those who favor native or heirloom grape varieties (*vitigni autoctoni*) and highly typified, old-fashioned wines made with native yeasts, using large, seasoned oak barrels and cement-lined vats, or stainless steel. The spreading use of selected, high-performance yeasts and new-oak casks results in what Italians call *vini tecnici*—technical wines, the opposite of *terroir* wines.

Genuino means both genuine and authentic, and is often used to describe cooking, wines and foodways. *Naturale* is a buzz word in the ice cream world, designating ice creams that are handmade from scratch using only fresh, wholesome ingredients (i.e. no concentrates, colorings, artificial flavorings, preservatives, thickeners, emulsifiers or other industrial or semi-industrial products).

Cucina casalinga means home cooking. Its opposite is *cucina creativa* or *cucina innovativa*, what we would call nouvelle cuisine, *cuisine d'auteur* or fusion cooking.

TABLES WITH A VIEW

The Italian Riviera is among Italy's top tourist attractions, drawing millions of visitors each year. Italians (Milanese and Turinese) account for the highest number of tourists, followed by the English, Germans, Scandinavians and Americans. In July and August, it's difficult to get great service and excellent food in resort areas on the coastal strip, because of the crowds. Most popular of all are seaside restaurants with a view, and the general rule is, the more spectacular the panorama, the less attention is paid by chefs and diners to what's on the plate. Some restaurants, *trattorie* and *osterie* with a remarkable view are listed in these pages. By and large, however, serious-food restaurants, and eateries of all kinds popular with local food lovers, are up and away from tourist crowds. The great Italian tourism cities Rome, Venice and Florence lead double lives—one for natives, another for visitors—but no other Italian region in its entirety is as clinically schizophrenic as Liguria.

TOP TABLES NOT
IN THIS GUIDEBOOK

. . . .

THE ITALIAN RIVIERA HAS MANY EXCELLENT, SOPHISTICATED AND SOME INTERNATIONally celebrated restaurants. Most are not included in this guidebook. These establishments may well be gastronomic pilgrimage sites worthy of toques, stars, bow ties, snails and other symbols of distinction. Some offer a sampling of "updated" or "personalized" Ligurian cooking. However, when the authenticity, regional tipicity, and simplicity of the cooking are outweighed by the restaurant's décor or setting and, above all, when the bravura of chefs focuses on innovative, creative or international cooking, the establishment does not correspond to the spirit of terroir. Restaurants of this kind are listed below, by area. Most are extremely expensive (70 to 90 euros per person without beverages), some are astronomically expensive (over 90 euros per person without beverages).

FROM TUSCANY AND EMILIA TO LA SPEZIA—LA LUNIGIANA

Capitelli

PIAZZA MATTEOTTI 38, SARZANA ✦ TEL: 0187 622892
DINNER ONLY WEEKDAYS, LUNCH WEEKENDS *and*
HOLIDAYS, CLOSED MONDAY *and* 3 WEEKS IN FEBRUARY
EXPENSIVE

Locanda dell'Angelo

VIALE XXV APRILE 60, AMEGLIA
TEL: 0187 64391 ✦ WWW.PARACUCCHILOCANDA.IT
CLOSED MONDAY *from* SEPTEMBER *to* JUNE *and* JANUARY
EXTREMELY EXPENSIVE

Locanda delle Tamerici

VIA LITORANEA 106, LOCALITÀ FIUMARETTA , AMEGLIA
TEL: 0187 64262 ✦ WWW.LOCANDADELLETAMERICI.COM
CLOSED MONDAY, TUESDAY *and* 1 WEEK IN OCTOBER,
and FROM CHRISTMAS *to* MID JANUARY
EXTREMELY EXPENSIVE

Locanda Miranda

VIA FIASCHERINO 92, LOCALITÀ TELLARO, LERICI
TEL: 0187 968130 ✦ WWW.LOCANDAMIRANDA.COM
CLOSED MONDAY AND FROM DECEMBER 15 *to* JANUARY 15
EXTREMELY EXPENSIVE

SESTRI LEVANTE TO
CHIAVARI—IL CHIAVARESE

Ca' Peo

STRADA PANORAMICA VIA DEI CADUTI 80, LEIVI
TEL: 0185 319696 ✦ WWW.CAPEO.INFO
CLOSED TUESDAY *and* WEDNESDAY LUNCH *and* MONDAY
EXTREMELY EXPENSIVE

RAPALLO, PORTOFINO PENINSULA,
CAMOGLI TO SORI

Ardiciocca

VIA MARAGLIANO 17, SANTA MARGHERITA LIGURE
TEL: 0185 281312 ✦ WWW.ARDICIOCCA.IT
CLOSED MONDAY ✦ EXTREMELY EXPENSIVE

La Terrazza

HOTEL SPLENDIDO, VIALE BARATTA 16
TEL: 0185 267801 ✦ CLOSED NOVEMBER THROUGH MARCH
EXTREMELY EXPENSIVE

Oca Bianca

VIA XXV APRILE 21, SANTA MARGHERITA LIGURE
TEL: 0185 288411 ✦ DINNER ONLY JULY *and* AUGUST,
CLOSED MONDAY, LUNCH WEEKDAYS EXCEPT FRIDAY, *and*
EARLY JANUARY *to* MID FEBRUARY ✦ VERY EXPENSIVE

Splendido Mare

VIA MARE 2, PORTOFINO ✦ TEL: 0185 267802
EXTREMELY EXPENSIVE

Zeffirino Portofino Kulm

VIALE BERNARDO GAGGINI 23, RUTA DI CAMOGLI
TEL: 0185 7361 ✦ WWW.PORTOFINOKULM.IT
EXTREMELY EXPENSIVE

GREATER GENOA

Antica Osteria del Bai

VIA QUARTO 8, GENOA-QUARTO
TEL: 010 387478 ✦ WWW.OSTERIADELBAI.IT
CLOSED MONDAY ✦ EXPENSIVE

Baldin

PIAZZA TAZZOLI 20R, SESTRI PONENTE
TEL: 010 653 1400 ✦ WWW.RISTORANTEBALDIN.COM
CLOSED SUNDAY *and* MONDAY ✦ EXPENSIVE

Da Giacomo

CORSO ITALIA 1R, GENOA
TEL: 010 311041 ✦ WWW.RISTORANTEDAGIACOMO.IT
CLOSED SUNDAY ✦ EXTREMELY EXPENSIVE

Edilio

CORSO A. DE STEFANIS 104R, GENOA
TEL: 010 880501 ✦ CLOSED SUNDAY DINNER *and* MONDAY
MODERATE *to* EXPENSIVE

Franca

VICO DELLA LEPRE 4R, GENOA
TEL: 010 247 4473 ✦ CLOSED MONDAY *and* MID
AUGUST *to* EARLY SEPTEMBER ✦ EXPENSIVE

Gran Gotto

VIALE BRIGATE BISAGNO 69R, GENOA
TEL: 010 583 6400 ✦ DINNER ONLY, CLOSED
SUNDAY *and* AUGUST ✦ EXTREMELY EXPENSIVE

La Bitta nella Pergola

VIA CASAREGIS 52R, GENOA ✦ TEL: 010 588543
CLOSED SUNDAY DINNER, MONDAY, THE FIRST WEEK
IN JANUARY *and* AUGUST ✦ EXTREMELY EXPENSIVE

Papageno

VIA ASSAROTTI 60R, GENOA
TEL: 010 839 2999 ✦ WWW.RISTORANTE-PAPAGENO.COM
DINNER ONLY, CLOSED WEEKENDS *and* AUGUST
MODERATE *to* EXPENSIVE

Saint Cyr

PIAZZA MARSALA 8, GENOA ✦ TEL: 010 886897

CLOSED WEEKENDS ✦ VERY EXPENSIVE

Zeffirino

VIA XX SETTEMBRE 20, GENOA

TEL: 010 591990 ✦ WWW.RISTORANTEZEFFIRINO.IT

EXTREMELY EXPENSIVE

GREATER SAVONA—IL SAVONESE

A Spurcacciun-a

HOTEL MARE, VIA NIZZA 89, SAVONA

TEL: 019 264065 ✦ WWW.MAREHOTEL.IT

CLOSED WEDNESDAY *and in* AUGUST

EXTREMELY EXPENSIVE

Antico Arco

PIAZZA LAVAGNOLA 26R, SAVONA

TEL: 019 820938 ✦ WWW.RISTORANTEANTICOARCO.IT

DINNER ONLY, CLOSED SUNDAY ✦ VERY EXPENSIVE

Antico Genovese

CORSO COLOMBO 70, VARAZZE

TEL: 019 96482 ✦ WWW.ANTICOGENOVESE.IT

CLOSED MONDAY LUNCH *and* SUNDAY, *and* ONE WEEK EACH
IN FEBRUARY *and* OCTOBER ✦ EXTREMELY EXPENSIVE

Fundegu

VIA SPOTORNO 87, ALBISOLA SUPERIORE

TEL: 019 480341 ✦ WWW.FUNDEGU.COM

DINNER ONLY, CLOSED WEDNESDAY ✦ VERY EXPENSIVE

La Fornace di Barbablù

VIA LAZIO 11A, LOCALITÀ SANT'ERMETE, VADO LIGURE

TEL: 019 888535 ✦ WWW.LAFORNACEDIBARBARBLU.COM

CLOSED MONDAY *and*, IN WINTER, TUESDAY, *and* 2
WEEKS IN OCTOBER ✦ EXTREMELY EXPENSIVE

Mse' Tuta

LOCALITÀ MONASTERO 8, MILLESIMO ✦ TEL: 019 564226

DINNER ONLY, CLOSED WEDNESDAY *and* 2 WEEKS IN JANUARY

VERY EXPENSIVE

Quintilio

VIA GRAMSCI 23, ALTARE ✦ TEL: 019 58000
DINNER ONLY *except* SUNDAY, CLOSED MONDAY
EXPENSIVE

FINALE LIGURE—IL FINALESE

Claudio

VIA XXV APRILE 37, BERGEGGI
TEL: 019 859750 ✦ WWW.HOTELCLAUDIO.IT
DINNER ONLY, CLOSED MONDAY ✦ EXTREMELY EXPENSIVE

DOC

VIA VITTORIO VENETO 1, BORGIO VEREZZI
TEL: 019 611477 ✦ WWW.RISTORANTEDOC.IT
CLOSED MONDAY *and* TUESDAY *from* SEPTEMBER *to* JUNE
VERY EXPENSIVE

Lilliput

REGIONE ZUGLIENO 49, FRAZIONE VOZE, NOLI
TEL: 019 748009 ✦ DINNER ONLY, CLOSED MONDAY, 3 WEEKS
IN JANUARY *and* THE LAST 3 WEEKS IN NOVEMBER
VERY EXPENSIVE

Muraglia-Conchiglia d'Oro

VIA AURELIA 133, VARIGOTTI
TEL: 019 698015 ✦ WWW.VARIGOTTI.IT
OPEN DAILY IN SUMMER, CLOSED TUESDAY *and* WEDNESDAY
THE REST OF THE YEAR, *and* 1 MONTH *from* MID JANUARY *to*
MID FEBRUARY ✦ EXTREMELY EXPENSIVE

ALBENGA TO ALASSIO

Baia del Sole

CORSO MARCONI 30, ALASSIO ✦ TEL: 0182 641814
DINNER ONLY, CLOSED MONDAY *and* TUESDAY
EXTREMELY EXPENSIVE

La Prua

PASSEGGIATA BARACCA 25, ALASSIO
TEL: 0182 642557 ✦ WWW.LAPRUADIALASSIO.IT
CLOSED WEDNESDAY *and* NOVEMBER
EXTREMELY EXPENSIVE

Palma

VIA CAVOUR 5, ALASSIO ✦ TEL: 0182 640314

CLOSED WEDNESDAY *and* SECOND HALF OF

JANUARY *and* NOVEMBER ✦ EXTREMELY EXPENSIVE

Il Rosmarino de l'Hotel la Meridiana

VIA AI CASTELLI 11, GARLENDA ✦ TEL: 0182 580271

CLOSED MONDAY LUNCHTIME ✦ EXTREMELY EXPENSIVE

GREATER IMPERIA—L'IMPERIESE

Agrodolce

VIA DES GENEYS 34/CALATA CUNEO 25, IMPERIA-ONEGLIA

TEL: 0183 293702 ✦ WWW.RISTORANTEAGRODOLCE.IT

CLOSED SUNDAY LUNCH *and* WEDNESDAY, LATE

MAY *and* IN NOVEMBER ✦ EXTREMELY EXPENSIVE

Lanterna Blu

VIA SCARINCIO 32, MARINA DI PORTO MAURIZIO,

IMPERIA-PORTO MAURIZIO ✦ TEL: 0183 63859

CLOSED WEDNESDAY ✦ EXTREMELY EXPENSIVE

Salvo Cacciatori

VIA VIEUSSEUX 12, IMPERIA-ONEGLIA

TEL: 0183 293763 ✦ CLOSED SUNDAY DINNER *and* MONDAY

EXPENSIVE

San Giorgio

VIA A. VOLTA 19, CERVO

TEL: 0183 400175 ✦ WWW.RISTORANTESANGIORGIO.NET

CLOSED MONDAY DINNER *and* TUESDAY, *with* SEASONAL

VARIATIONS, *and the* SECOND HALF *of* JANUARY

EXTREMELY EXPENSIVE

SAN REMO TO VENTIMIGLIA
AND THE BORDER WITH FRANCE

Baia Beniamin

CORSO EUROPA 63, LOCALITÀ GRIMALDI INFERIORE,

VENTIMIGLIA ✦ TEL: 0184 38002 ✦ WWW.BAIABENIAMIN.IT

CLOSED SUNDAY DINNER *and* MONDAY

ASTRONOMICALLY EXPENSIVE

Balzi Rossi

VIA BALZI ROSSI 2, FRONTIERA SAN LUDOVICO,
VENTIMIGLIA ✦ TEL: 0184 38132 ✦ CLOSED TUESDAY
LUNCH *and* MONDAY ✦ ASTRONOMICALLY EXPENSIVE

Carletto

VIA VITTORIO EMANUELE 339, BORDIGHERA
TEL: 0184 261725 ✦ CLOSED WEDNESDAY
ASTRONOMICALLY EXPENSIVE

Conchiglia

VIA LUNGOMARE 37, ARMA DI TAGGIA
TEL: 0184 43169 ✦ CLOSED THURSDAY LUNCH *and*
WEDNESDAY, *and* 2 WEEKS EACH *in* JUNE *and* SEPTEMBER
ASTRONOMICALLY EXPENSIVE

Giappun

VIA MAONAIRA 7, VALLECROSIA ✦ TEL: 0184 250560
CLOSED THURSDAY LUNCH *and* WEDNESDAY
and NOVEMBER ✦ ASTRONOMICALLY EXPENSIVE

La Via Romana

VIA ROMANA 57, BORDIGHERA
TEL: 0184 266681 ✦ WWW.LAVIAROMANA.IT
CLOSED THURSDAY LUNCH *and* WEDNESDAY,
and 1 WEEKEND MARCH *and* 3 WEEKS IN FALL
ASTRONOMICALLY EXPENSIVE

Paolo e Barbara

VIA ROMA 47, SAN REMO
TEL: 0184 531653 ✦ WWW.PAOLOBARBARA.IT
CLOSED WEDNESDAY *and* THURSDAY, IN
JULY OPEN ONLY FRIDAY *and* WEEKENDS
ASTRONOMICALLY EXPENSIVE

PRACTICALITIES

....

The four Riviera provinces, taken east to west, are officially abbreviated as follows: La Spezia = SP, Genova = GE, Savona = SV, Imperia = IM.

NORMAL RETAIL BUSINESS HOURS ARE MONDAY THROUGH SATURDAY 8/8:30AM to 12:30/1pm and 3:30/4pm to 7/7:30pm; few retail businesses stay open during lunch time.

Opening hours for bakeries and fish shops vary widely, sometimes starting early in the morning (6/6:30am). Wine shops and wine bars often open late (10/11am) and close late (8/9pm). Coffee shops (*caffè*) open early (7am), and remain open through lunch time, closing at 7/8pm. Restaurants seat guests for lunch from 12:30/1pm to 2/2:30pm; dinner is from 7:30pm to 9/10pm.

Important: Nine in ten businesses are closed Sundays and a half day or full day once a week, usually Monday, Tuesday or Wednesday, sometimes Thursday. Most businesses close for vacation for several weeks or a month, usually in fall/winter. Off-season hours are often shorter than spring/summer hours, particularly in resort areas. Unusual opening or closing hours of businesses are noted in guidebook entries.

Addresses

....

In Genoa and some other Riviera cities and towns, a double-numeration system exists. Certain Genoese *palazzi* cover an entire city block. Black numbers are "normal" numbers for buildings. Red numbers, marked with a red r or R, designate individual ground-floor street doors within a building. Confusingly, some addresses are given in black numbering, others in red, yet others in black and red.

The Via Aurelia

....

A two-lane coast highway, it runs the length of the region. The name changes locally dozens of times. Driving instructions in this guidebook are given starting at this highway.

The divisions in this guidebook reflect the geographical, cultural and/or administrative divisions of the Liguria region. For ease of use, they are listed from east to west. The twelve divisions are:

From Tuscany and Emilia to La Spezia – La Lunigiana
Greater La Spezia and Cinque Terre
Varese Ligure and Val di Vara
Santo Stefano d'Aveto
Sestri Levante to Chiavari – Il Chiavarese
Rapallo to Portofino and Camogli to Sori
Greater Genoa
Greater Savona – Il Savonese
Finale Ligure – Il Finalese
Albenga to Alassio
Greater Imperia – L'Imperiese
San Remo to Ventimiglia and the border with France

Listings
. . . .

Listings within each of the twelve divisions are alphabetical; an alphabetical index of place names, and thematic indexes, are found at the back of the book.

Prices
. . . .

For a three-course meal, per person, without beverages:
Inexpensive = under 25 euros; Moderate = 25 to 35 euros;
Expensive = 35 to 45 euros; Very Expensive = over 45 euros.

CHAPTER 1

....

Food

OLIVE OIL

....

ESIGNATING OLIVE OIL "EXTRA VIRGIN" IS NO LONGER A GUARANTEE OF EXCELLENCE, IT is merely a starting point. Any olive oil that does not make the extra virgin grade should be avoided. The best Ligurian olive oils are extra virgin, cold-pressed, centerfuged and decanted using only mechanical means—no chemicals or ultra-heat processing—from slightly immature, hand-picked olives as free as possible of defects and rot. Hot-pressing and re-filtering or heating oil or olive skins and waste to extract more oil, sometimes with the addition of solvents, are processes common in the making of all but virgin oils, and lower the quality below the point of reason. According to Italian law, an artisanal mill, called a *frantoio*, can use only mechanical means to make oils, whereas an *oleificio* can use solvents to refine or rectify oils.

These days it's fashionable to market top olive oils as *primu raggiu* (the spelling varies) or *mosto*, meaning, theoretically, they're the free run-off, or first oils skimmed off the top of the first light cold-pressing—the cream of the crop. A handful of oil makers still use stone wheels, coconut-fiber or hemp mats, vertical hydraulic presses and wooden or ceramic-lined vats, where the run-off and skimming techniques are possible. In reality, however, the vast majority of premium olive oil makers use high-tech, air- or water-cooled continuous crusher-presses with integrated centerfuges. The olives go in one end, the oil comes out the other. This isn't necessarily a bad thing. There's less oxidation because the processing is quick, in a closed environment, and the machinery can be thoroughly sterilized and therefore is less likely than traditional equipment to develop fungi. There's

also less effluent.

The gooseberry-sized Taggiasca and Lavagnina olives of the Italian Riviera produce a remarkably light, fruity, sweet oil that matches the region's delicate cooking style. The most typical flavors and scents of Ligurian oils evoke almonds, pine nuts, fresh-cut grass, wildflowers, oregano, citrus, raw bell peppers and chamomile.

Ancient Greek colonists probably planted the region's first domesticated trees; the Romans turned Liguria into one of Italy's most prolific olive-growing areas. With the collapse of the Empire, monastic orders took over. Around 1000 AD, monks in the Lavagna area, on the eastern Riviera, developed the Lavagnina variety of olive, while other monks in the Taggia area, on the western Riviera, cultivated the Taggiasca. Both are excellent varieties, are closely related and make up the bulk of Liguria's olive trees.

This isn't the whole story. As with wine and food, Liguria's olive culture is complex and characterized by highly local varieties, which engender a culture of *tipicità*. Wherever the monks went, they took olive trees with them, perfecting sub-varieties to thrive in specific microclimates, from the Island of Tino and Palmaria to Portofino, Varigotti and Dolceacqua. These lesser-known but excellent heirloom Riviera varieties are many, sounding when recited not so much like a Gregorian chant, but rather the *Catalogue Aria* from Mozart's *Don Giovanni*. Taken alphabetically they include Arnasca (also called Pignola), Castelnovina, Colombaia (alias Colombara, Culombera), Cozzanina, Cozzanone, Fiandola, Finalina, Gentile, Lantesco, Leccino, Lizzone, Merlina (aka Mortegna, Mortina), Moraiolo, Mortellina, Nostrale, Olivastro, Olivastrone, Olivella, Peranzana, Prempesa, Premice, Razzola, Rossese and Toso. Cross-breeds and unidentified cultivars related to the above are commonly called *frantoio*, though some olive growers claim that gene mapping shows the *frantoio* of Liguria to be a sub-species closely related to the multifarous *frantoio* group of varieties of Tuscany and central Italy. Reflecting this diversity, there are hundreds of ways to say both olive and olive tree in Liguria's many dialects.

As the Repulic of Genoa lost power and its overseas possessions, it concentrated on local farm products, turning Liguria into Italy's top olive oil-making area, starting in the 1700s. In the 1950s postwar economic boom, following a devastating frost in 1954, many Ligurian olive groves were destroyed, the land tranformed and used for building vacation homes, tourist hotels and cut-flower or live-plant nurseries. Since the 1990s, the region is once again considered among Italy's most distinguished, though not its most productive. Yields are low, because of the steep, terraced terrain and the nature of the olive varieties. That's why Ligurian oils are among the country's most expensive. Small harvests and high production costs mean top-quality Riviera olives cost twice as much as their Tuscan equivalent, and ten times that of north African blending olives (imported primarily from Morocco), which constitute about half the volume of most factory-produced European oils, including extra virgin oils.

With few exceptions, the most prized Ligurian olives are grown on hillside terraces near the olive-tree line, which traditionally runs at about 2,400 feet above sea level on the western Riviera near France, and 1,600 feet on the cooler eastern Riviera near

Tuscany. As a general rule, the higher the grove, the more delicate and subtle in flavor the oil produced from its olives. Mountain groves were long free of the Mediterranean olive fly, *dacus oleae*, whose larvae feed off the fruit and cause rot and therefore increase acidity. Global warming and the misuse of pesticides have helped propagate the fly; winters are no longer cold enough to kill its larvae, and chemical treatments have largely killed the beneficial pests that ate the larvae. The fly has spread inland. No region is free of it.

Traditionally, the olive harvest season runs from November through January, but climate change has forced many growers to start picking as early as the first or second week of October. This has influenced the color and flavor of many oils.

Orange, yellow and green nets stretch like hammocks under the groves, which cover thousands of seaside and interior valley terraces. The nets are picturesque, but the best oil is not made with the olives that fall into them (and rot or oxidize); premium oils are made exclusively from olives that are picked or knocked off the trees and rushed to the mill before they can get hot and begin to ferment.

Fall is the best time to visit the dozens of small-scale olive oil mills which operate seasonally on both sides of the Riviera; large industrial oil makers are concentrated on the western shore, primarily in the Province of Imperia, and some offer product tasting rooms and retail boutiques open year-round. While freshly extracted, spicy "new oil" (*mosto* or *olio nuovo*) can be excellent, reputable oil makers allow the majority of their oils to settle and mature in dark storage areas, and sell them when they are at their mellowest; for top oils, the DOP-certification process can also take weeks or months. Be warned: some unscrupulous olive oil mills sell oil leftover from last year's pressing as "new oil," and these millers also sometimes blend non-Ligurian oils into the mix. You should always demand oil freshly pressed from 100 percent local, Ligurian olives—better if they're DOP—and stick to the reputable firms listed here or belonging to the Consorzio per la Tutela dell'Olio Extra Vergine di Oliva DOP Riviera Ligure, an industry association that, while not perfect, does uphold quality. Many of the region's best olive growers and artisanal oil makers do not belong to the consortium, but all consortium members make or sell high-quality oils.

THE THREE DOP "OLIO EXTRAVERGINE DI OLIVA RIVIERA LIGURE" CLASSES OF OIL

Trustworthy oil makers are careful to use only Riviera olives in their oils, but the only way to be absolutely sure you're getting Ligurian oil from Ligurian olives grown on Ligurian trees is to buy a DOP-certified oil. The regulations are straightforward. The three growing areas are: "Riviera dei Fiori," which corresponds to districts within the province of Imperia, "Riviera del Ponente Savonese," which includes districts within the province of Savona, and "Riviera di Levante," which includes districts in the provinces of Genoa and La Spezia.

The composition of Riviera dei Fiori oil must be at least 90 percent Taggiasca from the growing area plus 10 percent other varieties also from the area. Riviera del Ponente Savonese has to be at least 60 percent local Taggiasca and the rest other local varieties. Riviera di Levante must be at least 65 percent Lavagnina and/or Razzola and/or Pignola, and the rest a mix of other local varieties. For all three DOPs, none of the olives can be imported from other growing areas.

To wear the DOP label, the olives must also be crushed and pressed and the oil bottled in the growing area. The olives must be harvested directly from the trees either by hand or using machinery (in other words, they can't be picked up from the ground or left to collect in nets) before January 30 of each calendar year. The oil has to be extracted without denaturing the olives — meaning no chemical extraction or ultra-heat-treating.

DOP, d'origine protetta

LABELING THAT INDICATES PRODUCTS "PROTECTED" BY EUROPEAN UNION REGULATIONS, CURRENTLY the most prestigious guarantee of quality found in Italy. DOP candidates must not only be excellent but also have a unique flavor or other unique characteristics. Currently, the only DOP labels in Liguria are for olive oil and basil; DOP status is being sought for pesto; Sant'Olcese and Orero salami; La Spezia mussels; and the cheeses called *formaggetta* and *zuncò (giuncata)*.

FUGASSA/FOCACCIA

P OCKED, PUCKERED AND OOZING OLIVE OIL, FOCACCIA IS MORE THAN JUST FLATBREAD, IT'S one of the Riviera's culinary icons and cultural touchstones, made from the border of Tuscany all the way to France. Ligurians call their flatbread *fugassa*, so the minute you open your mouth and ask for focaccia, or mispronounce *fugassa*, you give yourself away. Natives anywhere on the Riviera also spot each other in a crowd at breakfast, because while outsiders eat sweet brioche—the northern Italian version of croissant—locals opt for focaccia *con le cipolle*, aka *fugassa coë xipole* topped with sautéed white onions. And they wolf their *fugassa* with a tepid cappuccino. Any other time of day they go for plain focaccia. It's made with flour and yeast, water, salt and olive oil and no fancy ingredients.

To please *foresti*—non-Ligurians—some bakers now make focaccia with chopped olives, or herbs such as rosemary or sage, in the dough, not to mention other varieties crowned with cheese or pesto, tomato sauce or zucchini flowers. They're swell, and visitors love them, but when it comes to Ligurian focaccia, less is more. Recco's cheese-filled focaccia *con formaggio* is something entirely different.

Ideal *fugassa* must be crisp outside without being leathery or tough, and porous and fluffy inside. It's half an inch thick, with an unmistakable moonscape texture derived from fingertip

kneading. The most irresistible, lusciously unctuous yet airy focaccia of all is baked along a strip of coast about twenty miles long, starting east of Genoa at Recco and running to Sestri Levante.

Focaccia is found in other regions of Italy, and all over America, but Ligurian *fugassa* is hard to beat, and the reason remains mysterious. Nor is it clear why seaside Recco, Camogli, Santa Margherita, Rapallo, Chiavari, Lavagna and Sestri Levante are its true homeland. Some pundits say it's the microclimate and the natural yeast in the briny air, others insist it's the water, or the olive oil, which, on the eastern Riviera, is made primarily from Lavagnina and other local olive varieties. The multi-generational passion and skill of specialized bakers may be the real secret.

SAVORY VEGETABLE TARTS

T HE HOLY TRINITY OF RIVIERA FOOD IS PESTO, FOCACCIA, AND CHICKPEA *FARINATA*—FLANKED by a host of thin, supple, unusually flavorful savory tarts that hardly anyone outside Liguria knows: *torta salata*. They're served at any time of year as an hors d'oeuvre, first course or picnic food. Full of fresh vegetables and herbs, trimmer and lighter than most Italian or French savory tarts, *torta salata* is round and about half an inch thick, with a delicate crust envelope and springy texture. It may contain zucchini and other squash, spinach, onions, mushrooms, artichoke hearts and mixed field greens. But the classic and most popular ingredient is chard — not the broad, white-stemmed Swiss chard widely available in the United States but the rustic, thin-stemmed, leafy green variety, called in Italian *bietola*. With it, the tart becomes *torta di bietole*.

Some Ligurians like to imagine their pre-Roman forebears savoring *torta salata*, but its origins are more likely tied to the maritime exploits of the medieval Republic of Genoa, whose borders and those of modern Liguria are nearly identical. Partly because the region has little arable land, for thousands of years the inhabitants took to the sea as fishermen, sailors, traders, colonizers, crusaders and explorers. In the Middle Ages, Genoa rivaled Venice for control of the Mediterranean. Ligurian seafaring ensured constant contact with other nations and therefore cross-pollination of cuisines. Basil, the foundation of Genoese pesto, originated in Persia. So did spinach, which, when mixed with ricotta or fresh *prescinsêua* cow's milk cheese, is a popular filling for ravioli, something the Genoese claim they invented. Both

Greece and Turkey have tarts, filled with a variety of greens, that are remarkably similar to *torta salata*. Many Ligurian ingredients and recipes come from or are shared by the Middle East, and it may well be that *torta salata* came to Liguria from there before or possibly during the Crusades. The first documented mention of a Ligurian savory tart appears in a fourteenth-century cookbook.

Like those other Ligurian culinary icons focaccia and *farinata*, *torta salata* is almost never made at home but rather purchased at bakeries and special shops, often called Torte e Farinata. The reason is simple: savory tarts come out best when baked in large, hot, bread ovens.

FARINATA

ANCY RESTAURANTS DON'T SERVE THE CRUSTLESS LIGURIAN SAVORY TART MADE from chickpea (aka garbanzo bean) flour, mixed with water, olive oil and salt, and called *farinata*, *fainâ* in Genoese dialect. It's made by specialized bakeries, *focaccerie*, *osterie* and hole-in-the-wall eateries known poetically as Torte e Farinata.

Humble the tart may be, yet *farinata* rivals focaccia and pesto — and savory tarts — as the Riviera's favorite regional food. Festivals celebrate its irresistible deliciousness. Associations promote and protect it: Genoa's chamber of commerce awards traditional *farinata* makers the honorary title "Maestro." Regionalists also brandish *farinata* in the battle against fast food, and some

Green Cuisine

LIGURIANS SPEND THEIR LIVES GAZING AT, SWIMMING OR FISHING IN AND CROSSING the sea. Paradoxically what they seem to love to eat above all are greens. This is explained not only by the excellence of local produce, wild field greens and savory vegetable tarts, but also by historical, atavistic, deeply rooted behavior patterns. The Republic of Genoa and the Ligurian tribal clans that came before it were nations of seafarers. For thousands of years, long-distance sailors craved vegetables after a sea journey. To this day, the constant presence of the sea gives locals a hunger for food from the land, especially greens and herbs, which explains the popularity among other things of basil pesto and vegetable tarts.

A more practical explanation is that field greens and wild herbs have always been free for the taking. Alongside the ubiquitous chard, those plants include borage, chicory, dandelion, thyme, oregano and marjoram. Even today, when cultivated chard is available year-round, many Ligurians gather greens and cook them following half a dozen tried-and-true recipes. Pleasantly bitter, the greens are boiled before use. Ligurians call them *preboggion*, which probably comes from the Latin *pro bollire*, meaning "good [only] for boiling." Ligurians believe *preboggion* has curative powers. The mixture winds up notably as the filling of *pansôti* ("purses" of fresh pasta, the country folks' version of ravioli). *Preboggion*, combined with mashed potatoes, eggs and grated cheese, makes a delicious baked vegetable loaf, with many variants, called *polpettone*; in essence, it is a *torta salata*—a savory tart—without a shell.

say it's the oldest of Mediterranean foods. Ligurian members of the prestigious Accademia Italiana della Cucina and the Tigullio area's Association for the Protection and Promotion of Farinata claim that Homer mentions the dish in *The Odyssey*, a claim firmly denied by Andrew Dalby, the food historian and author of *Rediscovering Homer*. "For the record, chickpeas are never mentioned in *The Odyssey*," he remarks.

It's incontrovertible, however, that ancient Egyptian and Roman farmers grew chickpeas and ate something similar. The Middle Ages were the dish's heyday in Italy. One of the many memorable episodes in Dante's *Inferno* features Farinata degli Uberti, a fierce Florentine damned to burn forever in a flaming sarcophagus. Farinata degli Uberti's name confirms that *farinata* was widely known in the 1200s in Florence, where it also goes by the name *torta di ceci*. Other Tuscans, Pisans in particular, call it *cecìna*, while Piedmontese prefer the evocative *calda-calda* or *bella-calda*. On the French Riviera near Nice the name is *soca*.

Farinata may not be unique to the Italian Riviera, but it's demonstrably excellent here, and has been around for at least 600 years. Ligurian *farinata* lovers cite a 1400s document relating to *scripilita*, the old Genoese name for the tart. Since the 1700s, roistering chickpea devotees have belted out a celebrated Genoese drinking song, whose primary refrain is *viva, viva, viva, viva, viva pur la farinata!* Despite ubiquitous MP3 players and cellphones, you still occasionally hear lubricated Ligurians intoning this tune in *trattorie*, such as century-old Sà Pesta, near Genoa's port, or Antica Osteria Luchin, under the arcades of medieval Chiavari.

Farinata fanatics only eat the dish in cool-weather months, from September to March, when fresh, local chickpea flour is available. The flour goes off quickly, turning rancid in hot weather, they claim, though proper storage and modern vacuum packing can prevent spoilage for months or years. Some time ago, a Ligurian poet named Vito Elio Petrucci penned what he called the Seven Sacraments of Farinata, which lay down the laws governing how it should be made, from the use of exclusively fresh chickpea flour on up. Petrucci and other persnickety experts insist *farinata* must be baked on rectangular or round iron or copper *teglie* (baking trays) in very hot, wood-burning ovens fueled exclusively with olive wood. The tart's ideal thickness is five millimeters, and the textures and internal/external humidity are key: tender inside, crispy and unctuous outside.

Farinata is gorgeous in its simplicity. The only herb used to season it is rosemary. In summer, when the local catch and the weather allow it, *farinata* baked in seaboard communities may be spiked with whitebait or *bianchetti*, which are just-hatched, inch-long, translucent anchovies or sardines. Nothing could be more exquisite or surprising in flavor — nutty, olive oily and delicately fishy — or startling to look upon.

TESTAROLI

*I*F YOU THOUGHT ONLY AMERICANS COULD BE PASSIONATE ABOUT PANCAKES, THINK again. The Lunigiana district straddling northwestern Tuscany and southeastern Liguria is the homeland of *testaroli*, pancakes by another name. They're the size of a 45 rpm vinyl record, and the thickness of a classic Italian pizza. The batter for contemporary *testaroli* is of the simplest kind, containing white flour, water and salt. In the days of yore, *testaroli* were made with ground hulled wheat (*farro*), spelt, emmer, einkorn and other grains grown in the area since Neolithic times. It's said the ancient Romans, established at the once-important city of Luni, which gives the district its name, ate *testaroli* and their cousins, *panigacci*, which are as thin as crêpes and the diameter of a long-playing 33 rpm record.

The disks used for cooking the earliest known *testaroli* and *panigacci* have been unearthed by archeologists who, over the last century or so, have revealed a vast, landlocked site at Luni, which once included a port. The sea has receded several miles because of silting from the Magra River. The area's earliest proto-pancakes were probably cooked on flat stones or slabs of slate called *ciappe*. Later, to cook them more efficiently, someone, presumably a Roman, invented the two-piece cooking set of terracotta bottom disk topped by a low dome-shaped lid and together called *tèsti di coccio*. Modern versions of these may be purchased in hardware stores in the area, though they are increasingly hard to find. Clicking forward to more recent centuries, the terracotta was largely substituted by pig iron, and these iron versions, called *tèsti di ferro*, are also found in a few local hardware stores.

Like many ancient foods, *testaroli* are usually cooked not once but twice. To make them, the disk and dome must be preheated in a hot fire, usually on an open hearth. The thin, runny batter is ladled atop the bottom disk, covered with the dome, and returned to the fire, where it cooks in a matter of minutes. The bottom of a *testarolo* is dark brown, from contact with the disk, whereas its top is pale, because it has been cooked by refracted heat from the dome. Once cooked, *testaroli* are allowed to cool, and then stored for future use, or immediately cooked a second time (boiled) before being served. Refrigerated in an air-tight container, or shrink-wrapped, they can be stored for days, weeks, even months. They're now sold by the stack — like tortillas — in Lunigiana-area supermarkets.

Before cooking the *testaroli* for a second time, they must be cut or snipped into lasagne-like strips or rectangles. A large pot of lightly salted water is brought to a boil and the heat turned off. The *testaroli* are dropped into the pot and stirred. They cook gently in the hot, but not quite boiling water, in about three minutes. The favorite sauce of the Lunigiana for dressing *testaroli* is pesto. Some purists prefer olive oil, salt, pepper and grated cheese, ideally a local aged *pecorino* ewe's milk cheese. Grated *parmigiano* atop *testaroli* is acceptable even to the strictest regional constructionists, because the province of Parma abuts the Lunigiana. The area borders not only the region of Tuscany, but also Emilia. Note: in some villages, locals call *testaroli panigacci*, and call *panigacci testaroli*. No one is wrong. Everyone is right.

CHESTNUTS

....

*I*N THE BAGGAGE TRAINS OF INVADING ROMANS WERE TWO TREES: THE OLIVE AND CHESTNUT. The olives were grown on the coast and low-lying areas, the chestnuts above, in colder altitudes over the olive-tree line. Liguria's mountainous topography forced those living in isolated spots to depend on local foodstuffs. In the chestnut-clad mountains of the eastern Riviera, the so-called Chestnut Civilization took root. The chestnut trees provided building materials, burning wood and food for animals and people. Peasants invented fresh or dried chestnut and chestnut-flour dishes. Fresh *picagge matte* pasta is a lasting reminder of those lean days. Sweet and nutty, they contain only chestnut flour (sometimes mixed with wheat flour), salt and water — no eggs — and were once sauced with garden vegetables and lard, or herb pesto. They're still served in rustic *trattorie*, particularly in the inland areas of the eastern Riviera behind the Cinque Terre. *Pan martìn*, made in many inland areas between the Tuscan border and Genoa, are rustic buns baked with wheat flour mixed with chestnut flour. Another chestnut-flour specialty that has survived into the twenty-first century is *panella* (also called *castagnaccio*), a flat, elastic, crustless cake studded with pine nuts and fennel seeds, containing olive oil, salt and water. It's naturally sweet, moist and delicious, and tastes like semi-sweet chocolate. Often baked at home, it is also sold in Torte e Farinata shops and some bakeries, and simple inland *trattorie*. Chestnut flour is available widely at Ligurian specialty food shops, particularly in the Chiavari area on the eastern

Riviera di Levante (**Drogheria Giovanni Ameri**, Piazza Roma 27, Chiavari (GE), Tel: 0185 309438, closed Sunday), or direct from producers such as **Attilio Noceti**, in hills east of Chiavari (Via alla chiesa 2, Carasco (GE), Tel: 0185 383238, www.noceti. it). The municipality of Chiavari (Tel: 0185 325 198, info@comune.chiavari.ge.it, www.comune.chiavari.ge.it) and nearby villages including Carasco (Tel: 0185 350793) host chestnut fes-

tivals in mid to late October.

On the western Riviera di Ponente, the hillside village of Calizzano is the biggest producer of chestnuts, and its highest-quality sources are **Azienda Agricola Jole Buscaglia** (Via Matteotti 59/2, Tel: 338 176 2650), and **Santamaria & C.** (Via Sforza Gallo 12, Tel: 019 790 6065). Makers of chestnut ice cream are few; some of the freshest, most flavorful *gelato di castagna* comes from **Pinotto** (Piazza San Rocco 16, Calizzano, Tel: 019 79533). The Calizzano chestnut festival, Festa d'Autunno, is held the third Sunday in October.

SEAFOOD

L IGURIANS HAVE LONG HAD A LOVE-HATE RELA-TIONSHIP WITH THE SEA AND, BY ASSOCIATION, with seafood. Despite its limited size, the Mediterranean is a temperamental body of water, capable of turning within hours from the comfortable bathtub locals call *mare nostrum* — our sea — into a maelstrom of towering whitecaps. Sonar and GPS have helped ease atavistic fears, but to many sailors and fishermen the sea is still a threatening, bottomless abyss, where ships sink and people drown and are eaten by scavengers — including fish. It was primarily for this reason that once upon a time, better-off Ligurians ate only freshwater fish, such as salmon, sturgeon and trout. They were plentiful in the region's rivers and streams, and farmed for household consumption in the fish ponds with which most noble villas were equipped.

Seafood has never been more popular in Liguria than it is today, which is ironic, given that over-fishing and pollution have reduced fish stocks to an all-time low. Wild Mediterranean blue-fin tuna, swordfish, flounder and seabass are ever rarer and more expensive. It would seem at first glance to confirm the medieval slur about the Gulf of Genoa, *mare senza pesci*, a fishless sea, wrongly attributed to Dante, and inaccurate. Big market fish may be scarce; 90 percent of the Ligurian catch is trucked to Turin and Milan. However, even today, Ligurian waters produce reasonable quantities of small to medium-sized fish. Many are spiny but flavorful. Among them are anchovy, garfish, mackerel, mullet, piper, rockfish, sardines, tub-fish, spotted and greater weavers, scorpion fish, star gazers and tuna. Octopus, squid and shellfish still abound, especially in the deep waters of the eastern Riviera.

La Spezia in particular is renowned for its mussels and clams.

ANCHOVIES

S OME LIGURIAN RECIPES LEAD TO ANCIENT ROME, AND THIS IS CLEARLY THE CASE WITH SALTED anchovies and anchovy-based creams and spreads. In classical times, patricians devoured anchovies and related fish fresh or preserved, plus a variety of fermented fish sauces, brines and pastes called *garum, liquamen, muria* and *hallex.* The Empire's scattered descendants continue to do so today, Ligurians among them.

In Italian, anchovies and sardines are called *pesce azzurro* (bluefish), for their pronounced blue coloring. They've been a specialty of Liguria for millennia, and go into a dozen favorite recipes. When Thomas Jefferson put ashore at Noli, west of Genoa, on his 1787 voyage along the Riviera, he lodged in "a miserable tavern" that made up for its discomforts with "good fish, namely sardines, fresh anchovies."

Anchovies, though small, swim great distances. As adult fish they move from the Atlantic into the Mediterranean starting in April, and reach western Liguria in late May or early June. By the end of June they arrive off the Cinque Terre. Those not netted by *lampare* — small fishing boats with powerful lamps, which attract fish at night — spawn in coastal waters. A few fishermen in the Cinque Terre continue to salt and bottle anchovies. Several sell their catch to the national park, which has a salting facility in Monterosso, **Centro Salagione di Monterosso** (Via Servano 2/4, no telephone, behind city hall, open 9am to 2pm daily except Sunday). The national park's anchovies are sold at the train station boutiques in each of the Cinque Terre's five villages, and in some local gourmet shops.

Liguria also produces tiny amounts of a peculiar, fishy spread, used like Provençal *tapenade* or *anchoïade*, usually called *machetû* or *macheto* or *machetto*, sold in only a handful of gourmet shops (such as Salsamenteria Antica in Savona) or served in restaurants as an antipasto. It's delicious, and, food historians say, a close relative of ancient Roman *hallex.* Both *hallex* and *machetû* were made with fermented anchovy discards (including heads and viscera, undersized or damaged anchovies and transparent newborns); the salty paste was thinned with olive oil. Most people who enjoy *machetû* do not realize how it used to be made. Nowadays *machetû* is made with fresh, whole anchovies.

BASIL AND PESTO

. . . .

N O ONE IN LIGURIA BOTHERS ANYMORE TO SPECIFY "BASIL PESTO." THAT WASN'T always the case. Until the postwar economic boom and its year-round Riviera tourist masses demanding Genoa's green sauce, pesto was made not only with basil but, especially in winter, with other herbs, among them parsley and marjoram. *Pisto castarnoésa*, from the Castelnuovo Magra district on Liguria's southeastern frontier, near Tuscany, combines walnuts with parsley and marjoram. Half a dozen other rustic variants continue to be made in the Ligurian outback — the *entroterra*.

Pesto is an obsolete past participle of the verb *pestare*, to crush. There are dozens of types of pesto in Italy and elsewhere. Sicilians make their pesto with dried tomatoes, Neapolitans (and some other Italians) have *salsa verde* — crushed parsley, capers, olive oil and anchovies — and Provençal *pistou* is similar to its Genoese cousin except that it doesn't have pine nuts and usually doesn't have cheese either.

Some Ligurians claim basil pesto has been made in the region since the Phoenicians or Greeks founded Genoa, others limit themselves to a medieval pedigree. That may be, but gastronome Giovanni Battista Ratto wrote the Riviera's earliest regional cookbook, *La Cuciniera Genovese*, in 1865, and it has the oldest known recipe for pesto. Ratto calls it *battuto alla genovese*, subtitled *Pèsto*, and it makes uncomfortable reading for purists, calling for butter and Dutch cheese.

Genetic science confirms that the dozen or so Genovese basil cultivars currently available indeed have different fingerprints from other sweet basil cultivars, of which there are scores worldwide. Though there are no known ancient or medieval references to the Riviera's basil, it's widely agreed that the Greeks probably brought the herb to Italy from Persia. The botanical name, *Ocimum basilicum,* derives from the classical Greek meaning "swift" and "kingly," suggesting that basil germinates and grows quickly and is of noble or refined character. The Romans popularized it throughout the Italian peninsula and in other temperate regions of the Empire,

which led in time to countless local genotypes. (See sidebars on pages 111 and 272.)

GARLIC

THE MEDIEVAL MOTTO ABOUT THE PORTABILITY OF PAPAL POWER, *UBI PAPA, IBI ROMA,* MEANing "where the pope is, there is Rome," has often been transliterated and transmogrified by the irreverent to apply to garlic—*alium* in Latin—and Italian food. Hence *ubi alium, ibi Roma,* where goes garlic, there you'll find Italian food, or vice versa. Ironically, today's Romans have a light touch with garlic, whereas certain Ligurians (not to mention Frenchmen, Catalonians and Californians) seem to relish heavy doses of the bulb.

Two typically Ligurian sauces call for garlic raw. The medieval mariner's condiment *aggiàda* is a palate-bucking blend of pounded garlic, vinegar and salt, sometimes with pounded anchovies added. It's spooned into soup or slathered on fish, bread, sea-biscuits, boiled beef and whatever else a hungry seaman or peasant can get hold of. It is similar to *salsa verde,* without the green parsley component. As any Ligurian or Catalonian will tell you, the most efficacious way to make raw garlic easier to digest is to eat it with large quantities of raw parsley—which also helps tone down garlicky breath. Taken together, *aggiàda* and crushed raw parsley make either *salsa verde* or parsley pesto, a direct ancestor of basil pesto. Food experts have long wondered whether some shipwrecked sailor added basil—fresh or preserved in olive oil—to *aggiàda* instead of the parsley, thereby unwittingly creating Genoa's cult basil pesto sauce.

Be that as it may, in the kind of pesto Ligurians love, and most other Italians disdain, garlic and pesto march in lockstep like jackbooted Roman soldiers. The late, great Vittorio G. Rossi, an opinionated regional writer popular from the 1950s to '70s, lamented how mass tourism, driven by prosperous Milan, was taming and transforming pesto beyond recognition. "The tender mouths of the Milanese," he scoffed, not only prefer minty basil grown in the sun, instead of the pale, tender young basil for which the Genoese have a predilection. Worse, Milan shuns strong garlic.

Old-fashioned pesto devised for the local palate indeed some-times tastes like *aggiàda* with a little basil added. It is the spe-cialty of many unpretentious roadside *trattorie*. Even unbending garlic lovers must admit, however, that too much of a good thing masks the aroma of the basil and makes pesto hard to digest. (See Garlic of Vessalico, page 330.)

CHEESE

R IVIERA CHEESES ARE DELICIOUS BUT FEW, AND NONE IS KNOWN BEYOND THE REGION. THERE ARE two reasons for this surprising fact. First, the lack of pastureland in mountainous Liguria means there is little fodder grown, and very little room for dairy farms, which

require sizable acreages. Once upon a time, rural households kept a few cows, goats and ewes for home consumption, and farmers made simple farmstead cheeses with any extra milk these animals produced. The typical Ligurian cheeses of a century ago were, therefore, fresh *caprino* goat's milk cheese, *formagetta* of mixed milks, and cow's milk *prescinsêua*, *San Stè* and *stracchino* — all mild, soft and conceived to be eaten young. Until the post-World War Two period, the famous cheese focaccia of Recco was made with *prescinsêua*, for instance, which is similar to cottage cheese. For the last half century it has been made with thicker, elastic *stracchino*.

The second reason Liguria produces relatively little cheese is that, bordering the region, are cheese-rich Piedmont, Emilia and Tuscany. La Spezia borders northern Tuscany and is also closer to the Province of Parma (source of *parmigiano*) than it is to Genoa; Savona, Imperia and San Remo have the pastures of Piedmont in their backyard. Further, for centuries, Genoa was linked politically and by sea trade with Sardinia, the Mediterranean island where excellent, aged ewe's milk *pecorino sardo* is produced. It has always been more practical for Ligurians to import cheeses from these nearby regions, rather than to make cheeses at home

COFFEE, CAFÉ AND CAFFÈ

. . . .

*I*N STANDARD, MODERN ITALIAN, *CAFFÈ* MEANS COFFEE, THE SUBSTANCE, WHILE "BAR" MEANS café, as in coffee shop or espresso bar. However, many cafés have *caffè* in the name, such as Caffè Mangini in Genoa or Caffè Defilla in Chiavari. To avoid confusion, the cafés/espresso bars in this guide are referred to as *caffè*; so, too, is coffee. On the Riviera, *caffè* is often outstanding. Dozens of artisanal or medium-sized coffee roasters produce blends you will find here and nowhere else.

"ARTISANAL" ICE CREAM

. . . .

*M*ANY SMALL ITALIAN ICE CREAM MAKERS CALL THEIR PRODUCT *GELATO ARTIGIANALE*, meaning artisanal ice cream. Often the only artisanal or craft element lies in the dexterity with which the ice cream makers—*gelatai*—open the packages of the powdered, freeze-dried or concentrated ingredients which they use, to save time and money. The resultant ice creams are unnaturally showy and colorful, stiffly whipped and cloyingly sweet; they often contain colorings, preservatives and chemical stabilizers.

To distance themselves from unscrupulous *artigiani*, some honest artisans now describe their product as *gelato artigianale naturale*. Until Italian or European legislation defines exactly what "artisanal" and "natural" mean, the ancient Latin motto applies: *Caveat Emptor*. Let the buyer beware.

Unless otherwise noted, the ice cream makers in this guide make authentic, "natural" ice creams, *semifreddi*, ices and sorbets. Some use ready-made, semi-processed pastes for non-fruit flavors: crushed pistachios, hazelnuts and almonds, or liquified chocolate and Nutela. For fruit flavors, only fresh fruit is used. It's worth noting that "ice cream" is a misnomer for *gelato*; milk, not cream, is used to make nearly all Italian non-fruit *gelati*; fruit flavors are made from water, sugar and fruit, with no dairy products. That's the main reason why Italian *gelati* are lighter and less caloric than their northern European or American counterparts.

CHAPTER 2

Wine

LIGURIANS LOVE GENEOLOGY AND ETYMOLOGY, THE MORE INTRICATE THE BETTER. THOSE bent on grounding Ligurian wine in Antiquity insist the name "Giano"—Janus—the mythical founder of Genoa, means "wine" in Aramaic and Hebrew. Leaving aside the veracity or utility of the claim, what link it might have to the city's current vocation for winegrowing is unclear. Genoa is named for the Genuati, a Ligurian tribe established in the area from the seventh century BC. By no stretch of the imagination has the city ever been renowned for its wines, which are pleasant, and getting better, but limited in their range and register.

With few exceptions, traditional Riviera wines are light bodied. The climate and soil lend themselves to white wines, and reds that verge on rosé in coloration. Whatever the color, they're best drunk on the spot within a year of bottling, because they don't travel or age well. They're also relatively expensive compared to other Italian wines. The Riviera's grape varieties have small yields. The steep, terraced landscape imposes hand harvesting. Riviera winegrowing estates are small and don't benefit from economies of scale.

Paradoxically, hand harvesting, smallness and high price favor quality. Ligurian *terroir* is unmistakable, lending a lean, clean character to wines, which make the ideal complement to Riviera foods. Most Ligurian wines are named for the varietal from which they're made. The main grape varieties for whites are Vermentino and Pigato, the main red variety is Rossese (also called Ormeasco); Piedmont's Dolcetto is a cousin. Bigger, inkier Granaccia/Alicante was brought to the Finale Ligure area in the 1600s by Spanish occupiers, and has become almost native, with dozens of local sub-varieties, the best of which are in the

Province of Savona. A score of other, lesser varieties are also grown. It is now fashionable to add specific vineyard or dialect names to labels, in an effort to emulate Piedmontese or Tuscan winemakers.

The Italian wine industry in general and Ligurian winemakers in particular are in tumult, as quality and marketing ploys increase in lockstep, sometimes at the risk of compromising *tipicità*—the wine's typicity or *terroir*. At the top of the heap are wines labelled DOC (*d'Origine controllata*—made with a "controlled" quantity of grapes of specific origin) and DOCG (*d'Origine controllata e garantita*—controlled and guaranteed origin, quantity and winemaking processes). When *riserva* (reserve) follows DOC or DOCG, it means the wine has met additional ageing requirements. The lesser IGT label guarantees geographical provenance and typicity, without the stringent rules of a DOC/DOCG appellation. Dozens of table wines—*Vini da tavola*, V.d.t.—rarely leave the region; they're often served in *osterie* and *trattorie*, and sold in local wine shops. Locals refer to them as *nostralino* or *nostrano*—"our" wine. Some wines that don't fit into traditional classifications can be very good. Their makers may have vineyards outside DOC or IGT boundaries, or they may have opted to avoid the restrictions imposed by the Italian wine labeling bureaucracy. Note that the term *produttore* means a winegrower or winemaker (or maker of foodstuffs), while *cantina* means winery (or cellar), and *azienda agricola-vinicola* or *azienda vitivinicola* means a grape grower, winemaker, winery or winery-farm.

WINES OF THE EASTERN RIVIERA DI LEVANTE:

RIVIERA DI LEVANTE GRAPE VARIETIES

....

Whites: Albana, Albarola, Bianchetta genovese, Bosco, Greco, Malvasia bianca lunga, Pigato, Rollo, Trebbiano toscano, Vermentino

Reds and rosés: Cabernet, Canaiolo nero, Ciliegolo, Dolcetto, Granaccia, Merlot, Pollera nera, Sangiovese

C OMPARED TO THE WESTERN RIVIERA, THE EASTERN RIVIERA IS COOLER, MORE HUMID, BREEZIER AND has many more microclimates, which lend complexity to the area's wines. Starting in Tuscany and crossing the border north into Liguria, the Riviera di Levante's most promising new vineyard area is Colli di Luni. It spreads across gentle hills behind Luni, La Spezia and Sarzana, on both sides of the Magra River Valley. Fine wines were made here in Antiquity: Luni is a Roman city, extensively excavated last century and open to visitors, like Pompeii. The Renaissance of the area's wines began in the 1990s. Colli di Luni Bianco, a dry white with a flowery nose and fresh taste, is composed of Vermentino, Trebbiano toscano and other indigenous white grape varieties. It goes well with fish, pasta and vegetable dishes. Colli di Luni Vermentino is a pure (or almost) varietal wine, usually made with select grapes, and possesses greater intensity than generic Colli di Luni Bianco.

Colli di Luni Rosso (red wines) are more complex than the area's whites, and show the potential to develop into excellent wines rivaling those of Italy's great winegrowing regions. Colli di Luni Rosso is made with Cabernet or Merlot, Ciliegiolo, Canaiolo, Pollera nera and Sangiovese. Peppery and spicy, with cloves and plenty of red-fruit in the nose and mouth, it gets its pleasant cherry undertones from Ciliegiolo (which means "cherry grape"). You can keep good bottles of Colli di Luni Rosso for two or three years. It's delightful with pasta, poultry and meat, and with rich fish dishes with sauce.

Northwest of the Lunigiana and La Spezia are the Cinque Terre, where Liguria's best-known white wines originate. They don't go by varietal name, but rather are called Cinque Terre, and grown on terraced vineyards above the five seaside villages of Riomaggiore, Manarola, Vernazza, Corniglia and Monterosso. Forty years ago, Waverly Root noticed that most of the Cinque Terre's vineyards were abandoned, and 80 percent of the Albarola, Bosco and Vermentino grapes that go into Cinque Terre were grown elsewhere. The DOC appelation put an end to fraud. Monorails installed in the 1980s and '90s have eased access to vineyards, and the creation of the Cinque Terre National Park has further boosted winegrowing by providing subsidies for vineyard maintenance. The bulk of Cinque Terre wine is made by the area's co-op winery. Independent winegrowers are few. Wind is the main challenge faced by winemakers; upper terraces can be markedly cooler than those close to the sea. Cinque Terre is a pale straw-colored white wine, which is dry yet aromatic and fruity, with a pleasing bittersweet finish. It goes well with pesto and fish.

Sciacchetrà is the Cinque Terre's powerful dessert wine made from sun-dried Bosco grapes. Traditionally, twenty-four kilos (about fifty-three pounds) of fresh grapes yield eight kilos of

Bosco raisins, which in turn yield one liter of Sciacchetrà. In theory it must age for six years or more before being drunk. Good vintages keep for decades. Beware of imitations, which often are made from fortified wines. Authentic Sciacchetrà is very expensive. Only a handful of winemakers continue to produce it. Slightly chilled, Sciacchetrà is exquisite with *castagnaccio*, almond cookies and *pandolce*.

Colline di Levanto DOC covers territory immediately north of the Cinque Terre, in the communes of Levanto, Framura, Deiva and Bonassola, which produce whites, rosés and reds. Until the 1990s, these were simple table wines. They have come a long way and are now capable of excellence, at reasonable prices. The grape varieties are those of the Cinque Terre.

Vermentino di Verici, a little-known non-DOC wine from northeast of the Colline di Levanto, near the village of Casarza Ligure, can be as good as many DOC Vermentino wines. Also made in and around Verici is Passito, a sweet wine served with dessert.

Chiavari, which is about halfway between Levanto and Genoa, is gaining a reputation as the main city of the relatively new DOC Golfo del Tigullio, which includes thirty-six towns and villages, and produces still, sparkling and sweet whites (Bianco, Bianchetta Genovese, Moscato, Vermentino, Spumante, Passito), rosé (Rosato) and reds (Rosso, Ciliegiolo). They vary widely in quality; a handful are very good to excellent.

Genoa is among Italy's only major cities to produce its own wines. The Val Polcevera (sometimes spelled in one word, Valpolcevera) is a wide river valley directly behind Genoa, and it grows the same typologies as Golfo del Tigullio, from white to rosé and red, using the same classic grape varieties of the Levante. One of the many smaller valleys breaking off from Val Polcevera forms the sub-appellation Valpolcevera Coronata, a peculiar white wine. In the postwar period, Coronata wines had all but disappeared. Their nuanced sulfur undertones, from the valley's peculiar *terroir*, impart an unmistakable nose and flavor much sought after by the Genoese. It is reputed to be the perfect foil for unctuous, sumptuous pesto, specifically the pesto of nearby Prà.

WINES OF THE WESTERN RIVIERA DI PONENTE:

RIVIERA DI PONENTE GRAPE VARIETIES

Whites: **Lumassina, Pigato, Vermentino**
Reds and rosés: **Dolcetto, Granaccia, Ormeasco, Rossese**

LIKE THE CLIMATE AND THE NUMBER OF GRAPE VARIETIES USED, THE DOCS OF THE WESTERN Riviera are comparatively simple. The entire area is designated Riviera Ligure di Ponente DOC, with a handful of sub-areas identified as Albenga or Albenganese, Finale or Finalese, and Riviera dei Fiori; wines so labeled are made exclusively from grapes grown in the sub-area. A separate DOC is Rossese di Dolceacqua or simply Dolceacqua, which is a small inland growing area around the medieval town of Dolceacqua. (Other Rossese wines come from Savona to the French border.)

West of Genoa, in the Province of Savona, the white wines begin to get seriously good. This is the homeland of the indigenous Pigato grape variety, which goes into Liguria's most interesting and muscular dry white wines. Pigato grows from Savona to France, and thrives in baking heat on shoreline terraces and inland river valleys. Good vintages keep for up to two years. Pigato has an intense straw color. The nose is fruity and flowery, evoking jasmine, peaches and, in some bottlings, wild herbs. Ligurians drink it happily with fish, savory vegetable tarts, pasta dressed with butter and sage or rosemary, and lean ravioli or vegetable-filled *pansôti*. Vermentino often grows alongside Pigato, in vineyards that receive less sun or get more wind, and has an agreeable bittersweet resin aftertaste, possibly derived from the pine trees it grows near. Like the Vermentino of the eastern Riviera, it should be drunk young.

Ormeasco is a medium- to full-bodied red made from a relative of the Dolcetto grape, which is usually associated with neighboring Piedmont, and comes from hills behind Imperia and San Remo. With blackberry overtones and plenty of fruit, Ormeasco can keep for two or three years. It goes with hearty pasta dishes, poultry and meat. Despite the name, Ormeasco Sciac-trà has nothing to do with the sweet wine, Cinque Terre Sciacchetrà. Instead it is a light-bodied rosé made from Ormeasco grapes but like a blush wine, is taken off the skins after a matter of hours.

A Grab Bag of Remarkable Riviera Wines

....

Andrea Bruzzone

The winery's best: Valpolcevera DOC Bianchetta Genovese, Coronata Assûie, Trei Paexi

VIA BOLZANETO 94/R, GENOVA-BOLZANETO

TEL: 010 7455157

Domenico Barisone Cooperativa Viticoltori Coronata

The winery's best: Valpolcevera Coronata DOC

VIA MONTE GUANO 1/A, GENOVA-CORONATA

TEL: 010 6516534

Bisson

The winery's best: Golfo del Tigullio DOC Bianchetta Genovese, Cinque Terre Marea

CORSO GIANNELLI 28, CHIAVARI, (GE) ✦ TEL: 0185 314462

WWW.BISSONVINI.IT

La Cantina Levantese di S. Lagaxie

The winery's best: Colline di Levanto DOC Bianco

VIA ZOPPI 11, LEVANTO (SP) ✦ TEL: 0187 807137

CANTINALEVANTESE@LIBERO.IT

Durin

The winery's best: Colline Savonesi IGT Alicante/ Granaccia, Riviera Ligure di Ponente Rossese DOC

VIA ROMA 202, ORTOVERO (SV) ✦ TEL: 0182 547007

AA.DURIN@LIBERO.IT

Enzo Guglielmi

The winery's best: Rossese di Dolceacqua DOC

SOLDANO (IM) ✦ TEL: 0184 289042

Ruffino

The winery's best: Colline Savonesi IGT Mataossu

VARIGOTTI (SV) ✦ TEL: 019 698522

Walter De Battè

The winery's best: Cinque Terre DOC, Cinque Terre Sciacchetrà DOC

VIA TRARCANTU 25, RIOMAGGIORE (SP)

TEL: 0187 920127

Drink it young, with light pasta dishes and fish.

Rossese di Dolceacqua is usually lighter in color and structure than Ormeasco, more complex, with occasional undertones of violet, and a pleasant flowery nose. It goes with everything from savory tarts or pasta to fish, poultry and meat dishes.

Granaccia is the Ligurian name for Alicante, a Spanish grape, introduced in the 1600s and now considered "native." It's big-bodied, and makes sunny wines, the best of which come from the Province of Savona.

Top Winemakers Overall, Riviera di Levante

FROM LUNI TO GENOA

....

Azienda Vitivinicola La Baia del Sole

VIA FORLINO 3, ORTONOVO (SP) ✦ TEL: 0187 661821

Bisson

CORSO GIANNELLI 28, CHIAVARI, (GE) ✦ TEL: 0185 314462

WWW.BISSONVINI.IT

Luciano Capellini

FRAZIONE VOLASTRA, VIA MONTELLO 240B, RIOMAGGIORE

(SP) TEL: 0187 920632 ✦ WWW.VINBUN.IT

La Colombiera Di Ferro Pieralberto

VIA MONTECCHIO 92, CASTELNUOVO MAGRA (SP)

TEL: 0187 674265 ✦ WWW.LACOLOMBIERA.COM

Cooperativa agricoltura Cinque Terre

LOCALITÀ GROPPO DI RIOMAGGIORE, (SP)

TEL: 0187 920435 ✦ WWW.CANTINACINQUETERRE.COM

Walter De Battè

VIA TRARCANTU 25, RIOMAGGIORE (SP) ✦ TEL: 0187 920127

Lunae Bosoni

LOCALITÀ LUNI, VIA BOZZI 63, ORTONOVO (SP)
TEL: 0187 669222 ✦ WWW.CANTINELUNAE.COM

Il Monticello

VIA GROPPOLO 7, SARZANA (SP) ✦ TEL: 0187 621432

La Pietra del Focolare

VIA DOGANA 209, ORTONOVO (SP) ✦ TEL: 0187 662129

La Polenza di Lorenzo Casté

VIA FIESCHI 107, CORNIGLIA (SP) ✦ TEL: 0187 821214

Ottaviano Lambruschi

VIA OLMARELLO 28, CASTELNUOVO MAGRA (SP),
TEL: 0187 674261 ✦ WWW.OTTAVIANOLAMBRUSCHI.COM

Pino Gino

LOCALITÀ MISSANO, VIA VITTORIO PODESTÀ 31,
CASTIGLIONE CHIAVARESE (GE) ✦ TEL: 0185 408036

Santa Caterina

VIA SANTA CATERINA 6, SARZANA (SP) ✦ TEL: 0187 629429

CHAPTER 3

···························

From Tuscany and Emilia to La Spezia– La Lunigiana

Province: La Spezia. *Includes:* Bocca di Magra,
Bolano, Castelnuovo Magra, Lerici, Luni, Montemarcello,
Nicola, Ortonovo, Sarzana, Vincinella.

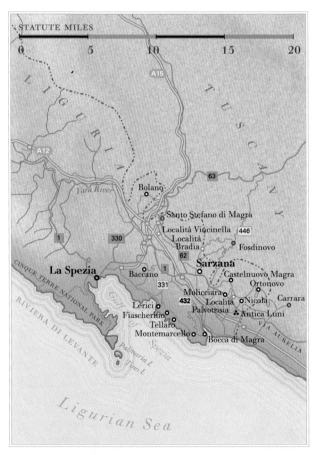

BORDER REGION WITH THE OVERLAPPING CHARACTERISTICS OF TUSCANY, EMILIA AND Liguria, the Lunigiana is named for the ancient Roman city of Luni, founded in 177 BC, primarily as a port facility to ship marble from the Apuan Alps to Rome, and import goods from Roman colonies. The moody, mossy ruins of Luni stand on the south bank of the Magra River and are worth visiting. In addition to being a natural crossroads at the convergence of several valleys, the Lunigiana was therefore further shaped by Mediterranean trade. The hills of the Lunigiana, terraced with olive groves and vineyards, are more rounded and less steep than those of either the rugged Apuan Alps, a few miles south at Carrara, in Tuscany, or the sheer cliffs of the Cinque Terre, northwest in Liguria. The cooking reflects the traditions of all three regions, with many ancient holdovers. While the sea is visible from almost every point in the Lunigiana, fish does not play a major role in the cuisine. Cooking with terracotta and iron *testi* is still common at home and in many restaurants, particularly those with fireplaces or large, wood-burning ovens. Sarzana is the biggest, most authentic town of the Lunigiana. Lerici — and the abutting villages of Tellaro, Fiascherino and Montemarcello — is a major, upscale tourist resort. North of the Lunigiana is La Spezia, among Italy's biggest military and industrial port cities.

BOCCA DI MAGRA

HIS RESORT ALONG THE NORTHERN BANK OF THE FAST-FLOWING MAGRA RIVER (THE NAME means Mouth of the Magra) is fashionable, with a marina and many vacation villas owned by wealthy Tuscans and Milanese. Of the chic fish restaurants, **Ristorante Capannina Ciccio** — around since 1951 — is reliably good and very pleasant (Via Fabbricotti 71, Tel: 0187 65568, www.ristoranteciccio.it, expensive). Gone are the days when Ciccio ran his eatery out of a reed shack on the beach. Today his son Mario and daughters Graziella, Giovanna, Ornella and Rosangela oversee the operation, which fills a rambling building on the seafront. There are the usual picture windows with views of the river and coast, the giant aquarium full of lobsters ready to sacrifice, and tables in a huge dining room where overly tanned owners of speed boats admire one another. Yet the fish is always fresh and simply prepared, the seafood pasta tasty (especially the miniature *lasagnette* with baby squid and the delicate *tagliolini* with squid ink and baby octopus). The ice cream is housemade and very good. You will find many of the area's best wineries on the wine list, with Vermentinos from Giacomelli, Il Torchio, La Pietra del Focolare and Il Monticello.

CASTELNUOVO MAGRA

L IKE MOST OF THE FORTIFIED HILL TOWNS OF THE LUNIGIANA, CASTELNUOVO MAGRA—"NEW castle on the Magra"—was built from the ruins of ancient Luni, and lived its heyday in the Middle Ages. The ruined castle at the atmospheric, perched village's highest point is imposing, with see-forever views. The castle of Castelnuovo Magra is famous among Italian literati because in it, in 1306, Dante Alighieri mediated a peace accord between rival clans. Another cavernous, vaulted, stone-paved building, this one from the 1500s and called Palazzo Amati-Ingolotti-Cornelio, houses the regional **Enoteca Pubblica** wine information center, which is behind the parish church, flanking the town hall. Here, in theory, you can taste and buy the wines of thirty growers from the province of La Spezia, plus those of about 130 others from the rest of Liguria, including both the eastern and western Rivieras (Via Vittorio Veneto 2, Tel: 0187 694182, www.enotecapubblica.it; call ahead to make sure someone is there, and ask how many wines are in stock). Unfortunately, the *enoteca* is only open to the public from 3pm to 7pm weekdays from June through September, the rest of the year 3pm to 7pm weekends only. The wines available for tasting are DOC or IGT, and range from a handful of bottles in winter, to dozens in the high season. Also sold are the very good bottled pesto and *rucola* sauces made by Anfossi, and *pandolce* from the local Terarolli bakery.

The church of Santa Maria Maddalena fronting the *enoteca* is worth a look: it houses a Calvary said to be by Bruegel the Younger (copied from Bruegel the Elder), and the crucifix is, with equal confidence, attributed to Van Dyke; both are remarkable, whoever painted them. Castelnuovo is the home of focaccia *castelnovese*, a semi-sweet dessert cake originally made with cornmeal, olive oil, butter and pine nuts, but now more commonly made with bleached wheat flour, butter, candied fruit, raisins, pine nuts and walnuts, and glazed on top. In the 1990s, local ham-and-salami-maker Mirco Bertini, a peerless marketing man, invented *la prosciutta castelnovese*, a boned, air-dried raw ham, which has received recognition from EU headquarters in Brussels.

RESTAURANT

Trattoria Armanda

T HOUGH THIS LEGENDARY, FAMILY-RUN *TRATTORIA* ON A CURVE AT THE ENTRANCE TO THE VILLAGE has been around for a century, and started out as an authentic *osteria* serving strictly regional food, it's in the process of morphing into an upscale restaurant that caters more to yuppie gastronauts than to savvy locals. The legendary Armanda is no longer. Her daughter-in-law Luciana does the cooking, which ranges from excellent in the starters and desserts departments to over-ambitious when it comes to second courses. Armanda's son, Valerio, who has been here forever, runs the small, narrow dining room. It has only a handful of tables, all draped in canary yellow tablecloths. Recent remodeling has given the interior a faux-Art Deco quality that seems to carry forward to some of the dishes, such as duck breast with citrus fruit, or suckling lamb cooked "in three ways" — fried chops, roasted other parts and *coratella* (stewed inner organs). None has anything to do with the Lunigiana, and each is underwhelming. However, the appetizers are very good, starting with the housemade rosemary-perfumed focaccia with Colonnata lard (Colonnata is only a few miles south), or the sumptuous savory tarts and *baccalà* fritters. The *panigazzi* are made on iron disks (on the stovetop) and dressed with good olive oil and grated cheese, or with flavorful pesto (which has walnuts in it). Best of all is the hard-to-find *lattughe ripiene in brodo*, which are tiny purses of lettuce stuffed with meat and vegetables and braised in a flavorful meat broth. The housemade *semi-freddi* — with cinnamon and hot chocolate sauce, or drizzled with honey and sprinkled with hazelnut *torrone* — are delicious, though they're served, for some reason, on platter-sized glass plates. This must be the only restaurant left in Liguria without a bar-style espresso machine, but the Illy coffee, from an old-fashioned Moka stovetop model, is excellent. The wine list includes bottlings from Santa Caterina and Ottaviano Lambruschi, among many other top growers.

PIAZZA GARIBALDI 6 ✦ TEL: 0187 674410

TRATTORIAARMANDA@LIBERO.IT ✦ CLOSED WEDNESDAY

MODERATE *to* EXPENSIVE

BAKERY, GOURMET FOODS, ICE CREAM,
PASTRIES, SALAMI AND HAM MAKER

Antica Salumeria Elena e Mirco

I N THE LATE 1960S, ELENA BERTINI OPENED A HUM-
BLE SALAMI, HAM AND CHEESE SHOP ON THE NARROW
road from the Via Aurelia to Castelnuovo Magra, in the
rough-edged farming and industrial area south of Sarzana called
Molicciara. Under her stewardship and that of her ambitious son,
Mirko, now in his forties, the shop has evolved into an artisanal
salami-and-ham-making operation and upscale gourmet food
boutique selling everything from the finest dry pastas, olive
oils and sweets to local wines and bottled sauces. Mirko did his

apprenticeship with sev-
eral ham-makers in the
Parma area, and came
home to create what
he dubbed *la prosciutta
castelnovese.* Liguria isn't
know for its meat prod-
ucts, largely because of
damp sea breezes, which
do not aid the curing process; further, there was no
way for Mirko to compete
with Parma in the realm
of classic prosciutto, with
an "o." However, the
porkers Mirko buys come
from Parma, Modena and
Reggio Emilia. Mirko
removes the bone from
the thigh, dresses the
thigh with herbs, spices
and extra virgin olive oil,
and hangs it in a climate-
controlled workshop (in
the garden behind the

boutique) for a year or more. The result is flavorful ham that's not overly salty and avoids the sweetness of lesser Parma ham. It has a hint of the local wild herbs—marjoram, tarragon, myrtle, rosemary, thyme—that hang in big cloth bags from the rafters of the workshop. Along the walls of the workshop are small coffin-like vats carved from solid Carrara marble, in which Mirko brines what he calls *larsciac*, which is similar to Colonnata lard but is prepared "dry" with coarse salt and the lees of Colli di Luni wine. There are many other delicious salamis and *salamini* made here and nowhere else. Phone ahead and request to be shown around the workshop.

VIA CANALE 56, MOLICCIARA/CASTELNUOVO MAGRA
TEL: 0187 673510 ✦ WWW.PROSCIUTTACASTELNOVESE.DOC
CLOSED WEDNESDAY AFTERNOON *and* SUNDAY

Magnani Salumi e Formaggi

ON THE BUSY, BLIGHTED VIA AURELIA HIGHWAY FOOT-ING THE PERCHED VILLAGES OF ORTONOVO AND Castelnuovo Magra, near the Bosoni winery and Terarolli bakery, this upscale, well-stocked delicatessen features dozens of excellent hams, salamis and cheeses from the best makers in Italy, with a good selection of local delicacies. Also sold are many fine Colli di Luni wines, olive oils and sweets.

VIA AURELIA 168, ORTONOVO ✦ TEL: 0187 66507
CLOSED MONDAY AFTERNOON *and* SUNDAY

Panificio Cudi dei Fratelli Lorenzini— Alimentari Gisella

ON A NARROW BACK ROAD LEADING UP TO ORTONOVO FROM THE VIA AURELIA, NOT FAR FROM THE SPORTS field and industrial park of Isola, this family-run bakery in a modern brick building turns out some of the area's best focaccia both plain or with herbs, baked in a wood-burning oven, plus deli-cious, simple pastries. Also sold are good pasta *fresca*, salami, hams and cheeses and everything you need to put together a picnic.

VIA ISOLA 42, ORTONOVO ✦ TEL: 0187 66701
CLOSED WEDNESDAY AFTERNOON *and* SUNDAY.

Panificio Pasticceria Fratelli Terarolli

ANCIENT LUNI IS LITTLE MORE THAN AN OPEN-AIR ARCHEOLOGICAL SITE, BOUNDED BY THE rough-and-tumble suburbs, highways and frontage roads of the area's many spreading towns and villages. There is no there there. However, about a hundred yards south of the Luni train station, in an unprepossessing modern shopping complex, with the Gelateria Alice ice cream parlor downstairs (perfectly good ice creams, and Illy coffee), Terarolli is a bakery with remarkably good focaccia *dolce*, a light, slightly sweet coffee cake similar to Genoese *pandolce*, also known as focaccia *castelnovese*, and other pastries with dry fruits, such as plum cake. Luckily, you can buy Terarolli products sold locally in many easier-to-find gourmet shops, so if you miss the bakery itself, don't worry.

VIA AURELIA KM 391, LUNI/CASTELNUOVO MAGRA

TEL: 0187 675640 ✦ CLOSED IN JANUARY

WINE BAR AND WINERIES

Il Mulino del Cibus

SOUTH OF SARZANA ON THE ROAD LEADING UP FROM THE OLD VIA AURELIA HIGHWAY AT MOLICCIARA TO perched Castelnuovo (take Via Aurelia to Via Canale, past Antica Salumeria Elena e Mirco, and keep heading north), this small, free-standing millhouse is an unexpectedly classy wine bar with an insiderish atmosphere. There are three small rooms indoors and a small covered terrace, open in warm weather. In some ways Il Mulino del Cibus does what the regional wine information and tasting room in Castelnuovo should be doing more efficiently: offering a Bacchic panorama of the area's wines, not to mention the wines of the rest of Italy. You can spend hours talking to the passionate staff, the same polished professionals who run the Enoteca Mulino del Cibus in Sarzana. You can also spend hundreds of euros, if you wish, tasting and buying the very best vintages from the best wineries in the country. The food ranges from salami, hams and cheeses to tasty daily specials, chalked up on a blackboard.

VIA CANALE, MOLICCIARA/CASTELNUOVO MAGRA

TEL: 0187 676102 ✦ OPEN FOR DINNER ONLY, CLOSED MONDAY

Azienda Agricola Giacomelli

A SMALL WINERY OWNED BY ROBERTO PETACCHI, WITH A HANDFUL OF VINEYARDS SCATTERED around the Lunigiana totaling twenty-five acres, Giacomelli is up and coming and worth seeking out. Its winery facility is basic—and difficult to find. When driving south from Sarzana on the Via Aurelia, the old coast highway, look for the Giacomelli sign, near a gas station; turn left, past the glitzy Lunae Bosoni winery, and continue uphill. Winemaker Andrea Farina will show you around, and give you a tasting. The Golfo dei Poeti whites are refreshing and delicious, while the reserve Vermentino Boboli is unexpectedly huge with a mineral nose and flint on the tongue, the result of the area's complex soil, and of a thirty-six-hour maceration of the skins. The official alcohol content is 13.5 percent, but the actual strength is probably higher. The reds, made with Sangiovese and Merlot, are also complex and potent. Giacomelli also makes good extra virgin olive oil.

VIA PALVOTRISIA 134, LOCALITÀ PALVOTRISIA,
CASTELNUOVO MAGRA ✦ TEL: 0187 674155, CELL: 349 630 1516
OPEN DAILY EXCEPT SUNDAY 8AM *to* 5PM *and* BY APPOINTMENT

Cantine Lunae Bosoni

THE NAME, PHILOSOPHY, WORKS AND DAYS OF OWNER PAOLO BOSONI ARE WRIT LARGE AT THIS winery, conference center and food-and-wine boutique, just off the Via Aurelia south of Sarzana. Paolo took over the century-old family business in 1966, and now has a hundred acres of vineyards made up of fifteen distinct parcels, where local winegrowers work on his behalf. Tuscany is only two miles south; one senses the presence of big-money wineries and their Super Tuscans, not to mention the long shadow of Napa Valley. Despite Bosoni's use of local grape varieties, and his family's experience in the business before the New World overtook the old, the winery feels like the glitzy set of the soap opera *Falcon Crest*. It will appeal to travelers who favor ease of parking, tasting and shopping. The wines at Bosoni come in a wide range of colors and flavors, some with fanciful names such as Leukotea (Golfo dei Poeti Bianco IGT) or Divina Contessa (a rosé table wine). A few are very good; all are well made. Also sold are liqueurs (a fine Grappa di Vermentino), Bosoni's own extra virgin olive oil, cooking knives and accessories, jams that follow the seasons and sweets and packaged cakes (including the excellent focaccia *dolce* of the nearby Fratelli Terarolli).

VIA PALVOTRISIA 2, LOCALITÀ PALVOTRISIA,
CASTELNUOVO MAGRA ✦ TEL: 0187 693483 ✦ WWW.CALUNAE.IT
OPEN DAILY, INCLUDING SUNDAY MORNING

Ottaviano Lambruschi

UNTIL HE BECAME A PROFESSIONAL WINEMAKER IN 1982, OTTAVIANO LAMBRUSCHI WORKED IN THE marble quarries of nearby Carrara, and readied his "retirement" among the vines that stretch below the perched villages of Ortonovo and Nicola, near Castelnuovo. He proved himself a talented, self-taught oenologist, but his fortunes really took off when his son Fabio joined him in the 1990s. The winery, up the road from Giacomelli, and just as difficult to find, is spartan and modern, with stainless steel tanks, one step up from a garage operation. But Lambruschi is widely recognized as among the region's best makers of Vermentino, and his two flagship wines are the single-vineyard crus, Sarticola and Costa Marina. The wines are as close to organic as the Lambruschis can manage. One secret to their success is staggered harvesting of perfectly ripe grapes, which usually starts in mid September and continues into October. The other secret is respecting the natural delicacy of the variety, and making it in stainless steel, not oak (which can mask Vermentino flavors). The reds—Sangiovese, Merlot and Cabernet—are big bruisers, and while they're well made, they're outshown by Lambruschi whites. Lambruschi also makes good extra virgin olive oil.

VIA OLMARELLO 28, LOCALITÀ PALVOTRISIA, CASTELNUOVO MAGRA ✦ TEL: 0187 674261, CELL: 338 441 3761 OTTAVIANOLAMBRUSCHI@LIBERO.IT ✦ BY APPOINTMENT

OTHER WINERIES AROUND CASTELNUOVO MAGRA, LUNI AND THE NEARBY VILLAGES OF ORTONOVO and Nicola include **La Baia del Sole** (Via Forlino 3, Antica Luni di Ortonovo, Tel: 0187 661821, www.cantinefederici.com), **La Colombiera** (Via Montecchio 92, Castelnuovo Magra, Tel: 0187 674265, www.lacolombiera.com), **La Felce di Marcesini Andrea** (Via Bozzi 36, Ortonovo, Tel: 0187 66789), and **Azienda Agricola La Pietra del Focolare** (Via Dogana 209, Ortonovo, Tel: 0187 662129, lapietradelfocolare@libero.it). Though most wineries welcome drop-by visitors, opening hours vary widely. It's wise to make an appointment.

Lerici

A MASSIVE MEDIEVAL CASTLE BUILT BY THE PISANS IN 1241 GLOWERS OVER THIS PROSPEROUS AND handsome seaside village, set in a cove along the Gulf of Poets, so named for Byron and Shelley, the first of many celebrity residents. Lerici and the nearby perched hamlets of Fiascherino and Tellaro are every bit as attractive and upmarket as the

Portofino Peninsula north of them. They're also cursed by too much of too many good things — gorgeous weather, inspirational views, dreamy villas, tangible wealth and tourism. Between the eat-and-run joints and the glitz, a handful of authentic places serve locals and the savvy owners — most of them Milanese — of holiday homes. The local outdoor market is held on Saturday morning on the seaside promenade, and includes as much clothing and household goods as it does food.

RESTAURANT, PIZZERIA

I Pescatori

IN LERICI, TOSS A COIN AND IT WILL LAND ON A "FISH RESTAURANT" WITH A VIEW, A FILIGREED MENU WITH predictable seafood classics and the occasional creative dish, tables of foreigners and well-heeled out-of-towners more interested in the scene than the food, and stellar prices. The only *trattoria* in town regularly used by Ligurians is this hard-to-find hole in the wall, hidden up an alleyway (a hiking trail that leads from the main square, Piazza Garibaldi, toward Montemarcello). There's no sign on the door, just a gray stone plaque on the wall. The interior is simple, the menu set — you get what's fresh that day, and hasn't been sent by truck to Milan; the fate of 90 percent of the fish caught along the Riviera is to be trucked to the city of fashion.

VIA ANDREA DORIA 6 ✦ TEL: 0187 965534
CLOSED MONDAY ✦ MODERATE

Bontà Nascoste

"BONTÀ NASCOSTE" MEANS "HIDDEN DELIGHTS," AN APT DESCRIPTION OF THIS MODEST EATERY'S location, on a pedestrian-only alley in the oldest part of Lerici, about 150 yards north of the main square, Piazza Garibaldi. The décor is minimal, there's no view or terrace, and the fancier the recipe the less successful it is, but locals come for the *farinata* and pizza, which are both very good.

VIA CAVOUR 52 ✦ TEL: 0187 965500 ✦ CLOSED TUESDAY
INEXPENSIVE *to* MODERATE

FRESH PASTA, ICE CREAM, GOURMET FOODS AND WINES

Arcobaleno Gelateria

THIS SMALL ARTISANAL ICE CREAMERY IS ON THE NORTH SIDE OF LERICI'S MAIN SQUARE, AND though it's not as chic as the *gelaterie* on the seaside promenade, it has better ice creams, in all the classic flavors. Buy a cone and walk with it.

PIAZZA GARIBALDI 20 ✦ NO TELEPHONE
CLOSED MONDAY AFTERNOON *and* WEDNESDAY

Enoteca Baroni

DON'T COME TO BARONI TO GET A SUNTAN. IN 1961 FRANCO BARONI OPENED THIS GROTTO-LIKE WINE shop, specialty foods store, snack bar and coffee shop, in the dark pedestrian alleyway that was for centuries Lerici's main north-south street. Nowadays, Franco's children, the three smiling Baroni sisters, Simonetta, Alessia and Laura, run the show. There are three shiny stainless steel tables on the sidewalk, and Illy coffee on offer. The dust on many of the old bottlings predates the young ladies. Locals come in to buy "birthday bottles"—a Barbaresco from the late 1950s or 1960s—plus more modern wines, like a 2001 Amarone Rocca Sveva. Many of the best Riviera wineries are represented, perhaps with just one

bottle from each—space is limited, and this really isn't a fancy place for tourists. The house red, served by the glass, is a characterful Poggio dei Magni from nearby Il Monticello winery, which you won't find elsewhere. The commitment to local producers extends beyond the wine. The back room is where locals shoot the breeze, sip wine or good coffee and nibble sandwiches made with excellent salamis, hams or headcheese from Antica Salumeria Elena e Mirco of Castelnuovo Magra. Canned and bottled specialty goods include the whole range of Antichi Sapori Liguri sauces, plus an unusual but tasty pesto, made by L'Aromatica, also in Castelnuovo, which, in addition to the usual ingredients, has walnuts, butter and, bizarrely, traces of sunflower seed oil.

VIA CAVOUR 18 ✦ TEL: 0187 966301
OPEN DAILY, *including* SUNDAY MORNING

Pasta Fresca Franzi

TUCKED INTO AN OLD BUILDING IN THE MEDIEVAL ALLEYS OF LERICI, ABOUT FIFTY YARDS WEST OF Via Cavour, and a hundred yards north of the seaside, this is where locals buy good, fresh pasta, including unusual *gnocchetti* filled with pesto—found nowhere else. Everything is handmade by the owners, and while the selection is small, the quality is high. Also sold are olive oils by small, excellent (and large, competent) oil mills, sauces and the peculiar, pungent arugula pesto of Il Frantoio Sant'Agata di Oneglia.

VIA FORNARA 7/9 ✦ TEL: 0187 968662
CLOSED SUNDAY AFTERNOON *and* MONDAY

MONTEMARCELLO

MONTEMARCELLO IS THE NAME OF A DOME-SHAPED MOUNTAIN, NOW A REGIONAL PARK, as well as the village that sits atop its northwestern side, surrounded by the olive groves and pine forests that spill seaward to Tellaro, Fiascherino and Bocca di Magra. It's a magical spot. The hiking trails are lovely, with see-forever views, but most visitors drive up and stroll around the alleyways, towered over by medieval houses, that vein the oval-shaped *borgo*—the core—of Montemarcello. Permanent residents are few, and you're likely to hear mostly foreign voices wherever you go. No matter. There's a nice old *trattoria* (and B&B) here serving regional classics (plus lentil soup, dried chestnuts and *baccalà* cooked in milk) in a rustic-elegant dining room, with old prints and white tablecloths and bentwood chairs (**Trattoria dai Pironcelli**, Via Delle Mura 45, Tel: 0187 601252, moderate, closed Wednesday, open for dinner only, except Sunday), and a neo-*osteria* with a glassed in dining room and small terrace (**Marcellino Pane e Vino**, Via delle Mura 7, Tel: 0187 65364, www.marcellinopanevino.it, closed Monday, moderate).

The honorary keeper of this castle-village is nonagenarian Signora Velia. With a warbling siren's voice, she sells olive oil, local herbs, jams and bottled mushrooms, picked and pickled by her daughter, which line the walls of a one-room, ground-floor apartment on the corner of Via Grande and Via della Chiesa.

NICOLA DI ORTONOVO

WHEN ROME CRUMBLED AND WITH IT CRUMBLED OUTPOSTS SUCH AS LUNI, THE locals arrived with pickaxes and wagons, and carted off the stones. They built hilltop aeries such as Ortonovo and Nicola, stony bird's nests atop hills away from marauding pirates and migratory barbarians. Nicola is only a few hundred yards around its perimeter, a pocket-sized perched labyrinth, with keyhole views of Luni and the flood plain of the Magra River, the marble mountains of Carrara and other castle-in-the-air villages bordering Tuscany, not to mention the innumerable light industrial plants, strung out along the highways on the flatlands, which have made this part of Italy prosperous.

Nicola's main square is the size of two tennis courts, an operetta set, framed by a mustard-yellow baroque façade, trimmed in cream, which was applied 400 years ago to the much older church behind it. Most visitors head for the **Locanda della Marchesa** (Piazza della Chiesa 20, Tel: 0187 660491, moderate, closed Monday, October and November), which sits on the square, and has a handful of tables outside in good weather. The establishment used to be an authentic, helter-skelter *trattoria* on several levels of an ancient building, called Locanda Cervia, but times have changed. While the food is still good, and the menu includes many local dishes, the lace and cuteness and inventiveness have driven some former clients elsewhere.

The humble bar-*trattoria* on a curve in the very curvy road to the village is run by Fiorella Cappetta and her family, and called **Da Fiorella Ristorante-Bar** (Via Per Nicola 46, Tel: 0187 66815, closed Thursday). Fiorella buys bulk olives—local ones when available, otherwise olives from central/southern Italy—and has them cold-pressed down the road to make the restaurant's oil, which dresses many dishes. She and the crew make the giant *ravioloni*, filled with zucchini and dressed with raw oil and walnuts, or stuffed with ground meat and minced chard and sauced with rich meat-and-tomato *sugo*. There are savory vegetable tarts and *testaroli* with pesto or mushroom sauce. The boned, fried rabbit, and fried tidbits of lamb, are delicious. Of the simple, housemade desserts, the most unusual is the moist rice cake, *torta di riso*, the most delicious the classic *crostata* jam tart. Recently renovated, with an increase in comfort but a loss of rough-edged charm, the dining room is long and cavernous, but has many windows, with lovely views, and the atmosphere is as jovial as it was in the old, less properous days. There's a tiny bar area where locals hang out, sip coffee (or something stronger) and play cards.

SARZANA

O F ANCIENT ROMAN ORIGIN AND ASTRIDE THE VIA AURELIA, THOUGH LESS IMPORTANT IN ANTIQ-uity than nearby Luni, Sarzana became a key fortified city during the Middle Ages. The Magra River runs nearby, and so too do the once-important valley roads into Tuscan and Emilian territory. This is a border city, long contested by three regions.

Sarzana's walls and fortress are largely intact, and lend character to this handsome, unsung town which would be wonderful even if the food and wine were unremarkable. They are not. Food lovers make special trips here to savor the *spungata*, a delicious dessert that's been baked in and around Sarzana for centuries, possibly millennia. Within the pie's puffy pastry shell is a rich mince meat of raisins, nuts and candied or dried fruits, and sometimes jam. Many local restaurants serve *testaroli*, another local specialty (hardware stores sell the terracotta or iron *testi* needed to make them). The local pesto often contains wal-nuts. Another local specialty, usually made in simple *farinata* or

9

pizza joints, is a savory rice tart, *torta sema*. In the vicinity of Sarzana and Castelnuovo Magra are many good wineries and olive oil mills.

RESTAURANT AND PIZZERIA

Giraresto da Paolo

WITH A SMILE ON HIS BEARD-FRAMED LIPS, AFFABLE CARLO ALBERTO CARGIOLLI, HIS gentle mother and charming daughter run this humble country-style *trattoria* about a mile-and-a half north of Sarzana on the narrow, two-lane back road to Fosdinovo. The easiest way to find Da Paolo is to follow the Torrente Calcandola, a creek that parallels the city walls on the southern side of town. If you get lost, ask. Da Paolo has been in business since the 1950s. Locals love it. There's a television hanging from the ceiling in the sprawling dining room, which is panelled in knotty pine, and a roaring fireplace, guarded over by a stuffed badger. The big, glassed-in terrace is wrapped by a garden for fine weather dining. Blue-collar workers from the olive oil mills and small industrial plants nearby, white collars from Sarzana, winemakers from Castelnuovo and lively Italian families find their way to Da Paolo. On the menu are giant ravioli stuffed with greens and ground meat and topped with red meat sauce, giant *testaroli* daubed with pesto and *mesciua* mixed-bean soup. The wild boar, which marinates overnight and then is slow-cooked in *salmì* to form a thick, dark sauce, comes with slabs of polenta. The house specialty, however, is *pollo in testo*. The *testo* is usually a flat cooking tool of terracotta or iron used for the pancake-like *testarolo*, but it's also a heavy, shallow cast-iron casserole with a thick lid, used for baking meat. In this case, whole chickens are cut into small pieces and baked slowly in the *testo*, with sweet peppers, rosemary, carrots, garlic and potatoes. Everything on the menu is simple, local and good, including the tiramisu or chestnut-and-ricotta *cannolo*-like dessert and the inky Colli di Luni house wines served by the carafe.

VIA DEI MOLINI 388, LOCALITÀ BRADIA, SARZANA
TEL: 0187 621088 ✦ CLOSED WEDNESDAY *and* HOLIDAYS
INEXPENSIVE

Da Silvio

SISTERS PAOLA AND LARA GARBATI RUN THIS HUMBLE OLD PIZZERIA, WITH EXCELLENT PIZZA, ABOUT fifty yards south of Sarzana's main square, Piazza Matteotti, and are adamant that they also make several local baked specialties. The first is *torta sema* (or *torta scema*), a savory rice tart about half an inch thick, with a kind of rice pudding that sandwiches baked ham and mozzarella. The *castagnina* (called *castagnaccio* elsewhere) is a slightly sweet tart of chestnut flour, pine nuts and fennel, and comes in two versions, thick or thin. The *farinata* chickpea tart is made with extra virgin olive oil, and can be ordered as a rib-sticking *rotolo* — a strip of *farinata* with baked ham and *stracchino* cheese rolled up. The savory vegetable tarts are also delicious. You can eat in the simple, barrel-vaulted dining room, or buy your snacks to go.

VIA MARCONI 14 ✦ TEL: 0187 620272 ✦ CLOSED SUNDAY
INEXPENSIVE

COFFEE, ICE CREAM, GOURMET FOODS,
PASTRIES, SNACKS, WINE

Caffè Costituzionale

THE OWNERS OF THIS HISTORIC *CAFFÈ*, ON THE CORNER OF VIA MAZZINI AND THE MAIN SQUARE, ignored the commonsense expression "If it ain't broke, don't fix it." In 1999 they remodeled, and killed the magic. The additional choice of adopting Covim coffee as the bar blend hasn't done much to improve the situation, though loyal customers continue to fill tables indoors and on the square. The real draw here is the fresh fruit-flavored ice cream, made by a Sicilian master. Buy a cone and walk with it.

PIAZZA MATTEOTTI 65 ✦ TEL: 0187 620051
OPEN 7AM *to* 9PM (2AM IN SUMMER), CLOSED WEDNESDAY

Le Due Lune

SAVVY LOCALS COME TO THIS SIMPLE GROCERY STORE ON A BACK STREET NEAR PIAZZA CALANDRINI to stock up on wines from the region. You'll find bottlings from wineries such as Santa Caterina, Conte Picedi Benettini, La Felce and La Pietra del Focolare, plus Walter De Battè's innovative PrimaTerra wines. Le Due Lune also sells canned or bottled gourmet delights, and a small selection of otherwise unfindable local cheeses—*formagella, caciotta, pecorino, tre latti* (mixed milk) and ricotta—made for the shop by a shy little old shepherd. The housemade savory vegetable tarts are very good, though you'll need to reheat them at home, and the pesto, also good, has walnuts in it.

VIA GIUSEPPE MAZZINI 21 ✦ TEL: 0187 620165
OPEN 7AM *to* 10PM, CLOSED MONDAY

Gemmi Pasticceria Bar Confetteria

IF YOU STEP THROUGH ONLY ONE THRESHOLD IN SARZANA, MAKE IT THAT OF GEMMI, THE TOWN'S famed *caffè* and pastry shop, on the main drag, near Piazza Calandrini and the church of Sant'Andrea. Founded in 1840 by the Robbi family, it was bought in 1934 by Silvano Gemmi, and is run today by his daughter, Fiammetta Gemmi. Though restored and expanded in recent years—Silvano died in 1996—the shop is much the same as ever, with delicately frescoed vaulting, marble floors, antique wooden display cases with matching tables and chairs and crystal chandeliers hanging from the surprisingly low ceilings. Locals of all ages and descriptions come here to enjoy a wide variety of snacks and housemade pastries, from the delicious *spungata*—sold by the pie or the mini serving—to the excellent, airy focaccia and breakfast rolls, to the cookies, cakes and candies that have earned the establishment its well-deserved reputation. The coffee is supplied by Bei e Nannini of Lucca, and is remarkably good; the cappuccinos made with it are excellent.

VIA CASTRUCCIO 24 ✦ TEL: 0187 621700
CLOSED SUNDAY AFTERNOON

Bugliani Panificio Pizzeria

*I*N A ONCE-NOBLE BUT LONG-BEDRAGGLED OLD BUILDING FACING SARZANA'S MAIN TRAFFIC circle, on the edge of the historic part of town, this bakery-cum-pizza-and-*farinata* shop has been in business since the 1940s. In nice weather there are a few tables for clients, set under the portico, but the traffic noise is such that you're better off taking a walk with your delicious *farinata* or focaccia, savory vegetable tarts or pizza, all baked in an old wood-burning oven.

PIAZZA SAN GIORGIO 20 ✦ TEL: 0187 620005. OPEN 6:30AM *to* 1PM *and* 4:30PM *to* 8PM (*from* 5:30PM *to* MIDNIGHT IN JULY/ AUGUST), CLOSED SUNDAY

Enoteca Il Mulino del Cibus

*S*POTLIT, SPARKLING, ELEGANT AND CHIC, THIS UPSCALE WINE SHOP IS AFFILIATED WITH THE Mulino del Cibus wine bar-restaurant in nearby Castelnuovo Magra. Among the hundreds of wineries represented are a handful of top local producers, including Giacomelli and Ottaviano Lambruschi. Their hard-to-find reserve wines—mostly single-vineyard crus—are available here. This is a serious boutique run by serious wine experts, a good place to learn about Lunigiana wines or the latest developments in Italian winemaking.

VIA CIGALA 20 ✦ TEL: 0187 621656. CLOSED MONDAY

WINERIES IN OR NEAR SARZANA

Azienda Agricola Il Monticello

*J*EFFERSON WOULD APPROVE. THIS SMALL WINERY A FEW MILES NORTHEAST OF TOWN MAKES A NICE RED reserve, Poggio dei Magni, and other good local DOC and IGT wines, plus the unusual, only-in-Groppolo wine called, simply, Groppolo. The owners are Davide and Alessandro Neri.

LOCALITÀ GROPPOLO 7, BRADIA-SARZANA ✦ TEL: 0187 621432 SUB@LIBERO.IT ✦ OPEN BY APPOINTMENT

Top Olive Oil Makers of the Eastern Riviera di Levante

Azienda Agricola Orseggi

VIA CACCINI 4, LOCALITÀ SANTA GIULIA DI LAVAGNA (GE)

TEL: 0185 390164 ✦ ORSEGGI@ALICE.IT

Cà Bianca di Francesco Bruzzo

VIA RIVAROLA 69, CHIAVARI (GE) ✦ TEL: 0185 309795

Frantoio Bo

VIA DELLA CHIUSA 70, SESTRI LEVANTE

TEL: 0185 481605 ✦ WWW.FRANTOIO-BO.IT

Lucchi e Guastalli

LOCALITÀ VINCINELLA 19, SANTO STEFANO MAGRA (SP)

TEL: 0187 633329 ✦ WWW.FRANTOIOLG.COM

Massimo Solari

VIA CAPERANA CASE SPARSE 26, CHIAVARI (GE)

TEL: 0185 382036

Pino Gino

VIA VITTORIO PODESTÀ 31, LOCALITÀ MISSANO,

CASTIGLIONE CHIAVARESE (GE) ✦ TEL: 0185 408036

Azienda Agricola Santa Caterina

ANDREA KIHLGREN, GRANDSON OF COUNT PICEDI-BENETTINI, TOOK OVER ONE PART OF THE FAMILY oil and wine business, and now makes big, flowery Colli di Luni wines at this winery in the northern outskirts of Sarzana, near the Ipercoop megamarket. The Vermentino comes in at 13.5 percent alcohol yet is rich, fruity and well balanced.

VIA PRIVATA SANTA CATERINA 6, SARZANA ✦ TEL: 0187 629429

OPEN BY APPOINTMENT

VINCINELLA AND BOLANO

....

ONE OF LIGURIA'S MOST POLISHED AND PROFES-SIONAL PRODUCERS OF EXTRAORDINARY EXTRA virgin olive oils, **Lucchi e Guastalli** (Località Vincinella, Santo Stefano Magra, Tel: 0187 633329, cell 333 852 0734, www.frantoiolg.com, open 8am to 7pm weekdays and 8:15am to noon on Saturdays or by appointment), is very difficult to find, but worth the effort. Located in a small industrial park, it is reached via a back road between Via Cisa Sud (the main two-lane highway between Sarzana and Santo Stefano Magra) and the A12 autostrada. If you're coming from the A12 autostrada, get onto the La Spezia superstrada, head east, turn southeast on Via A. de Gaspari, jog west as the road changes name to Via U. La Malfa, turn west on Via Vincinella and when you see a sign that says Vetreria, you'll see the facility on your left amid the industrial sheds. The surroundings are anything but attractive. No matter. Though created only in 2002, Lucchi e Guastalli have won many of the prestigious European awards for their light but highly flavorful and herby oils, DOP and extra virgin, made from Razzola, Lavagnina, Leccino, Gentile and Peranzana olives grown nearby. They're also certified organic (for some, not all, of their products), and make a line of delicious olive patés, pitted olives packed in oil, and flavored oils (rosemary, lemon, truffle, porcini and *peperoncino* chili). Lucchi e Guastalli have state-of-the-art milling equipment, including a two-phase crusher and continuous press which produces no effluent. The residues are recycled for bio-mass. The plant is set up to receive visitors, and the young, enthusiastic owners are glad to give you a tour and let you taste their oils; if you visit in the harvest season, you can watch them making oil.

Northwest of the oil mill several miles, between the Magra and Vara rivers south of La Spezia, on the old highway to Genoa, near the bus station on Via Francesco Petrarca and the Via Cisa main highway, is **Il Mattarello Pazzo** (Via Romana 32, Bolano, Tel: 0187 933485, closed Monday), one of the Lunigiana's best pasta *fresca* shops and delicatessens, where the Cardelli family handmake all the local and pan-regional variations on ravioli, which are filled with field greens or meat, plus classic pasta shapes. The shop stocks fine hams, cheeses and specialty foods, and also sells delicious take-out dishes.

Two Local Indigenous Grape Varieties

....

AMONG THE LEAST-WELL-KNOWN AND LONG- EST-ESTABLISHED HEIRLOOM WINE GRAPES of the Lunigiana is Ruzzese, probably not its original name, since *ruzzese* is a corruption of *rossese*, a very different, light red-wine grape that grows on the western Riviera. Ruzzese is found only in the neighbor- hood of Baccano, a hamlet within the commune of Arcola, near Montemarcello. "Baccano" derives from Bacchus and means the noise Bacchus' drunken followers made; the grapevines may have been brought here by the ancient Romans of Luni. The dry white wine made from Ruzzese is straw yellow, and the nose and taste are flowery, herby and sometimes reminiscent of the citrus fruit grown in nearby groves. The only winery that makes Ruzzese is **Conte Picedi Benettini** (Fattoria il Chioso, Baccano di Arcola, Tel: 0187 967110, www.picedibenettini.it, by appointment), a long- established and very good producer of olive oil and Colli di Luni DOC and IGT wines, not to mention the unusual Vino del Chioso, made with late-harvest grapes and aged in wood barrels for at least two years, not in the cellar, but rather in the attic of this handsome farm-winery (where it alternately gets very cold and very hot, thus producing an oddball, amber-colored nectar).

Another heirloom white-fleshed grape, from the suburbs of Sarzana, in the area where you'll find the restaurant Girarosto da Paolo, is called Groppolo, from Groppolo di Bradia. It's a paler shade of white, almost greenish, or hon- eysuckle yellow, is also very light on the palate, and known only to initiates. The only commercial winery that makes it is **Il Monticello** (Località Groppolo 7, Bradia-Sarzana, Tel: 0187 621432, sub@libero.it, by appointment).

CHAPTER 4

Greater La Spezia and Cinque Terre

Province: La Spezia. *Includes:* Cinque Terre (Riomaggiore and Riomaggiore-Volastra, Manarola, Vernazza, Corniglia, Monterosso and Monterosso-Beo), Greater La Spezia, Levanto, Portovenere

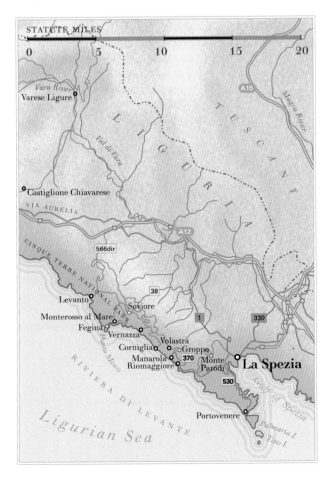

CINQUE TERRE

. . . .

IVE DRAMATICALLY POISED SEASIDE VILLAGES—
AND THE UNCOUNTED, UNSUNG HILLSIDE HAMLETS
above them—comprise the self-styled Cinque Terre,
which does not mean "five lands" but rather "five communities" or, in standard modern English, "five villages."

Many Riviera villages are authentically isolated, so it is surprising that travel writers and otherwise level-headed commentators haven't debunked the Cinque Terre isolation myth: trains reached this stretch of coast in the 1870s, and each village has its own station. Ferry boats chuff from port to port. A wide, modern highway from La Spezia curls in from above to Riomaggiore, and each village is easily reached by car and regular bus service. A final touch: starting in the 1990s, dozens of mini-monorails were installed to facilitate access to vineyards and the handful of authentically isolated houses, hamlets and sanctuaries far above the sea.

However, if the estimated 2.3 million annual visitors to this UNESCO World Heritage Site of genuine beauty wish to believe in isolation, so be it. The sheer number of hikers on the roller-coaster trails that climb from the craggy shoreline through tiered vineyards and olive groves to hogback ridges, is hair-raising. In the dry season, meaning much of the year, the dust clouds produced by hikers' boots can be seen from miles out to sea, and if you arrive by ferry boat you can also see the bumper-to-bumper backpacks. That's why as of 2001 the entire Cinque Terre district is a national park, and it's also why hikers must now pay trail fees: the funds raised go in part toward restoring dry walled terraces

and maintaining trails and infrastructure. There used to be a low season, but these days spring, fall and even winter see droves of eager visitors. The resultant prosperity has brought with it a bloom of mediocre eateries, ice creameries, pizzerias, restaurants and wine bars. With few exceptions, the area's best food and wine are to be found not in the Cinque Terre themselves, but rather in La Spezia (precisely seven minutes from Riomaggiore by local train). Happily, a handful of eating spots have survived the onslaught.

From southeast to northwest, following the sun, the five villages are Riomaggiore, Manarola, Corniglia, Vernazza and Monterosso. They are listed in that order. This is also the best direction in which to hike if starting in the morning, so that the sun is not in your eyes. For information about the national park, trails and recreation, transportation, restaurants, lodging, wine and food, contact Parco Nazionale delle Cinque Terre, Via Telemaco Signorini 118, Riomaggiore, Tel: 0187 760000, www.parconazionale5terre.it.

RIOMAGGIORE

THE SOUTHERNMOST OF THE CINQUE TERRE, RIOMAGGIORE IS LINKED TO LA SPEZIA BY A highway and has several big parking lots. As the main wine- and olive oil-producer of the five villages, with the National Park headquartered here, it feels like a real working town. The Via dell'Amore runs from Riomaggiore north half a mile to Manarola.

RESTAURANTS

Ripa Del Sole

SET ABOVE RIOMAGGIORE ON THE PAVED ROAD LEADING NORTH FROM THE MAIN PARKING LOT, this well-established and well-liked restaurant seems to prove the old Riviera adage that the farther you are from the sea, the more likely you are to find great food. The place is modern, sunny, with a small terrace and a large, glassed-in dining room that looks out at parked cars, the surreal tip of Riomaggiore's tallest *campanile*, and the Mediterranean away and below. Owned and operated by the Bertola family, Daniela cooks and Matteo, her brother, manages and takes orders. The menu is strong on seafood, and changes with the catch, and the mood of the chef. Expect to find variations on the theme of anchovies, octopus-and-potato salad, linguine with seafood and shellfish sauce, and baked whole fish *alla ligure* with olives, pine nuts and potatoes. The *zabaione* (not always available) is made not with Marsala but Sciacchetrà, and all the desserts are housemade and delicious. The wine list features Cinque Terre and other Ligurian bottlings.

VIA DE GASPERI 4 ✦ TEL: 0187 920143 ✦ OPEN FOR DINNER ONLY TUESDAY *through* SATURDAY, SUNDAY LUNCH ONLY CLOSED JANUARY *and* FEBRUARY ✦ MODERATE

Cappun Magru

IN A VILLAGE HOUSE NICKNAMED *CASA DI MARIN*, BETWEEN THE CINQUE TERRE CO-OP WINERY AND Volastra, above Riomaggiore, this stylish restaurant is where owner-chef Maurizio Bordoni's grandparents lived in rustic simplicity. He's upgraded the furniture, adding Chiavari chairs and old buffets, and original artworks. Unlike many hereabouts, this house isn't hidden in the dark fold of the mountainside; there's a keyhole view to the Mediterranean. There's something survivalist about the cooking, with many ingredients (beans, squash, wild herbs, olives, shade-grown basil and olive oils) from nearby terraced kitchen gardens and olive groves. The anchovies and other fish are from Riomaggiore. The best way to eat the *acciughe* here is marinated in fresh lemon juice. Don't shun the fish soup, made from small, unmarketable but flavorful fish.

GROPPO ✦ TEL: 0187 920563 ✦ OPEN FOR LUNCH SUNDAY *and* BY ARRANGEMENT, FOR DINNER WEDNESDAY *through* SATURDAY CLOSED MONDAY *and* TUESDAY ✦ MODERATE *to* EXPENSIVE

Bar-Ristorante dell'Amore

ONE OF THE WORLD'S MORE SPECTACULAR SEASIDE PROMENADES CLINGS TO THE ZIGZAGGING, FRACtured coves and striated cliffs separating Riomaggiore from Manarola. Almost precisely halfway, about a quarter-mile from either direction, you come upon this improbable, casual snack bar and lunch spot. The indoor dining room is welcoming; usually it's empty. That's because a handful of tables under a shaded awning are perched on metal grates overhanging the shore, which is too far below for comfort. Owned and built by the national park authorities, Via dell'Amore is run by a group of young women, who make the *bruschetta*, pesto, linguine with seafood, swordfish with olives and potatoes, stuffed local anchovies, and mixed small fry. The salted anchovies (de-salted before being served, with sliced tomatoes and oregano), smoked swordfish and *pecorino* ewe's milk cheese (accompanied by local honey and walnuts) come from the national park's supplier. Everything is highly edible, fresh, and simple, and the view from the outdoor tables simply cannot be beat. The white wines are local, from the Cinque Terre co-op and Colli di Luni.

LOCALITÀ VAILUNGO, VIA DELL'AMORE (PEDESTRIAN WALKWAY *from* RIOMAGGIORE *to* MANAROLA) TEL: 0187 921026 ✦ OPEN DAYLIGHT HOURS, USUALLY 8:30AM *to* 10:30PM IN SUMMER, UNTIL 6:30PM IN WINTER ✦ INEXPENSIVE

Colle del Telegrafo

THE OLD TELEGRAPH LINE FROM THE COAST TO LA SPEZIA USED TO CROSS THE RIDGE AT THIS POINT, and the views from nearly 1,800 feet above sea level are amazing. National park employees run this tasteful glassed-in restaurant and information center, open since April 2003. Given its remoteness, at the end of scores of switchbacks on a tiny paved road, and crisscrossed by long-distance hiking trails, you're entitled to be astonished to find succulent swordfish carpaccio, calamari salad with walnuts, and regional classics like Cinque Terre co-op pesto, fried small fry, and *mesciua* white bean soup, the specialty of La Spezia. Everything tastes better than merely good, many of the ingredients are organic, and everything is strictly local. Wines include bottlings made up and down the coast, among them, the crisp whites of the Cinque Terre co-op.

LOCALITÀ COLLE DEL TELEGRAFO, MONTE PARODI
TEL: 0187 760561 ✦ MODERATE ✦ OPEN *from* 10AM *to* 5PM
MONDAY, TUESDAY, WEDNESDAY *and* FRIDAY, CLOSED
THURSDAY, OPEN FOR LUNCH *and* DINNER WEEKENDS

Gli Ulivi

VOLASTRA, A COMPACT VILLAGE ON TILTING STREETS, PERCHES HALFWAY UP THE STEEP terraces hemming in Riomaggiore. This has been olive oil country since time immemorial. The village's name is said to derive from the Roman *Vicus oleaster*—the place of olive trees—and this restaurant has followed suit. Owned and operated by the national park, the food and wine is very similar to that of Colle del Telegrafo, the cooking good, the atmosphere jolly. There's a small outdoor terrace and a handsome dining room. The pesto is usually made here by the chef, though sometimes it comes from the nearby farm co-op (growers of organic basil).

Other restaurant-refreshment facilities owned and operated by the national park and open seasonally (hours/days vary widely, phone ahead): **Ristorante Bar Santuario di Montenero** (Tel: 0187 760528), in the arcaded former refectory of this splendid church complex, perched far above Riomaggiore, and reached only by hiking trails or monorail. Call ahead to reserve lunch or dinner, which is usually made for overnight guests only. **Ristorante Bar**

Monesteroli (Via Litoranea 801, Tel: 0187 758214) is a simple roadside eatery between La Spezia and Riomaggiore, a good place to stop for a snack, light meal or coffee.

VIA NOSTRA SIGNORA DELLA SALUTE 114, VOLASTRA
TEL: 0187 920158 ✦ MODERATE ✦ OPEN DAILY

COFFEE, HONEY, ICE CREAM, PASTRIES

Non Solo Vino

O N THE MAIN STREET FROM THE PARKING LOT TO THE SEA, THIS WELL-STOCKED BOUTIQUE HAS every imaginable Ligurian sauce, plus local wines, honeys and salted anchovies.

VIA COLOMBO 180 ✦ TEL: 0187 760558
OFF-SEASON HOURS VARY WIDELY

Panificio Rosy

O WNERS THE SACCHELLI FAMILY ARE FROM LA SPEZIA, AND HAVE RUN THIS HOLE-IN-THE-WALL bakery since 1997. They bake the bread and focaccia served at many of the village's hotels, bars, B&Bs and restaurants, which explains why Riomaggiore is credited with having the best focaccia for miles around. Mauro Sacchelli makes a delicious five-cereal loaf, firm and flavorful focaccia and crisp *schiacciata*, a focaccia-like flatbread. Rosetta Sacchelli makes the classic cookies, *crostata* with walnuts, savory vegetable tarts and the house specialty, *torta Cinque Terre*, a caloric bomb fashioned from fractured sponge cake, pastry cream and chocolate chips, perfected, she claims, in the 1950s.

VIA COLOMBO 188 ✦ TEL: 0187 920775 ✦ OPEN 7AM *to* 8PM DAILY

Bar Centrale

A LOCAL HANGOUT ON THE MAIN DRAG FROM THE PARKING LOT TO THE SEASIDE PROMENADE, BAR Centrale serves a decent cup of espresso and outstanding fruit ices and fruit ice creams. The lemons used to make that flavor are grown locally by a cousin of the owner.

Grab a cone of *gelato al limone* and stroll with it.

VIA COLOMBO 144 ✦ TEL: 0187 920208

OPEN 8AM *to* 8PM, CLOSED MONDAY

WINERIES

Luciano Capellini

L UCIANO CAPELLINI (WITH ONE "P"—NOT TO BE CONFUSED WITH GIACOMO CAPPELLINI, WHOSE winery is in nearby Manarola), a passionate winemaker, grows and bottles small quantities of distinctive Cinque Terre wines. The Casata dei Beghee, for instance, is a brilliant straw color, full of herbal notes, and fills under 4,000 bottles a year. Capellini is also winning fame for his mellow Sciacchetrà, and what he's designated Vino di Buccia. This peculiar wine, derived from the second pressing of Sciacchetrà skins (*le bucce*), is still sweet and powerful, but looser and less alcoholic than Sciacchetrà. The cantina is small, and rough and ready. Capellini will gladly show you around his winery and, if he has time, his vineyards; tastings can be arranged and are held at Cappun Magru restaurant in Groppo.

FRAZIONE VOLASTRA, VIA MONTELLO 240B ✦ TEL: 0187 920632
CAPELLINI@VINBUN.IT, WWW.VINBUN.IT. TO MAKE AN
APPOINTMENT: INFO@ARBASPAA.COM ✦ TEL: 0187 760083

*Cantina Cooperativa
Agricoltura Cinque Terre a.r.l.*

A HUNDRED YEARS AGO THERE WERE 4,000 ACRES OF THE VERMENTINO, BOSCO AND ALBAROLA grapes that go into Cinque Terre DOC wines. Of them only about 250 acres are left, worked by around 160 active co-op growers aged an average seventy-five (the total membership is 300, but not everyone is active), and a handful of independents. The good news is, the national park authorities are helping to reverse the trend, have reclaimed scores of acres of vineyards so far for the co-op, and are growing organic basil (for Genoese pesto) alongside the grapevines. The wines made by this modern facility, built in 1982, are clean and precise, without being overly technical, meaning, the typical herbal notes of the Cinque Terre shine through. The Costa de Campu di Manarola is often the best of the three vineyard crus, which also include Costa de Sera di Riomaggiore and Costa dá Posa di Volastra. Vineyard visits are by appointment only; you must have your own car. There is a charge for wine tastings and snacks. The co-op has a well-stocked boutique, which sells not only wines, but pesto, oils and olives, salted anchovies under oil and other specialty foods of the area.

LOCALITÀ GROPPO ✦ TEL: 0187920435
WWW.CANTINACINQUETERRE.COM ✦ OPEN 7AM *to* 7PM
MONDAY *through* SATURDAY, *and* BY APPOINTMENT
(PHONE AT LEAST 3 DAYS AHEAD; GROUP VISITS, MINIMUM 15)

Walter De Battè

D E BATTÈ IS WIDELY RECOGNIZED IN ITALY AS THE FINEST MAKER OF SCIACCHETRÀ. WITHOUT HIS resolve, the wine may well have disappeared or become a run-of-the-mill fortified wine. His cantina is modest, as is he, located off the main drag (from the main parking lot to the seaside). Many of his grapes come from high terraces, topping 1,600 feet, where wild boars sometimes destroy the harvest; they did in 2005. De Battè makes classic Cinque Terre white, which is three-quarters Bosco grapes, twenty percent Albarola and only five percent Vermentino. He also makes Cerricò, which is full-bodied and sure to please those unfamiliar with Riviera wines. It strays from native varieties, and is made almost entirely from Granaccia (Alicante), with a touch of Syrah. De Battè's other big, New World-style wines are marketed under the label PrimaTerra, and made at a separate winery in Brugnato (inland, near La Spezia).

VIA TRARCANTU 25 ✦ TEL: 0187 920127 ✦ BY APPOINTMENT

MANAROLA

WINERY

Forlini e Cappellini

G IACOMO CAPPELLINI (WITH TWO "P"S, NOT TO BE CONFUSED WITH LUCIANO CAPELLINI OF VOLASTRA) is the second generation in his family to make wines in a small cantina in Manarola. He's upgraded from his parents' day, with temperature-controlled stainless steel and a handful of oak casks, which he uses judiciously. Look for the typical herbal notes, straw color and hints of iodide in his Cinque Terre whites. The Sciacchetrà Riserva is remarkable, with a honeyed mellowness and depth not often found in this difficult-to-make sweet wine.

VIA RICCOBALDI 45 ✦ TEL: 0187 920496 ✦ BY APPOINTMENT

CORNIGLIA

THE HIGHEST OF THE CINQUE TERRE'S NESTED VILLAGES, CORNIGLIA SITS ATOP A RIDGE precisely 382 steps up a zigzag stairway from the curling road behind the train station. Tiny, with just a handful of shops and the smallest of the area's ports, Corniglia is slightly less clogged with foot traffic than its four sisters. The outdoor *caffè* and restaurants in the main square are pleasant but not distinguished in gastronomic terms. Try **A Cantina de Mananan** (Via Fieschi 117, Tel: 0187 821166, closed Tuesday, inexpensive to moderate). Agostino and Marianne Galletti own and operate this neo-*osteria* on Corniglia's single main alleyway. There is no terrace or patio, so tourists head elsewhere. The heavy wooden tables and wooden shelves filled with bottles, the white walls and a bar-counter at one end of the room match the simplicity of the menu. Its offerings range from platters of hams, salami and cheeses to good local anchovies served with a pinch of oregano, or marinated with onions, and savory tarts. The *testaroli* daubed with pesto or porcini-and-tomato sauce, and *pansôti* with walnut sauce, are housemade. Second courses include rabbit *alla ligure* with olives, pine nuts, rosemary and potatoes. The desserts are simple—*crostata*, almond cookies—and many of the area's independent wineries are on the wine list.

Gelateria Zico (Via Fieschi 98, no telephone, open seasonally), is across the alleyway from the *osteria*. A tiny take-out *gelateria*, run by Alberto and Cristina Zico, it makes good artisanal ice creams and sorbets. Buy a cone and walk across the village square to the panoramic point where the alley deadends.

Winery **La Polenza di Lorenzo Casté** (Via Fieschi 107, Tel: 0187 821214, by appointment), a small, artisanal operation making classic Cinque Terre wines, is a separate entity from La Polenza di Maria Rita Rezzano in Vernazza.

VERNAZZA

THE MOST PICTURESQUE AND POPULAR OF THE CINQUE TERRE, VERNAZZA HAS A SCALLOP-shell-shaped harbor and a handsome Romanesque church perched over it. The main square is perpetually mobbed. Two respectable restaurants, both with outdoor seating on the square, serving fish and local specialties, are **Trattoria Gianni Franzi** (Piazza Marconi 1, Tel: 0187 821003, www.giannifranzi.it, closed Wednesday and January 8 to March 8, moderate to expensive), in the same family since 1960; and a fall-back, **Taverna del Capitano** (Piazza Marconi 21, Tel: 0187 812201, closed Tuesday, moderate to expensive). Keep it simple. Service is hectic much of the time. Relax and enjoy the atmosphere.

In the Middle Ages, Vernazza was a prime winemaking village, and may well lie at the origin of Vernaccia, the wine now associated with San Gimignano in Tuscany. One good winery making classic Cinque Terre wines is based here: **La Polenza di Maria Rita Rezzano** (Via San Bernardino 24, Tel: 0187 821214, lapolenza@libero.it, call ahead). The Cinque Terre's other wineries are in surrounding villages, though some of their vineyards encircle Vernazza.

You'll find bigger and better-stocked wine shops elsewhere, but **Enoteca Sotto l'Arco** (Via Roma 70, Tel: 0187 812124, closed Monday, seasonal hours vary widely) offers a good selection of bottlings from local winemakers (and others in farther-flung regions), plus many Ligurian delicacies, including pesto and salted anchovies.

MONTEROSSO

THOUGH STILL REFERRED TO AS A VILLAGE, MONTEROSSO IS ACTUALLY A FAIR-SIZED TOWN, divided into three parts, the oldest and most interesting of which — *il centro storico* — is to the east. The train station is in the middle, between the *centro storico* and the late 1800s resort area of Fegina (where Nobel-winning Genoese poet Eugenio Montale spent his boyhood summers). All of the best restaurants, wine bars and shops are in the *centro storico*, north of the elevated railway viaduct. Monterosso Beo and the monastery of Soviore are high above town.

RESTAURANTS

Il Ciliegio

PERCHED AT ABOUT 600 FEET ABOVE SEA LEVEL, THIS FAMILY-STYLE RESTAURANT IS WHAT YOU WISH you could find in one of the villages below. It's comfortable — white walls, open timbers, white tablecloths, prints and original, motel art, plus a wrap-around terrace under pines and shady trees — and serves delicious, simple, housemade Riviera food, from marinated or stuffed Cinque Terre anchovies to stuffed mussels in the style of La Spezia, *trofie* with pesto, *cima alla genovese* or baked whole fish with olives and pine nuts. The desserts are homey and simple — *crostata* and other tarts — and the wine list features local bottlings and quaffable house wines. If you're on foot, call ahead and ask to be picked up; the restaurant has a free shuttle service to Monterosso.

LOCALITÀ BEO 2 ✦ TEL: 0187 817829 ✦ CLOSED MONDAY
and NOVEMBER 1 *to* LATE DECEMBER ✦ MODERATE

Santuario Nostra Signora di Soviore

THIS MEDIEVAL PILGRIMAGE SITE PERCHED ON A RIDGE BEHIND MONTEROSSO, EVEN HIGHER UP than Beo, houses a miracle-making sculpture of the Madonna in a gold-encrusted church, but it also has a simple pilgrims' restaurant flanking a sixteenth-century hostel. The regional specialties are designed to please groups of hungry visitors, but they're suprisingly good and authentic, from the pesto on up, and very reasonably priced.

SOVIORE, MONTEROSSO ✦ TEL: 0187 817385
WWW.SOVIORE.ORG ✦ OPEN DAILY ✦ INEXPENSIVE

COFFEE, PASTRIES, SNACKS, WINE

Enoteca Ciak

WELL-STOCKED WITH MOST OF THE WINES, INCLUDING SCIACCHETRÀ, MADE IN THE CINQUE Terre, from De Batté to Forlini e Capellini or the Cinque Terre cooperative, Ciak also sells jams and honey, bottled pesto or anchovies, and olives, olive oil and olive pastes. A recent and welcome addition is **Ciak Wine & Food**, across the street to the west, on Via Vittorio Emanuele (same telephone). Here you can taste wines by the glass, and snack on simple Ligurian specialties — from savory tarts and pasta with pesto to squid-ink risotto, seafood salad or skewered, grilled octopus — or sip a decent cup of coffee. There's a pleasant sidewalk terrace.

VIA ROMA 4 ✦ TEL: 0187 817345 ✦ CLOSED WEDNESDAY

Enoteca Internazionale

S USANNA BARBIERI AND HER FAMILY OWN AND RUN THIS OLD WINE SHOP AND WINE TASTING BAR, WITH a handful of tables inside and a pleasant terrace out front. You'll find all the best wines of the area, plus many Italian and even a few foreign labels. Barbieri always has a small stock of hard-to-find De Batté Sciacchetrà, very good olive oils, dry pasta and a small selection of specialty foods. Snacks served range from platters of ham, salami and cheese, to salads.

VIA ROMA 62 ✦ TEL: 0187 817278 ✦ WWW.CINQUETERRENET.COM
OPEN DAILY APRIL *to* NOVEMBER, CLOSED *from* JANUARY 6
to MID FEBRUARY, *and* ON TUESDAYS *the rest of the year*

Pasticceria Laura

W ITH ITS KITCHENS ON ONE SIDE OF A TINY *PIAZ-ZETTA* WEDGED BETWEEN TALL BUILDINGS, AND the pastry shop-cum-*caffè* on the other, this old, family-run *pasticceria* makes very good shortbread cookies, *crostate* jam tarts and the mind-bogglingly rich, pastry cream-and-chocolate *monterossina* tart. The coffee served is strong and dark-roasted, and best consumed in the form of a cappuccino.

VIA VITTORIO EMANUELE 59 ✦ NO TELEPHONE ✦ OPEN DAILY
8AM *to* 7:30PM, CLOSED MONDAY *from* SEPTEMBER *through* JUNE

Four More Cinque Terre Independent Wineries

. . . .

Bonanni Fellegara

VIA DI LOCA 189, RIOMAGGIORE ✦ TEL: 338 406 3383

Buranco

VIA BURANCO 72, MONTEROSSO ✦ TEL: 0187 817677

WWW.BURANCO.IT

Molinari & Pasini—M&P

SALITA CASTELLO 137, RIOMAGGIORE ✦ TEL: 335 836 3708

Natale Sassarini

LOCALITÀ PIAN DEL CORSO 1, MONTEROSSO

TEL: 0187 817034 PHONE AHEAD *and* MAKE AN APPOINTMENT

LA SPEZIA

. . . .

A MAJOR NAVAL PORT AND RAIL HUB, HOMELY LA SPEZIA IS OFTEN OVERLOOKED BY VISITORS, who pass through on the way to the Cinque Terre, which are a few miles northwest over a ridge. Yet La Spezia's grid of mostly nineteenth-century streets, lined by stately *palazzi*, and its landscaped seaside promenade, are handsome, pleasant and free of the less attractive aspects of mass tourism. Likewise, most *spezzini*, as residents are known, seem extraordinarily welcoming and helpful. This is a very good food city, with what might be the region's best *farinata*, delicious if unpronouncible *mesciua* mixed-bean soup, locally cultivated mussels and clams, abundant fresh fish, and many of the specialties of the abutting Lunigiana region, including *testaroli* and *panigacci*. The city is named for the spices — *spezie* — traditionally shipped through the port, before it became a naval facility, and a possible reminder of this is the local love for chocolate. A chocolate festival is held at many different venues in the center of the city each year in October and November. The covered market, in Piazza Mercato, though not antique or aesthetic, is among the

biggest and best stocked in the entire region, and opens earlier than most, at about 6am, closing at 1pm. From La Spezia you can take buses to Portovenere, Lerici, Sarzana and the Cinque Terre (and direct trains to just about anywhere in Italy).

RESTAURANTS, *FARINATA*, WINE BAR

Antica Osteria da Caran

ARRIVING BY CAR FROM THE NORTHWEST, ON THE OLD HIGHWAY, YOU COME UPON THIS AUTHEN-tically old *trattoria*, which once sat in the landscaped garden of a sprawling villa, and now occupies a slice of land between busy trunk roads and a traffic circle on La Spezia's outskirts. Walking to it from the train station is another, less pleasant matter. Happily, the patio is isolated from the surrounding blight, and is a lovely place to enjoy al fresco some of the area's best *farinata*, very good pizza, *mesciua* bean soup, savory tarts, lasagne sauced with tomatoes, not to mention very good meat-filled ravioli with meat sauce and platters of small fry or local mussels. The desserts are homey classics — jam tarts, apple pies and tiramisu.

VIA GENOVA 1 ✦ TEL: 0187 703777
CLOSED MONDAY ✦ INEXPENSIVE

Bellavista

AFFABLE ALESSANDRO TAVILLA RUNS THIS SIM-PLE *TRATTORIA* A HUNDRED YARDS SOUTHEAST of the market square. The wooden tables are covered with paper, the walls painted with naif seaside scenes and the clientele a mix of shopkeepers, blue-collar workers and neighborhood residents. The menu changes daily following the market, but you can expect to find a mix of fresh, well-made La Spezia favorites, from gnocchi with pesto to *stoccafisso* or stuffed anchovies, plus Italian classics from other regions.

VIA RATTAZZI 54-56 ✦ TEL: 0187 738720
OPEN FOR LUNCH DAILY EXCEPT SUNDAY, FOR DINNER
THURSDAY *and* FRIDAY ONLY ✦ INEXPENSIVE

Osteria all'Inferno

FIFTY YARDS EAST OF LA SPEZIA'S VAST MARKET SQUARE, YOU CLIMB DOWN FROM STREET LEVEL into a vaulted cellar that looks at first like a narrow tunnel, but turns out to sprawl to either side. Tall waiters and guests stoop to move under the vaults, which rise to about six feet at their apex. The establishment's name is appropriate only in a geophysical sense—an underworld—because the service is friendly, the interior unadorned but clean, white and brightly lit, and the food, while not heavenly, is very good, and authentic to the city's traditions. The recipes are as old as this *osteria*, founded in 1905 and still in the same extended family after four generations. Try the minestrone and *mesciua* bean soup, *stoccafisso* with olives and potatoes (plus a pinch of chili pepper and a dollop of tomato sauce), tripe and fresh fish. It's worth noting that the housemade pesto has both pine nuts and walnuts, which many Ligurians claim is closer to the original recipe. Beyond the well-made regional classics, you might find hearty wild boar stew, sausages with broccoli rabe, or, on the lighter side, delicious *taglierini* with seafood and tomato sauce. Desserts are homey and tend to be rich (*zuppa inglese* or scoops of mascarpone with cream, apple pie). The market is next door, all' Inferno always packed, with quick turnaround, and the food therefore very fresh. Stick to the house carafe wines, which are quaffable Colli di Luni white and red.

VIA COSTA LORENZO 3 ✦ TEL: 0187 29458
CLOSED SUNDAY ✦ INEXPENSIVE

Party House Enoteca con Cucina

THIS WINE BAR WITH TABLES ON A RECENTLY PEDESTRIANIZED STREET A HUNDRED YARDS FROM the covered market has a good selection of Italian wines, but only a handful from the Riviera. They include Cinque Terre cooperative bottlings and Bruna. Locals lunch here on house-made gnocchi or *testaroli* with pesto and a variety of La Spezia classics, plus platters of cold cuts and cheeses.

VIA DEI MILLE 76 ✦ TEL: 349 345 7527
WWW.PARTYHOUSE.COM ✦ OPENING HOURS VARY
from NOON *to* 7PM, 8PM, 9PM OR MIDNIGHT (IN JULY
and AUGUST), CLOSED SUNDAY ✦ INEXPENSIVE

La Pia Centenaria

SEPARATED FROM THE SIDEWALK BY AN ALCOVE AND COUNTER, LA PIA'S PAIR OF CENTURY-OLD WOOD-burning ovens chug away, perfuming the alleyways of La Spezia surrounding this cult *farinata* joint. Ask anyone for "La Pia" and you'll be led there, approvingly, and probably joined by your guide. No red-blooded *spezzino* can resist *farinata*, morning, noon or night. There's a spartan, echoing sit-down dining room next door to the ovens, and a shaded outdoor terrace around

the corner, but La Pia is best for a take-out snack — hot slices of fragrant chickpea tart, pizza (the classics, plus pizza *con pesto*) or mildly sweet *castagnaccio*, wrapped in thick paper. The vegetable savory tarts (usually spinach) are very good. While the pizza is on the doughy side, the *farinata* that's baked patiently at off-hours might just be the region's most sumptuous. At lunch or dinner the crowds are huge and the pressure to feed them is such that, occasionally, the insides of the tart are still tacky when served. At its best, it's about a quarter-inch high, crisp on top, cooked through without being dry, firm on the bottom, and rich in oil. It has just the right amount of salt, not to mention a smoky flavor from the roaring ovens. Don't forget to sprinkle some black pepper on your slice before you walk away.

VIA MAGENTA 12 ✦ TEL: 0187 739999 ✦ WWW.LAPIA.IT
OPEN 8AM *to* 10PM DAILY *except* SUNDAY ✦ INEXPENSIVE

CHOCOLATE, FOCACCIA, ICE CREAM, GOURMET FOODS, PASTRIES

Armando — Pasticceria, Gelateria

GISELLA BRIZZI DOES THE BAKING AND RUNS THIS SPARTAN PASTRY SHOP THAT FACES LA SPEZIA'S busy market. The pine nut-studded *pinolata* cookies and fresh *savoiardi* — the keystone ladyfinger cookies used in many Italian cake recipes — are remarkably good. From March to October, Gisella makes about a dozen natural fruit ice creams, following the ripe, seasonally available fruit she finds at the market.

VIA DEI MILLE 55/PIAZZA MERCATO ✦ TEL: 0187 24513
OPEN DAILY, *including* SUNDAY MORNING

L'Artigiano del Cioccolato

FOR SOMETHING APPROACHING THIRTY-FOUR YEARS, GIORGIO BENETTI WAS ONE LA SPEZIA'S TOP pastry chefs before he turned his hand to making only chocolate, and, with a partner, took over this small boutique about halfway between the train station and the shipyard, in the center of town. Benetti, an artist and perfectionist, uses forty different types of base chocolates from the world's best suppliers because, he feels, each of his creations—filled chocolates, chocolate bars, chocolate sculptures, chocolate-dipped candied orange slices—requires a specific percentage of cocoa, the right chemical makeup, texture and appearance. Many of his chocolate sculptures seem too elaborate and too beautiful to be edible, but he swears that customers, including men of the cloth, devour the gilded Cinderella-style carriages, the old-fashioned Singer sewing machines, the fierce-looking eagles and even the Baby Jesuses nested in their creches. Luckily, the ordinary chocolates are also exquisite—never too fatty or sweet—and the humble chocolate "salami" looks so real you'll have no qualms slicing it into dark, chocolatey rounds.

VIA NINO BIXIO 46 ✦ TEL: 0187 715966
CLOSED SUNDAY *and* MONDAY

Cioccolateria Dolce… più Dolce

THIS NEW CHOCOLATE BOUTIQUE ABOUT A HUNDRED YARDS NORTH OF THE MARKET MAKES A wide variety of good, classic filled chocolates and very crisp yet buttery shortbread cookies, all of which tend to the sweet side of the spectrum. The shop also supplies the equally cute **Caffè Mozart**, on the northwest side of the market (Corso Cavour 112).

VIA DEI MILLE 66 ✦ TEL: 329 388 1397
CLOSED MONDAY AFTERNOON *and* SUNDAY

L'Isola delle cose buone

THE QUINTESSENTIAL BOUTIQUE, WHERE EVERYTHING IS DONE UP LIKE A BERIBBONED GIFT, THIS self-styled "food island" about 150 yards north of the market may just be the diamond cutting-head of the gentification that's transforming rough-and-ready old La Spezia into something cozy and welcoming. Luckily the selection of wines, grappas, olive oils, jams, dry pastas and rice, anchovies in olive oil and prettily wrapped sweets—including candied fruit from Romanengo and *pandolce* from Confetteria Rossi, both in Genoa—is excellent, and the elegantly dressed owner helpful and friendly.

VIA DEI MILLE 103 ✦ TEL: 0187 751503
WWW.FOODISLAND.IT ✦ CLOSED SUNDAY

Panificio Rizzoli Marcello

SMALL, FAMILY-RUN, SPARTAN AND ON A TRAFFIC-CLOGGED ARTERY LEADING WEST TOWARD GENOA, this neighborhood bake shop turns out remarkably good classic focaccia, crispy *schiacciata* and savory vegetable tarts. Rizzoli is now into its second generation of bakers, with no descernible lowering of quality, and continues to make focaccia in the triangular format which founder Marcello Rizzoli first created decades ago. The bakery supplies some of La Spezia's best bars and restaurants with bread and focaccia, and is worth seeking out, especially if you're planning to walk from the station to Antica Osteria da Caran, which is another 300 yards west.

VIA FIUME 108 ✦ TEL: 0187 743168 ✦ CLOSED SUNDAY

Stampetta—Panificio, Pasticceria

THIS IS AN ALADDIN'S CAVE OF PASTRIES, COOKIES, CAKES, BREADS AND FOCACCIAS OF VARIOUS kinds, all of them good and beautifully displayed, at two almost identical shops a few blocks apart on one of La Spezia's main east-west arteries. But it's the giant loaves of local *pandolce*, which are rich in raisins, and less sweet than most *pandolce*, which distinguish Stampetta from the city's many other competent bakeries. The focaccia tends to be firm, almost crisp, and dry, and Stampetta sells it in the small triangles that are now common to La Spezia, but which, it's widely believed, were invented by rival baker Marcello Rizzoli.

CORSO CAVOUR 245 ✦ TEL: 0187 24502
(SECOND SHOP AT CORSO CAVOUR 375) ✦ CLOSED SUNDAY

TESTI FOR MAKING TESTAROLI

Granbazzar

RUN BY THE SAME FAMILY SINCE THE 1920S, THIS HARDWARE AND VARIETY STORE SELLS THE terracotta or iron *testi* needed to make *testaroli*, the pancake-like pasta.

CORSO CAVOUR 262/254 ✦ TEL: 0187 718155
CLOSED MONDAY MORNING *and* SUNDAY

LEVANTO

MEDIEVAL, WITH PARTS OF ITS CITY WALLS INTACT, LEVANTO IS A HANDSOME SMALL town just north of Punta Mesco and the Cinque Terre. The seaside walk is paved in slate, and provides views of the rugged mountains framing the scene. Most of the atmospheric old streets and alleys of Levanto are closed to traffic. It's a pleasure to stroll amid the old buildings, many of which are painted in pastel shades. Fewer tourists swarm Levanto compared to the Cinque Terre, and there is a sizeable, year-round population of residents, but to claim Levanto is undiscovered would be stretching things. Most restaurant menus come in several languages, and the concentration of B&Bs, hotels, pizzerias and cutesy boutiques is high. The perched Romanesque church of Sant'Andrea is particularly handsome, with black-and-white stripes. Levanto has two gastronomic specialties of its own: *gattafin*, a savory pastry purse stuffed with chard and sautéed minced onions which is deep fried; and *torciglione*, a sweet pastry made with strands of sugary dough and shortbread dough twisted together to form a loose knot, with chocolate powder, raisins and sugar mixed in. One of the region's better pesto makers is here, there's delicious ice cream and you can taste local wines direct from the co-op makers. The weekly street market is held Wednesday mornings from 8am to 1pm in Strada del Mercato, which is halfway between the sea and the train station; the covered market is also found here, and is open weekday and Saturday mornings. The tourist information office is on Piazza Mazzini (Tel: 0187 808125) in the former train station, on the western end of the seaside promenade.

In terms of authentic regional cooking, the restaurant scene is a challenge. The two long-established fish restaurants, La Loggia and Osteria Tumelin, facing each other across Piazza del Popolo, are interchangeable. There's a chic, very expensive new restaurant, L'Oasi, on the main square, Piazza Cavour, facing city hall, which serves sophisticated, seafood-based cuisine but could be in San Francisco, Syndey or Paris. Kitty corner to it, with a nice terrace on the square, directly behind the monument to Count Camillo Benso Cavour, is the old-fashioned, century-old **Trattoria Cavour** (Piazza Cavour 1, Tel: 0187 808497, closed Monday, moderate to expensive). It has curmudgeonly notices, written in English, that state: "No pizza, No party," a reaction, the waiters explain, to the demands of foreign tourists. Happily, the octopus with potatoes is good, the mixed grilled fish is, too, and so is the lemon sorbet (made with local lemons) and *semifreddo* with *torroncino*. Another locale serving the closest thing Levanto gets to *terroir* cooking is **Antica Trattoria Centro** (Corso Italia 25, Tel: 0187 808157, closed Tuesday, moderate to expensive). Here you can enjoy anchovies marinated in lemon juice, savory vegetable tarts, minestrone *alla genovese* and the only-in-Levanto specialty *gattafin*, plus housemade ravioli, stuffed anchovies or "black" *mandilli* lasagne with squid ink and baby *moscardini*. The *trattoria* is located one street in from the seaside roadway, near Piazzetta della Marina, and has a covered back terrace.

COFFEE, GOURMET FOODS, ICE CREAM, PASTRIES, PESTO, WINE

Caffè Le Clarisse

UNDER THE ARCADES OF THE MAIN SQUARE, FACING CITY HALL, THIS CLASSY *CAFFÈ* WITH CHANDELIERS, armchairs and couches inside, and a covered terrace outside, serves a good cup of espresso and offers a wide range of snacks.

PIAZZA CAVOUR 7 ✦ TEL: 0187 804020

OPEN 8AM *to* 2AM DAILY *except* WEDNESDAY

La Cantina Levantese di S. Lagaxie

ON A BACK STREET DOWNTOWN BETWEEN CORSO ITALIA AND VIA JACOPO DA LEVANTO, THIS CO-OP winery's tasting and sales room is a good place to try remarkable white DOC Colline di Levanto (plus single-vineyard crus Costa di Brazzo and Costa di Montaretto, and the reserve black-label red). In fall, if you enjoy zingy new wine, you can taste the *vino novello* direct from the stainless steel tanks. Also sold are the full line of *sottoli* made by Frantoio Sant'Agata d'Oneglia, plus the co-op's own good extra virgin olive oil, *limoncino* and white wine vinegar aged in new oak casks.

VIA ZOPPI 11 ✦ TEL: 0187 807137

CANTINALEVANTESE@LIBERO.IT

CLOSED WEDNESDAY AFTERNOON *and* SUNDAY

Enoteca Coop Vallata di Levanto

THERE ARE TWO CO-OP WINERIES IN LEVANTO, AND THIS ONE IS ALSO A FARMING CO-OP. TO BRING in the walk-by business, in fall 2007 they opened this handsome wine-tasting and sales room on Piazza del Popolo, facing Osteria Tumelin and the ramp leading up to the seaside roadway. Sit on the slate-paved terrace and sip the co-op's many DOC wines—red, white and rosé—by the glass. A wide range of other Ligurian wines—from Cooperativa Cinque Terre to Ottaviano Lambruschi, Il Torchio, Santa Caterina and Bosoni—are available by the bottle. Snacks range from cold cuts and cheeses to the many delicious bottled vegetables under oil—artichokes, olives and more—made by the co-op's members and available for purchase. Also sold are the co-op's fine extra virgin DOP olive oils, grappas and *limoncino* made with local organic lemon peels infused in alcohol.

PIAZZA DEL POPOLO/VIA D. E. TOSO 1 ✦ TEL: 0187 807001
WWW.COOPAGRICOLTORILEVANTO.IT ✦ CLOSED THURSDAY

Enoteca Vinum

ON THE WIDE, TRIANGULAR SQUARE THAT SERVES AS LEVANTO'S CENTRAL PARK, THIS TINY WINE SHOP is about an arm-span wide, but sells over 500 different wines, including fifteen to twenty of Liguria's best, plus liqueurs, excellent olive oils and a small selection of delicious sweets (*torrone* from Rossignotti in Sestri Levante) and bottled sauces and pesto from Frantoio Sant'Agata d'Oneglia. The shop is run by affable Paolo and Vittorio Bertonati.

PIAZZA STAGLIENO 34 ✦ TEL: 0187 800141
CLOSED MONDAY MORNINGS

Gelateria Il Porticciolo

THIS SIMPLE LITTLE ICE CREAMERY IS TUCKED BETWEEN THE ELEVATED SEASIDE ROAD AND Corso Italia, on a small square with an underpass leading to the seaside promenade. It's not the fanciest place in town, but makes the best ice cream, using only fresh, natural ingredients—no

shortcuts—most of which follow the seasons. The day's flavors—about ten in winter, more in summer—are chalked up
outside on a board, and might include rich chocolate, hazelnut or
cream, banana, lemon or strawberry. Get a cone and walk with it,
or take a seat at one of the tables in the pocket-sized, shaded
garden wedged between the shop and the elevated roadway.

PIAZZETTA DELLA MARINA ✦ NO TELEPHONE
CLOSED MONDAY

Il Laboratorio del Pesto

LABORATORIO MEANS "WORKSHOP" IN ITALIAN.
LUIGINA AND MARCO ROMANO RUN THIS GOUR-
met food boutique, specialized in fresh or bottled pesto,
on the main road in Levanto's historic town center. The pair have
been perfecting their pesto for decades, and have adopted a classic
recipe including basil from Prà and plump Tuscan pine nuts; the
curiosity is, the oils they use are about seventy to seventy-five
percent excellent extra virgin from Ardoino, and twenty-five to
thirty percent plain olive oil from Aclova (in Ortonovo). While
most non-virgin olive oils are to be avoided, Romano claims the
use of this higher-acid but neutral-tasting oil is the secret to the
deliciousness of his sauce, which is indeed remarkably good. The
shop also sells good bottled pesto made for Il Laboratorio by an oil
producer from the western Riviera, and a wide range of specialty
foods, from artisanal pasta and excellent Lucchi e Guastalli or
Ardoino oils, to *sottoli* of all kinds, cookies and sweets, and the
hard-to-find organic rose water syrup of Il Giardino dei Semplici.
Note that Levanto's other fine gourmet food and pesto boutique,
Enoteca La Nicchia (Corso Italia 26, Tel: 0187 802638), on the
corner of the public park nearest the seaside, is owned by the
same family. There you'll also find a good selection of wines from
the area.

VIA DANTE ALIGHIERI 16 ✦ TEL: 0187 807441
WWW.LEVANTO.COM ✦ CLOSED WEDNESDAY
AFTERNOONS *from* NOVEMBER *to* MARCH

Pasticceria Bianchi

PATTERNED TILES, CHIAVARI CHAIRS PAINTED GOLD
AND A WIDE COUNTER OF RED GRANITE, PLUS OLD-
fashioned display cases and mirrored advertisements from

a century ago, lend atmosphere to this pastry shop-cum-*caffè*. The classic Ligurian pastries and cookies are delicious, but the best thing of all is the *pinolata*, a shortbread cup filled and studded with pine nuts, and the chocolate-covered *nocciolato* cake, sold by the slice. The coffee, supplied by ItalCaffè, is perfectly good, especially when softened with milk in the form of a cappuccino. Bianchi is in the center of old Levanto, on the corner of Via Dante Alighieri.

VIA VINZONI 33 ✦ TEL: 0187 808183. CLOSED MONDAY

PORTOVENERE

A T THE TIP OF THE PROMONTORY SEPARATING LA SPEZIA FROM THE CINQUE TERRE, facing Palmaria Island across a narrow straight, Portovenere is a handsome village of tall buildings rising over rocky shoals. The ubiquitous Lord Byron was a regular (as was fellow poet Shelley, who drowned while trying to swim here from Lerici). The black-and-white-striped Romanesque church of San Pietro sits atop a buried Roman temple at the peninsula's fingerlike extremity. In recent decades, Portovenere has morphed from rough-edged Genoese fortress-village to seaside resort. Its 1,000-year-old house-towers wear pastel tones, the alleys below them are paved with slate. *Caffè* and restaurant tables fill sun-washed piazzas watched over by sculpted saints and Virgins. Like Portofino,

and despite or perhaps because of the history and beauty, this is not a gastronomic pilgrimage site.

However, there is one particularly pleasant *caffè* with shaded tables facing Portovenere's marina (**Bar Gelateria Lamia**, Piazza Marina, no telephone, closed Tuesday), and it serves excellent coffee roasted by Bei e Nannini (in Lucca) and makes excellent ice cream. **Antica Osteria del Caruggio** (Via Cappellini 66, Tel: 0187 790617, www.anticaosteria.com, closed Thursday, inexpensive to moderate) serves Ligurian classics and the *mesciua* of La Spezia. **La Pizzaccia** (Via Cappellini, no #, Tel: 0187 792722, in summer open 9am to 9pm daily except Thursday, in winter hours vary widely) has good pizza and *farinata*. A gourmet food boutique set between the marina and the village gate is **Ä Posa-a** (Piazza Bastreri 2, Tel: 0187 791466, closed Monday, winter hours vary); though it looks like the predictable tourist trap, it actually sells fine wines, olive oils and dry pasta (from Pastificio Santa Rita). On the port, near the yachts and fishing boats, you'll come across an unexpected automatic dispenser, the "Pesto Mat," not for soda pop or candy but pesto, made by industrious Laura Massa, owner, since 1947, of **Bajeicò** (Via Capellini 70, Tel: 0187 791054, www.bajeico.it). Her boutique and "Oleoteca" with many extra virgin olive oils, is on the main alleyway near La Pizzaccia. Whether the basil is grown and handpicked in Portovenere, and whether the 30,000 jars' worth of pesto produced annually is actually made in a mortar, as claimed by some food writers; how the olive oil can be "cold pressed" though not virgin let alone extra virgin; are mysteries known only to Massa and her assistants.

Organic Shade-Grown Basil from the Cinque Terre

·····················

ART OF THE AMBITIOUS PLAN OF THE CINQUE TERRE NATIONAL PARK IS TO RESTORE TERRACED farmlands, replant olive trees and grapevines, and, in their shade, grow certified organic garlic and basil. They are transformed by a local food processing firm into classic pesto, which is served in the park's concessionary restaurants and sold at the Cinque Terre co-op winery (which sells wine, pesto and other park products) and the park's shops in the train stations of each of the five seaside villages.

The basil plantations are on the Costa del Corniolo, a slope between Riomaggiore and Manarola, not far from the co-op winery. The basil grows tall, large and healthy here in the sea breezes, and is darker and more powerful in flavor than the tiny hothouse basil of Genoa's Prà peninsula. But it's much less strong than most full-sun, garden-grown basil. Direct sun gives basil what's often described as a "minty" flavor, which Ligurians dislike. Scientists in Genoa have isolated and identified eugenol as the culprit. It is the active chemical substance in mature, sun-grown plants. Shade-grown basil has little or no eugenol, and is high in methyleugenol, which gives it a pleasant citrus scent and taste.

Riviera Terraces

MOUNTAINOUS AND ROCKY, LIGURIA HAS LITTLE ARABLE LAND. FARMERS HAVE been reclaiming wild, steep slopes for at least 2,000 years. Some 25,000 miles of dry wall terraces built with field stones contour the Riviera end to end, an unmistakable, unifying trait. Ligurians call them *fasce*, literally "bands." Each averages twelve feet wide, with stone walls six to ten feet high. The effort that went into building them was collosal, took centuries and is comparable, it's said, to the building of the Great Wall of China or Machu Pichu. Virgil in *The Georgics* refers to an already-old saying, *Adsuetum malo Ligurem*: Ligurians are accustomed to toil and hardship.

The terraces strung from sea level to crest on precipices between the Cinque Terre's five villages of Monterosso, Vernazza, Corniglia, Manarola and Riomaggiore are among the Riviera's most spectacular. There are an estimated 1,250 miles of them, many in ruin, others planted with grapes and olive trees. They're a UNESCO World Heritage Site. One of the more ambitious tasks the Cinque Terre National Park has set for itself is the restoration of these terraces. Government and private funding have helped by subsidizing wall-building campaigns, the installation of monorails and the growing of olive trees, organic basil and grapes. Other parts of the coast have not been as fortunate; it's nothing another millennia of toil won't fix.

CHAPTER 5

....

Varese Ligure and Val di Vara

*Province: **La Spezia**. Includes: **Calice al Cornoviglio,
Maissana (Cembrano, Ossegna, Tavarone, Torza), San Pietro
Vara, Sesta Godano, Varese Ligure.***

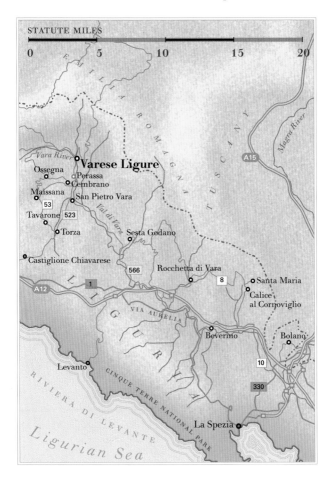

UNSUNG AND OFF THE BEATEN TOURIST TRACK, VARESE LIGURE AND THE VAL DI VARA, A LONG, wide river valley, are remarkably lovely. Many of the creeks and rivers that flow from abutting Emilia into Liguria wind up in the Vara River. It flows south into the Magra River, which debouches on the border of Tuscany. The valley's fields and forested hillsides, from which tons of chestnuts and mushrooms are harvested, seem greener than those of the rest of rugged, rocky Liguria (with the exception of Santo Stefano d'Aveto). That's the main reason why the Vara's headwaters are the eastern Riviera's cattle and cheese country, though the quantities of beef raised and cheeses made are tiny. A constellation of hamlets fills the valley and the many smaller valleys branching off it. Varese Ligure is the biggest town, and its municipal district is vast, the biggest in the whole Liguria region. Though it belongs to the Province of La Spezia, the closest cities are actually Sestri Levante, Chiavari and Lavagna, which lie due west and are linked by regular bus service—a hair-raising ride on chase-your-tail two-laners—and historical affinities. Varese Ligure was a fief of the powerful Fieschi clan, which had bases in the Chiavari-Lavagna-Sestri area.

A ROAD TRIP TO VARESE LIGURE

Note: Because of the scattered locations of fine food producers, shops and restaurants in the Val di Vara and surroundings, the best way to discover them is to budget a day, rent a car and take the road trip inland. The distances are relatively short, but roads are narrow with many curves. Expect to spend a pleasant, whole day for a round-trip tour.

Driving north from the Lunigiana, go past Bolano, Beverino and Rochetta Vara, and follow highway SP10 up the Val di Vara on the riverside to highway SP8, which climbs to Calice al Cornoviglio. Follow signs to the hamlet of Santa Maria, where you'll find a remarkable honey maker, **Apicoltura Ribaditi** (Via S. Maria 44, Frazione Santa Maria 12, Tel: 0187 936346, www.apiriba.itgo.com, drop by or make an appointment). Monica Coselli and Ennio Ribaditi make cold-extracted rosemary, acacia and mixed wildflower honeys, propoli, dried fruit in honey and lovely beeswax candles. No heat is used in the honey-making process, and the powerful flavors are preserved. You can also buy their honeys at the La Spezia open market on Wednesday and Saturday.

Further north up the Vara, follow signs toward perched Sesta Godano, and amid the modern, free-standing houses surrounding the old part of town (make time for a visit), find **Ristorante La Margherita** (Via Caduti della Libertà 77, Tel: 0187 891233, closed Monday and in November, inexpensive to moderate). Run by Gianni and his wife Francesca (the cook), this cozy, simple *trattoria* serves homey dishes that unite the traditions of the Lunigiana, La Spezia and Val di Vara. Try the brined lard with sweet-and-sour onions and porcini in olive oil. There's also smoked swordfish, however, and classic anchovies marinated in lemon juice. The pasta includes *pansôti* with walnut sauce, but also *testaroli* with pesto, or minestrone thickened with fresh pasta. The flash-fried eels from the Vara River are a rare treat (not always available), and though you can get grilled saltwater fish or seafood, the meat dishes are best, from the breaded and pan-fried lamb chops to the grilled beef *tagliata* with porcini. The desserts are housemade, and include delicious tarts and fruit pies. Wines are from the Bosoni winery in the Lunigiana.

Further up the valley, between Varese Ligure and the coast, and also accessible from Sestri Levante or Chiavari, Maissana is a cluster of scattered hamlets—Cembrano, Ossegna, Tavarone, Torza—straddling the Val di Vara and the abutting Val Petronio. This is where many Ligurians, especially residents of Greater La Spezia, take their rural vacations. Borsa Creek runs through a valley named Valle dei Mulini (Mill Valley). For centuries, the grain from nearby fields, and the chestnuts from the thick woodlands around, were ground into flour here. Mushrooms, chestnuts and beans (a variety known as *la fagiolana*) are prized in the area, and game is plentiful in season.

Due south of Maissana, near the junction of highway SP53, Tavarone hosts a variety of food-related events, including a mushroom festival (Sagra del Fungo) during the last week of August, theoretically after the first rains; unfortunately, global warming means the weather does not always cooperate, so before making plans, phone ahead to ask whether the *funghi* have sprung up. There's also a hayseed feeding frenzy in late July (Sagra dei frisceu, testaieu e zuppa de faxeu) during which locals and vacationers feast on fritters, the local version of *testaroli* called *testaieu*, and bean soup. There's even an Apennine cheese festival in the first week of August, a good place to sample many mountain cheeses, including those of Varese Ligure. Don't miss the only hotel-restaurant in Tavarone, **La Veranda** (Via Mario Padovani

26, Tel: 0187 845629, open daily, inexpensive), a family-run, old-fashioned place with a veranda and delicious, simple food, including housemade ravioli filled with borage, *taglierini* with meat sauce, stewed rabbit, roast chicken or pork, veal stew, and luscious housemade desserts—fruit pies and *crostatas*.

A mile south of Tavarone is Torza, whose bean festival features stands at which you can eat *la fagiolana* (including with *stoccafisso*); it's held the first week of October. For info on all these events, call 0187 845617, comunedimaissana@libero.it .

Northeast of Maissana and due south of Varese, in the hamlet of Cembrano, by the village church, Graziella Giambruno's **Azienda Agricola Le Rattatuie** (Via XXIII Marzo 16, Tel: 0187 847650, always open) is a working farm that sells (when available) home-baked bread made with the farm's flour; always sold are delicious homemade jams, pickled vegetables, dried or pickled mushrooms and herb or wildflower syrups.

On the main highway from La Spezia to Varese Ligure (SP523), in San Pietro Vara, just north of the creek, is **Panificio Battalini & Ginocchio** (Via Provinciale, Tel: 0187 847590, closed Monday), a traditional bakery with local breads and sweets. Nearby, the simple **Trattoria Picchetto** (Via Vara, Tel: 0187 847731, closed Monday, dinner served only on Friday and weekends in winter, inexpensive to moderate), by the Vara River, just east of the center of the village, serves local mushrooms and specialties plus pan-Ligurian food such as *trenette* or other pasta with pesto.

For outstanding organic cow's milk cheeses made from local milk, a few miles south of Varese Ligure, just off the highway, is the **Cooperativa Casearia Val di Vara** (Località Perassa, Tel: 0187 840507, www.coopcasearia.it, closed Sunday afternoon). Here you can get fresh, light ricotta, flavorful *fior di latte* cow's milk mozzarella and creamy Ugo e Luigia organic *formagetta*, aged just one month, plus firm but mild *stagionato de Vaise*, also organic, and aged for two months, or the remarkable *stagionato di Varese Ligure affinato nelle vinacce dello sciacchetrà*, a wonderfully flavorful hard cheese aged for a year before being soaked for two months in the lees of Cinque Terre Sciacchetrà. The co-op also sells their cheeses (plus a small selection of salamis) at the weekly open markets of the region, including those in Camogli and Recco.

VARESE LIGURE

FOR THOUSANDS OF YEARS, THE SALT ROUTE FROM THE MEDITERRANEAN TO EMILIA RAN through the Val di Vara and its main town, Varese Ligure, founded in pre-Roman times by the Veleiates tribe. It was and still is a center for trade. Under the arcaded, medieval central square, called Borgo Rotondo, which is actually shaped like a horseshoe, mule trains loaded with salt and other goods would take shelter. Nowadays the portico, built by the Fieschi clan in the 1200s, has handsome shops, and a favorite *enoteca* and *trattoria*. The oldest part of town around the square and castle, and the narrow alleyway across the highway from them, are full of charm.

Food is taken seriously in Varese Ligure. There are local strawberry and *porchetta* (stuffed, spit-roasted pig) fairs in early and late August. The best time to visit is August 16, for the Festa di San Rocco, a religious procession with a blessing for dogs (a dog brought San Rocco food when he was dying of the plague); it includes a feed at the local sports field, where you can gorge on classic Ligurian dishes and sweets. November 11, the feast of Saint Martin, is also colorful and authentic; the streets fill with stands selling local produce, including quantities of dried mushrooms. For information, phone 0187 842094 or 0187 842505, www.prolocovavareseligure.it and www.comune.vareseligure.sp.it.

Hotel food is often forgettable; an exception is **Amici** (Via Garibaldi 80, Tel: 0187 842139, www.albergoamici.com, open daily in July and August, closed Wednesday the rest of the year). Family-owned and operated by Enrico and Gianna-Enrica Marcone, whose son Marco helps them do the cooking, while daughers Alessandra and Michela run the dining room, this pleasant, cheerful old restaurant with high ceilings, mirrors and white-draped tables, serves delicious, traditional Ligurian food, starting with stuffed, baked vegetables or Genoese ravioli with meat sauce, and including *corzetti*, *pansôti* with walnut sauce, mushroom-filled *testaieu* (*testaroli*), mushroom-and-potato casserole, *cima*, *stecchi* and *tomaxelle* veal rolls. The very good organic cheeses come from the local co-op, and the jam tarts, *gobeletti* and *semifreddi* are housemade. Similar fare is served at **Taverna del Gallo Nero** (Piazza Vittorio Emanuele 26, Tel: 0187 840513, closed Thursday), a recent restaurant and wine bar on the main square as you enter the oldest part of town.

The real favorite of savvy locals is tucked away down a narrow alleyway, a hundred yards from the castle, on pocketsized Piazza Mazzini: **Osteria Du Chicchinettu** (Piazza Mazzini 5, Tel: 0187 842052, closed Tuesday dinner and Wednesday; in winter, dinner is served on weekends only, inexpensive). This tiny *trattoria* was opened in 1910 by the great-grandfather of current owner and cook Monica di Venanzo, whose husband and son run the dining room. The savory tarts of rice, potatoes and onions or chard are exquisite. The salamis, *coppa* and head cheese come from local producers (including the organic co-op). Only two or three starters are available on a given day, but each is housemade and delicious: meat or lean ravioli with mushroom sauce, or pine nut sauce, *pansôti* with walnut sauce, slabs of old-style polenta with wild boar or porcini, classic long-stewed rabbit with pine nuts and olives, fried mushrooms, or the house specialty, generously served *fritto misto all'italiana*—fried vegetables and meats. The jam tarts, *semifreddi*, honey-and-pine nut tart and local organic ricotta with *amaretti* are outstanding, and all housemade. There are a few bottled wines available, but the carafe wines from Bosoni are perfectly quaffable.

Facing the *trattoria* is **Parmiggiani Fratelli** (Piazza Mazzini 11, Tel: 0187 842106, closed Wednesday afternoon and Sunday), a well-stocked grocery and pasta *fresca* shop with local cheeses from the co-op. Near the Hotel della Posta and Taverna del Gallo Nero is local grocery shop **Alimentari Andrea de Vincenzi** (Piazza Vittorio Emanuele 54, Tel: 0187 842492, closed Wednesday afternoon year-round and Sunday in winter). Here you'll find fresh mushrooms in season and dry mushrooms the rest of the year, plus local salami and cheeses. The best bakery in town, with a variety of breads, good focaccia and savory tarts, is **Il Forno di Germano** (Piazza Vittorio Emanuele 5, Tel: 0187 842517, closed Monday).

The Val di Vara cattle rancher's beef co-op, **Coopertiva San Pietro Vara** (Via Municipio 1, Tel: 0187 842501, closed Sunday), on the main street facing the forestry service HQ near city hall, sells excellent local, organic meat and salamis.

CHAPTER 6

Santo Stefano d'Aveto

*Province: Genova. Includes: Borgonovo Ligure,
Borzonasca, Santo Stefano d'Aveto.*

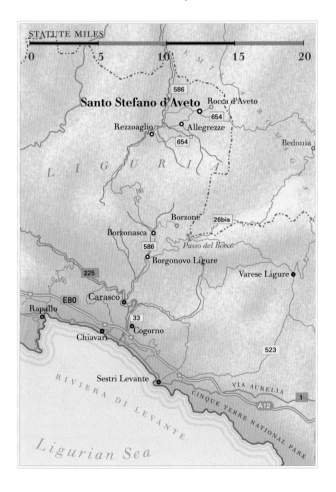

S ANTO STEFANO D'AVETO IS A SMALL APPENINE MOUNTAIN RESORT DUE NORTH OF CHIAVARI, AT the north end of the Val d'Aveto (Aveto River Valley). The highest peaks are snow-bound in winter, and there are several ski resorts. Many coast dwellers spend July and August here to beat the heat. Like the Val di Vara, this is cattle and cheese country. Wild game and mushrooms are plentiful, and trout are farmed or live wild in rivers and lakes. The population density is extremely low. Foreign tourists are few. Beyond the remarkable scenic beauty of the district, the real reason to travel here is to eat in the country or village *trattorie* serving mushrooms, wild boar, trout and other hearty dishes, and try the local cheeses, generically called San Stè.

A ROAD TRIP FROM CHIAVARI TO SANTO STEFANO D'AVETO

Note: Because of the scattered locations of fine food producers, shops and restaurants in the area, the best way to discover them is to budget a day, rent a car and take the road trip inland. The distances are relatively short, but roads are narrow with many curves. Expect to spend a pleasant, whole day for a round-trip tour.

From Chiavari, take highway SS225 or SP33 north about five miles to Carasco (see Sestri Levante to Chiavari entries). Follow signs to Borzonasca and Santo Stefano d'Aveto (on highway SP586) for another five miles, following the river to Borgonovo Ligure. This valley village is strung out along the road, with the river to the west. Family-style **Trattoria Marchin** (Via Ginocchio Mario 201, Tel: 0185 336097, closed Monday, inexpensive) is just north of the village, across the bridge. Worth going out of your way to find, Marchin has been around for a hundred years, in the same family, and is known for its outstanding, handmade, delicious ravioli and other homey *cucina casalinga* favorites. The ravioli are filled with chard, meat, *parmigiano*, egg and breadcrumbs and topped with wild mushroom or long-stewed tomato-and-meat sauce. The mushrooms are found locally, in the chestnut- and oak-covered hills around Borgonovo. Try some, served in a blue glass bowl full of oil, as an appetizer. There's sumptuous, long-stewed rabbit with pine nuts and olives, roast guinea fowl, delicious *cima* and more. With the exception of the ice cream, everything, including the desserts (don't miss the *panna cotta*), is made by Adriana Graffigna and her sister. The house wines are innocuous. A handful of regional bottlings are

also available. Marchin is comfortable, homey, squeaky clean and incredibly affordable, and therefore draws crowds of savvy locals. Reserve ahead (for Sunday lunch, reserve a week ahead).

From Borgonovo, do not take the looping highway uphill to Passo del Bocco. Drive due north to Borzonasca, less than three miles away on SP586. For those who can't get into Marchin, the best fallback is here: **Antica Trattoria Rocchin** (Piazza Marconi 2, Tel: 0185 340147, closed Wednesday, inexpensive to moderate). It's just west of the main road, near town hall and the big Banco di Chiavari building. Rocchin is modern and comfortable, with the feel of a high-end pizzeria, and is equipped with a wood-burning oven. Baked in it are good stuffed vegetables and lasagne with meat sauce, and roasts. As at Marchin, the pasta and desserts are housemade, classic and delicious.

If you're interested in church history or architecture, or just want to enjoy the view, detour uphill about two miles from Borzonasca, following the creek at the south end of the village, and be careful to follow inadequate signage to the moody, medieval Borzone Abbey. It's flanked by an imposing, rusticated Romanesque belltower and surrounded by terraces and woodlands. The abbey church is over 1,000 years old, and has several remarkable side altars and a mix of tenth-century brickwork and eleventh-century stonework. Back in Borzonasca in the river valley, follow signs north on highway 586 to Rezzoaglio and Santo Stefano d'Aveto.

At over 2,200 feet above sea level, Rezzoaglio has a mountain climate and atmosphere, and is surrounded by forested peaks and pasturelands. The district's modern co-op cheese factory and retail shop is near here: **Caseificio Val d'Aveto** (Via Rezzoaglio Inferiore 35, Tel: 0185 870390, www.caseificiovaldaveto. com, closed Tuesday afternoon). To find it, drive into town and turn left at the crossroads in the square, still following the highway to Santo Stefano d'Aveto for about two miles. The cheeses are made from the milk of Razza Bruna (Italian-Swiss Brown) cows. They include delicious rounds of pale San Stè, fresh ricotta and *prescinsêua*, and a variety of other mild mountain cheeses including Crescenza, Montello, Sarazzu, Morbidezza, Formaggetta and Tosella. The compact, almost flat Tomino is coated with wild herbs.

From the cheese factory, Santo Stefano d'Aveto is another eight miles or so northeast by steep, curving roads. About two-thirds of the way there, at over 3,000 feet above sea level, stop at the junction of highway SP654 at the medieval hamlet of Allegrezze and visit third-generation dairy farmer-cheesemaker Massimo

Monteverde of **Azienda Agricola Mooretti** (Località Allegrezze 21, Tel: 0185 899502, 347 305 5802 mooretti@hotmail.com, open Monday, Wednesday and Friday morning or phone their cellular and they will meet you). The farm has been here since 1895. Massimo's handsome, friendly brown cows range free from May to November, gorging on wild flowers and grass. They're kept in barns in winter, and fed the organic grasses, hay and grains that Massimo grows on the farm, which covers about fifty acres. The cheeses he makes are mild, especially the fresh *stracchino* (the cheese that goes into Recco's focaccia *con formaggio*), ricotta and *prescinsêua*. The Avetina is ready after fifteen days, while the so-called Formaggio del Pastore or shepherd's cheese ages for a month, firming up. Stagionato ranges from two to three months and is firm and flavorful. Also sold are organic leaf and root vegetables, flour and barley, all from the farm, and chestnut flour from a local producer.

SANTO STEFANO D'AVETO

LALOM A FEW MORE MILES UPHILL TO SANTO STEFANO D'AVETO AND GET A MAP FROM THE TOURIST office in the center of the handsome, sunny village (Piazza del Popolo 6, Tel: 0185 88046, 887007, www.comune.santostefanodaveto.ge.it). It sits in wide, open high pastures with fir and broadleaf forests on the mountains behind. Though parts of town have been around since the twelfth century, the feel is that of a modern mountain resort. If, for a lark, you'd like to visit a centuries-old watermill that still grinds grain, corn and chestnuts (using granite millstones), ask at the tourist office about taking a tour. Owned by farmer Attilio Monteverde, in the outlying hamlet of Gramizza, the mill is used nowadays to show schoolkids how a mill functions.

May is a lovely time to visit the area; if the rain has been abundant, you can hope to find plenty of the local spring mushrooms, *spinaroli*. The Sagra dello Spinarolo food festival is held during the first three weekends of May, and most local restaurants offer special *spinarolo*-theme menus. Late summer and fall are also good times to visit Santo Stefano d'Aveto. The second Sunday in September is when the Sagra della Trota festival is held, with a trout fly-fishing and spin-casting contest in nearby Lago delle Lame (a resort lake). Contestants take the rainbow or spreckled trout they've hooked to a local *trattoria* and have it cooked for them; anyone can join in for the big trout feed, which starts at about 12:30 in the afternoon. If you don't happen to have a trout with you, the chef will oblige.

Gone are the days when thousands of cows, sheep and goats were moved on the hoof from high pastures down to the valleys. However, on the last weekend in October, the hayseed Festa della Transumanza nods to the times of yore: at about nine in the morning cows are herded by local dairy ranchers from pastures at Crociglia, over the border in the Province of Piacenza, about six miles to the center of Santo Stefano, with tourists in tow. The party starts around noon, when the cows clomp into town, and everyone heads to a *trattoria* for a special meal.

During the first half of November, it's the Sagra della Castagna, a chestnut extravaganza, which starts at noon with a long, lubricated lunch in one of the village's chummy eateries, and then gets going in earnest at about three o'clock on the streets, where the locals sing, dance and make merry. You'll see huge roaster-tumblers that look like the insides of industrial washing machines, used here to roast whole chestnuts (*caldarroste*) over a roaring fire. You'll also find boiled and peeled chestnuts (*pelate*), chestnut fritters (*frittelle*) and rustic, flavorful *polenta di castagne*.

There are many good restaurants and *trattorie* in and around Santo Stefano d'Aveto. On the northwest side of the village, with a clean, rustic, white interior, ceiling timbers painted brown, a roaring fireplace and white tablecloths on the heavy wooden tables, is **Hostaria della Luna Piena** (Via Ponte dei Bravi 7, Tel: 0185 88382, closed Monday except in July and August, inexpensive to moderate), run by Maria Tilde Barattini. Alongside the pan-regional Genoese classics — savory tarts, housemade lasagne with pesto — you can order good pizza (served in the evening only, and in winter on Friday, Saturday and Sunday nights). During the May mushroom festival you'll find housemade polenta or *taglierini* sauced with *spinaroli*. For the trout festival, the restaurant usually has trout *al cartoccio* (in an aluminum foil bag). For the cowboys of October and the chestnut lovers of November, the menus might feature savory tarts, baked porcini and potato casserole, veal roast and chestnuts done in half a dozen ways.

Stock up on fresh or dry mushrooms, chestnuts, chestnut flour, cheeses and picnic supplies, including wine at **Vini Liquori e Funghi Pareti Biagio** (Via Razzetti 19, Tel: 0185 88550, closed Monday and Wednesday afternoons), on the main street. Signor Biagio is a mushroom hunter, and collects the *spinaroli* and porcini (and many others) himself. For delicious bread, focaccia, savory tarts and pastries, try award-winning **Pasticceria Alimentari Chiesa** (Via al Castello 27, Tel: 0185 88056, pasticceriachiesa@ libero.it, closed Monday and Wednesday afternoons). Now into its third generation, this friendly, authentically great bake shop, founded in 1920, is celebrated locally for its *pandolce*, apple tarts and irresistible cookies (*canestrelli*, *baci di dama*, tender, slightly sweet *amaretti*, pine nut-studded *pinolata* and others). Also sold are groceries and dry local mushrooms.

If you want to get into the mountains around Santo Stefano d'Aveto for a hike, or a panoramic lunch or dinner, drive to the ski resort at Rocca d'Aveto, at over 4,000 feet above sea level, where you'll find **Trattoria La Rocca** (Via Rocca d'Aveto 97, Tel: 0185 88596, open daily June through August; Friday dinner, weekends and holidays the rest of the year, inexpensive to moderate). A Ligurian version of a Swiss ski chalet, flanking the slopes, with motel art on the walls and kitsch objects to match, the tables are heavy wood, the atmosphere jolly. Stick to simple savory tarts (including rice tart), ravioli and *pansôti* with meat, sausage or mushroom sauce, grilled or baked mushrooms and grilled trout or meat. Desserts are creamy, rich and homey — tiramisu, *panna cotta*, apple crumble. La Rocca also serves special menus to coincide with local festivities: in May, *spinaroli*-and-vegetable frittata, *spinaroli*-and-potato stew, risotto or spaghetti with *spinaroli*; in September, baked or stewed trout; in October/November, *tagliolini* or polenta with porcini. The wines are primarily Piedmontese or Lombard, with a few Ligurian bottlings. The view is stunning.

CHAPTER 7

Sestri Levante to Chiavari–Il Chiavarese

Province: **Genova.** *Includes:* Carasco, Castiglione Chiavarese, Chiavari, Lavagna, Né, Sestri Levante.

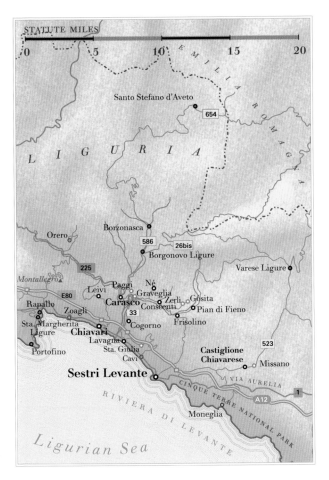

*I*L CHIAVARESE IS THE AREA STRETCHING FROM THE COAST AT SESTRI LEVANTE INLAND TO Borzonasca, up the Val Graveglia and Val Fontanabuona, to the ridge of steep coastal mountains separating Chiavari from Zoagli and Rapallo. A small, prosperous city, Chiavari has some of the best food shops, *caffè* and ice creameries on the Riviera. Dramatic headlands and cliffs frame the area on either end. The coastal strip has long, straight beaches swirled with sun umbrellas. It seems to have been lifted from the western Riviera di Ponente. The medieval center-cities of the area are atmospheric, and the hilly hinterland is striking, with vineyards and olive groves backed by soaring, chestnut-clad mountains.

CARASCO

*D*UE NORTH OF CHIAVARI WHERE THE VAL FONTANABUONA AND VAL GRAVEGLIA MEET, Carasco is near the enchanting medieval chapel of San Salvatore dei Fieschi, and good food destinations Né, Borgonovo Ligure and Santo Stefano d'Aveto. Carasco itself is unattractive, strung out on busy two-lane highways in the valley bottom. However, the Gravelia area of Carasco is home to the artisanal pasta-maker **Pastificio Artigianale Fiore** (Via Prioria 20, Località Graveglia, Tel: 0185 381222, www.pastificiofiore.it, closed weekends), on highway SP33 on the east side of the Entella River. The easiest way to get there from the Via Aurelia seaside highway is to skirt Chiavari, following signs to Cogorno, on the east side of the river; a few hundred yards after the junction for Né you'll see the building. Founder Maria Lucia Fiore, now in her eighties, is still at the helm. Pasta Fiore white or spinach *trofie*, made with durum wheat, take twenty minutes to cook, and are very flavorful, possibly the best dry *trofie* in Liguria. Indeed, Fiore might just be the region's top dry pasta maker, with all the classic shapes and more, made with choice ingredients and no colorings or preservatives. Among many other types, you'll find three kinds of *corzetti*, *trine* (fettuccine-like ribbon pasta) made from chestnut flour, basil-infused *trofiette*, durum wheat *trenette* and *trenette avvantaggiate* made with white and whole wheat flour.

Practically next door is the old-fashioned, family-run **Trattoria Settembrin** (Via Vecchia Provinciale 34, Località Graveglia, Tel: 0185 380703, closed Monday and February, inexpensive to moderate), where you'll choose from a long list of delicious regional classics, all housemade, served in a comfortable setting packed with vociferous locals.

Also in Località Graveglia, about a quarter mile west of Settembrin on highway SP33, below the church of Paggi, is chestnut, pine nut, bean and walnut grower-wholesaler **Attilio Noceti**, (Via alla Chiesa 2, Tel: 0185 380700, www.noceti.it). He also sells chickpea and corn flour, split peas, pearl barley, *farro*, soy beans and hazelnuts. In theory, Attilio doesn't retail; however, if you're going to purchase olive oils or eat nearby at **Agriturismo-Azienda Agricola Roberto Noceti** (Località Dotta 1, Paggi, Tel. 0185 350115, cell 392 830 4279, always open, www.youritaly.com, inexpensive to moderate), by request Attilio will sell his goods to you via Roberto Noceti, who has a retailer's license. The two Noceti are not related, though they live within a few hundred yards of each other.

Robert Noceti's farmstead and *trattoria*, which is up the hill from the bridge and highway SP33, above the church of Paggi (follow signs to "Agriturismo Noceti"), serves delicious, homemade food using produce from the farm or local growers. In addition to classic stuffed vegetables and plates of cold cuts, you'll find pasta filled with the *preboggion* which plump, cheerful Roberto, his mother and his family gather. There are rustic *picagge* with chestnut flour (from the other Noceti) or *mandilli de saea*, sauced with pesto or *salsa di pinoli*. Noceti raises the chickens and rabbits, using them to make succulent stews with pine nuts, olives and herbs, or simple, flavorful grilled or spit-roasted *pollo ruspante* — free-range poultry; when available, he also serves spit-roasted suckling pig. The desserts are homey (jam tarts, *panna cotta*, tiramisu). The wine list is surprisingly long, with over fifty bottlings from the region, Italy and abroad. Originally a winemaker and acclaimed olive grower-oil producer, Roberto Noceti continues to make excellent cold-pressed, unfiltered oils from his 3,000 Lavagnina, Razzola and Pignola trees. The olive type and specific grove are indicated on the label. He sells the oils to restaurants and specialty food boutiques, or direct from the farm.

Another fine, artisanal olive oil maker nearby, on the opposite side of the Entella River, practically facing Settembrin, is **Massimo Solari** (Via Caperana, Case Sparse 26, Tel: 0185 382036, cell 339 3735410, by appointment). The Solari family have about 800 Lavagnina, Pignola and Razzola trees, and make about 1,000 liters per year of classic DOP and non-DOP extra virgin oils.

CASTIGLIONE CHIAVARESE

ASTIGLIONE CHIAVARESE IS FAR FLUNG BUT WORTH STOPPING IN IF YOU'RE DRIVING ON THE corkscrew highway from Sestri Levante to Varese Ligure. Once an important stronghold of the Fieschi clan, it is set in hills due north and several ridges inland of Moneglia. West of town on the main road, near Piazza Nostra Signora del Carmine, is the celebrated salami factory **Antico Salumificio Castiglione**, also a butcher shop, run by the Perazzo family (Via Canzio 62-64A, Castiglione Chiavarese (GE), Tel: 0185 408025, closed afternoons on Sunday and Monday). Try the many varieties of salami, and the firm, small, flavorful *salamino*.

Olive oil producer and winemaker **Pino Gino** (Via Vittorio Podestà 31, Località Missano, Tel: 0185 408036, by appointment), also located west of town, about one mile, in the outlying hamlet of Missano, is worth seeking out. In good years Pino Gino makes DOP extra virgin oil with the Lavagnina olives he grows, plus non-DOP oils from a mix of local olive varieties. The oils and wines sell out to top restaurants (such as Nonna Nina, in San Rocco di Camogli), wine bars (Ö Caratello, in Lavagna) and wine shops, so little is left for direct sale from the winery; phone ahead to make sure stock is available. A tasting will be offered.

FARINATA BAKING PANS

Over seventy years old but as volcanic as ever — he's nicknamed Vulcan — **Mario Mattoli** (Piazza San Giacomo 5, Chiavari

[GE], Tel: 340 791 8118) is one of the last smiths on the Riviera who makes and restores everything from wrought-iron bedsteads to pergolas, plus lined copper pots, cooking pans and heavy baking dishes called *teglie* for *farinata* and focaccia. His clients are restaurateurs and individuals, and while he makes most pieces by special order (in a day or two), he always has a small selection of *teglie* for sale at his cluttered, wonderfully ungentrified workshop on old Chiavari's northern edge, about 200 yards from celebrated *farinata* eatery Luchin (see page 136).

CHIAVARI

H EMMED BY UNATTRACTIVE MODERN APARTMENT BUILDINGS, THE BUSY COAST HIGHWAY, and a glitzy marina developed in recent decades, Chiavari is not on the Riviera's international tourist beat. But it's among the region's great food cities, famed for its *farinata* among other things, and it also has an attractive historical district, made up of arcaded medieval streets and handsome piazze laid out in a chessboard pattern. The seventeenth-century palazzo Costaguta Rocca (filled with regional artworks, furniture and archeological finds) sits at the base of a nicely landscaped, hilly park, and several churches are remarkable for their architecture and artworks. The city's name means "key [city] of the valleys," from the Latin *clavarium*. The River Entella marks Chiavari's southeastern border, and separates it from rival Lavagna, on the opposite bank. Parts of Chiavari's medieval castle and one crenellated tower are the backdrop to the lively fruit-and-vegetable market, held in the main square, Piazza Mazzini, daily except Sunday, from 5:30am to 1:30pm. It's one of the Riviera's most authentic, with fine produce grown locally, and a good selection of specialty foods, honeys, wines and baked goods. The last weekend of each month sees the Mercatino dei Sapori e delle Tradizioni. This itinerant gourmet market boasts a handful of stands that sells top-quality olives and olive oil, cookies and cakes, salamis and cheeses and local wines (held in Piazza Fenice and the attiguous Piazzetta Verdi, both in the medieval part of town). The local tourist office is at Corso Assarotti 1, near the train station, Tel: 0185 325198, www.comune.chiavari.ge.it.

RESTAURANT, *FARINATA*, WINE BAR

Caffè Defilla

T HE WINE BAR-RESTAURANT ATTACHED TO CAFFÈ DEFILLA (SEE 141) LOOKS AND FEELS LIKE an old-fashioned library, but where books would normally be, stand hundreds of bottles. Top regional wineries such as Santa Caterina, Bruna and La Polenza are represented. The snacks (Ligurian savory tarts, cold cuts, cheeses) and meals are delicious, changing daily. You might find a pasta-and-seafood dish such as *taglierini al sugo di gambero* or an oven-roasted sea bass, a hearty Piedmontese beef stew such as *brasato al Barolo*, or succulent braised guinea fowl. The long tables are shared, but there's no crowding, and no benches: the rounded wooden chairs have comfortable cushions.

CORSO GARIBALDI 4 ✦ TEL: 0185 309829
WWW.GRANCAFFEDEFILLA.IT ✦ CLOSED MONDAYS
INEXPENSIVE *to* MODERATE

Luchin

THE FOUNDER OF THIS MULTI-GENERATIONAL, CENTURY-OLD *OSTERIA* UNDER THE ARCADES OF medieval Chiavari was Luca Giobatta Bonino, alias Luchin. His great grandsons Antonio Bonino and Nicola Mangiante, and Nicola's son Luca, now run it. The scent of burning wood and baking chickpea flour, and oven-baked soups, fills nearby streets — the perfect outdoor advertising. The place is mobbed at lunch and dinner. Many connoisseurs insist Luchin makes the region's best, most flavorful *farinata* from the highest-quality, freshest chickpea flour, using very good olive oil. It is unquestionably among the Riviera's most sought after, and is baked in an old wood-burning oven in the requisite huge, round copper pans, of the kind made by artisan Mario Mattoli, whose workshop is about 200 yards away. Luchin was the first *farinata* maker to receive the approval of the Accademia Italiana della

Cucina and the unbending Associazione per la Tutela e la Valo-
rizzazione della Farinata del Tigullio, a local watchdog set up to
defend *farinata* from fast food oblivion. The *farinata* comes in
various versions, with herbs or *bianchetti* (in season), and there
is also delicious *panissa*, the related chickpea polenta (served
with raw green onions and olive oil), plus a selection of Ligurian
osteria favorites, starting with savory vegetable tarts, and pre-
ceeding through plump ravioli with meat sauce, to stewed baby
squid and more. The minestrone with pesto—cooked in a big
pot in the wood-burner—is luscious, the *stoccafisso* tender and
flavorful, and, when they're available, the stuffed, fried anchovies are sublime. Dessert is of the simplest. Don't miss the house
specialty, a kind of *castagnaccio* chestnut-flour tart with lots of
plump raisins, pine nuts and fennel seeds, different from others
because it's leavened and more like a cake. If there's one sour
note to this symphony, it's the crush of bodies trying to get a table
on Saturdays and holidays, and the consequent pressure on the
cooks to bring out the *farinata* before it's cooked through. Pick a
weekday if you can, and get there early—service starts at noon,
sharp. Even if the food weren't delicious, a meal at Luchin would
be worth traveling out of your way to experience. The wine list
is longer than those of most *farinata* places. Good bottles of local
Vermentino or reds from the Golfo del Tigullio or Luni are on
offer, by winemakers Bisson and Ottaviano Lambruschi, plus
Riviera di Ponente reds and whites by Fèipu dei Massaretti.

VIA BIGHETTI 53 ✦ TEL: 0185 301063 ✦ CLOSED SUNDAY
(*and* SEVERAL WEEKS *from* LATE OCTOBER *to* MID NOVEMBER)
INEXPENSIVE *to* MODERATE

Il Portico

T HIS IS THE KIND OF SERIOUS, FOR-SAVVY-LOCALS
RESTAURANT YOU'D WALK RIGHT BY ON CHIAVARI'S
porticoed main street, the Via Aurelia coast highway
(called Corso Assarotti here), a hundred yards southeast of the
train station. Intimate, quiet, conservatively modern and neu-
trally decorated in white tones with touches of red, it has only
a dozen or so tables set at a discreet distance from each other. Il
Portico serves extremely fresh fish, brought in by sports fishermen and professionals based at the marina, across the highway.
You'll pay premium prices for it, and can be sure it's the best
available. But fish isn't the only draw. The Ligurian specialties

are also remarkably good, from the simple pesto and fresh house-made pasta, to the roasts and pork shanks. The wine list includes many local bottlings, among them those by Bisson, whose winery is on the same street, about 300 yards northwest.

CORSO ASSAROTTI 21 ✦ TEL: 0185 310049
CLOSED TUESDAYS ✦ EXPENSIVE

CHESTNUT FLOUR, COFFEE,
ICE CREAM, PASTA *FRESCA*, PASTRIES

Drogheria Giovanni Ameri

THIS SMALL, TRADITIONAL DRY GOODS, HERBS, SPICES, WINE AND SUNDRIES SHOP, RUN BY A diamond in the rough, sells good candied fruit at Christmastime and, in fall and winter, the excellent, fresh chestnut flour of local producer Attilio Noceti. It's located between the medieval center of town and the river, about a hundred yards west of landmark Gelateria Davide (see page 141).

PIAZZA ROMA 27 ✦ TEL: 0185 309438 ✦ CLOSED SUNDAY

Caffè Bocchia

LITTLE ATMOSPHERE, BUT A FINE PLACE TO THROW BACK A REMARKABLE HOUSE-ROASTED ESPRESSO, or buy ground coffee to go. See Recco entries (beginning on page 189) for a full description of this successful local mini-chain.

PIAZZA MATTEOTTI 16 ✦ TEL: 0185 368070
WWW.BOCCHIACAFFE.IT ✦ CLOSED SUNDAY

La Bottega del Formaggio
(aka The Best) Formaggi e Salumi

IN CHIAVARI'S MAIN EAST-WEST *CARUGGIO*—A NARROW STREET IN THE MEDIEVAL CENTER OF TOWN— this small but remarkable *gastronomia* shop is bursting with delicacies. Affable owners Gian and Mauro stock 300 cheeses (including San Stè, from Santo Stefano d'Aveto) and wines from 300 wineries, plus dozens of hams, salamis and ready-to-savor regional foods, all of the highest order.

VIA MARTIRI DELLA LIBERAZIONE 208 ✦ TEL: 0185 314225
WWW.THEBEST.IT ✦ CLOSED SUNDAY

Copello Pasticceria

B ACK IN 1826, THE COPELLO FAMILY OPENED A
HUMBLE BAKERY AND SWEETS SHOP UNDER THE
arcades of Chiavari's medieval heart. About a century
later, in 1911, the heirs redecorated with what's called "Liberty
Floreale" style — the typical Italian Art Nouveau, with squarish
flowers and interlocking motifs. And time stopped. Rising over
the colorful tile floor and nearly reaching the fifteen-foot ceilings
are Liberty cabinets filled with bottles of liqueur, or boxes of
chocolate and candy. Locals read newspapers at the three small,
marble-topped round tables, or prop up the granite-topped bar as
they sip cappuccinos or hot chocolate. Premodern cookies, breakfast rolls and pastries — some the size of thimbles — beckon from
refrigerated display cases. The *bigné allo zabaione* is a walnut-
sized puff filled with rich Marsala-embued eggy cream, mounted
on a tiny shortbread base. The dozen types of *pasticini* — mini-

pastries—made with almonds and almond paste are addictive. Equally irresistible are the *dolcezze di Chiavari*, luscious lumps of toasted hazelnut and sponge cake soaked in liqueur, encased in chocolate and then wrapped in yellow or green printed paper. The Antonini family took over in 1972, was smart enough to leave a good thing unchanged, and is now well into its second generation. The atmosphere is chummy. The coffee served is Illy.

VIA MARTIRI DELLA LIBERAZIONE 162 ✦ TEL: 0185 309837
CLOSED TUESDAYS IN FALL *and* WINTER

Bar Gelateria Davide

O N THE EASTERN EDGE OF CHIAVARI, A FEW BLOCKS FROM THE ENTELLA RIVER, BAR DAVIDE IS A CHIAVARI institution, a nicely preserved *caffè* and ice creamery from the 1940s, with a handsome tin-topped bar, polished stone floors and a spacious back parlor where locals gorge on frozen fantasies, many of them combining fresh fruit and fruit *gelato*. Simple regional foods are also served. The house coffee is Illy, and the house coffee ice cream is particularly good. Davide *gelati* are soft, fluffy (without being overly whipped) and tend to the sweet side of the spectrum. The current owners have been at the helm since the 1960s, and are secretive about their recipes, techniques and ingredients, insisting only that everything they make is natural and without preservatives. Certain Riviera ice cream lovers claim this is the best *gelato* "for 200 kilometers around," and that might well be, though the local competition is stiff. It is unquestionably very tasty, extremely well made and generously served ice cream. However, the less trumpeted ice creamery a mere fifty yards away, Bar Gelateria Verdi, makes less sweet ice creams, and those of Caffè Defilla are certainly a match for either.

CORSO DANTE 80 ✦ TEL: 0185 300050 ✦ WWW.BARDAVIDE.COM
OPEN DAILY 7AM *to* 1AM ✦ CLOSED TUESDAYS

Caffè Defilla

U NDER THE ARCADES OF CHIAVARI'S ELONGATED "MODERN" PIAZZA GARIBALDI, BUILT IN THE LATE 1800s, Defilla has been more than merely a coffee house and tearoom since it opened in 1914. The great and good of the Riviera di Levante have long gravitated here to meet, discuss politics, business and culture, and, above all, enjoy a dizzying variety of treats, from egg to apple. The establishment is not only gorgeous to behold but impressive in size, occupying the length of a city block. From the arcaded terrace, via the spacious bar area, you come upon the pastry-and-ice cream area, and another salon filled with boxed chocolates, wines, liqueurs and gift items. Beyond them, through a curtained threshold, lies a suite of wonderfully fuddy duddy rooms with parquet floors, tables draped with white tableclothes and hundreds of handsome Campanino-style chairs made by local artisans nearly a century ago. The chairs of Chiavari — built like musical instruments, with wooden frames assembled under tension, and finely woven seats — were particularly popular in the nineteenth and early twentieth centuries. At teatime, a pianist tinkles the ivories of a black baby grand, and you might think you're on the deck of the Titanic. What's startling about Defilla is it's continuing popularity. No dusty landmark, the décor is original and in extremely good condition. The coffee, supplied by Covim, a Riviera roaster, is perfectly good but not distinguished, but the ice creams are remarkable, from the bittersweet dark chocolate to the luscious nut flavors and fresh fruit flavors. They're natural ice creams, with no colorings or preservatives, and many of the fruit flavors

are made for diabetics, without added sugar. The coffee flavor is made with soya milk, for those who can't eat dairy products. Defilla pastries, cakes and butter cookies, and chocolates, are excellent. *Sorrisi di Chiavari*, the house specialty, come wrapped in green or red foil. Inside the wrappers are egg-sized, chocolate-coated mounds filled with light and dark creamy chocolate layers and maraschino cherry liqueur. Defilla is no longer owned by the founding family, but rather by the energetic, mustachioed Mauro Pietronave, who took over in the 1990s. He regilded the Defilla lily, and also turned the Enoteca con ristoro del Caffè Defilla wine bar (flanking the bar area) into one of the region's best places to sample wines from all over Italy.

CORSO GARIBALDI 4, CHIAVARI (GE) ✦ TEL: 0185 309829
WWW.GRANCAFFEDEFILLA.IT ✦ OPEN DAILY 7:30AM *to* 1AM
CLOSED MONDAYS ✦ ENOTECA: MODERATE

Pastificio Prato

CHIAVARI'S BEST AND LONGEST-ESTABLISHED PASTA *FRESCA* SHOP IS ON THE EDGE OF ITS MAIN MARKET square, facing city hall. It was founded way back in 1810, and its succession of owners have been using the same recipes for centuries, to turn out exquisite *corzetti, tortelloni*, ravioli, *pansôti* and other classic Riviera pasta shapes. The fresh take-out sauces include very good pesto, creamy walnut *salsa di noci*, tomato-and-porcini *sugo di funghi* and a remarkable tomato-and-meat *tôccu*, which, in fall, is made with wild boar. Bottled sauces range from *sugo dei Fieschi*—an unusual blend of veal, duck, guinea fowl, seasoned with herbs and Marsala—to *crema di zucca*, which is made with pumpkin, cream, butter and onions.

2 VIA CITTADELLA ✦ TEL: 0185 309424
CLOSED WEDNESDAY *and* SUNDAY AFTERNOONS

Bar Gelateria Verdi

PROXIMITY TO GREATNESS CAN BREED GREAT- NESS, AS IS PROVED BY THIS NEIGHBORHOOD ICE creamery on the eastern side of town, located about fifty yards west of the more famous Bar Gelateria Davide (see above). Verdi's premises are not grand, though the curving bar and old wooden built-ins are handsome. The ice cream concoctions here can be very elaborate, with fruit and *gelato* and whipped cream, but since the ambience isn't thrilling, you're better off getting a cone or a paper cup (*coppetta*) of ice cream to go, and enjoying it as you walk across town under Chiavari's medieval porticoes. The house coffee is ItalCaffè, a medium-sized, regional roaster, and it's perfectly good; the coffee ice cream reflects this, so if coffee is your passion, head to Bar Gelateria Davide instead. Verdi's award-winning pistachio ice cream is rich, intense, creamy and nutty, and made with a top-quality paste of pistachios from Bronte, the celebrated pistachio growing area on the slopes of Etna.

CORSO DANTE 74 ✦ TEL: 0185 306703 ✦ CLOSED MONDAY

WINERY

Enoteca Bisson

THE HOUSE MOTTO IS "WATER WAS MADE FOR THE PERVERSE; THE DELUGE PROVED IT." BISSON'S combination winery and wine sales room is on Chiavari's porticoed main highway, the Via Aurelia (here called Corso Giannelli), about 150 yards northwest of the train station. Ask for a tour and the staff will gladly show you the tanks and handful of oak casks, used exclusively to make muscular Mosaico, a blend of thirty percent Dolcetto—called "Munferrà" in local dialect—and seventy percent Barbera grapes, and intense, herby Granaccia. Bisson sells two grades of wine: drinkable bulk, on-tap wines from second pressings, bought by restaurateurs, barkeepers and locals who bring in their own jugs; and premium bottled "*primo fiore*" wines from the first pressing. Among the remarkable ones that owner-winemaker Pierluigi Lugano produces is Cinque Terre Marea (Albarola twenty percent, Bosco sixty percent, Vermentino twenty percent). It's grown in coastal vineyards just west of Volastra, above Riomaggiore, and is an intense straw color, with distinctive floral and herby notes typical of the best Cinque Terre wines. Another delightful surprise is the Golfo del Tigullio DOC Bianchetta Genovese—easy to drink, flowery and fresh. Bisson's Ciliegiolo is entirely made of this inimitable local grape variety, which lives up to its name, derived from *ciliega*, cherry. Somewhere between a dark rosé and a light red, it has lots of red fruit and berries to its nose and a full, cherry and berry taste. Bisson also sells other wines by top wineries from the Riviera (Santa Caterina, Fèipu dei Massaretti, Terre Bianche) and the rest of Italy. Also available are bottles of fruit preserved in vodka or liqueur, vegetables packed in olive oil, pesto and other sauces and bottled olives and excellent organic olive oil from makers Lucchi & Guastalli of Santo Stefano di Magra in the Lunigiana.

CORSO GIANNELLI 28 ✦ TEL: 0185 314462

WWW.BISSONVINI.IT ✦ OPEN DAILY

OLIVE OIL MAKER

Cà Bianca di Francesco Bruzzo

WITH PUTATIVE RETAIL SALES FROM HIS SUMP-TUOUS VILLA IN THE CENTER OF CHIAVARI, ON the narrow road running east-west to the open market and city hall, Francesco Bruzzo is often busy at the DOP consortium, which he presides, or in his olive groves perched high above town to the west, along the Costasecca hills, in the municipality of Leivi. They and he are unfindable. Bruzzo makes about 3,000 liters in a good year of exceptional, complex DOP Riviera Ligure di Levante extra virgin oils, from Lavagnina olives grown on trees that are 200 years old or more. Bruzzo harvests using a rake and a hand-held mechanical picker. Once off the trees, the olives are milled within a day; the milling equipment is state of the art. Bruzzo oils have a greenish cast, with lovely herby, grassy notes and, in some years, a distinctive lemony, pleasantly bitter flavor and nutty aftertaste. This is a small operation, and, be warned, Bruzzo is frustratingly hard to track down.

VIA RIVAROLA 69 ✦ TEL: 0185 314140
and LOCALITÀ COSTASECCA, LEIVI (GE) ✦ TEL: 0185 309795
BY APPOINTMENT

WOODEN *CORZETTI* PASTA STAMPS

Franco Casoni

CASONI IS A CABINETMAKER AND RESTORER, AND HAS PRESIDED OVER THE PROVINCIAL CRAFTS Guild. His small workshop is on a tiny square on the northern edge of Chiavari's arcaded medieval center. Casoni's passion is bringing back to life valuable Genoese antiques. He also creates contemporary furniture, sculpts wood and makes figureheads for boats, figurines for Nativity scenes and, for cooks, the traditional wooden stamps needed to make *corzetti* pasta. The silver-dollar-sized flat pasta rounds are impressed on both sides with geometrical patterns, coats of arms or personalized symbols.

73 VIA BIGHETTI ✦ TEL: 0185 301448 ✦ CLOSED SUNDAY

LAVAGNA

T HIS SEASIDE TOWN ON THE SOUTHEAST BANK OF THE RIVER ENTELLA IS, LIKE ITS NEIGHBOR, Chiavari, a wonderful sleeper. Its medieval historic center is wrapped in unappealing postwar apartment buildings, and a vast marina and boat-building district stretches along the coastal strip. It's a good place to savor authentic Ligurian delicacies. *Lavagna* means "slate"; the town lived for centuries off its slate industry. Many medieval buildings are made of slate, and most roofs are, too. The church of Santo Stefano must be among the most elaborately gilded on the Riviera. Arcaded streets provide a pleasant shelter from sun or rain.

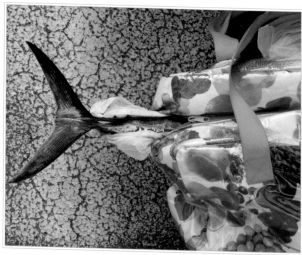

This was the fief of the powerful Fieschi clan, which, over the centuries, gave Italy two popes, scores of cardinals and bishops and untold merchants and sea captains. Nowadays the marina's boat facilities turn out speedboats and luxury motor yachts of unrivaled hideousness, but the area is still a good place to eat fresh fish. Pick any of the restaurants on the rough-and-ready strip — Via dei Devoto — south of the coast highway, and keep it simple: flash fried *fritto misto* of tiny squid and fish, mixed grilled fish or whole roasted fish. The restaurants are interchangeable, with locals favoring the very simple, impossible-to-pronounce **Ca' Du Luasso** (Via Devoto 141, Tel: 0185 303557, closed Tuesday, moderate).

Lavagna's annual blowout is held on the evening of August fourteenth each year, and is known as the Torta dei Fieschi, the Fieschi clan's cake. It recalls the legendary wedding, in the year 1230, of Opizzo Fiesco and a Sienese noble woman, during which the city's starveling subjects were presented with an enormous wedding cake. The cake that's baked today is actually composed of many small cakes, and like most such confections is not the object of the exercise. At around 8:45pm, partygoers buy tickets at the entrance to Piazza Vittorio Veneto — blue tickets for males, pink ones for females — and the lucky couples who manage to find in the crowd their mystery mate — i.e. he or she with matching numbers or symbols on the ticket of the opposite color — are entitled to a slice and who knows what else. Needless to say, those officiating in the parade and performances wear silly, mock-medieval costumes. Locals and out-of-town adolescents seem to enjoy the mating dance and the cake, too (www.tortadeifieschi. com). The local tourist office is at Piazza della Libertà 48/A, Tel: 0185 395070, www.comune.lavagna.ge.it. The Chiavari fruit and vegetable market (mornings, except Sunday) is a mile north.

TRATTORIA

Da Ö Pescòu

FAR FROM THE GLITZY HARBOR, UNDER THE MEDI-EVAL PORTICOES ON THE NORTH SIDE OF TOWN, near the church of Santo Stefano, this cozy, casual neighborhood *trattoria* of very long standing serves delicious Ligurian classics, from stuffed vegetables or anchovies to savory tarts, *trenette al pesto*, ravioli with meat or walnut sauce, rabbit with herbs and good fresh fish when it's available. The produce—fresh chard, zucchini, lettuces and local fruit—is remarkable. There's a pleasant back garden with a glassed-in dining room. The wine list is short; stick to local bottled reds and whites.

VIA DANTE 70 ✦ TEL: 0185 392727 ✦ CLOSED WEDNESDAY *and* THE SECOND HALF OF OCTOBER ✦ INEXPENSIVE *to* MODERATE

COFFEE, GOURMET FOODS, ICE CREAM, PASTRIES

Caffè Bocchia

AS IN EACH OF ITS OUTLETS, THERE'S LITTLE ATMOSPHERE, BUT BOCCHIA IS A FINE PLACE TO throw back a remarkable house-roasted espresso or buy ground coffee to go. See Recco for a full description of this local mini-chain.

VIA ROMA 43R ✦ TEL: 0185 390790 ✦ WWW.BOCCHIACAFFE.IT CLOSED SUNDAY AFTERNOON

Pasticceria Caffetteria Monteverde

A TIME-WARP PASTRY SHOP AND *CAFFÈ* ON THE MAIN ALLEYWAY OF MEDIEVAL LAVAGNA, Monteverde has been around for over 120 years. The décor is original, with a lovely bar and shelves lined with glass jars full of candies and chocolates. Rich creamy cakes and eclairs beckon, but the house specialty is the *torroncino*, which is unlike other *torroncini* found in Italy, because it is not a nougat, but rather a slender, small *millefoglie* layered pastry with heavy cream sandwiched by leaves of crispy hazelnut pastry. Exquisite! The other house delicacy is an ethereally light *amaretto*, made here like a meringue, but tender and airy instead of being stiff, and flavored with almonds and almond essence.

VIA ROMA 99 ✦ TEL: 0185 393667 ✦ CLOSED TUESDAY

WINE BARS

LAVAGNA HAS TWO *ENOTECHE*, NEITHER OF WHICH HAS A VAST CHOICE OF LIGURIAN WINES. **MONNA Bianca** (Via Dante 56, Tel: 0185 395452, closed Sunday afternoon), near the church of Santo Stefano, under the arcades, opened in January 2007 and is run by eager young Paola Cozzolino. It stocks the finest bottlings of Conte Picedi Benedettini, and some good Cinque Terre wines (and many Tuscan and Piedmontese bottlings), and serves tasty cold cuts and cheeses. **Ö Caratello** (Via Roma 86-88, Tel: 0185 395794, closed Sunday afternoon and Monday), on the main alleyway between the church and main square, has wines by top local winemaker Pino Gino, and serves very good, simple food, housemade by the owners, the Solari sisters; the minestrone is thick with beans and pasta with lots of good pesto, and the ravioli are stuffed with borage and sauced with cracked pine nuts, marjoram and excellent olive oil. The wine list changes often, but isn't long, and it's the food that draws regulars. Both *enoteche* are inexpensive.

OLIVE OIL MAKERS

Azienda Agricola Orseggi

FARFLUNG BUT WORTH THE EFFORT: THIS OIL IS OUTSTANDING. FROM THE CAVI DI LAVAGNA TRAIN station (southeast a few miles from Lavagna), head inland to Borgo di Cavi, find the pharmacy in the center of the village, and take the scenic, two-lane Strada Panoramica about halfway up the hillside toward Santa Giulia; if you phone or email ahead, the owners will drive down and meet you in Borgo di Cavi and lead you uphill. Unsung, Silvio and Federica Raggio make only about 3,700 liters of exceptionally fine organic extra virgin olive oils from their nearly 2,500 Lavagnina olive trees, with a tiny amount of Rossese, another, rare local olive variety, and some Pignola. They have about eighteen acres of groves in all, and their own traditional mill, with granite millstones, and welcome visitors year round (it's best to make an appointment, however). If you don't manage to make it to the mill, you can buy Orseggi oils at EVO in Genoa and Parlacomemangi.com in Rapallo, or taste them when you eat at cult *trattoria* La Brinca in nearby Né.

VIA CACCINI 4, LOCALITÀ SANTA GIULIA DI LAVAGNA (GE)

TEL: 0185 392009, CELL: 334 344 2990 ✦ ORSEGGI@ALICE.IT

CLOSED SUNDAY

Cooperativa agricola lavagnina

FROM THE LAVAGNA TRAIN STATION, DRIVE INLAND, FOLLOWING SIGNS TO SANTA GIULIA ON VIA SANTA Giulia. This farmers' co-op produces and sells good honeys, olives, oil and wine, and welcomes visitors.

VIA SANTA GIULIA 15 ✦ TEL: 0185 391497

CLOSED SATURDAY AFTERNOON, WEDNESDAY *and* SUNDAY

ROSE-PETAL SYRUP AND HERBAL PRODUCTS MAKER

Il Giardino dei Semplici

ON THE WESTERN EDGE OF CHIAVARI, INLAND AND BORDERING THE LEIVI MUNICIPAL AREA, THIS small, organic producer of rose-petal syrup (from *Rosa gallica officinalis*), herbs (oregano, marjoram, rosemary, thyme), chili peppers and herbal liqueurs grows most of its roses and aromatic plants on terraced olive groves in Leivi. To get to the retail shop, from the Chiavari exit of the autostrada, take the second street down, past Piazza Franca, go by the Leivi sports field, double back beyond the autostrada on the viaduct, and when you see the big Lames auto accessories outlet you'll see the shop. From central Chiavari, follow signs to toward Leivi, Piazza del Popolo and the autostrada.

VIA SAN RUFINO 26 ✦ TEL: 0185 300752

WWW.ILGIARDINODEISEMPLICI.IT ✦ CLOSED WEEKENDS

NÉ AND CONSCENTI DI NÉ

*I*N THE NARROW VAL GRAVEGLIA RIVER VALLEY NORTHEAST OF CHIAVARI AND LAVAGNA, THE village of Né is strung along an unprepossessing two-lane highway. Marble and slate quarries in the hills are still active. The area is ungentrified, rough-and-ready and authentic, the opposite of gorgeous Portofino. Its many outlying hamlets perch on olive- and vineyard-clad hills. The roads leading here twist and climb, but the driving time is worth the effort. Very good olive oil and wine come from here, as well as old-fashioned dry pasta, chickpea flour and farm produce. Two upscale restaurants serve excellent regional dishes, and there are half a dozen *trattorie* offering authentic *cucina casalinga*. In the tiny square between the town hall and gas station, the local farmer's market is held each Saturday morning, from about 8am to 1pm. Don't be surprised if you see scores of statues of Italian independence hero Giuseppe Garibaldi, and see his name everywhere: his family was from the Val Graveglia. "Garibaldi" is the area's most common last name.

RESTAURANTS

Antica Trattoria dei Mosto

*T*HIS IS NOT A *TRATTORIA*, BUT RATHER AN UPSCALE RESTAURANT, AND IS NEARLY AS CELEBRATED AS LA Brinca. Back in the 1980s, Catia Saletti was a housewife and her husband Franco Solari sold Christmas tree ornaments in nearby Chiavari. Her kitchen talents led Catia to partner with another housewife and start cooking professionally, and Franco's passion for wine (and food), plus courses with Ligurian wine master Virgilio Pronzati, helped him mature into a fine sommelier. In 1989 they bought what was a humble hotel in a charmless, drive-through village inland from Lavagna, a rustic place one flight up from a *caffè* and butcher's shop. They restored and transformed it into a high-end property; nonetheless, it serves authentic (if rich) Ligurian food. The atmosphere is that of a bourgeois home. The floors are tiled, the wooden beam in the dining room contrasts with the white walls, the tablecloths are patterned and light blue in color and there are lace curtains on the windows.

The menu changes often. However, Catia always makes luscious flash-fried *fritelle*, three-inch-long fritters of dough, which she serves with translucent strips of *lardo di Arnad* (a village in the Val d'Aosta); and *mandilli di saea*, which, only here, have parsley sprigs integrated into the pasta dough. They're sauced with outstanding pesto, made using strong, dark, local basil (Catia shuns the hothouse variety), excellent Ligurian oil and *parmigiano*, and, surprisingly, no garlic. Alternatively, she sauces the *mandilli* with porcini, in a creamier sauce than you'd normally find (Parma is as close as Genoa). The baked corn-flour cannelloni stuffed with heirloom black cabbage and sausage meat, topped with cheese from the Val Graveglia, are exquisite (and very rich). Main courses range from flavorful *cima alla genovese*, which Catia bakes instead of boiling, to herbed flash-fried rabbit, which is surprisingly tasty and not dry. Desserts range from light hazelnut cake or persimmon pie, topped with a dollop of hot, melted chocolate, to the house specialty, *gallane pinn-e* (sweet cannoli-like pastries filled with pastry cream). The remarkable wine list features scores of regional bottlings, from Bisson, Bruna or Capellini to De Batté, Durin and Rocche del Gatto, plus a hard-to-find Tolceto (a blend of Sangiovese and Ciliegiolo) made by La Ricolla.

PIAZZA DEI MOSTO 15, CONSCENTI DI NÉ (GE)

TEL: 0185 337502 ✦ TRATTORIAMOSTO@VIRGILIO.IT

WWW.TRATTORIAMOSTO.IT ✦ CLOSED WEDNESDAY

RESERVE AHEAD ✦ MODERATE *to* EXPENSIVE

La Brinca

L A BRINCA IS A CULT RESTAURANT; IT DRAWS GAS-TRONAUTS FROM FAR AND WIDE. HOWEVER, YOU can still experience the authentic peasant cooking of old here in an upscale setting, on a hilltop far above Né, with sweeping views from the glassed-in veranda. Judging by the timbers and stone-clad arches, you'd never guess the place was once a stable. If only La Brinca would serve lunch on weekdays, too, and not just on crowded weekends: the post-prandial nighttime drive down the corkscrew road to Lavagna is an unwelcome challenge. Prepared by Franca and Roberto Circella, the menu follows the seasons, but the perennial *torta baciocca*, a savory tart of *quarantina* potatoes and Zerli red onions, both from the Val Graveglia, is superb, luscious and flavorful. The pesto is actually made with a mortar; many restaurants claim to do so, La Brinca does, without boasting. The pesto tops homemade *gnocchetti* of *quarantina* or *cannelline* potatoes mixed with chestnut flour (and served with fava beans, in season). Most of the produce is grown or (picked wild) by Carlo Circella, the *pater familias*, or his friends. The herbs and field greens come from the family's terraced property. The restaurant has a wood-burning oven, the secret to the smoky quality of many dishes. You might find roast veal lightly flavored with juniper berries, or roast suckling pig, or *cima* made not with veal but guinea fowl. The desserts, made by daughter-in-law Pierangela, include apple pies, *crostatas*, hazelnut cake and, in summer, sorbets or ice creams. The wine list is among the longest in the region, and nowhere else will you find more organic winemakers represented. A word to the wise: go easy on the appetizers, which are overabundant, and might keep you from discovering the full range of dishes.

VIA CAMPO DI NÉ 58, NÉ (GE) ✦ TEL: 0185 377480
WWW.LABRINCA.IT ✦ OPEN FOR DINNER ONLY
TUESDAY *through* SUNDAY; OPEN FOR LUNCH ON
WEEKENDS *and* HOLIDAYS ✦ EXPENSIVE

Il Minatore

HIDDEN WAY UP THE VALLEY, BEYOND TWO OTHER GOOD *TRATTORIE* (IL CAPPOTTO AND LA Teleferica), this simple, spartan, family-run spot is where savvy locals go to enjoy all the specialties of the Val Graveglia—from savory tarts and ravioli sauced with meat or mushrooms, to fried porcini and wild boar, plus roasts and housemade pies, tarts and *panna cotta* or tiramisu. Everything is locally grown, wholesome and made in-house. The name means "the miner;" the last slate and marble mines are nearby. You'll see blue-collar workers here at lunchtime, digging in, and spending for an entire meal what you'd spend for one dish at celebrated La Brinca or Antica Trattoria dei Mosto. Stick to the house wines, which won't hurt you.

VIA PIANDIFIENO 57, PIAN DI FIENO/NÉ ✦ TEL: 0185 339207
CLOSED MONDAY DINNER ✦ VERY INEXPENSIVE

FARM PRODUCE, OLIVE OIL, DRY PASTA, AND LUNCH OR DINNER AT THE FARM

Rùe de Zerli

FRANCA DAMICO, HER MOTHER AND UNCLE OWN AND RUN THIS FARM AND OLIVE OIL-MAKING PROPERTY named for a centuries-old oak tree—*rùe*, in dialect—which locals believe protects the hamlet of Gòsita, up the road a quarter mile. Damico, who's passionate about farming and enjoys sharing her knowledge with visitors, grows the celebrated heirloom red onions of Zerli, which she sells fresh in season or pickled and then bottled in her own olive oil, plus fresh heirloom *cannelline* and *quarantine* potatoes, herbs, hot chili peppers and other specialty farm produce, including dried chestnuts and remarkably good chestnut flour. Franca also makes a very good extra virgin olive oil from hand-picked Lavagnina, Leccino and Olivastro olives, which is sold at many gourmet food stores in the region, including EVO and Le Gramole in Genoa, and La Bottega dei Piaceri in Camogli. The farm is set high up in hills behind Chiavari and Lavagna, on a twisting back road that climbs from Conscenti di Né past Caminata and Zerli, and then branches west toward Gòsita, and is not easy to find. Rùe de Zerli is also a B&B, with two pleasant, nicely decorated rooms.

If you plan to visit Damico on a Friday or Saturday evening, or around lunchtime on Sunday, consider reserving a table at nearby **Ca' di Gòsita** (Via Zerli 57, Gòsita, Tel: 0185 339298,

inexpensive to moderate), an *agriturismo*, meaning, in this case, a farm serving homemade food. It's open for dinner Friday and Saturday night, and lunch Sunday, and only by reservation. Ca' di Gòstia is located about 250 yards west of Zerli, up and behind the Damico chestnut grove. You'll eat delicious local produce, the classic onion-and-potato savory tart called *baciocca*, exquisite pesto spread on homemade pasta (including *testaroli*, cooked in the fireplace), plus simple but flavorful stews and grilled meats.

LOCALITÀ ZERLI 51, STRADA PER GÒSITA, NÉ (GE)

TEL: 0185 339245 ✦ WWW.RUEDEZERLI.COM ✦ BY APPOINTMENT

Pastificio Santa Rita

SINCE 1989, THIS SMALL PASTA FACTORY, LOCATED ON A BACK ROAD 300 YARDS SOUTH OF THE village's main square, parallel to the highway, has been turning out a dozen types of typical Ligurian pasta shapes, such as *fèuggie d'oia* or *foglie d'ulivo* if you prefer (olive tree leaves), *trofie*, *taglierini* and *corzetti*, all of them made without eggs. The only ingredients are durum wheat, water and natural flavorings, such as cooked spinach or nettle-tops, squid ink, lemon juice or chili pepper. A few types are made with chestnut flour or whole wheat, mixed with durum wheat. There are also pastas made without wheat flour, for allergy sufferers. Alessio, Paolina,

Roberta and their mother Tea Pozzati work together, using small pasta machines and their hands, to twist or nest ribbon pasta, for instance, and lay the pasta on drying racks. The pasta is dried for twenty-four hours before being weighed and hand packaged. The Pozzatis sell their pasta at the local grocery store and bakery (**Panificio Sanguineti**, Tel: 0185 337187), and at open markets in Genoa and Chiavari, and through many gourmet shops in the region, including Armanino, Le Gramole, Magistrati and Rosticceria Bruciamonti, all in Genoa; Salumeria Valeria in Sarzana; and La Posa-a in Portovenere. To buy direct from the factory, be sure to call ahead to make an appointment.

VIA ALDO MORO 66, CONSCENTI DI NÉ (GE) ✦ TEL: 0185 337482
OPEN WEEKDAY MORNINGS ✦ BY APPOINTMENT

SESTRI LEVANTE

....

ESTRI, AS LOCALS CALL IT FOR SHORT, LEAVING OFF THE "LEVANTE," IS LESS FAMOUS THAN THE Cinque Terre and Portofino and is too large to be called a village, yet it packs plenty of charm and authenticity into its narrow medieval alleys. They run between two bays, one little more than a cove, and a pine-shagged promontory. Because of this spectacular setting, the town is also known to locals as Bimare — two seas — or Le Due Baie. Like many Riviera towns, Sestri Levante is best out of season; in summer it's packed with vacationers, and the quality of food and service can decline. Because it's a particularly wealthy town, even by Riviera standards, and has many apartments and villas owned by Milanese and Genoese, who are demanding customers, the number of fine restaurants, *caffè*, pastry and ice cream shops is out of proportion to Sestri's size.

RESTAURANTS AND WINE

La Cantina del Polpo

WHAT STARTED OUT IN THE EARLY 1990S AS A WINE BAR OWNED BY POLPO MARIO, THE RESTAURANT, has evolved into a full-scale restaurant, specializing in wines and local dishes. It's run by Andrea Ballarini, and offers cheek-by-jowl seating in a cool, cozy interior with heavy wooden tables and chairs, or on a covered rear terrace. Delicious Ligurian specialties — anchovies, pesto, ravioli — are served, accompanied by over a dozen of the region's best wines (Santa Caterina, La Polenza, Durin).

PIAZZA CAVOUR 2 ✦ TEL: 0185 485296 ✦ CLOSED TUESDAY

INEXPENSIVE *to* MODERATE

Polpo Mario

THE THEME OF THIS STRICTLY REGIONAL SEA-FOOD RESTAURANT IS OCTOPUS. THE COMIC STRIP character Polpo Mario for which it is named is also an octopus. Polpo Mario's head is the head of this unusual restaurant's owner, Rudi Ciuffardi. He owns his own fishing boat; the fish served is perfectly fresh. Though a consumate restaurateur, Ciuffardi is above all a world-class self-promoter, with a tentacular ego. The spacious, vaulted restaurant's walls are hung with darkly inked sketches illustrating the life and times of the fictional octopus hero; the effect of seeing them everywhere, and the owner's real, living head passing to and fro in front of them, is disconcerting. Luckily the food is excellent, starting with such only-in-Liguria delicacies as tender octopus with potatoes or translucent octopus carpaccio, parboiled *rossetti* drizzled with olive oil or baby squid with basil sauce — a pesto without pine nuts, garlic or cheese. The roasted or grilled fish is always fine, but more interesting is bream or wild seabass braised with sliced potatoes and slivered local artichokes. Desserts are few and simple, but rich, and while the chocolate soufflé is well made, it makes for an unusual ending to an otherwise light meal. The wine list is long, and includes some fine Ligurian bottlings, such as Pigato by Laura Aschero. But if it's wine you're after, you're better served by the nearby La Cantina del Polpo (above), owned but not operated by Ciuffardi.

VIA XXV APRILE 163 ✦ TEL: 0185 480203

WWW.POLPOMARIO.COM ✦ CLOSED MONDAY

MODERATE *to* EXPENSIVE

ANCHOVIES, COFFEE,
FOCACCIA, ICE CREAM, PASTRIES

Gelateria Baciollo

*I*F YOU LIKE RICH, FATTY, CREAMY ICE CREAMS BACI-
OLLO IS SURE TO PLEASE. JUDGING BY THE NUMBER
of gold and silver medals won by this small ice creamery
and *caffè* on Sestri's seaside walk (with a second entrance on the
caruggio), the region's judges prefer richness to precision. Baciollo's chocolate, coffee, pine nut, pistachio and other cream or nut
flavors are as Baroque and luscious as they come; the hazelnut,
however, stands out for its true nut flavor.

PIAZZA MATTEOTTI 55 ✦ TEL: 0185 41093 ✦ OPEN 8AM *to* 8PM
WEEKDAYS, 8AM *to* 1AM WEEKENDS, CLOSED THURSDAY

Balletin Pescheria

A THRIVING FISH SHOP IN THE CENTER OF OLD SES-
TRI, ON THE NARROW ROAD LEADING FROM THE
main *caruggio* east toward the Monastery of the Cappuccini, Balletin belongs to the local fishermen's cooperative,
which not only sells amazingly fresh fish, but also does its own
salting of anchovies. You can buy anchovy filets here packed in
salt or de-salted and packed in olive oil.

VIA PALESTRO 7/8 ✦ TEL: 0185 480961
OPEN 8AM *to* 1PM TUESDAY *through* SUNDAY *and*
SATURDAY 4PM *to* 7PM, CLOSED MONDAY

La Bimare Torrefazione

*I*N THE SAME HOLE-IN-THE-WALL SHOP SINCE 1955,
ON SESTRI'S MAIN SHOPPING STREET A HUNDRED
yards south of the Via Aurelia highway, this family-owned
coffee roasting establishment is one of a handful on the Riviera
to import its beans direct, and roast them daily right in the shop.

That's been the job of owner Augustina Gandolfo since she took over in 1977. Bimare offers nine different blends. The top 100 percent Arabica house blend contains four to five types of Central American beans—mostly from Costa Rica and Guatemala—and is outstanding. Augustina roasts only a few kilos a day, to ensure perfect freshness for her regular clients. Also sold: Panarello *pandolce*, candies, chocolates and jams.

CORSO COLOMBO 18 ✦ TEL: 0185 41405 ✦ CLOSED SUNDAY

Caffè Bocchia

LOCATED NEAR THE MAIN HIGHWAY THROUGH TOWN, BOCCHIA HAS EXCELLENT HOUSE-ROASTED espresso. Drink it on the spot or buy beans to take home, ground as you wait. See Recco (page 194) for a full description.

VIA FASCIE 2 ✦ TEL: 0185 43042 ✦ WWW.BOCCHIACAFFE.IT
CLOSED SUNDAY

Gelateria K2

A NO-NONSENSE MODERN ICE CREAMERY ON A CROSS STREET EDGING THE *CARUGGIO*, MANY locals feel K2 is Sestri's best, making well-balanced "natural" *gelati* in dozens of flavors without preservatives or colorings, and using only guar or carob to stabilize some of the cream- or nut-based flavors such as pistachio, hazelnut or chocolate. The *semifreddi* are totally natural, and particularly good. Buy a cone and stroll with it.

VIA ASILO MARIA TERESA 14 ✦ TEL: 0185 44604
WWW.GELATERIAK2.IT ✦ OPEN 11AM *to* 8PM DAILY *except*
WEDNESDAY, IN JULY *and* AUGUST DAILY 11AM *to* MIDNIGHT

Pasticceria Rossignotti

CLOSE YOUR EYES AND IMAGINE THE QUINTESSENTIAL ITALIAN PASTRY AND CHOCOLATE SHOP OF centuries past — with curving glass, molded ceilings, heavy wood-and-glass cases, and a wide, stone-topped counter, and you'll begin to form a picture in your mind of this gorgeous corner property in the center of old Sestri, facing the open market. Now add the sound of a grandfather clock ticking from its niche in the heavy woodwork, the smell of hazelnuts and chocolate, and the warbling, solicitous voice of Agnese Rossignotti. With her brothers and sisters, she's the fifth generation of Rossignottis since 1840 to own and run this shop (and a similar one, five miles

south in Riva Trigoso, plus landmark Caffè Mangini in Genoa). Everything is made here or at the family *torrone*—nougat—factory and coffee-roasting plant on the edge of town. The *torrone* is best in October and November, when the hazelnuts are freshest, and the luscious chocolate variety of it is to die for. So, too, are the *sestresi*—chocolate kisses—and the cakes, jam tarts and shortbread cookies. You'll be hard pressed to find better *cappellini di sacerdote*—tiny three-cornered shortbread purses filled with almond paste—or classic *gobeletti* filled with apricot jam.

VIALE DANTE 2 ✦ TEL: 0185 41034

CLOSED SUNDAY AFTERNOON *and* MONDAY MORNING

Panificio Tosi

FOCACCIA IS THE KEYWORD—THIS SIMPLE BAKERY ON THE NARROW *CARUGGIO* IN THE OLDEST PART OF town makes remarkably good classic focaccia and good focaccia *con formaggio* in the style of Recco.

VIA XXV APRILE 128 ✦ TEL: 0185 41090

CLOSED MORNINGS SUNDAY *and* WEDNESDAY

Gran Caffè Tritone Gelateria

BUILT IN 1946 AND RESTORED TO ITS ORIGINAL, SLEEK SPLENDOR IN 2001, THIS BIG, WRAP-around corner *caffè* has giant windows, period wooden furniture, plaster bas reliefs and an outdoor terrace on Sestri's tree-lined seafront. It's not only remarkably elegant. Il Tritone also serves very good coffee, and excellent housemade ice creams, brioches, pastries and *crostate*. Managed by affable Marco Cinia and Pier Enrico Bregante, a pair of polished professionals, and their wives, the owners are the Rossignotti family, who also own and operate Sestri's landmark pastry and candy shop, of the same name, and two of the resort's luxury hotels, not to mention Caffè Mangini in Genoa. Rossignotti's Arabica blends (one conceived for bar machines and served by Il Tritone, the other for home brewing) are sold here in vacuum-packed cans. The coffee roasting facility is on the edge of town. Though the coffee draws cognoscenti, Il Tritone is above all a hangout for well-healed locals and tony vacationers with holiday homes and villas. Many come here to hobnob and eat the *gelati*, which are particularly creamy and satisfying, without being fatty or cloyingly sweet. They're made daily, with six fruit flavors, three *granita* ices, three *semifreddi* and three classics—often rich chocolate, nutty pistachio and *panera* (lush, frozen cappuccino, made with freshly brewed Rossignotti bar-blend coffee).

PIAZZA BO 1 ✦ TEL: 0185 41169 ✦ OPEN 7:30AM *to* 8PM DAILY (UNTIL MIDNIGHT ON FRIDAY, SATURDAY, *and* DAILY IN JULY *and* AUGUST) CLOSED MONDAY *from* SEPTEMBER *to* JUNE

OLIVE OIL MAKER

Frantoio Bo

SESTRI LEVANTE IS SURROUNDED BY TIERED OLIVE GROVES AND VINEYARDS. FAMILY OWNED AND OPERated since 1867, Frantoio Bo is where locals take their olives to be pressed and bottled. The premises are on the edge of town, about 300 yards east of the main *caruggio*, an easy walk. The Bo family also owns hundreds of olive trees near the mill, and makes some of the finest extra virgin oils on the Riviera. They've won awards everywhere, in Italy and Germany in particular, plus a gold medal at the Los Angeles County Fair. The top of the line is called Le Due Baie — the two bays, a reference to the town's topography — and it's composed 100 percent of handpicked Lavagnina, Razzola and Pignola olives from Liguria. The acidity is a low 0.2-0.3 percent. Also excellent is La Ginestra, which is made from "net" olives that have been knocked off or fallen from the trees into nets stretched from trunk to trunk. The

acidity is higher — around 0.5 percent — but still low enough to allow the sweetness of these delicate, flowery oils to shine through. The current scion of the Bo dynasty is Carlo, flanked by his wife and son. Though the mill has been around for over 140 years, don't expect to see ye olde stone wheels and hemp mats; the equipment here is state of the art, manufactured by Alfa Laval. The olives are cold-crushed, pressed and centrifuged rapidly at precisely twenty-seven degrees Celcius. You can taste and buy Bo oils in the spacious boutique, and also pick up very good brined, bottled whole olives.

VIA DELLA CHIUSA 70 ✦ TEL: 0185 481605
WWW.FRANTOIO-BO.IT ✦ CLOSED SUNDAY

CHAPTER 8

························

Rapallo to Portofino and Camogli to Sori

*Province: **Genoa**. Includes: Camogli, Portofino, Punta Chiappa, Rapallo, Recco, Ruta di Camogli, San Massimo, San Rocco di Camogli, Santa Margherita Ligure, Sori, Sori-Capreno, Zoagli.*

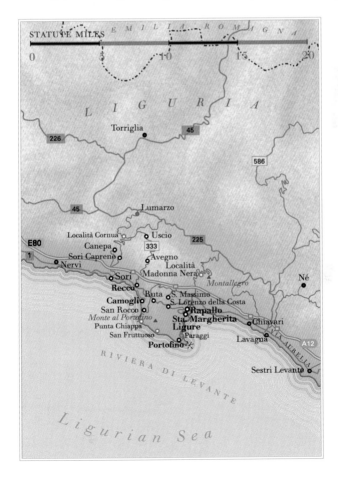

SCORES OF LUXURY HOTELS STUD THE ROCKY COASTLINE THAT RUNS WEST FROM RAPALLO'S handsome bay, past Santa Margherita and Paraggi to Portofino. The villas of billionaires rise amid olive groves and pine forests, and the sea is often filled with sailboats and motor yachts. This is the quintessence of the Riviera. Luckily, alongside the glitz, in many seaside communities you'll find authentically wonderful food, including the region's best focaccia and focaccia *con formaggio*.

CAMOGLI

A SMALL PORT TOWN, TOO BIG TO BE A VILLAGE, CAMOGLI USUALLY FEATURES ON THE INTERNAtional list of Riviera favorites, for its congenial atmosphere, curving beach, and well-preserved houses that are remarkably tall, handsome and gaily painted. The town's name is said to derive from *case delle mogli*—the wives' houses—presumably because the wives were alone, their husbands away at sea. In reality, the name is much older, and comes from the temple to Camuli, a Ligurian-Celtic deity, which once stood here. Still, the wives' houses makes for a nice story; in the nineteenth century, Camogli had the largest merchant fleet in the northern Mediterranean, most of its ships being moored in Genoa and other ports, including Marseille. Those days are long over. Tourism has been the main industry for the last hundred years (the tourist office is on the main street, Via della

Tables with a View and Good Food

MOST OF CAMOGLI'S SEASIDE RESTAURANTS ARE FOR TOURISTS WITH SLEEPY tastebuds. There are three exceptions to the rule. **Ristorante del Mulino Da Drin** (Via San Nicolò di Capodimonte 36, Località Punta Chiappa, Tel: 0185 770530, cell 347 124 8047, closed Tuesday in winter, moderate to expensive) is a small, family-run place in, a reconverted former watermill at Punta Chiappa, an isolated seaside hamlet east of town, reachable by a beautiful descent on a 1,000-step staircase from San Rocco di Camogli, or by ferry from Camogli. In fine weather you dine under a pergola, or climb to a rooftop terrace (half inside, the other half glassed-in) to eat local foods. The fish comes from Punta Chiappa, the basil, herbs and much of the produce is garden grown or from neighbors. About a hundred yards east, on the seaside walk to the ferry dock, **Do Spadin** (Via San Nicolò 55, Tel: 0185 770624, closed Mondays except in August, open from early April to early November, expensive to very expensive) is another magical spot, with shady terraces on the shoals. Stick to classics — *mandilli* with pesto, grilled fish, small fry. Transportation challenges make lunch your safest bet, unless you enjoy hiking. Reserve ahead. Ask if the ferry boats are running (or hire a fisherman at Camogli's port to take you to Punta Chiappa and back).

On the south end of Camogli, perched on a cliff above the port, **Rosa** (Largo F. Casabona 11, Tel: 0185 773411, closed Wednesday and in January, expensive) is a family-

run seafood restaurant founded in 1949, with a wrap-around indoor winter garden, with trees growing from the floor through the roof, and a terrace with plunging views of Camogli and the Monte di Portofino. Owned and managed by affable Maria Rosa Costa, who lives upstairs, it's heads above most such glitzy Riviera spots, though it also attracts clients with speed-boat suntans. Rosa gets its fish from the co-op in Camogli or the market in Santa Margherita Liguria, and it's flipping fresh, perfectly prepared and professionally served. Regional specialty is what sets this place apart. Rosa's assistant chef, Francesco Garibotti, was a finalist in the 2007 International Mortar-Made Pesto Championship in Genoa, and, surprising for a seafood restaurant, makes excellent pesto (order ahead to have it made with a mortar). The olive oils Rosa uses are remarkable, including La Baita (pure Taggiasca) and Chiavari-area maker Rùe di Zerli (Lavagnina). There's even a hard-to-find thyme liqueur made on the Monte di Portofino.

Repubblica, about 150 yards west of the train station). A handful of fishermen belong to the local cooperative, which operates the celebrated *tonnara di Punta Chiappa* (see page 179).

The outdoor market is held each Wednesday, from 8am to 1pm. The best food-related stands are near the train station. There you will find a handful of farmers who grow and sell their own produce, a woman who sells cheeses and salamis from the Santo Stefano d'Aveto area, and a seller of locally made honey. At the western end of the market is a stand from the Valle del Biologico, the "organic valley" of Val di Vara, in eastern Liguria, with a few good salamis and many delicious organic cheeses from Cooperativa Casearia Val di Vara.

If you're in the market for an olive wood cutting board, or an olive wood mortar and pestle, they may be purchased at **La Bottega di Mastro Antonucci** (Via P. Schiaffino 36, Tel: 0185 770519, opening hours vary). At this pleasantly hokey hole in the wall on the main drag, near the former covered market on the western side of town, above the port, ye olde craftsman toils amid clutter.

Camogli is the site of the annual Sagra del Pesce, a postwar phenomenon, originally a semi-religious celebration thanking the Madonna for helping local fishermen escape death, but nowadays a kitsch feeding frenzy. It centers on a giant frying pan, set up in the port, in which tons of fish are fried in small baskets set up along the edge of the whale-sized pan. People attend for the party atmosphere, not the food.

Camogli's authentic religious festival, which is deeply felt by locals, and also provides an excuse to eat well and watch evening activities from a convenient *trattoria* table, is Stella Maris. It's held the first Sunday in August. The sea is usually calm. Garlanded fishing boats, canoes, ferryboats, air mattresses and rafts leave Camogli's port to an altar on Punta Chiappa, south of town. Local priests bless the fleet there. In the evening, participants light 20,000 candles, which are set inside paper cups, and float them from the port and from Punta Chiappa. Each candle represents a mariner's soul. Tides bring them together in the middle of the Golfo del Paradiso, where they twinkle into the night.

ANCHOVIES, COFFEE, PASTRIES, ICE CREAM, GOURMET FOOD AND WINE

Choco Emotion

THE NAME MAY BE UNFORTUNATE, BUT THIS PINT-SIZED *CAFFÈ* ON CAMOGLI'S RECENTLY PEDESTRIANIZED main street serves good coffee, chocolates and delicious pastries made by one of the Riviera's top pastry makers, Budicin (see Ruta di Camogli, page 195).

VIA DELLA REPUBBLICA 55 ✦ TEL: 0185 770329 ✦ OPEN DAILY

Cooperativa Pescatori

ON A STEEP STAIRCASE THAT DESCENDS FROM VIA DELLA REPUBBLICA, NEAR THE FORMER CITY GATE, toward the port, this grotto-like fish shop is where the fishermen's co-op sells its fresh fish and salted anchovies, which are particularly delicious. They're prepared in the "traditional" manner, meaning they are headless and gutted, but still have bones and fins, and are packed in brine.

SALITA PRIARO 14 ✦ TEL: 0185 772513
CLOSED SUNDAY AFTERNOON

La Bottega dei Piaceri

ON CAMOGLI'S MAIN PEDESTRIAN STREET FACING ROCCO RIZZO'S BAKERY, THIS SMALL, NEW AND modish boutique, run by a trio of local food-and-wine experts, sells a fine selection of Ligurian wines (including those of Bruna and Santa Caterina, and Pigato by Laura Aschero), Riviera delicacies (anchovy-and-olive paste from Sommariva in Albenga, basil pesto and pesto "Portofino" mixed with tomatoes, *salsa di noci*, honey, jams, rose-petal syrup), and even thyme- and other herb-flavored liqueurs (and olive oil) from local producer Il Giardino del Borgo San Fruttuoso. Other Ligurian olive oils include excellent pure-Lavagnina olive oil from Rùe di Zerli near Lavagna, and Sommariva, in Albenga. This is the best source in town for bottled anchovies from the local co-op (which sometimes sells out). You can also pick up Revello's *camogliesi* sweets here: one of the owners is a member of the Revello family.

VIA DELLA REPUBBLICA 87
TEL: 0185 771520 ✦ WWW.BOTTEGADEIPIACERI.COM
OPEN 9:30AM *to* 1PM *and* 4PM *to* 7:30PM, CLOSED SUNDAY
(*and* THURSDAY, *from* JANUARY *through* MARCH)

Primula

THE DOLCE VITA CONTINUES AT THIS LONG-ESTAB-LISHED BAR, *CAFFÈ* AND TEA ROOM, ON CAMOGLI'S seaside promenade, a favorite of the Milanese who have bought up much of the town's prime real estate. Take a seat at a granite-topped table under the awnings and watch the world walk by, while enjoying one of the area's most luscious ice creams. They're handmade by the partners who've run Primula for decades. The *panera*—creamy cappuccino ice cream—is outstanding, but so too is the rich pistachio (made with the best pistachio pastes from Bronte, in Sicily), and the fresh fruit *gelati*. The texture is perfect—neither too stiff nor too soft—and the sweetness nicely balanced. Primula is also a great lunch spot, serving big seafood salads and simple Riviera classics of all kinds. Their pesto is particularly delicious and generously served—ask for an extra bowl of it, and the owners are happy to oblige. But nut-allergy sufferers be warned: the pesto is made not only with pine nuts, but also walnuts.

PASSEGGIATA MARE/VIA GARIBALDI 140 ✦ TEL: 0185 770351
SAMBELLAMY@LIBERO.IT ✦ OPEN 8AM *to* MIDNIGHT DAILY
EXCEPT THURSDAYS

Pasticceria Revello

THIS NARROW OLD SEASIDE SPECIALTY BAKERY IS OFTEN THREE-DEEP AT THE COUNTER WITH TOURISTS; somehow the Revello family and employees remain friendly and helpful, and their products authentic, from the delicious *pandolce* to the very good focaccia, plain or with cheese, in the style of Recco, and, in the fall/winter season, the *farinata* (afternoons only). Many Riviera towns have their specialty sweets, and Camogli is no exception. *Camogliesi* are irresistible rum-cream-filled pastry shells covered with chocolate, invented by Revello in the postwar period. They're now flanked by variations on the theme, also called *camogliesi* but without alcohol, flavored with almond, orange, amaretto or hazelnut instead, and which look surprisingly like pinched noses. (Revello has recently opened a bakery in Japan, where they make *camogliesi* with about half the dosage of rum.)

VIA GIUSEPPE GARIBALDI 183 ✦ TEL: 0185 770777
WWW.REVELLOCAMOGLI.COM ✦ OPEN DAILY

Panificio Rocco Rizzo

BAKER AND PASTRY-MAKER ROCCO RIZZO IS FROM PUGLIA. HE MOVED TO LIGURIA IN THE EARLY 1960S, and his simple *panificio-pasticceria* on the western end of Camogli's main street (which has recently been pedestrianized) is now the best in town. Rocco's cheese focaccia is closer in style to that of Genoa, meaning it's thicker and more bready on the bottom than what you get just a few miles away in Recco. The plain focaccia is excellent, with plenty of extra virgin olive oil — never the cheap bulk olive oils many bakers use in order to save money. In fact Rizzo, having visited an industrial seed-oil factory decades ago, decided he would only ever use extra virgin oils, even to oil his baking pans. When he runs out of the oil his family makes from his trees in Puglia, he buys it. The bread is reliably excellent, especially the sourdough Puglian loaves. But what the Rizzo bakery really excels at is *pandolce all'antica* — the low, dome-shaped Genoese dessert stuffed with candied fruit, raisins and pine nuts. Rizzo cookies and *crostata* jam tarts are also very good, and the extravagant *bocca di dama*, the only pastry from Puglia that Rocco Rizzo always makes, is guaranteed to surprise and delight: it's a bite-sized oval sponge cake filled with chocolate cream.

VIA DELLA REPUBBLICA 134 ✦ TEL: 0185 770247
CLOSED WEDNESDAY *and* SUNDAY AFTERNOONS, *and* NOVEMBER

The Tonnara of Camogli

....

A TONNARA IS A TUNA-FISHING NET. ITALY ONCE HAD MANY, BUT ONLY A HANDFUL remain, most of them off the southern coast or Sicily. The *tonnara* at Punta Chiappa, between Camogli and San Fruttuoso, on the north side of the Portofino Peninsula, has been around since the 1600s, and is used from April through September. Each year the *tonnara* is made anew from the nets and ropes on up, using natural coconut fibre. It's a complex weave of netting that forms a tunnel about 300 yards long, and hangs from floats, forming a trap. Tuna — *tonno* — and other medium-sized or large fish swim into the *tonnara* but can't find their way out; small fry escape unharmed. Fishermen in two wooden rowboats, one on each end, pull the net up and flip the catch aboard. Everything is done by hand, a picturesque though exhausting procedure repeated season to season by the handful of local fishermen who hold shares in the *tonnara* cooperative. Depending on the weather and catch, the *tonnara* is pulled up once or twice daily. The fish is unloaded startlingly fresh — often still flipping — in Camogli's port, usually mid-morning or late afternoon. The catch is sold through the co-op fish shop on a steep staircase near the port, or direct to professionals. The owners of certain seaside restaurants in the area are known to watch the *tonnara* through binoculars to see what the fishermen are hauling up. They then dispatch the chef to buy choice specimens.

PORTOFINO

ITH ITS ELABORATELY FRESCOED OLD HOUSES, TIDY OLIVE GROVES AND A striking setting at the tip of a curling, craggy peninsula, Portofino ranks among the world's most celebrated former fishing villages: the handful of fishing boats in the port are used to transport billionaires to and from their yachts or isolated seaside villas. Local income now comes from the dozen international fashion boutiques in reconverted fishermen's houses; several five-star luxury hotels; and the mooring fees paid by those who anchor their motor yachts in or near the small, horseshoe-shaped harbor. Portofino has long been ludicrously expensive and exclusive. Over 400 years ago, in the late sixteenth century, the traveling nobleman Giambattista Confalonieri noted that at the hostelry where he slept, "You were charged not only for the room, but for the very air you breathed." As has been remarked by many, that is called paying for the atmosphere.

The few year-round locals, most of them servants or gardeners at the villas of the rich and famous, go elsewhere when they eat out. Portofino is a gorgeous place for a picnic, however, which you can buy in Rapallo or Santa Margherita Ligure, on the way out. Savor it on a bench in the port, or on the *piazzetta* facing the pan-oramic church of San Giorgio, or at the lighthouse at the tip of the peninsula (in summer, a *gelataio* sells decent ice creams along the trail near the lighthouse). At a pinch, if timing, romance or wealth induce you to dine out in Portofino, the most authentic

Ligurian food is to be found at a chic restaurant with a lovely terrace on the port, **Puny** (Piazza Martiri Olivetta 7, Tel: 0185 269037, closed Thursdays and January and February, expensive to very expensive). Alongside the predictable international favorites, Puny serves *crostini* with *stoccafisso*, housemade *pappardelle* with pesto and tomato sauce (*pesto corto*), and whole fish with olives and bay leaves. Tiny and serving mostly savory tarts, pizzas and good first courses is **El Portico** (Via Roma 21, Tel: 0185 269239, closed Tuesdays and January to mid February, moderate), under the short portico on the main street from the parking lot to the port. There's a bakery facing El Portico, and a grocery next door to it, where you can buy focaccia and supplies, plus a sandwich shop next to the grocery.

RAPALLO

S ET IN A CURVING BAY HEMMED IN BY THE 1,900-FOOT MONTALLEGRO AND ITS LOVELY BAROQUE sanctuary, Rapallo was among the Riviera's proto tourist resorts, drawing European and Russian bluebloods, and American nouveaux riches, as early as the mid 1800s. Nietzsche wrote most of *Thus Spake Zarathustra* here. Fine villas dot the olive groves on tiered terraces around town, and hulking turn-of-the-century *palazzi* line Rapallo's small historic center, whose old house-towers rise around a cat's cradle of medieval alleys. In the 1960s and '70s Rapallo boomed, which accounts for the less attractive apartment complexes on the outskirts, and the Italian verb, *rapallizzazione*, coined in the 1970s and meaning "to over-build" or "build without planning." The seaside promenade and old part of town are charming, and packed with wonderful shops selling delicacies.

As in many Riviera resorts, the restaurants are expensive and those serving fish to the tourist trade are interchangeable. Locals in search of authentic fare go inland to San Massimo di

Rapallo or San Lorenzo della Costa, on hilltops nearby, or they head to Chiavari and Lavagna, a few miles south. The fruit-and-vegetable market is held on weekdays 8am to 1pm and on Saturdays from 8am to 7pm. It's in the center of the old part of town, on Piazza Venezia.

TRATTORIA

Ö Bansin

A CENTURY OLD, COZY, CLUTTERED WITH SHIP MODELS AND HUNG WITH OLD PRINTS, Ö BANSIN IS hidden down an untraveled back alleyway parallel to Rapallo's main *caruggio*, a few storefronts west of the Cantin-a du Púsu bottle shop, and has a small outdoor terrace in back. This is the only authentic *trattoria* in town serving exclusively Ligurian food, and the atmosphere is friendly. The simple fish dishes are good — anchovies marinated in fresh lemon juice, or stuffed and fried, plus classic *stoccafisso alla ligure* and *buridda* stew made with squid — but so too are the savory vegetable tarts, the delicious minestrone *alla genovese* and good fresh pasta, such as *trofie* with pesto or ravioli with meat sauce. The desserts are simple and housemade, and the wine list includes good regional bottlings.

VIA VENEZIA 105 ✦ TEL: 0185 231119
CLOSED ON MONDAY *and* FOR DINNER ON SUNDAY ✦ MODERATE

COFFEE, PASTRIES, ICE CREAM,
PASTA *FRESCA*, GOURMET FOODS

Baj Pasticceria

A HANDFUL OF SMALL TABLES WITH COMFORTABLE, OLD-FASHIONED CHAIRS SET OUT ON THE MAIN pedestrian alleyway, an even more old-fashioned interior with a composite marble floor and cold cases filled with pastries, and reliably good Illy coffee: this long-established pastry shop is a favorite with locals. The name is pronounced "bye," and the house specialty is *baci di Rapallo*—luscious chocolate-and-hazelnut "kisses."

VIA MAZZINI 13 ✦ TEL: 0185 50440
OPEN 7:30AM *to* 8PM DAILY *except* MONDAYS

Caffè Bocchia

TWO CENTRAL LOCATIONS IN RAPALLO FOR THIS SUC-CESSFUL LOCAL MINI-CHAIN OF COFFEE ROASTERS, based in Recco.

VIA GIUSEPPE MAZZINI 31 ✦ TEL: 0185 50009 *and* VIA MAMELI 261
TEL: 0185 232079 ✦ WWW.BOCCHIACAFFE.IT ✦ CLOSED SUNDAY

La Bottega dei Sestieri— Parlacomemangi.com, Salumeria Formaggeria

VIA GIUSEPPE MAZZINI 44 *and* PIAZZA MARTIRI
DELLA LIBERTÀ 11 ✦ TEL: 0185 230530 ✦ CLOSED SUNDAY

THE CRYPTIC WORDS *PARLA COME MANGI*—SPEAK LIKE YOU EAT—ARE SCRAWLED ON THE WINDOWS OF this well-stocked salami, cheese, specialty foods and wine shop that connects Rapallo's main pedestrian alleyway to a seaside *piazzetta*. The owner travels Italy selecting top products, and there are many remarkable ones from the Riviera. The only thing in short supply is modesty; happily the quality and range of offerings — including farmstead cheese from Stella, on the Riviera di Ponente — is excellent. Among the 1,000 or so wines you'll find most of the Riviera's best bottlings.

Cantin-a du Púsu

RUN BY THE CHATTY GUIDO TASSARA AND HIS AFFABLE, BESPECTACLED SON GIOVANNI, BOTH TOP wine experts, this handsome old bottle shop on a less-traveled alleyway in the center of old Rapallo has an astonishing 4,500 wines on display, including about a hundred of Liguria's best, from Laura Aschero to Bio Vio and the owners' favorite, Luciano Capellini of the Cinque Terre. Giovanni Tassara is a great believer in organic wines, and you'll find most of Italy's best here. Cantin-a du Púsu manages to merge professionalism with friendliness and a refreshing lack of pretention.

VIA VENEZIA 113 ✦ TEL: 0185 270891

WWW.CANTINADUPUSU.COM ✦ CLOSED SUNDAY AFTERNOON

Cantine d'Italia

A RAPALLO INSTITUTION THAT'S FULL OF PLEASANT SURPRISES, THIS CORNER *CAFFÈ* AND WINE BAR on the main pedestrian alleyway has been around since 1910, and was taken over in 1962 by the Raggi family. They still own and operate it, and the current generation has taken it upscale, remodeling and expanding the choice of gourmet foods and the remarkably wide range of wines. You can not only get a good cup of coffee, but buy a carton of milk at the bar. More profitably, you can take a seat at a table in the bustling *caruggio* and snack on something to accompany a glass of wine. The most pleasant surprise of all is that, among the 3,000 bottlings in stock are nearly sixty of the region's best. This is an authentically great place to taste a wide range of Riviera wines before buying in quantity, or driving to a winery for a visit.

VIA MAZZINI 59 ✦ TEL: 0185 50538 ✦ OPEN DAILY 7AM *to*
10:30PM (LATER IN SUMMER), CLOSED THURSDAYS IN WINTER

Pasta Fresca Dasso

THE LUXURY PASTA BOUTIQUE FOUNDED DECADES AGO AND STILL RUN BY OLGA DASSO AND A FLOCK of assistants makes some of the Riviera's highest-quality and most delicious fresh pasta and is famed among other things for *pansôti* (purses stuffed with *preboggion*, redolent of fresh marjoram), stamped, round *corzetti*, ravioli filled with meat or ricotta and spinach, and excellent pesto, creamy *salsa di noci* walnut sauce, and many other Ligurian pasta and sauce specialties. The location is handy, facing Rapallo's small fruit-and-vegetable market. Olga has another shop, equally good, in the center of old Lavagna.

PIAZZA VENEZIA 31 ✦ TEL: 0185 53309
CLOSED SUNDAY AFTERNOON *and* MONDAY

Gelateria Frigidarium

AT THE SOUTH END OF THE SEASIDE PROMENADE, FACING RAPALLO'S PINT-SIZED BUT FEARSOME castle, Frigidarium is by far the best ice cream parlor in town, and might just be among the region's top three or four. The ice cream is totally "natural," meaning no artificial anything, and no stabilizers or thickeners or colorings of any kind. Nothing but milk, cream and fresh fruit, or good-quality chocolate, hazelnut and pistachio pastes of the best types available, and little sugar, go into these memorable *gelati*. Fruit flavors follow the seasons—strawberries in late spring, pears in fall and dozens of others as the produce ripens.

LUNGOMARE VITTORIO VENETO 4, ✦ TEL: 0185 50044
OPEN DAILY IN HIGH SEASON 10AM *to* MIDNIGHT;
IN WINTER CLOSED ON WEDNESDAYS

Mazzini-Graglia Salumeria Rosticceria

AMONG RAPALLO'S MOST LAVISH AND GORGEOUSLY APPOINTED SPECIALTY FOOD SHOPS, with dozens of ready-to-eat dishes, from seafood salad to roast pork or rotisserie chicken, plus a wide selection of hams, salamis, cheeses, dry mushrooms, wines, sauces, vegetables packed in olive oil and canned goods. Truly a feast for the eyes, served up with a smile.

VIA GIUSEPPE MAZZINI 31 ✦ TEL: 0185 50303 ✦ CLOSED MONDAY

Torrefazione Caffè Pagliettini

FOUNDED IN 1925 AND INTO ITS THIRD GENERATION, THIS ARTISANAL COFFEE ROASTER ON RAPALLO'S market square has half a dozen blends, including several very good pure-Arabica blends. The best is "Super Dolce," which is 50 percent Colombia Excelso, 30 percent Costarica and 20 percent Caracolito Brasiliano. When the stock of roasted beans gets low, the owners remove the packages of candies, cookies and specialty foods from the basin of the old roaster, which sits in the middle of the shop, stoke the machine with charcoal, and toast away. The alleys of old Rapallo are soon perfumed.

PIAZZA VENEZIA 29 ✦ TEL: 0185 50023
CLOSED SUNDAY *and* WEDNESDAY

COPPER PANS

Roncagliolo e Simonetti

THIS LONG-ESTABLISHED HOUSEWARES AND GIFT SHOP ON RAPALLO'S MAIN SQUARE STOCKS EVERY-thing an Italian cook needs, including the big, handsome, tin-lined copper baking pans for *farinata* and savory tarts.

PIAZZA CAVOUR 16 ✦ TEL: 0185 60558
OPEN DAILY INCLUDING SUNDAY

OLIVE OIL MAKER

Agriturismo La Bicocca

LA BICOCCA IS A TWO-IN-ONE: A FARMHOUSE B&B (SERVING GOOD REGIONAL FOOD TO OVERNIGHT guests only) and micro olive oil-making concern. It's set on the coiling, panoramic road from downtown Rapallo to the perched sanctuary of Montallegro. The sweet, classic, cold-pressed extra virgin olive oil is labeled Madonna Nera and made with a blend of hand-picked Lavagnina, Pignola and other native varieties. Only 1,000 liters are produced a year. Buy the oil direct from La Bicocca or at La Bottega dei Piaceri in Camogli.

SALITA SANT'AGOSTINO 57, LOCALITÀ MADONNA NERA
TEL: 0185 272380, CELL: 347 211 6051 ✦ WWW.LABICOCCA.EU
BY APPOINTMENT ✦ OPEN DAILY YEAR-ROUND FOR OLIVE
OIL SALES; B&B CLOSED JANUARY 15 *to* MARCH 15.

RECCO

*I*N WORLD WAR II, USAF AND RAF BOMBERS FLAT-
TENED THE SEASIDE VILLAGE OF RECCO, 12 MILES
southeast of Genoa, in an attempt to take out the railway viaduct. Recco was hastily rebuilt in the 1950s and
'60s, which is why uncharitable English-speaking travelers think the name means "Wreak-oh!" Despite its lack of urbane charm, Recco has a lovely setting, with a small river and steep, olive-covered terraces. It's also known correctly as one of the Riviera's gastronomic pilgrimage sites, with many fine restaurants, gourmet shops, a world-class coffee roaster in its hinterland and local specialties, the most famous of which is focaccia *con formaggio* (also called *al formaggio* or *col formaggio*). This thin, pale savory tart is usually the diameter of a truck tire, sandwiching white, mild *stracchino* cow's milk cheese between two sheets of translucent, olive oil-based dough, similar to focaccia or pizza dough but without yeast.

The pesto of Recco (like that of Camogli, Santa Margherita Ligure and Rapallo) often includes tangy *prescinsêua*, a fresh cow's-milk cheese reminiscent of yogurt mixed with cottage cheese, and is paler in color than most other Ligurian pesto, but remarkably delicious. The best classic pesto and also the finest restaurant-made focaccia *con formaggio* are served by three of Recco's top luxury restaurants, **Manuelina** (see below), **Da Lino** (Via Roma 70-72, Tel: 0185 74336, closed Tuesday, expensive) and **Da ö Vittorio** (Via Roma 160, Tel: 0185 74029, closed mid November to early December, expensive to very expensive), and the much simpler **Ristorante Da Angelo** (see 193), a local favorite.

Recco's weekly Monday street market, which fills several city blocks under and around the railroad viaduct, from 8am to 1:30pm, offers some excellent deals on produce and packaged specialty foods, such as chestnuts and chestnut flour, pesto or handmade pasta, plus cooking utensils and accessories (and clothing). It brings even greater animation to this lively, if homely, town.

Like Vivaldi's *Four Seasons*, Recco hosts four week-long street fairs, La Settimana Gastronomica, held starting the 21st of March, June, September and December. They are a recent, professionally organized marketing gambit, but they do bring together scores of fine Ligurian food and wine producers and retailers. While they're on, you can be sure local shops will do their best to seduce you. The Festa della focaccia, an orgy of focaccia *con formaggio*-eating, is held the last Sunday in May; truth be told, in Recco, every day is focaccia day, with *panifici*, *pizzerie* and *ristoranti* busily baking away.

More traditional and heartfelt is the Sagra del Fuoco, a religious festival held since the 1820s in Recco in early September to celebrate the town's patron saint and protector, Nostra Signora del Suffragio (Tel: 0185 722 440 or 0185 729 1285, www.sagradel-fuoco.it). Nowadays it's an excuse to saunter among the town's seven *quartieri* (districts), from one food stand or sit-down, open-air feast to another. All the usual suspects are served, from focaccia *col formaggio* or puffy, cheese-filled *focaccette* fritters to *trofiette con pesto*, stuffed eggplants to mixed seafood fry, stewed baby squid and *stoccafisso*, plus creamy sweet rice tart or crusty *crostata* with lemon-flavored pastry cream and pine nuts.

FOCACCIA BAKERIES

Panificio-Pasticceria Moltedo

EW LIGURIANS CONTEST THE CLAIM MADE BY THE INHABITANTS OF RECCO THAT THE MOLTEDO FAMILY are the kings of focaccia, both classic and cheese filled. Moltedo owns and operates two bakeries in town, one of fairly recent creation on the coast highway, near the beach (Via Assereto 15, Tel: 0185 74202), the other a century-old outlet practically under the railway viaduct that flies over the center of town. Both are referred to in dialect as *dau Louensu* — Lorenzo's place — and are three-deep with customers waiting in line. The original location, which is also a regular bakery and grocery, turns out the best focaccia of all, because this is where focaccia master Bruno Conti, who married into the Moltedo family, has been working wonders since 1969. Why are Moltedo focaccias so good? They're crisped

to perfection not only on top but also on the bottom, which is rare. The pores are compact, the pockmarks on the surface small and regular. The amount of salt inside and out is balanced, and there's plenty of good quality olive oil.

Try to get to the bakery early, because the Moltedos always sell out, and they often bake plain, herb-flecked or onion-topped focaccia in the morning only. Happily the Moltedos' fabulous focaccia *con formaggio* is baked throughout the day — Conti and his sons and helpers turn out about 110 cheese focaccias per day. People drive here from far and wide to buy it. Compared to other focaccias in town, which are nearly always very good and sometimes excellent, Moltedo focaccia *con formaggio* is thinner, lighter and perfectly cooked on the bottom. The secret is the coarse polenta the baker scatters onto his paddle and across the oven's cooking surface. The focaccia *con formaggio* slides from the paddle onto the surface and cooks in direct contact with the oven. Almost all other focaccia bakers use baking pans. The other secret

is the oven itself, which has a built-in rotating mechanism like a printer's platen; the focaccia turns with the platen, browning evenly, without damage.

VIA XX SETTEMBRE 2/4 ✦ TEL: 0185 74046

WWW.MOLTEDO.COM

CLOSED WEDNESDAY AFTERNOON *and* SUNDAY

Tossini

A FALL-BACK IN CASE YOU CAN'T GET TO MOLT-EDO, RECCO-AREA RESIDENTS SWEAR BY THIS successful local mini-chain. The most convenient location is on the main drag, Via Roma, about a hundred yards north of the Via Aurelia highway. The focaccia *con formaggio* is thicker, with more crust, and is cooked darker, than that of Moltedo. The regular focaccia is very good, and so is the bread.

VIA TRIESTE 14 *and* VIA ROMA 17 ✦ TEL: 0185 74314

(*plus other locations* IN RAPALLO, AVEGNO *and* SANTA MARGHERITA
LIGURE) ✦ CLOSED WEDNESDAY AFTERNOON *and* SUNDAY

Ü Fainottö—Da Franco

A NOTHER FALL-BACK IN CASE YOU CAN'T GET TO MOLTEDO FOR THE CHEESE FOCACCIA. DA FRANCO would be considered a great spot for focaccia *con for-maggio* if it didn't live in the shadow of Moltedo. The *farinata* is well cooked and highly popular. This is a spartan, simple take-out place located on the first road inland from the Via Aurelia, parallel to it.

VIA IV NOVEMBRE 3A ✦ TEL: 0185 74326 ✦ CLOSED MONDAY

RESTAURANTS

Ristorante Da Angelo

*I*NLAND SEVERAL MILES ON THE BUSY TWO-LANE HIGHWAY TO USCIO, BEYOND THE SOARING UPRIGHTS OF the autostrada, Da Angelo doesn't have a winning location. There's no view. However, the interior is comfortable, sunny, simple and clean. Run by Angelo and his brother, the chef, Da Angelo has some of the best focaccia *con formaggio* anywhere, and serves many regional classics, plus very fresh, well-prepared fish (the chef is also a fisherman). You're unlikely to encounter business tycoons or tourists, just savvy locals, and if all you want to eat is focaccia *con formaggio* that's fine, Angelo won't pressure you to have a full meal.

VIA SAN ROCCO 86 ✦ TEL: 0185 76719, CELL: 348 864 4459
CLOSED MONDAY; LUNCH SUNDAY ONLY
INEXPENSIVE *to* MODERATE

Manuelina and La Focacceria

*R*ECCO'S MOST CELEBRATED RESTAURANT WAS FOUNDED IN 1885 BUT THERE'S LITTLE LEFT OF the humble eatery of old. The current generation runs the operation with professionalism and panache. Manuelina lives off its reputation, but few say the reputation isn't deserved—starting with the focaccia *con formaggio*, which was invented here. The pesto is remarkably good, the seafood and other Ligurian specialties well prepared and of the highest quality, though verticality has snuck in—the crustaceans in your *cappon magro*, for instance, will come mounted at a daunting height. Prices are also high. Locals come to celebrate anniversaries, weddings and birthdays, and Genoese businessmen bring in their out-of-town clients to impress them. The restaurant is located several miles inland, on Recco's main thoroughfare linking the coast to the autostrada, so it gets no walk-by customers and has no view. The luxury is palpable, the service smooth. Next door to the main restaurant is the lower-priced, more casual *focacceria*, which is a better place to sample Manuelina's sumptuous focaccia *con formaggio*. The dish as served at either is softer and richer and cheesier than what you'll taste in Recco's many bakeries. The wine list features a fine selection of Ligurian and other Italian wines, including many from Tuscany.

VIA ROMA 278 ✦ TEL: 0185 74128 *or* 0185 75364
WWW.MANUELINA.IT ✦ MAIN RESTAURANT: EXPENSIVE *to*
VERY EXPENSIVE; FOCACCERIA: INEXPENSIVE *to* MODERATE

COFFEE, ICE CREAM, PASTRIES

Caffè Bocchia

OWNERS RAFFAELA AND EMANUELA BOCCHIA ARE THE SECOND GENERATION OF THE BOCCHIA FAMILY, which opened this coffee and tea shop back in 1958. The coffee-roasting facility is a few miles inland, at Avegno, and supplies the original Recco location plus identical Bocchia coffee shops in Chiavari, Rapallo and Sestri Levante. The house special blend is called I Magnifici Sette, the magnificent seven. It contains Puerto Rican Fino AA Yauco Selecto, Costarican SHB Tournon HT/M, Mexican Altura Superior, Brasilian Santos N.Y. Cerrado dulce, Nicaraguan Matagalpa, Guatemalan Estrellas and Ethiopian Moka Sidamo. Smooth, rich and without a trace of bitterness, this blend is excellent. Buy a kilo of beans and take them with you, or enjoy the coffee in situ. Bocchia also sells irresistible chocolate-covered coffee beans, *canestrelli* and *anicini* cookies made by a local bakery, and, at the bar, to accompany your espresso or cappuccino, very good pastries, including *fagottini con le mele*, which are sumptuous envelopes of pastry wrapped around chunky apple sauce. This is strictly a local hangout, on Recco's busy main north-south axis, with no tables inside and no sidewalk terrace either, which is why vacationers pass it by.

VIA ROMA 40R ✦ TEL: 0185 730058 ✦ WWW.BOCCHIACAFFE.IT
CLOSED SUNDAY

Gelateria Cavassa

UNDER THE ARCADES OF RECCO'S SHORT AND HUM-BLE SEAFRONT, THIS FAMILY-RUN ICE CREAMERY has been around since 1971, hand-making the best *gelati* in town, with good ingredients, and no colorings or preservatives. The fruit flavors are excellent — fresh fruit, water and sugar. You can enjoy them at a table facing the children's playground and the beach, or take a cone and walk with it.

VICO SAPORITO 8 ✦ TEL: 0185 74280

OPEN 9AM *to* MIDNIGHT DAILY EXCEPT THURSDAY,

CLOSED LATE-JANUARY *to* LATE-FEBRUARY

Pasticceria Bar Riviera

RIVIERA WAS IN BUSINESS BEFORE WORLD WAR II RECONFIGURED RECCO, BUT THE CURRENT OWNERS, the Barone family, have been here for about thirty years. They're known among local connoisseurs for their *pandolce*, both the low and dense variety (*all'antica*) and the tall, doughy type. They also make giant, creamy *meringata* — a confection resembling baked Alaska — plus aniseed-flavored *anicini* dry biscuits and luscious butter cookies, not to mention a wide assortment of exquisite cream-filled *bigné* pastry puffs. The place has a wonderfully old-fashioned feel, with a zinc-topped bar, where you can enjoy a pastry and a cup of good coffee. Locals prefer this spartan locale to the seaside or sidewalk places where tourists hang out.

VIA ROMA 2 ✦ TEL: 0185 74296

CLOSED SUNDAY AFTERNOON *and* TUESDAY

RUTA AND SAN ROCCO DI CAMOGLI

ON THE EASTERN SLOPES OF THE BOWL SUR-ROUNDING CAMOGLI, ABOUT A THIRD OF THE way up the west side of the Monte di Portofino, the hamlets of Ruta and San Rocco di Camogli are wrapped in tiered olive groves and strung out along the tilting Via Aurelia (Ruta) and a looping two-laner lined with thick old umbrella pines

(San Rocco). People come to both for the views, the richly adorned churches, and because several hiking trails into the Monte di Portofino regional park run through. Though tiny, each hamlet has several restaurants, snack bars and food shops of note.

RESTAURANT

La Cucina di Nonna Nina

A COZY, COMPACT, WHITE-WALLED RESTAURANT ON THE SECOND-FLOOR OF A TURN-OF-THE-nineteenth-century building, with a pleasant outdoor terrace but no stunning views to distract you, Nonna Nina serves authentic cooking of the kind found a century ago in middle- or upper-class Ligurian homes. *Nonna* means grandmother. "Nonna Nina" is none other than Paolo Dalpian the chef, and his wife Rosalia Musumeci, who runs the dining room. Together they assembled heirloom recipes and have spent the last several decades earning a well-deserved reputation as keepers of the flame of Riviera food. That doesn't mean what they make is out of date, rather, that it's timeless. The ingredients are of the highest quality, from the olives and oils to the cheeses and basil. The herbs are homegrown or supplied by neighbors. Paolo handmakes everything, including *fugasette cö-u formaggio* — tiny cheese fritters fried in olive oil — fabulously good pastas stuffed with field greens or nettle tops, or linguine sauced with fresh seafood, or *corzetti* with walnut sauce, and *picagge avvantagge a-u pesto* — fresh pasta twists made partly with whole wheat flour and sauced with perfect pesto (which, if ordered ahead, can be made with a mortar and pestle). The *rosetti* and artichoke soup is exquisite and found only here. The tiny squid, gently stewed, stuffed or flash fried in olive oil, and the *fritelle di bianchetti*, also fried in olive oil, are exquisite. But so too are heartier dishes such as *coniggio ä ligure* — the classic Ligurian-style rabbit with olives and pine nuts. The desserts — simple jam tarts made with Paolo's own fig jam, or a lemon-perfumed pastry cream tart with pine nuts — are ethereal, the ice creams wholly natural, simple and among the best in the region, period. Even the fragrant bread is homemade. The wine list is short, but features a handful of top Riviera bottlings. Reserve ahead. Note: on sale at the restaurant are the organic rose-water syrups and jams of Paolo's brother, Luca Dalpian, whose company, **Il Sottobosco**, is in the northwestern hinterland of Genoa (Località Acquabuona, Tel. 010 929298, Tiglieto, Genoa).

VIALE FRANCO MOLFINO 126, SAN ROCCO DI CAMOGLI (GE)

TEL: 0185 773835 ✦ WWW.NONNANINA.IT

CLOSED WEDNESDAY ✦ MODERATE *to* EXPENSIVE

COFFEE, SEA BISCUITS, PASTRIES, PICNIC SUPPLIES

Pasticceria Bar Budicin

ARCO BUDICIN, THIN AND WIRY, AND RIGHTLY CONSIDERED ONE OF THE REGION'S GREAT pastry makers, was born in Rovigno, Istria, when the city still belonged to Italy. It's been part of Croatia since the end of World War II. Marco's family, like many Italian families, starting with settlers from the Republic of Venice forward, had lived there since the Middle Ages. He's been in Liguria since 1949, but the slight lilt in his accent, and his looks, give away his northern origins. So, too, does the excellence of certain cream-filled pastries he makes, including *cannoli*. But his *pandolce*, shortbread cookies, *crostata* and *pinolata*—buttery cookie clusters studded with pine nuts—are pure Riviera. This *caffè*-pastry shop on the Via Aurelia highway that cuts across Ruta is tiny and dark, and it's easy to miss, near a butcher shop and hardware store. You'll recognize it by the wall posters of lovely Rovigno, the Venetian island city of Croatia, and, near them, the awards and certificates from the Italian government declaring Budicin a *cavaliere del lavoro*—the highest recognition given to business people and artisans. Budicin's pastries are also available in Camogli, on the main pedestrianized street, at a pleasant little coffee and chocolate shop with outdoor tables and the unfortunate name, Choco Emotion (see page 176).

VIA AURELIA 186, RUTA DI CAMOGLI (GE)

TEL: 0185 770523 ✦ OPEN DAILY

Da Nicco

ICCO MAGGIOLO AND HIS SON MARCO OWN AND OPERATE THIS CLASSY *CAFFÈ*, COCKTAIL BAR and all-around upscale hangout perched high above

Camogli and blissfully off the busy Via Aurelia. Illy coffee is served, as well as very good snacks and simple hot dishes. Da Nicco also sells gourmet chocolates, cookies and candies. Bearded, devoted to the cause of Bacchus and highly professional, Marco makes dozens of exotic cocktails, stocks an astonishing number of world-class beers, 120 different whiskies and scotches, and also has a fine selection of about a hundred different Italian wines served by the glass or bottle. Ligurian wines are not his strongest suit, but he does carry Vermentino and Pigato by respected olive-oil and winemaker Domenico Ramoino, and Sciacchetrà by La Polenza, plus the Cinque Terre cooperative's whites. The ice cream is house-made and delicious, especially the creamy chocolate and coffee flavors. Da Nicco's outdoor terrace has comfortable wooden chairs and built-in benches, with see-forever views down the coast to Genoa.

VIALE FRANCO MOLFINO 7, RUTA ✦ TEL: 0185 770128

OPEN 7:30AM *to* 1:30AM, CLOSED TUESDAYS

and MID JANUARY *to* MID FEBRUARY

Macelleria Paolucci

*I*N THE SAME BUILDING AS RESTAURANT NONNA NINA, AFFABLE ARTURO AND ANTONIETTA PAOLUCCI'S butcher-and-grocery shop keeps locals in good supply of everything from egg to apple. Arturo is known for his *testa in cassetta*, a particularly luscious head cheese made with pork cheeks and other parts of the head. He's also mastered *cima alla*

genovese, the delicious breast of veal stuffed with a mix of eggs beaten with grated *parmigiano*, peas, ham and spices, and slow-boiled for several hours (he uses less egg than most, and more of the delicious and costly ingredients that give it flavor). Food lovers travel far to buy both, and the timing of a visit is important. Arturo

makes *cima* on Friday evenings, selling out over the weekend. A few doors down, Arturo and Antonietta's son Stefano runs **Bar Pippi** (Viale Franco Molfino 144), which serves good sandwiches, *bruschette*, snacks, coffee and ice cream.

VIALE FRANCO MOLFINO 126, SAN ROCCO ✦ TEL: 0185 770681

CLOSED AFTERNOONS ON WEDNESDAY *and* SUNDAY

Panificio Lippi

T HE SIZE OF A LARGE BROOM CLOSET, THIS NEIGH-BORHOOD BAKERY NEAR THE TUNNEL ON THE MAIN road in Ruta makes very good plain focaccia and *castagnac-cio* using extra virgin oil, and, in winter, on Tuesdays and Fridays only, delicious *farinata*.

VIA AURELIA 217, RUTA ✦ TEL: 0185 770714

CLOSED WEDNESDAY AFTERNOON, SUNDAY *and* IN JANUARY

Panificio Maccarini

S EMI-RETIRED, ITALO MACCARINI IS A 'SECOND-GEN-ERATION BAKER SPECIALIZED IN THE NOW-RARE mariner's sea biscuit, *la galletta del marinaio*, which was the staple of Camogli's seafarers for centuries. Italo's father learned from a family who started making *gallette* in 1885, and is practically the only baker left in the region who knows

how to make true hard tack — another name for sea biscuit. Italo in turn trained his younger cousin Remo in the art, and so the tradition continues. The *gallette* at Panificio Maccarini are hard enough to break your teeth, and are rarely eaten as is, but rather used moistened or fractured to make a dozen classic Riviera recipes. The bakery also turns out very good olive-pulp bread, a specialty of Levanto and certain western Riviera villages, and delicate focaccia *al formaggio* in the style of Recco. Wife Anna and daughter Valeria excel with classic savory tarts, stuffed vegetables

and delicious, crusty shortbread pies with apples, peaches and other fresh fruit. Excellent dry pastas from Pastificio Fiore and Martelli, olive oils, jams, local honey and other gourmet foods are also stocked. It's pleasant to sip an espresso or cappuccino at the bakery's single table on a narrow terrace in the alley that leads from San Rocco down to Camogli.

VIA SAN ROCCO 46 ✦ TEL: 0185 770613

WWW.PANIFICIOMACCARINI.COM

CLOSED TUESDAYS *and* WEDNESDAYS

SAN MASSIMO DI RAPALLO

TINY AND ISOLATED ON A HILL INLAND FROM RAPALLO, NEAR THE ANCIENT ROMAN ROAD TO Ruta di Camogli, San Massimo is known for one thing only, cult restaurant **Ü Giancu** (Via San Massimo 78, Tel: 0185 260505, www.ugiancu.it, dinner daily except Wednesday, lunch on Sunday or by reservation, closed two weeks in October or November, moderate, reserve ahead). Fausto Oneto — alias Ü Giancu, the white one, presumably because of his light complexion — is a *fumetti* — comic book — fanatic, and when this postmodern *osteria* opened decades ago, it was known as *il ristorante a fumetti*. Fausto's comic book collection is vast and valuable, and much of it hangs on the cluttered walls of this unusual spot on a hilltop about five miles northwest of Rapallo (follow signs inland toward the autostrada and then take the twisting two-lane road behind the golf course and shooting range). It's favored by Riviera insiders, and still run by Fausto and his family. Once upon a time the cooking was provocatively vegetarian, and the restaurant had the first nonsmoking room in the land. Now all Italian restaurants are smoke-free, and Ü Giancu serves free-style variations on local game (in season), plus succulent stewed rabbit with local black olives and oven-roasted or herb-battered suckling lamb, or slow-cooked pork. Vegetables, field greens (*preboggion*) and herbs are still king — the sautéed spinach would keep Popeye smiling — and most come from the kitchen gardens or olive groves of San Massimo and surrounding villages. The homemade desserts are simple, light — often fruit based — and include a perfect *crostata* jam tart, shortbread cookies and ice creams. A selection of local cheeses is also offered, French style. There's a pleasant garden for fine weather dining, and an equally nice terrace-like dining room with lots of light. The wines are reasonably priced, and you'll find many Ligurian bottlings, especially those from the Riviera di Levante.

SANTA MARGHERITA LIGURE

BBREVIATED AS SML AND CALLED "SANTA" FOR SHORT BY LOCALS, THIS DELIGHTFUL bourgeois enclave is nicknamed "the Port of Milan," because it's popular with wealthy Milanese. Wealth is writ large in the frescoed villas, fashion boutiques, 4- and 5-star luxury hotels and, above all, the number and quality of the food shops of all kinds. The tiny outdoor market is held weekday and Saturday mornings in the main square fronting the outsized Rococo church. Local producers sell garden-grown lettuces, tomatoes, peppers and basil, and excellent honey from surrounding hills. SML has a fleet of fishing boats, which supply most of the top fish shops and restaurants in the district, as far north as Recco and Sori. The fish market, facing the port on Via T. Bottaro, is clean, orderly and open to the public weekdays from 5pm to 8pm only. The fish restaurants in town are interchangeable—stick to simple, fresh fish and you'll be fine, though possibly bankrupted; expect to spend upwards of fifty euros per person without wine. A handful of new restaurants recommended by luxury hotel concierges offer *cucina creativa*—delicacies such as raw fish and shrimp with translucent slices of radish. For authentic Ligurian specialties, locals dine in the hills—at San Lorenzo della Costa, on a ridge above town, or in San Massimo, behind Rapallo—or stick to pizza, focaccia and *farinata*.

RESTAURANTS

La Palma

NDER THE ARCADES OF THE SEASIDE DRIVE, FACING THE STATUE TO CHRISTOPHER COLUMBUS, this upscale, highly professional pizzeria-restaurant has sidewalk tables and two comfortable, vaulted dining rooms. You can get all the well-made Riviera classics if you want, starting with anchovies, but the real draw here is the very good pizza, particularly the pesto-topped pizza. It's one of the few restaurants around that's always open, and has friendly, efficient service.

PIAZZA MARTIRI DELLA LIBERTÀ ✦ TEL: 0185 287436
OPEN DAILY ✦ INEXPENSIVE *to* MODERATE

Il San Lorenzo

NEAR A MOTORCYCLE DEALERSHIP AND GAS STATION ON THE MAIN HIGHWAY FROM SML TO RUTA di Camogli, this restaurant looks like a big white chalet from the outside, but is simply and elegantly furnished inside. Locals from Camogli, Santa and Rapallo flock here for the cheerful atmosphere and generously served food. Start with *frisceu* fritters, or housemade ravioli filled with borage and sauced with classic meat sauce, *pansôti* with walnut sauce or lasagne or *gnocchetti* with pesto. The focaccia *con formaggio* is sensational. Second courses are simple — barbecued steaks, mixed grilled meats and chicken or fish. The desserts are housemade, also simple, and very good (jam tarts, tiramisu, walnut-and-pine nut pie, chocolate cake). The wine list has a few good Riviera bottlings.

VIA AURELIA OCCIDENTALE 117, SAN LORENZO DELLA
COSTA (SANTA MARGHERITA LIGURE) ✦ TEL: 0185 262691
DINNER ONLY, CLOSED TUESDAY *from* OCTOBER *to* JUNE
MODERATE

ANCHOVIES, COFFEE, ICE CREAM,
GOURMET FOODS, PASTRIES, WINE

Bardi

ON THE PORT, ABOUT A HUNDRED YARDS PAST THE FISH MARKET ON THE WAY TO PORTOFINO, THIS century-old fishmonger's shop run by Gianni and Giuseppe Bardi salts its own anchovies, which it sells in small plastic tubs. If a tub-full is too much for you to pack, many local restaurants, including the seafood spot **La Paranza**, on the port, serve Bardi anchovies.

VIA T. BOTTARO 23 ✦ TEL: 0185 287085
CLOSED SUNDAY AFTERNOON

Bar Colombo

O N THE MAIN SEASIDE ROAD FACING THE STATUE OF CHRISTOPHER COLUMBUS, THIS *CAFFÈ* HAS BEEN around since the 1890s, and the lavishly sculpted wooden built-ins and stone-topped bar are original. New owners have added designer chairs with reddish velvet, and the music can be louder than a thinking person might appreciate, but the coffee is very good (from l'Aromatica, a Genoa-based roaster), and so are the house *gelati*, made with fresh ingredients.

VIA PESCINO 13 ✦ TEL: 0185 287058

CLOSED WEDNESDAY IN WINTER

Fiordiponti

O N THE CORNER OF THE ARCADED PIAZZA FRATELLI BANDIERA A BLOCK IN FROM THE FISHING PORT, AND therefore off the tourist track, this is the locals's best-kept-secret bakery, a no-nonsense place where everything Alberto Fiordiponti makes is good, from the cookies and jam tarts to the bread. Focaccia is the bakery's strongest suit. Take a number and stand in line. The focaccia *con formaggio* is excellent, as good as the best of it found outside Recco. The plain, herb-flecked and olive-pulp focaccias are remarkable too.

VIA RUFFINI 26 ✦ TEL: 39 0185 283971

CLOSED SUNDAY AFTERNOON

Pestarino

P ESTARINO IS THREE STORES IN ONE—PASTRIES AND COFFEE, GOURMET FOODS AND WINE, TAVOLA calda—all owned and operated by the cheerful, tireless and talented Irma Pestarino and her family, on the town's main pedestrian shopping street, about fifty yards northwest of the church. The *caffè-pasticceria* has two inside salons and tables in the street, amid the bustle of shoppers, and serves excellent cappuccinos made with Illy coffee. The housemade pastries, which are as good as they get in the region, meaning fabulous, include *gobeletti* filled with apricot jam and single-serving *pandolce alla genovese*. There's also a slimming *sacripantina*—pound cake

with pastry cream, liqueur, chocolate and almond paste—and exquisite cookies, jam tarts and cakes. Though there are several very good *gelaterie* in Santa Margherita Ligure, Pestarino makes some of the best in town, the real thing, using natural ingredients and no shortcuts, no colorings, no preservatives and no stabilizers. The cream-based flavors are rich and satisfying without being cloying (the coffee, made with freshly brewed Illy, is fantastic). A few doors down, on both sides of the street, you can pick up everything from a roast chicken (the business started in the

1960s as a take-out chicken rotisserie) to fresh pasta, Sant'Olcese salami to fine Ligurian wines and, especially, cheeses, specifically those from Santo Stefano d'Aveto (il San Stè), plus an otherwise unfindable "Divino" (a flavorful organic cow's milk cheese from the Val di Vara, aged for three months in the lees of Ciliegiolo wine), and *caprino* goat's cheese from the village of Stella, on the western Riviera di Ponente. Handily, at the *caffè*, you can order and enjoy anything from the three shops for a snack, lunch or early dinner (including very good focaccia *con formaggio*, or *trenette* with housemade pesto).

VIA PALESTRO 5, 10-12 *and* 20 ✦ TEL: 0185 287055
OPEN DAILY 6AM *to* 8PM, CLOSED TUESDAYS IN OCTOBER,
NOVEMBER, JANUARY *and* FEBRUARY

Pinamonti

IN BUSINESS SINCE 1899 (THOUGH THE CURRENT, IMPOSSIBLE-TO-FIND PREMISES ARE ONLY FIFTY years old, tucked away down an alley near the Lido Hotel and train station), Pinamonti makes remarkably good focaccia. Many claim it's the best on the Riviera; it's certainly excellent, firm and nicely browned on top, with larger pockmarks than most, indicating lots of lively, natural yeast, and less salt or oil than you would general find elsewhere. Consistently, the dough is softer in the center than it is around the edges, so savvy locals request slices according to doneness.

VIA DELL'ARCO 24 ✦ TEL: 0185 287552
CLOSED WEDNESDAY AFTERNOON *and* SUNDAY

Seghezzo

FAMILY-RUN AND ESTABLISHED FOR THE BETTER PART OF A CENTURY, SEGHEZZO HAS MORPHED from a simple dry goods and sweets shop (candied violets, bonbons and chocolates of all kinds) into a luxury mini-supermarket of gourmet delights. It sells everything from cornflakes and milk to fine wines (though only a handful of Ligurian bottlings), cheeses, meat, salami and pastries, fruits and vegetables, and even has a tiny at-the-counter bar area. The house olive oil, a pure Taggiasca made on the western Riviera di Ponente, is flavorful and unfiltered. The house amaretto cookies, which earned Seghezzo a name decades ago, come individually and beautifully wrapped in old-fashioned paper, and are called *ricci*— sea urchins or hedgehogs— though no one seems to know why. They merge honey and almonds, and are delicious.

VIA CAVOUR 1 ✦ TEL: 0185 287172 ✦ CLOSED WEDNESDAY

Vineria

IN EARLY 2007 A CREW OF YOUNG WINE EXPERTS TOOK OVER FROM THE MACCHIAVELLO BROTHERS, who for decades ran this wonderful old wine shop and local boozer's bar. It's now a classy, professionally run wine bar offering hundreds of top bottlings from all over Italy and elsewhere. This is a fine place to try a dozen or more Riviera wines, because most of the best winemakers' best products are carried, served by the glass or bottle (Bisson, Laura Aschero, Durin, Fèipu dei Massaretti, La Polenza, Lupi). Reserve ahead and a theme tasting can be organized. Vineria is on the narrower of SML's two main old shopping alleyways, about a hundred yards northwest of the church.

VIA CAVOUR 17 ✦ TEL: 0185 286122 ✦ CLOSED SUNDAY MORNING

Bar Vittoria

RUN BY THE SAME DIAMOND-IN-THE-ROUGH FAMILY SINCE 1941, THIS ULTRA OLD-FASHIONED ICE creamery has tables on a shaded veranda on the traffic island facing SML's small swimming beach. Get a cone to go, with a scoop of luscious pistachio, or *panera*—cappuccino ice cream, which is made with Covim espresso and lots of cream. All the ingredients are fresh, everything is made from scratch, and the fruit flavors are excellent. The only stabilizer Bar Vittoria uses is natural guar.

VIA GRAMSCI 43 ✦ TEL: 0185 286676
OPEN 8AM *to* 7:30PM, CLOSED MONDAYS

SORI

THE FIRST THING IN SORI THAT MOST TRAVELERS SEE IS THE TOP OF THE HANDSOME, PAINTED *campanile*. That's because it rises higher than the railway viaduct and Via Aurelia. Both flyovers keep traffic and noise out of this fishing village, which is molded into the contours of the steep Sori Creek Valley. The flyovers also keep out tourists, so that, even in high season, you rarely feel overwhelmed by crowds of sunseekers. Sori is small and most of its businesses are on the southeast side of the valley, away from the pocketsized beach. On it you'll find the requisite one-man fishing boats and tangles of nets. What the few remaining fishermen bring in isn't enough to meet even local demand. There's one *trattoria* on the port, **Scandelin** (Via Stagno 1, Tel: 0185 700963, closed Wednesday and in November, inexpensive to moderate). The risotto with

flavorful fish stock, and the grilled calamari or whole roasted fish, are fine; the best offerings aren't *piscine*, but rather the house-made *pansôti* (dressed with walnut sauce) and focaccia *al formaggio* in the style of Recco.

Sori is the homeland of *trofie* pasta twists usually sauced with pesto or walnuts. Recco has claimed them as its own, but they come from Sori, and the best place to buy them is **Pastificio Novella** (Via Roma 14, Tel: 0185 702045, closed afternoons on Wednesday and Sunday). Novella has a small shopfront on the creekside road, but its pasta factory, which turns out a wide variety of Ligurian pasta types, and supplies many local restaurants, is upstream about half a mile (and not open to the public).

Two *gelaterie* turn out better-than-average product. **Bar Crovetto** (Via Garibaldi 1, Tel: 0185 700907, closed Sunday) is inland, on the corner of the main shopping street, Via Garibaldi, and the road leading to the car bridge over the creek, and is a favorite of locals; it serves decent Portioli coffee. On the beach-front, the hole-in-the-wall, no-name ice creamery marked with the sign **Granite/Gelati** (Via Cavour 1, no telephone, open daily late morning to late at night, from May through September), has luscious fruit ice creams made from ripe, fresh local fruit.

Sori may be small, with few shops, but the restaurant scene is satisfying, especially if you like hearty *entroterra* food, as opposed to fish. The *farinata*, savory tarts, fried herbed fritters and fried potato dumplings, not to mention the chestnut-flour *castagnaccio*, all cooked in wood-burning ovens, are delicious at **Edo Bar** (Via Mazzini 5, Tel: 0185 700856, closed Monday, inexpensive), which is also a simple *trattoria*, with a handful of roadside tables. It's fifty yards inland from the only gas station in town, on the right bank of the creek.

If not to Edo Bar, workers, fishermen and locals head for the fixed-price lunch at **Antica Trattoria delle Rose** (Via Trieste 6, Tel: 0185 700968, closed Sunday, inexpensive). This casual, old-fashioned place is on the main road inland, on the southeast side of the valley. It has a small terrace with tables for al fresco dining. The menu changes daily; you'll always find homey pasta with garlicky housemade pesto, delicious roasts or long-stewed pork short ribs, an excellent baked potato-and-salted-codfish casserole with onions and piquant parsley sauce, and fresh fish for dinner on Friday and Saturday.

Further up the scale in décor and ambiance, but on the same winding, narrow road (it changes name), about a quarter mile inland, is **Al Boschetto** (Via Caorsi 44, Tel: 0185 700659, closed Tuesday and from mid September to mid October, moderate to expensive). Clinging to the roadside above the creek, it's been run since 1962 by affable Ugo Moltedo and his sister Luciana, and has a big, comfortable, recently renovated dining room with tile floors and open timbers, and tables covered with starched yellow cloths. You can get everything from focaccia *al formaggio* to *pansôti*, or ravioli filled with ricotta and spinach, *tagliolini* with mushroom sauce, spaghetti with seafood, plus stewed baby squid, grilled or fried porcini, and grilled or baked swordfish or seabass. The cakes and pies are housemade and delicious. Across the street, where the original restaurant used to be, is the pizzeria; it's open in the evening only, and, like the restaurant, has a good selection of top Ligurian wines, including those by Laura Aschero, Fèipu dei Massaretti and Maria Donata Bianchi.

About three miles farther inland, up the same twisting road, at the perched hamlet of Capreno, is **Osteria Tabacchi Da Drin** (Frazione Capreno 66, Tel: 0185 782210, closed Wednesday and mid September to mid October, moderate, reserve ahead). Da Drin started out in the early 1900s as a tobacco shop and grocery store, morphed into an *osteria*, and, still in the same family, is now a full-blown, upscale *trattoria*, with grandmother and mother in the kitchen, and sons out front. The views from the outdoor or glassed-in terrace reach back to Sori and the sea. Like the former tobacco shop-grocery, which is still intact, the food is from yester-year, starting with the baked stuffed vegetables, fried *focaccette* with *stracchino* cheese, or housemade *pansôti* with walnut sauce, to the fresh *taglierini* with dense, tomato-and-mushroom sauce, *cima alla genovese*, slow-stewed rabbit with herbs and olives, or the abundant mixed fry—bits of lamb or veal with flash-fried

fresh vegetables, a kind of Ligurian tempura. The pies and cakes are luscious (try the single-serving apple or pear *tortino* with chocolate and a ball of vanilla ice cream), and so are the tiramisu and *panna cotta*. Everything is made from scratch, using local ingredients, from the olive oil and wild greens on up, with the single exception of the ice cream. As the affable, garrulous owners say, "If we have to start buying in, we'll change jobs." The wine list is short; stick to local bottlings.

Ristorante Nestin (Frazione Canepa 67 , Tel: 0185 700791, moderate) is also high above Sori, accessed via the hamlet of Sussisa, or more directly on roads on the west side of valley, which are not so much a corkscrew as a tangled spider's web or cat's cradle. This panoramic restaurant with a mountain feel is even higher up, and has a classic interior: half panelling, copper pots on the walls and open timbers. The terrace is shaded by horse chestnut trees. Locals drive up here for the focaccia *col formaggio*, fried rabbit and seasonal specialties such as mushrooms or wild boar.

Wild Boar

....

THE INLAND HILLS OF LIGURIA—THE *ENTRO-
TERRA*—ARE FULL OF WILD BOAR. HUNTERS
and forestry officers cull them by the hundred each
fall and winter. The boars have no natural predators—the
bears of the Appennines disappeared long ago. Wolves have
been reintroduced in certain areas, but so far there are too
few in Liguria to bring down rampant boar overpopula-
tion. With their snouts and tusks, the boars are eroding
steep, fragile hillsides and knocking down thousands of
dry walls.

Many *trattorie* in the *entroterra* are run by hunter families and frequented by locals. In addition to Ristorante Nestin, another favorite is even higher up, on the panoramic
highway behind Recco and Sori. The road links Uscio to
Genoa across the Monte Fasce, that massive mountain
bristling with radio and television antennas on the eastern
edge of town, behind Nervi. Only the adventurous need
apply: tourists rarely set foot around here. The food is rustic
but authentic and delicious, and now that smoking is not
allowed, it's a pleasure to join the good ol' boys at **Trattoria
Cornua** (Località Cornua, Strada Panoramica del Monte
Fasce, Lumarzo (GE), Tel: 0185 94049, lunch only, Tuesday
to Sunday). The best time to visit is hunting season—October, November, December. Faded black-and-white photos
and hunting trophies decorate walls. Garrulous Elmer
Fudds with shotguns toss back rough local wines, and the
atmosphere is surprisingly convivial.

On the way up, as you drive through Uscio, stop at pastry
shop **Dolci Delizie** (Via V. Veneto 133, Tel: 348 661 4965,
closed Monday). Young Serena Soghe makes exquisite
baci di dama and other shortbread cookies and confections
using centuries-old or brand new recipes (for *castagnello* or
maronsini), plus *pandolce* with chestnut flour and chunks
of cooked chestnuts, and other wholesome, delicious
delights you'll find nowhere else (including treats for diabetics and allergy sufferers). No shortcuts are used, and no
transfats—just top-quality ingredients.

La Casetta (Via Cappelleta 14, Avegno—Recco, Tel:
0185 781145) is a bit more up the scale from Cornua,

though the watchwords are still rusticity, simplicty, authenticity and affordability. They make this spartan spot worth the corkscrew drive—turn on your GPS and good luck to you! The *trattoria* is hidden several miles behind Recco, off the main road to Uscio; follow the signs to Avegno and look for the white house at the top of a steep driveway. That's the restaurant. Call ahead to reserve a table—opening hours and days closed are flexible. The chef is a big-time boar hunter, and a story hangs from each boar-head trophy on the walls.

In a rustic hinterland suburb about ten miles east of downtown Genoa, perched far above Pontedecimo, is award-winning butcher shop **Macelleria Angelo Torrazza** (Via Conte E. Lombardo 4R, Gazzolo/Campomorone, Tel: 010 780433, open Thursday, Friday and Saturday, closed Wednesday all day and afternoons on Sunday, Monday and Tuesday). The Torrazza family, originally from the salami-making village of Orero, is specialized in flavorful boar salami (and sells fresh boar meat, which is supplied by a farm and forest rangers from the nearby Parco di Capanne di Marcarolo, or by local hunters). The shop has been around for about 120 years, and the quality of its products is exceptionally high. Everything is done by hand, in the old-fashioned way; the hanging/drying room is heated by a wood-burning stove. Torrazza makes several unusual, original salamis with "pesto," using basil from Prà, *parmigiano*, pine nuts, garlic and salt but no olive oil, which would accelerate spoilage; to it are added trace amounts of honey and royal jelly (*propoli*), which make it more luscious and longer lasting. Other only-in-Campomorone salamis are made with chili, garlic or truffles.

Also in the Compomorone area, on the main square of the perched hamlet of Isoverde, is **Trattoria Iolanda**, (Piazza N. Bruno 6/7R, Isoverde/Campomorone, Tel: 010 790118, closed Tuesday dinner and Wednesday), you can savor many Ligurian classics—from *panissa* and *mandilli* with pesto, to dry cod with olives and potatoes—plus wild game, including boar, which is usually available in fall months. Take the two-lane highways SP5 and SP35 and follow the signs to Campomorone and then Isoverde.

CHAPTER 9

·····················

Greater Genoa

Province: Genova. Includes: Genoa, Mele, Nervi, Prà, Sant'Olcese.

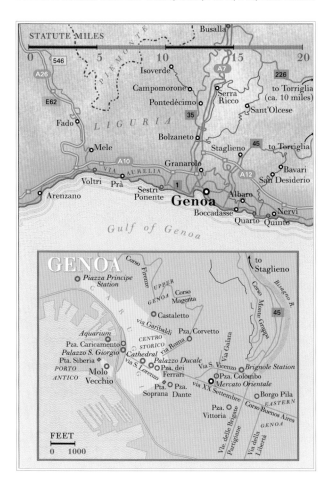

ENOA—GENOVA TO ITALIANS—LEADS MULTIPLE LIVES. IT'S THE REGIONAL CAPITAL, A BUSY, prosperous, modern city of 632,000 (about 800,000 if you include adjoining suburbs). Museums and scores of palaces stud its historic core, which is still girded in places by medieval walls. But Genoa is also a seaside resort: the Albaro, Boccadasse, Quarto, Quinto and Nervi neighborhoods on the east side of town are stuffed with villas, dotted with public parks and have seaside promenades and swimming beaches of startling beauty. On the opposite end of the spectrum, on the western side of the city, places like Sampierdarena, Pegli, Sestri Ponente and Voltri are crisscrossed by railroads and spaghetti bowl freeways and continue to struggle to remove rust-belt industries, while upgrading the giant ferry and container ports. For decades, Genoa has been transitioning from heavy industry, shipping and petroleum to high tech and cultural tourism, with surprising success. Renzo Piano's urban renewal plans—some excellent, others questionable—are well underway, despite the celebrated Genoese talent for stonewalling and sandbagging. Happily, this wonderfully underrated city maintains its authenticity and, in some areas, a distinctive urban edge. It is among the great food cities of Europe. While most Italian food is regional, Genoa, like Rome, has its own civic cuisine, which has shaped the cooking of the entire region.

GENOA'S HARBOR AND MEDIEVAL CITY

Includes: Porto Antico, Molo, Sottoripa, Caruggi, Via Garibaldi, Via San Lorenzo

HE OLDEST PART OF GENOA'S *CENTRO STORICO*—THE HISTORIC CENTER-CITY DISTRICT—STARTS at Porto Antico, the harbor redeveloped in the last twenty years by Renzo Piano. With the aquarium and a shopping mall, restaurants and hotels, this is the part of Genoa most visitors see. On its eastern edge, beyond the fortified gateway called Porta Siberia (now a museum), is the Molo district, a narrow peninsula with a grid of medieval streets around the former arsenal. Due north of Porto Antico is the pedestrianized Piazza Caricamento and Palazzo di San Giorgio, backed by

Sottoripa, and Via Turati, which are arcades lined with stores, fry shops and bars. Behind them, the medieval alleyways or *caruggi* begin. They spill outwards in an uneven oval, reaching as far west as the Piazza Principe train station; east to the Porta Soprana city gate; and north to Via Garibaldi and Piazza De Ferrari. This is the largest medieval neighborhood in Europe. Most *caruggi* are too narrow for cars. Teeming with daytime shoppers, merchants, office workers and visitors, many alleys are ghostly by night. The wider streets and *piazze* near the harbor, cathedral and ducal palace are always lively; a few of the narrowest, darkest back alleys are best avoided. The city's greatest concentration of fine food shops, *caffè*, *trattorie* and wine bars is in the *caruggi*, which must be explored on foot. Pick up a free, detailed map from one of the train station tourist offices (look for the APT sign), or the APT info booth on Via San Lorenzo facing the main stairway into Palazzo Ducale.

RESTAURANTS, TRATTORIE, FARINATA, TORTE SALATE, TRIPPERIA

Antica Osteria di Vico Palla

NEAR THE FORMER ARSENAL IN THE MOLO DIS-TRICT, THIS ROUGH-AND-READY OLD *OSTERIA* WAS completely remodeled in 2002 in shades of white. The wooden furniture is solid. Codfish is the decorative leitmotif. Owner Maurizio Capurro chose to leave the stone and brick-work in place, preserve the egalitarian, raucous atmosphere, and stick to traditional Genoese cuisine without frills (and a wine list strong on regional bottlings). You'll find *stoccafisso* prepared in various popular ways, from classic *accomodato* with olives, potatoes and pine nuts, to codfish fritters, and the less common puréed variety called *brandacujun*, plus minestrone with pesto, spinach-and-ricotta-filled ravioli *di magro* with but-ter and herbs, or *mandilli* with pesto, chickpea-and-chard *zemin* stew, squid stewed in its own ink, and whole fish *alla ligure* with olives and pine nuts. The desserts are homey, and feature a good apple tart and tiramisu.

VICOLO PALLA 15/R ✦ TEL: 010 246 6575

CLOSED MONDAY. INEXPENSIVE *to* MODERATE

Antica Sciamadda

A CLASSIC *TORTE E FARINATA* HOLE-IN-THE-WALL SHOP, BETWEEN PORTO ANTICO AND POCKETSIZED Piazza San Giorgio, Antica Sciamadda was founded in the 1850s, and restored and reopened in 1999 by young Umberto Prestigiacomo, who does the cooking, aided by Rogeria Ramos, his friendly Brazilian wife. The dialect name *sciamadda* means "nice little fire," and in the unheated days of yore, neighbors would gather here to warm themselves and have a bite. Some things never change. The wood-burning oven still chuffs away in view of passersby, and locals perch on the four stools set against the spartan, white-washed walls and gobble tasty snacks such as

herbed fritters, or buy take out foods. The savory vegetable tarts are light and flavorful, made with fresh produce supplied by the green grocer around the corner, and the *farinata* chickpea tart is nicely crisped on top and cooked through as tradition requires. Prestigiacomo buys his dry herbs and spices from historic Torielli, right up the street.

VIA SAN GIORGIO 14R ✦ TEL: 010 246 8516 ✦ OPEN 10AM *to* 3PM *and* 5PM *to* 7:30PM DAILY EXCEPT SUNDAY ✦ INEXPENSIVE

Antica Trattoria Sà Pesta

DUE NORTH, A FEW HUNDRED YARDS, OF PORTO ANTICO AND PIAZZA SAN GIORGIO, THIS CAVernous, landmark *trattoria* famed for its *farinata* is run by the third generation of the founding Benvenuto family. A mixed bag of local bluebloods, blue- or white-collar workers, students from the nearby architecture department of Genoa University, business people and visitors, share the long wooden tables and benches in the *trattoria*'s two echoing, tiled rooms. The service, straightforward, is supplied with smiles and jocular asides in Genoese dialect. The *farinata* is baked in an antique wood-burning oven, in seasoned antique pans, and is crispy on top, cooked through, and firm on the bottom. It may well be the best in town. Reliably good are the savory tarts and traditional pasta dishes — from *pansôti* filled with wild greens and sauced with walnut sauce or herbs and butter, to classic Genoese lasagne with pesto — not to mention the *stoccafisso* with olives, pine nuts and potatoes, stuffed anchovies and codfish fritters.

16R VIA GIUSTINIANI ✦ TEL: 010 246 8336
OPEN NOON *to* 2PM FOR LUNCH MONDAY *through* SATURDAY *and* FOR DINNER BY RESERVATION ONLY *from* TUESDAY *through* SATURDAY, CLOSED SUNDAY ✦ INEXPENSIVE

Le Cantine Squarciafico

PROOF THAT *TERROIR* AND TRENDINESS CAN SOME-TIMES GO HAND IN HAND IS PROVIDED BY THIS neo-*trattoria* in a Gothic cellar. The menu is in part remarkably traditional, with very good *stoccafisso* with olives, pine nuts, potatoes and a trace of tomato; housemade fresh pasta topped with good pesto; and a variety of light salads and snacks. The cathedral is about fifty yards north, and the rabbit's warren of old Genoa's alleys spreads on all sides.

PIAZZA INVREA 3R ✦ TEL: 010 247 0823
WWW.SQUARCIAFICO.IT ✦ OPEN DAILY *from* NOON *to* MIDNIGHT

Caffè degli Specchi

SPECCHI MEANS MIRRORS, AND THERE ARE MANY ON THE WALLS OF THIS 1890S *CAFFÈ*, NEIGHBORHOOD hangout and popular lunch spot about a hundred yards east of Palazzo Ducale, with a small terrace on a busy pedestrian alley. Artists, boutique keepers and university professors drift in at all hours to sip cappuccinos — the "Smeraldo" blend of coffee, supplied by Covim, is dark and strong — and nibble good focaccia plain or topped with sautéed minced white onions. There's a cozy upstairs salon, but the ground floor is the most desirable place to sit and watch the regulars. Remodeled in the early 1990s, Caffè degli Specchi helped spark a rebirth of local businesses in this formerly rundown area. Scores of trendy restaurants, bars and boutiques have followed. The tasty Genoese daily snack or luncheon specials range from savory tarts to generously filled focaccia sandwiches, *trenette* with pesto, and meat-filled ravioli sauced with a rich meat-and-tomato sauce.

SALITA POLLAIUOLI 43R ✦ TEL: 010 246 8193
OPEN 7AM *to* 8:30PM ✦ CLOSED SUNDAY

Da Rina

ATOP WHAT WERE THE PORT-SIDE CITY WALLS OF THE MIDDLE AGES, FACING THE FISH MARKET, elevated highway and Porto Antico (and a gas station), this handsome, family-run restaurant has been in business since

1946. It's now well into its second generation. The founder, Rina Rapetti, officially remains present and at the helm despite her years. The big, vaulted dining room is paved in black-and-white marble and held aloft by massive, short columns. Prints of old Genoa hang on the white walls, and the tables, comfortably spaced, are draped with yellow cloths. Long a hangout for the great and good, Da Rina is now a low-key family restaurant favored by locals, and the prices are surprisingly reasonable. Don't be put off by the kitsch miniature fishing boat in the entrance, from which sea bass, monkfish, squid and swordfish stare out. If you are seeking fresh, simply grilled or roasted fish and traditional Ligurian starters — *trofie* or minestrone with pesto, lasagne with meat or mushroom sauce, fish-filled ravioli — and luscious desserts — housemade *semifreddo* with crunchy nougat and chocolate sauce or creamy pudding cakes and jam tarts — Da Rina is an excellent choice. The wine list includes many good Riviera bottlings.

MURA DELLE GRAZIE 3R ✦ TEL: 010 246 6475

WWW.RISTORANTEDARINA.IT

CLOSED MONDAY *and* AUGUST ✦ MODERATE *to* EXPENSIVE

Ombre Rosse

A SMALL, STYLISH RESTAURANT THAT OPENED IN EARLY 2007 IN A CAREFULLY RESTORED BUILDING from the early thirteenth century, on a tiny square in the *caruggi*, about halfway between the cathedral of San Lorenzo and the old port, Ombre Rosse looks like a trendy hot spot but is actually very quiet, frequented by studious locals, and serves remarkably good, simple Genoese food. Owned and operated by a husband-and-wife team (Enrico and Isabella), their daughter (Marianna), a partner (Elide) and an assistant (Patrizia), the library-cum-antique shop décor betrays the team's past careers as university professors and dealers of collectibles. The menu changes often, but hearty vegetable soups, savory tarts and platters of cold cuts and cheeses are always to be found, plus a handful of homey desserts such as apple-and-walnut pie with cinnamon. Everything is homemade except the pasta, which comes from a nearby pasta *fresca* shop. The *torta di bietole* with chard and fresh *prescinsêua* cheese is flavorful, light and perfectly cooked. In winter, the spinach-and-ricotta-filled ravioli are sauced with an unusual and deliciously perfumed pesto of fresh marjoram, not basil. The wine list is short, with only a handful of Ligurian bottlings (including good Ormeasco from Lorenzo Ramo, and several wines from Bisson).

VICO INDORATORI 20-24R ✦ TEL: 010 275 7608

CLOSED SATURDAY LUNCH and SUNDAY

INEXPENSIVE to MODERATE

Il Ristoro dei Grimaldi

HIDDEN DOWN A DOG'S-LEG ALLEY ON THE WEST SIDE OF THE SAN LUCA CHAPEL, TWENTY YARDS off Via San Luca (in Palazzo Grimaldi), this hole-in-the-wall pizza and focaccia joint makes some of Genoa's best plain focaccia and focaccia *al formaggio* in the style of Recco, using good fresh ingredients and extra virgin oil. Also available are pizzas with arugula and bacon, and a variety of *calzoni*, plus *crostata* and *baci di dama* cookies, all housemade. Perch on a stool, admire the vaults and massive column of the medieval, many-times remodeled building, or get a slice and meander through the *caruggi*.

VICO SAN LUCA 3 ✦ TEL: 010 251 4179 ✦ OPEN DAILY 10AM to

2:30PM and 5PM to 9PM ✦ CLOSED WEEKEND MORNINGS

La Taverna di Colombo

DOWN AN ALLEYWAY ABOUT A HUNDRED YARDS EAST OF THE MUSEO NAZIONALE DI PALAZZO SPINOLA, in the bull's eye of the *caruggi*, this cavernous *trattoria*-cum-wine bar occupies the vaulted ground floor of a medieval *palazzo*. Young and with a casual atmosphere, with burnt Siena-colored walls, and simple wooden booths and tables, it's a good place to have a light lunch or dinner and a glass of wine (the list is long, and includes bottlings from all over Italy) after visiting nearby museums, galleries and antique shops. The menu is traditional, and there's a special every weekday. On Monday: *bollito misto* (mixed boiled meats served with *salsa verde* and other condiments); Tuesday: *baccalà* prepared in a variety of ways; Wednesday: *buridda di seppie* (thick, delicious squid stew); Thursday: *trippe accomodate* (long-cooked tripe with tomatoes and potatoes); Friday: *stoccafisso* with pine nuts, olives and potatoes. You can also have classic ricotta-and-spinach ravioli with walnut sauce, gnocchi with basil pesto or unusual and flavorful artichoke "pesto," and a handful of other simple, homey but tasty Ligurian dishes. The desserts include a creamy *bianco mangiare* with almonds.

Note, the Taverna di Colombo is not affiliated with **La Cantina di Colombo** (Via Porta Soprana 55-57R, Tel: 010 247 5959, www.lacantinadicolombo.it, closed Saturday lunch and Sunday, moderate), a new, modish wine bar-restaurant, which has about 1,000 different bottlings on its wine list, and serves updated regional and creative cuisine.

VICO DELLA SCIENZA 6R ✦ TEL: 010 246 2447

CLOSED SATURDAY LUNCH *and* SUNDAY

INEXPENSIVE *to* MODERATE

Trattoria della Raibetta

STENCILED ON THE STONE ARCADES OF THE ALLEYWAY LEADING FROM VIA TURATI TO THIS *TRATTORIA* YOU can still make out a warning from the 1940s: THIS STREET OFF LIMITS TO ALL ALLIED TROOPS. By Raibetta standards that was yesterday. The massive black-stone column in the *trattoria*'s cozy main room dates to circa 1000 AD. For nearly 300 years, eateries of many kinds have occupied the L-shaped, vaulted, ground-floor premises of the medieval building near Porto Antico, gussied up and run since 1999 by Carlo Bruzzo and his wife Chiara, the art-loving owners of Trattoria della Raibetta. "Perennial" and "pan-regional" would be a good way to describe the delicious classic Ligurian dishes they serve, from the *testaroli* sauced with pesto (or puréed almonds) of the Lunigiana district, to the housemade fresh *trenette avvantaggiate* with pesto, green beans and potatoes, or the *mosciamme* of tuna from Favignana, the *mesciua* soup of La Spezia, the *cima alla genovese*, the *tomaxelle* veal rolls of the mountainous *entroterra*, hearty *zemin* from the Riviera di Levante, stewed baby octopus, or rabbit slow-cooked on the stovetop with pine nuts and olives. The roll call of Riviera delicacies continues with roasted whole fish *alla ligure* (also with pine nuts and olives), stuffed anchovies, and more. The luscious desserts are housemade, though none is particularly Genoese (creamy tiramisu, *panna cotta* or refreshing fruit sorbets). The wine list is strong on Riviera and Piedmont wines.

VICO CAPRETTARI 10R ✦ TEL: 010 246 8877

WWW.TRATTORIADELLARAIBETTA.IT

CLOSED MONDAY AND AUGUST ✦ MODERATE

Trattoria Da Ugo

THE EXTENDED PARISI FAMILY, NOW INTO ITS THIRD GENERATION, HAVE OWNED AND RUN THIS SIMPLE, family-style *trattoria* since 1969. Don't be put off by the unattractive façade. The interior is spotless, cheerfully decorated and packed with locals, whether white- or blue-collar workers, captains of industry, or university professors, and many speak to each other in rough-edged Genoese dialect. The menu changes according to the availability of seasonal produce and fish, but you can expect to find fried anchovies filled with herbed *parmigiano* and breadcrumbs, plump *tortelli* or *pansôti* filled with field greens and dressed with delicioius pesto or black pepper and herbs, cod-fish fritters, baby octopus or squid in a spicy tomato sauce, rabbit or fish *alla ligure* with herbs and pine nuts, or stuffed, boned veal shoulder, and very fresh seafood.

VIA GIUSTINIANI 86R ✦ TEL: 010 246 9302

PROSPERINO@LIBERO.IT ✦ CLOSED SUNDAY,

MONDAY *and* HOLIDAYS ✦ MODERATE

BREADSTICKS, CANDY, COFFEE, FOCACCIA, GOURMET FOODS, ICE CREAM, PASTA *FRESCA*, PASTRIES, TRIPE, WINE

Antica Drogheria Ferrea

THIS OLD VARIETY STORE IN THE *CARUGGI*, FACING THE *GELATERIA* PROFUMO, ABOUT A HUNDRED YARDS due south of Via Garibaldi, is a slice of Genoa circa

1950. The handsome window display of candied and dried fruit—including delicious dried bilberries—contrasts with the brooms and mops hanging opposite. Inside are shelves of delicacies and oddments. The excellent and hard-to-find *Rossignotti torrone* of Sestri Levante is sold here, and locally roasted Tober coffee, which the friendly owners will happily grind for your home espresso machine.

VICO SUPERIORE DEL FERRO 19R ✦ TEL: 010 2474177
CLOSED SUNDAY AFTERNOON *and* WEDNESDAY

Antica Drogheria M. Torielli

HUNDREDS OF DIFFERENT SPICES, DRIED HERBS, TEAS AND FRESHLY ROASTED COFFEE SCENT THIS legendary hole-in-the-wall boutique owned, operated and unchanged since 1920 by the Torielli-Cavanna family. The shop is on a narrow, dark alley about 300 yards inland from Via

Turati and the port, and is itself narrow and dark, crammed floor to ceiling with wonderful displays, and elbow-to-elbow with locals and immigrants. This is old Genoa incarnate; don't miss it.

VIA SAN BERNARDO 32R ✦ TEL: 010 246 8359

CLOSED WEDNESDAY AFTERNOON *and* SUNDAY

Antica Tripperia la Casana

ITH YOUR BACK TO THE FAÇADE OF THE OPERA HOUSE, THE ALLEYWAY DIRECTLY IN FRONT of you is Vico Casana. If you follow it downhill into the teeming tangle of *caruggi*, on the eastern side of the alley you'll see the sculpted white marble shopfront and dangling white tripe of this historic hole-in-the-wall *tripperia*, a Genoa institution since the 1800s. The tripe arrives fresh and is boiled in big copper vats, and then hung on steel hooks. Below the tripe is a platter of boiled white beans, which, when dressed with olive oil and salt, accompany the tripe. Locals, many long in tooth, feed at marble-topped old wooden tables, in the cool, stone-paved interior. Other customers select strips of tripe to take home, and usually have them run through the cutter, which slices them into

perfect bite-size pieces. How this last of the great Genoese tripe shops from the days of hunger has survived into the age of fast food is a mystery. Experience it while you can.

VICO CASANA 3R ✦ TEL: 010 247 4357
CLOSED SATURDAY AFTERNOON *and* SUNDAY

Armanino

BACK IN 1905 THE ARMANINO FAMILY OPENED THIS NARROW-BUT-DEEP SHOP UNDER THE PORTICOS of Sottoripa facing Porto Antico, and the Armanino family still owns and operates it. Famous for its candied fruit, hand-made by a candymaker in Savona, Armanino also sells dozens of excellent Ligurian specialty foods such as Santa Rita dry pasta, unfiltered extra virgin olive oil from the Frantoio di Borgomaro, Savona anchovies bottled in olive oil, locally made bottled pesto and chickpea or chestnut flour.

VIA SOTTORIPA 105R ✦ TEL: 010 247-6905
CLOSED WEDNESDAY AFTERNOON *and* SUNDAY

Boasi Caffè Torrefazione

NOT TO BE CONFUSED WITH THE POPULAR BOASI CAFFÈ ON VIA XX SETTEMBRE, THIS TINY DRY goods store hidden in the *caruggi*, about a hundred yards north of Piazza dei Macelli di Soziglia, is not a *caffè*; it sells the coffees roasted by one branch of the fractious Boasi family. This is the original outlet, founded in 1930, and the 100 percent Arabica blend, roasted at a suburban facility, is very good. You can also stock up on everything from breakfast cereal to canned tuna or candy. A charming, old-fashioned hole-in-the-wall.

VICO INFERIORE DEL FERRO 5R ✦ TEL: 010 247 7777
CLOSED SUNDAY

Bottega dello Stoccafisso

THIS CULT, MARBLE-CLAD OLD CODFISH SHOP IS HUNG WITH ENOUGH AIR-DRIED OR SALT COD TO flare nostrils for miles around. *Stoccafisso* and *baccalà* also soak in tubs, where cold water trickles constantly. Serious eaters

pay premium prices for whole fish, heads or prized *budelli di stoc-cafisso*, which are none other than the fish's dried innards. Also sold are good vegetables packed in olive oil, sun-dried tomatoes, fresh housemade pesto, and a variety of canned goods including excellent tuna.

VIA DEI MACELLI DI SOZIGLIA 20/22R ✦ TEL: 010 247 6390
CLOSED WEDNESDAY AFTERNOON *and* SUNDAY

Canevello—Salumeria Sottoripa

A LONG, NARROW CAVERN UNDER THE ARCADES OF SOTTORIPA, THIS OLD-FASHIONED FISH, salami and ham specialty boutique opened in 1946, and has been owned and operated since 1982 by affable, blue-eyed Roberto Magistrati. Clusters of air-dried cod dangle above the door. Inside, you'll find a wide variety of pan-Italian hams and salamis—including both mortadella and sausages made with wild boar meat—and hard-to-find local octopus carpaccio, plus *bottarga di tonno, mosciamme*, sea biscuits from the Maccarini bakery of San Rocco di Camogli, several good Ligurian olive oils and wines, plus brined olives, fresh pesto and a range of bottled or canned specialty foods.

VIA SOTTORIPA 53R ✦ TEL: 010 247 6878 ✦ WWW.VIVIGENOVA.IT
CLOSED WEDNESDAY AFTERNOON *and* SUNDAY

Casa del Cioccolato

MASSIMO MIGLIARO AND HIS FAMILY MAKE SOME OF THEIR CHOCOLATES IN AN UPSTAIRS kitchen here, but most of the work is done at the Casa di Paganini chocolate-and-pastry works in outlying Bolzaneto, founded in 1893. Items sold at this tiny boutique (on a stairway near Genoa's medieval city gate) range from classic filled ovals to tablets and very thin, small squares of semisweet chocolate flavored with chili or basil and other herbs. The *pandolce all'antica* is very good: crunchy, full of raisins and candied fruit, and not overly sweet.

VIA DI PORTA SOPRANA 45R ✦ TEL: 010 2513662

WWW.CIOCCOLATOPAGANINI.IT ✦ OPEN 9:30AM *to*

7:30PM DAILY *except* SUNDAY

Claretta Panificio Grissinificio

THE PHILOSOPHY OF THIS OLD CORNER BREAD-STICK AND FOCACCIA BAKERY IN THE HEART OF the *caruggi*, about a hundred yards east of the Museo Nazionale di Palazzo Spinola, is "a few, well-made specialties and that's it." Since 1954, baker Piero Claretta has been hand-making and baking delicious pizza with red sauce, luscious, salty focaccia — plain or with minced white onions — and crispy, irresistible breadsticks with olive oil, plus Genoese *pandolce* and *canestrelli* cookies. That's it. They're all very good — the focaccia would be more wholesome if Piero used extra virgin oil, which he claims is "too strong" — and the shop itself is a time warp. Don't miss it.

VIA DELLA POSTA VECCHIA 12R ✦ TEL: 010 247 7032

CLOSED SATURDAY AFTERNOON *and* SUNDAY

Le Gramole Olioteca

IT HAD TO HAPPEN: AFTER THE GENTRIFICATION OF THE GOOD OLD ITALIAN *ENOTECA* — THE HUMBLE WINE shop — someone was bound to invent the *olioteca*, a boutique where customers taste and may buy olive oils. Le Gramole, run by eager young Norma Fedolfi and Francesca Femia, is a small but handsome operation in the heart of the *caruggi*, near the famed Bottega dello Stoccafisso. On offer are a handful of Ligurian olive oils (award-winning Olio Roi, plus La Baita, Rùe di Zerli, Lucchi & Guastalli) and many other Italian oils, some of which customers may taste. This is one of the few places where you'll find braids of Vessalico garlic and bottled pesto made with it, or bottled *stoccafisso alla brandacujon* (a creamy blend of boiled air-dried cod, garlic, parsley, pine nuts and potatoes), artichokes from Perinaldo packed in oil, an unusual, lightly sweet cream of heirloom potatoes with vanilla and milk (*crema di patata quarantina*), mini *pandolce* loaves from Borgomaro, and dry pasta from Pastificio Santa Rita. In the autumn, theme tastings of specialty foods are held starting at 5:30pm.

VIA DEI MACELLI DI SOZIGLIA 69R ✦ TEL: 010 209 1668
WWW.LEGRAMOLE.COM ✦ CLOSED SUNDAY

Enoteca Susto

ABOUT A HUNDRED YARDS WEST OF VIA ROMA AND THE OPERA HOUSE, ON THE WAY TO ANTICA TRIP-peria di Vico Casana, this old wine shop with vaulted ceilings and worn plank floors is stuffed with hundreds of top French and Italian bottlings, including a handful of the Riviera's best. Wine tastings can be arranged by appointment. Also sold is the full range of excellent olive oils, brined olives, vegetables packed in olive oil and sauces made by the Mela family of Frantoio di Sant'Agata d'Oneglia, plus other remarkably fine oils, bottled olives and olive paté from Dinoabbo, Piero Blengeri Leverone and Bosoni, pasta from Pastificio Santa Rita and other specialty foods.

VICO CASANA 24R ✦ TEL: 010 247 4570 ✦ CLOSED SUNDAY

Fratelli Klainguti Bar Pasticceria

A RELATIVE NEWCOMER TO THE NEIGHBORHOOD, KLAINGUTI WAS FOUNDED IN 1826 BY A PAIR of Swiss brothers, pastry makers who'd hoped to sail to America to make their fortune. They missed the boat, opened their shop here and the rest is history — a sweet tale of butter cookies and cakes such as the diabolically caloric but irresistible white *torta Zena* (rum *zabaione*, sponge cake and almond paste)

and *torta Engadina* (a variation on German chocolate cake, with heavy cream and sponge cake made from almond flour). In the year 2000 affable Sauro and Fabrizio Ubaldi, and Fabrizio's son Luca, took over, trimmed the sails, and got this wonderful landmark skimming along again. Everything is made in house. The *gobeletti* apricot-jam cookies are very good, the chocolate-dusted meringues are made to look like miniature porcini mushrooms, and the Falstaff, a croissant filled with hazelnut paste, is memorable and might even have been one of Giuseppe Verdi's favorites, as legend claims. The maestro was a regular, it's said, when in Genoa. If you can't handle a whole *torta Zena*, get an inkling of its deliciousness by trying a *patatina rosa*—a pink baby potato-shaped confection exploding with rummy *zabaione*. Alas, the coffee is the predictable Covim. The outdoor tables in the pocketsized piazza in the very heart of the heart of town are a great place from which to watch the world walk by. Klainguti also serves light lunches and snacks, and has a comfortable little backroom with crystal chandeliers and stone floors, a good place to get out of the weather.

PIAZZA DI SOZIGLIA 98/100R ✦ TEL: 010 860 2628
OPEN DAILY 7:30AM *to* 8PM, CLOSED SUNDAY

Migone Enoteca

ON A CORNER OF THE SMALL SQUARE FRONTING THE MEDIEVAL CHURCH OF SAN MATTEO, BEHIND THE massive Ducal Palace, this old wine shop with a popular wine bar next door (**San Matteo Osteria**, open daily noon to 3pm and 7pm to midnight, closed Monday and for lunch on Sunday) was one of Genoa's first serious attempts to showcase the wines of Italy and France in upscale surroundings. You step down from the square into a vaulted cellar and discover shelf upon shelf of bottles from top wineries, many of them Piedmontese or Tuscan (and lots of Champagne). The Riviera is represented by only a handful of fine winegrowers, including Maria Donata Bianchi, Laura Aschero, Bisson and Santa Caterina. You'll also find gifts and specialty foods, conserves and spirits. Step from the shop into the wine bar and take a seat under the timbered ceiling, amid old prints of Genoa and the sea, and enjoy the often-changing selection of classic Ligurian dishes in a cozy, congenial atmosphere. You can order wine by the bottle or the glass.

PIAZZA SAN MATTEO 4/6R ✦ TEL: 010 247 3282
CLOSED MONDAY

Gelateria Profumo

IN 2007, AMBITIOUS PASTRY-MAKER MAURIZIO PROFUMO OF GENOA'S CELEBRATED PROFUMO chocolate-and-pastries dynasty opened this stone-clad take-out *gelateria* in the alleyways of old Genoa, about 150 yards south of the family pastry shop and the palace-lined Via Garibaldi. Like the successful mini-chain GROM, based in Turin but now established in Genoa, Profumo clearly posts a list of ingredients and states his methodology. His ice creams are well-balanced, creamy without being fatty, exquisitely flavorful and, unlike some of GROM's flavors, are never overwhelmed by sweetness. They're made using the best ingredients available, including ripe fresh fruit, and no colorings or preservatives. Maurizio toasts and grinds the pistachios, hazelnuts and almonds that go into those exquisite flavors, shunning shortcuts and ready-to-use pastes, and the resultant *gelati* are wonderfully nutty and fresh-tasting. The *panera* flavor — a *semifreddo* combining freshly brewed coffee and whipped heavy cream — is the best of its kind in town, and among the best in Liguria.

VICO SUPERIORE DEL FERRO 14R ✦ TEL: 010 2514159

CLOSED SUNDAY *and* MONDAY

Panificio Fiore

A HOLE-IN-THE-WALL ON AN ATMOSPHERIC ALLEYWAY ONE EAST AND PARALLEL TO VIA SAN LORENZO, at about the level of Palazzo Ducale, this friendly neighborhood bakery was founded in 1914 and is now run by Sergio Tognoni, who uses sourdough and organic flours to make his breads, and extra virgin oil in his delicious, porous, crisp focaccia. The breadsticks are also remarkable, not to mention the plump, round *pinolata* pine nut-studded cookies, *occhio di bue* cookies with a "bull's eye" of jam or hazelnut cream, *baci di dama* and *canestrelli*.

VIA CANNETO IL LUNGO 79R ✦ TEL: 010 246 8521

CLOSED SATURDAY AFTERNOON *and* SUNDAY

Panificio Patrone

O N A CURVING MEDIEVAL ALLEY THAT RUNS FROM PIAZZA DI SARZANO (SITE OF THE MUSEO SANT' Agostino) to the castellated city gate at Porta Soprana, this humble old corner bakery with high-schoolers' graffiti scrawled on the walls is celebrated for its many types of focaccia — plain, with onion or wild field greens, and, occasionally, incorporating pesto, green beans and potatoes. The latter is worth trying as a curiosity; lightness is not an attribute. Patrone also makes good classic savory tarts, simple desserts, cookies and *pandolce*.

VIA RAVECCA 72R ✦ TEL: 010 251 1093

OPEN 7AM *to* 7:30PM CLOSED SUNDAY

Panificio Tumioli

A HUMBLE BAKERY FACING PORTO ANTICO, AT ABOUT THE LEVEL OF THE MOCK PIRATE galleon, Tumioli's baker Patrizia Ferretti makes surprisingly excellent bread and *grissini*, and perfectly porous and flavorful plain focaccia dressed with extra virgin olive oil. This is a good place to buy a snack and walk with it through the *caruggi* or into the port area.

VIA GRAMSCI 37R ✦ TEL: 010 246 5956 ✦ OPEN MONDAY *through* SATURDAY 8:30AM *to* 7:30PM *and* SUNDAY 8:30AM *to* 1:30PM

Pasticceria Profumo

*I*N AN ALLEYWAY RUNNING FROM VIA GARIBALDI TO PIAZZA PORTELLO, THIS LOVELY LANDMARK SHOP, founded in 1827, is widely and rightly considered the home of Genoa's most refined pastries and chocolates. The Profumo family, who have owned and operated it for decades, certainly turn out fabulously good *pandolce*, studded with house-made candied fruit, and their chocolates and candies are world class. Always elegant, Elena Profumo and her son Marco run things, while Marco's brother Maurizio is chef. Profumo's green or black "olives" have a hazelnut-flavored chocolate center and a lightly sweet candy shell, are crunchy and delicious and are found nowhere else. A sampler of Profumo chocolates includes seven types, from a 72 percent cocoa Aragnani and a 70 percent Guanaja, to a buttery white Ivoire. The candy-coated almond *confetti*, displayed in glass jars on shelves behind the marble-topped counter, are given out at weddings and for anniversaries, and come in a mind-boggling array of colors. Each is flavored naturally and pegged to an anniversary year. Like the shop itself, Profumo packaging is remarkable. Textile- or paper-covered boxes show the palaces of Via Garibaldi, or typical Genoese fabric patterns of centuries past.

VIA DEL PORTELLO 2R ✦ TEL: 010 2770002 ✦ CLOSED SUNDAY

Romanengo fu Stefano

*T*HREADBARE TERMS SUCH AS "JEWEL BOX"
INEVITABLY SPRING TO MIND WHEN GAZING AT THE
sculpted marble façade, painted glass and mirrors, crystal
chandeliers and plaster moldings and antique wooden display
cases of this family-owned shop opened in 1814. Cousins Paolo,
Pietro, Giovanni Battista and Delfina Romanengo are the current
generation of Romanengo owners and managers of what might
justly be Italy's most celebrated landmark *confetteria*, a shop
making candied fruit, chocolates and candy covered almonds.

Starting in the late 1700s, the Romanengos perfected the medieval techniques (learned by the Genoese from the Arabs during the Crusades) used to take fresh, ripe fruit and preserve it in sugar, so that the flavor and color remained intact. Romanengo still buys and candies the best, ripest Italian apricots, oranges, cherries, quinces, *chinotti*, figs, strawberries, melons, mandarin oranges, loquats, pears, peaches, plums and chestnuts, and imports exotic fruits such as pineapples. The recipes are a closely guarded secret. The almond-based sweets such as *quaresimali*, originally made for Lent, are available all year. Romanengo has another handsome shop, from the 1930s, on Genoa's elegant Via Roma, between the opera house and Piazza Corvetto (Via Roma 51R, Tel: 010 58 02 57, same hours).

VIA SOZIGLIA 74/76R ✦ TEL: 010 2474574

WWW.ROMANENGO.COM

CLOSED MONDAY MORNING *and* SUNDAY AFTERNOON

Serafina Artigiana Alimentari

THE WINDOW DISPLAYS OF EVERY IMAGINABLE VEGETABLE BATHING IN OLIVE OIL, PLUS DRIED mushrooms and dozens of sauces, are hard to pass by on this narrow alley about a hundred yards east of Via San Lorenzo toward its seaside end. Serafina's fresh pesto is made with Umbrian non-extra-virgin olive oil. Stick to the pickled artichokes, olives and other delicacies where the oil is a packing medium and not the object of the exercise.

VIA CANNETO IL CURTO 34 ✦ TEL: 010 246 8779
CLOSED WEDNESDAY AFTERNOON *and* SUNDAY

Vedova Romanengo

IN A MEADOW-LIKE CLEARING AMID THE TOWERING OLD *PALAZZI* JUST NORTH OF THE FORMER STOCK exchange and Piazza Banchi, this landmark *caffè*, chocolate and pastry shop was founded in 1805 by the same fractious family that runs the more famous Romanengo fu Stefano candied fruit shop up the street a hundred yards or so. The tale of the family's split, estrangement and the continuing confusion the names and proximate locations create among the uninitiated, would be long to tell. Suffice it to say that the butter cookies here are delicious—especially the daisy-shaped *canestrelli*—the candied fruit and chocolates very good, the coffee perfectly all right (supplied by the ubiquitous Covim), and the interior wonderfully weathered, with period display cases, creaking floors and a solicitous shopkeeper who, alas, stiffens when asked about the rival Romanengo. The handful of tables outside are convenient for a rest, especially in Genoa's roasting summer heat.

VIA OREFICI 31/33R ✦ TEL: 010 247 2915
OPEN 7AM *to* 7PM, CLOSED SUNDAY

Romeo Viganotti di Alessandro Boccardo

FOUNDED IN 1866, CURRENT OWNER, CHOCOLATIER EXTRAORDINAIRE ALESSANDRO BOCCARDO, CAME on board and bought out the business in the 1990s. His specialty is dark chocolate. Shy and meticulous, he buys

direct from a Genoese importer, and uses antique machinery and molds from the mid 1800s to make his luscious, wonderfully traditional chocolates. The shop is spartan, with a wide wooden counter and wooden shelves. Try the classic dark, filled *cioccolatini*, bonbons, *torrone*, pure chocolate bars, chocolate-dipped oranges and old-fashioned chocolate-dipped cherries called *boeri*. Don't miss it.

VICO DEI CASTAGNA 14R ✦ TEL: 010 2514061

CLOSED SUNDAY *and* JULY-AUGUST

GENOA'S CENTRAL BUSINESS AND NINETEENTH-CENTURY DISTRICTS

Includes: Via San Vincenzo, Piazza Colombo, Via XX Settembre, Piazza De Ferrari, Via Roma, Piazza Corvetto, Piazza Dante

ALSO PART OF THE *CENTRO STORICO*, THOUGH NOT NEARLY AS OLD AS THE *caruggi*, the streets above the medieval tangle are lined by imposing *palazzi* dating mostly to Genoa's heyday in the mid to late 1800s, when the city was part of Italy's industrial triangle (Milan, Turin, Genoa). The streets are straight and wide — and some are remarkably noisy, especially Via XX Settembre (the double X is pronounced *venti*). Most of the city's department stores, supermarkets, office buildings and elegant shops are found here, and so is the covered municipal market, *il mercato orientale*, so called not because of "oriental" exoticism, as some visitors think, but because it's on the eastern side of town. The entrances to the market are on Via XX Settembre near the church of La Consolazione, and on two alleyways leading off Via Galata, between Via XX Settembre and Piazza Colombo. The market is open from 7:30am to 1pm and 3:30pm to 7:30pm, and has two levels. Most of the best food stands are on the ground floor, and that's where you'll find an amazing assortment of fruit and vegetables, a dozen or more types of tomatoes, chard, peas, artichokes from Albenga, basil from Prà, fish from the Gulf of Genoa, chestnuts and mushrooms from the hills on both sides of the city, plus dry goods, herbs, spices, pine nuts, oils, conserves and the usual meats, poultry, hams, cheeses and other delicacies found in the market stalls of other Italian cities. **Fiorella d'Amore**, in stall #B184, is among the few green grocers to sell the wild field greens known as *preboggion* and bunches of wild and/or domestic borage, which are essential to authentic Genoese cooking.

FARINATA, FRIGITTORIA, TORTE SALATE

Farinata

A THROWBACK TO THE 1800S, THIS NO-NAME HOLE-IN-THE-WALL *FARINATA* SHOP ON A SMALL SQUARE in what passes as Genoa's theater district hasn't changed in decades. Locals, blue-collar workers and theater-goers flock here for a quick snack. There's a marble counter, an oven and a scale and that's about it. Get a slice of hot, unctuous *farinata* and walk with it.

PIAZZA MARSALA 5 ✦ NO TELEPHONE
OPEN WEEKDAYS 8AM *to* 2PM *and* 6:30PM *to* 8:15PM

Ostaja San Vincenzo

O N THE EASTERN END OF VIA SAN VINCENZO, A PEDESTRIAN-ONLY FOOD-AND-SHOPPING STREET, this *osteria*-cum-fry shop is a favorite among insiders for its *farinata* and savory tarts, fried *panissa* and codfish or herbed *frisceu* fritters. It's the kind of place you'd probably never enter, unless accompanied by a Genoese friend. You step down from the street into a grotto where a handful of shared, wooden tables face a counter arrayed with delicious vegetable tarts. Take-out customers line up starting in the morning. Sit-down clients can choose between the rough-and-ready entrance, or they can opt for a nicely dressed table in a big back dining room, or a tiny back-back dining room. To reach both, you walk by the roaring, wood-burning oven where the tarts are cooked. Regulars know this as one of the only places where you can ask the baker to give you a slice of *farinata* that's *ben cotta*, meaning well done — crisped and firm on top and bottom — as opposed to *normale*, meaning, at this establishment, that it's tender and soft inside and on the bottom. Unusually, the *farinata* also comes optionally with *stracchino* cheese, sautéed white onions, codfish or sausage meat. The delicious chard tart is about three inches thick, with a head of *prescinsêua* cheese. Other menu items include pasta with pesto and roasts. There are few places left in town that are more authentic, simple and local than this homey old fry shop.

VIA SAN VINCENZO 64R ✦ TEL: 010 565765
CLOSED SUNDAY ✦ INEXPENSIVE

COFFEE, PASTRIES, ICE CREAM,
PASTA *FRESCA*, GOURMET FOODS

Caffè Gelateria Balilla

IEWED FROM THE HISTORICAL AND POLITCAL STAND-POINT, BALILLA IS AN AMBIGUOUS CHARACTER, A Genoese adolescent who, during the Austro-Hungarian occupation of the Republic of Genoa in the 1740s, refused to carry out the occupiers' order to drag an artillery piece across town. Like David fighting Goliath, Balilla flung a stone at them; his courageous act prompted a bloody uprising and the eventual (though short-lived) emancipation of the Republic. Mussolini appropriated Balilla as a symbol, and it was during the country's Fascist period, in 1934, that this handsome *caffè* opened for business. Nowadays politics seem of no interest to the mixed crowd of regulars, who stand three-deep at the bar clutching housemade almond croissants or slices of excellent focaccia, and order cappuccino. The barmen are known for their skill in frothing milk to perfection, and its richness meshes with the strong Covim Smeraldo coffee blend that Balilla uses. The décor is lavish, from the checkerboard black-and-white marble floor to the woodwork and crystal chandeliers. The enlargements of 1700s maps of Genoa, and drawings of Balilla, lend atmosphere. There's a pleasant, fuddy-duddy salon beyond the bar area, where well-healed Genoese sip tea and nibble pine nut-studded and other very good shortbread cookies or creamy Genoese desserts. Balilla is probably most revered as one of the city's top ice creameries, with a selection of about two dozen natural flavors in season, many of them fruit-based, others rich and creamy, such as white chocolate or cinnamon. Several are found nowhere else, including Spuma di Marsala or Spuma di Orange, two delicious *semifreddi* flavored, respectively, with Marsala and fresh orange juice. The Fatina al Cioccolato *semifreddo* is heavenly. There's also a selection of low- or no-sugar and low-calorie ice creams. Balilla is off the beaten track, at the southern end of Via Macaggi, about 150 yards west of Piazza Vittoria, but is definitely worth the detour.

VIA MACAGGI 84R ✦ TEL: 010 542161

OPEN DAILY 7AM *to* MIDNIGHT (10PM IN WINTER)

Boasi Caffè

SET UNDER THE HANDSOME ARCADES OF GENOA'S MAIN DRAG, THE TRAFFIC NOISE SENDS VIBRATIONS through the sidewalk tables of this popular *caffè* with a stylish interior. Locals and commuters stop by for a shot of excellent espresso at the bar — Boasi has one of the city's best bar blends, which is 100 percent Arabica, dark roasted and strong — or to pick up freshly roasted coffee beans to take home. They come from the Boasi *torrefazione*, the suburban coffee-roasting plant that supplies this mothership location and several other lesser bars serving Boasi coffee in and around Genoa. Like most Italian cities worth their millennial pedigrees, Genoa is a fractious place, so don't be surprised if you see a dry goods shop and *torrefazione* in the tangled medieval *caruggi* nearby, which is also called Boasi (it's owned by a relative and also sells very good coffee beans, but is not a *caffè*).

VIA XX SETTEMBRE 266R ✦ TEL: 010 540131

OPEN 7:15AM *to* 8PM, CLOSED SUNDAY

Bonanni — Antiche Bottiglierie Genovesi

A FEW HUNDRED YARDS WEST OF THE BRIGNOLE TRAIN STATION, ON ONE OF GENOA'S BUSIEST and most attractive pedestrianized shopping streets, this bottle shop has been around for the better part of a century. The elaborate cast-marble floor is decorated with the names of famous Italian drinks companies. It's been run for the last 50 years or so by Anna Napoletano and her husband, owner Flavio Bonanni. Locals allergic to gentrified wine bars and newfangled *enoteche* shop here. The selection of Ligurian wines includes fine bottlings by Terre Bianche and Laura Aschero, plus Sciacchetrà from the Castello di Riomaggiore. Bonanni also sells very good olive oils by Isnardi.

VIA SAN VINCENZO 60R ✦ TEL: 010 580088
WWW.BONANNI.IT ✦ CLOSED SUNDAY

Bruciamonti

O N GENOA'S FASHIONABLE VIA ROMA, WHERE OLD-MONEY FAMILIES LIVE AND SHOP, THIS CORNER gourmet food boutique, rotisserie and delicatessen, family-run by the Bruciamontis since 1885, makes delicious *torta pasqualina*, *cima alla genovese* and *cappon magro* (sold in individual servings), using original, nineteenth-century recipes. The pesto is excellent, made with high-quality extra virgin olive oil, Ligurian basil, Tuscan pine nuts, and a mix of *parmigiano* and *pecorino sardo* cheeses; Bruciamonti ships it worldwide to restaurants and private clients. Also sold are dry pastas by Pastificio Santa Rita, and the hard-to-find, *pandolce*-like *pandolio* and *pane del pescatore* of San Bartolomeo al Mare, near Imperia, which are made primarily with oil and vegetable fats instead of butter.

VIA ROMA 81R ✦ TEL: 010 562515
WWW.BRUCIAMONTI.IT ✦ CLOSED SUNDAY

Buffa—Fabbrica Cioccolato, Confetteria

T HIS POCKETSIZED, FAMILY-RUN CHOCOLATE AND CONFETTI SHOP OVERFLOWS WITH IRRESISTIBLE handmade treats. It has been around for decades, and serves the prosperous neighborhood south of Via XX Settembre and west of Piazza Vittoria. Buffa uses high-quality ingredients to turn out classic Genoese filled or solid chocolates, which are well-balanced and never too fatty or sweet. The candied fruit and candy-coated almonds are excellent.

VIA D. FIASELLA 9R ✦ TEL: 010 542370
CLOSED MONDAY MORNING *and* SUNDAY

Chicco Caffè

STACKED FLOOR-TO-CEILING WITH DRY, CANNED AND BOTTLED GOODS, FROM CANDIES AND CHOCOLATES to honey, cookies, jams, herbal teas and breakfast cereal, this classic old Genoese grocery shop, owned and run since the 1950s by Stefano Toncini and his family, also happens to sell outstanding coffees, which are roasted for it at the Rostkafé factory on the outskirts of town. The blend of Arabicas sold as Arabica *dolce* is one of the city's best—mild, aromatic, redolent of chocolate. The Arabica Kenya blend is also excellent. The only drawback is that there's no in-house coffee shop. Buy some beans to go, and, if you're staying in a rented apartment on the Riviera, ask Toncini to grind them for your home-style Moka machine. You will discover a remarkable, unsung brew.

PIAZZA COLOMBO 9-11R ✦ TEL: 010 542252 ✦ CLOSED SUNDAY

Cremeria Colombo

SINCE 1985, FRANCO ALESSANDRI AND HIS FAMILY HAVE RUN THIS FRIENDLY NEIGHBORHOOD *CAFFÈ*, lunch spot and ice cream parlor just off Piazza Colombo, and they've made a name for themselves with their flavorful and totally natural handmade ice creams. No preservatives, colorings or stabilizers are used, only fresh, ripe fruit and high-quality milk, cream and natural flavorings—freshly brewed coffee, chunky chocolate and good pistachio or hazelnut pastes.

VIA COLOMBO 37-39R ✦ TEL: 010 588466
OPEN 6:30AM *to* 7:30PM DAILY EXCEPT SUNDAY

Danielli

THIS POPULAR NEIGHBORHOOD PASTA *FRESCA* SHOP'S AFFABLE OWNER, ANTONIO DANIELLI, has been at the helm since 1975, turning out remarkably good ravioli, *pansôti*, *taglierini*, *gnocchetti* and other classic Genoese pasta shapes, and making the sauces to go with them: pesto, long-cooked *tôcco* meat sauce, walnut sauce, and others. The *mercato orientale* is across the street, and Piazza Colombo just two shopfronts north.

VIA GALATA 41 ✦ TEL: 010 562383 ✦ CLOSED SUNDAY

Enoteca Sola

OWNED BY THE SOLA FAMILY (SEE EASTERN GENOA ENTRIES, PAGE 262), THIS UPSCALE BOTTLE SHOP and wine-tasting bar next door to Chicco Caffè has thousands of bottlings from all over Italy (and abroad), including about 20 of the Riviera's best. To participate in thematic wine tastings, or try the dozen wines on offer daily by the glass, you must pay an annual fee, for which you receive a "Vinotecard." With the card you also benefit from reduced prices. For the casual visitor, however, it's more convenient to taste wines and eat at the Sola restaurant across town, and make your purchases there.

PIAZZA COLOMBO 13R ✦ TEL: 010 561329

CLOSED MONDAY MORNING *and* SUNDAY

EVO Oleo Granoteca

IN 2005 ROBERTO PANIZZA, SCION OF THE FAMILY THAT OWNS CONFETTERIA ROSSI, THE MAN BEHIND Genoa's "mortar-made pesto championship," decided to create a specialized olive oil boutique where clients could taste oils before buying them. A selection of Ligurian (and other oils) is uncorked, so to speak, and poured daily, with tasting cups and hunks of bread at the ready. Many of the region's best oil makers are represented, so if you want to give yourself an education, and avoid driving 200 miles or more to seek out producers, you can taste and buy their product here. From the eastern Riviera di Levante you'll find Lucchi & Guastalli, Orseggi, Buranco, Cooperativa Vallata di Levanto, Rùe de Zerli, Cooperative Olivocoltori Sestresi; from the Ponente come Valle Ostilia, Cooperativa di Arnasco (from 100 percent *arnasca*, aka *pignola* variety, olives), Laura Marvaldi, Ranise, Fratelli Lupi, Tre Fasce, Frantoio Benza, Anfosso and Olio Roi. The boutique also calls itself a *granoteca*— another trendy neologism, this one meaning dry goods or grain shop. It sells excellent risotto rice, specialty grains, flours and dry pasta by a dozen small makers, from Pastificio Setaro in Campania to Felicetti in Trentino-Alto Adige, or Fabbri (Tuscany), Mancini (Marche) and Cavalier Cocco. To go with them are bottled sauces of all kinds.

VIA GALATA 46R ✦ TEL: 010 542019

WWW.PALATIFINI.IT ✦ CLOSED SUNDAY

Fratelli Centanaro

O N THE GROUND FLOOR OF AN ARCHITECTURAL EYESORE FROM THE 1970S DROPPED BY "URBAN planners" into this historic neighborhood, about half-way between the Brignole train station and Via XX Settembre, it's easy to walk past this excellent fresh meat and fine foods shop, which makes some of the best pork sausages and smoked pork products in the region, and also has a fine selection of cheeses, including, when available, a few from Liguria. Giuseppe Centanaro is the last of the family to run this century-old business, and with his wife keeps up the quality. There are no chemicals or artificial ingredients used in the pork smoking process, just firewood (mostly oak and olive). Centanaro pork products contain no artificial anything, and no fillers or by-products, and are delicious, particularly the *zampone*, which is traditionally eaten at Christmastide. Also sold are a few good Ligurian wines from Foresti, and extra virgin DOP olive oil, bottled sauces of various kinds including good pesto, all from Magé in Arma di Taggia.

VIA SAN VINCENZO 103-105R ✦ TEL: 010 580841
WWW.CENTANARO.IT ✦ CLOSED SUNDAY

Gelateria GROM

B ASED IN TURIN, THIS CHAIN OF HIGH-END GOURMET ICE CREAM SHOPS HAS OVER TWO DOZEN OUTLETS in Italy, plus several abroad, including one in New York City, and claims to make the best ice cream in the world. Maybe. The GROM formula is the same everywhere: excellent ingredients (hazelnuts from Piedmont's Langhe district, pistachios from Sicily), high-quality, extra rich milk for the cream flavors, San Bernardo mineral water for the sorbets and fresh, seasonal fruit. The operational philosophy aims at environmental and political correctness, and largely succeeds. GROM ice creams are very good, some, such as *caffè*, are excellent, though many flavors tend to the sweet side of the spectrum, which might account for their popularity. With luck, competition from GROM will stimulate local, family-run *gelaterie* — many of which currently take shortcuts — to return to the artisanal methods of decades past: the home-toasting and hand-crushing of nuts, for instance, and the refusal to use emulsifiers, colorings, stabilizers and preservatives.

VIA SAN VINCENZO 53R ✦ TEL: 010 565420, WWW.GROM.IT
OPEN DAILY 11AM *to* 10PM (11PM FRIDAY *and* SATURDAY)

Gerolamo Pernigotti—Gamalero

*T*HIS CENTURY-OLD SHOP FAVORED BY SERIOUS COOKS AND RESTAURATEURS STOCKS EXCELLENT split peas, black-eyed peas, the makings of *antica minestra genovese* (mixed beans for Genoese minestrone), La Spezia's *mesciua* mix and top-grade chickpeas.

VIA GALATA 32R ✦ TEL: 010 591673 ✦ CLOSED SUNDAY

Caffè Pasticceria Mangini

*G*ENOA IS A CITY OF TUNNELS, PHYSICAL AND TEMPORAL, AND THIS TEMPLE OF COFFEE AND PASTRIES burrows back to the city's late nineteenth-century heyday. The show starts the moment your shoes pass the threshold and touch the marble floor. The bar is of inlaid wood, topped with beaten zinc, the tables draped with yellow tablecloths and surrounded by cane chairs. Mangini's plates, saucers, espresso and cappuccino cups are gorgeous, hand-painted Herend porcelain,

with floral or butterfly patterns (they're sold next door to the *caffè* at the swank Issel boutique, at Via Roma 89R). Waiters in livery move graciously among the regulars and the well-heeled out-of-towners who know Mangini is still, after 120 years, *the* place to meet and talk politics, art and culture—or observe Genoa's old, plutocratic families. Managed and part-owned (with his extended clan) by Giacomo Rossignotti, whose family created Mangini and a handful of other memorable *caffè* and pastry shops on the Riviera, this landmark has no dust on its shoulders. Mangini serves the family's own 100 percent Arabica blend, very dark-roasted at the Rossignotti coffee and nougat factory in Sestri Levante. It's potent, lending itself to transubstantiation with milk as cappuccino. The hazelnut-and-chocolate *Baci di Dama* cookies, jam tarts, brioches and creamy cakes and candied fruit are all housemade—the Rossignotti are a clan of pastry and candy makers since 1840—and scrumptious.

PIAZZA CORVETTO 3R ✦ TEL: 010 564013

OPEN 7:30AM *to* 8PM, CLOSED MONDAY

Panarello

A CENTURY OLD, PANARELLO IS STILL AMONG GENOA'S MOST FAMOUS AND BEST-LOVED PASTRY shops, now a local chain, celebrated for having perfected the classic *pandolce alla genovese*. The mini *pandolcini*—the diameter of a coffee saucer—are a delicious mid-morning snack, just the right size for two. They have the advantage of being lightly sweet, and pleasantly bready. The coffee bar isn't striking to look at and there's nowhere to sit, but the coffee is noticably good, a blend of central American Arabicas roasted exclusively for Panarello by local coffee company Romoli. You can buy packages of Panarello coffee to go, but you might want to save room to load up instead on the irresistible cookies, cakes and jam tarts, from lifesaver-shaped *ciambelline*, to *gobeletti* filled with apricot jam, pine nut-studded *pinolate*, tiny fan-shaped *ventagli*, or aniseed *anicini*. This is a good place to stop on the way to or from the *mercato orientale*, the municipal covered market, which is about 150 yards south of Panarello's Via Galata location.

VIA GALATA 67R ✦ TEL: 010 562 238 (*and* NEARBY AT 154R VIA XX SETTEMBRE) ✦ OPEN 7:30AM *to* 7:30PM, CLOSED SUNDAY

Confetteria Rossi

THIS MINI-CHAIN OF CANDY STORES, LOCALLY OWNED BY THE PANIZZA FAMILY, BELONGS TO THE more-is-more school: counters and shelves are stacked high with every imaginable form, shape and color of candy. The real draw is the handmade cookies such as hazelnut-cream-filled *baci di dama*, buttery *canestrelli di Torriglia*, and beautifully wrapped, slightly sweet almondy *amaretti morbidi del Sassello*. The *tartufi di Rossi* are chocolate truffles with chunky hazelnut bits, and are also handmade by an artisan for Rossi shops. Rossi is famous for its beautifully packaged *pandolce*, *panettone* and *pandoro di Verona*—the wrappers show sailing ships, or have Rococo floral garlands—and does a booming business in gift packages, selling these and other goodies (wine and olive oil) by mail order and over the Internet. The same family runs the EVO olive oil tasting room and boutique on nearby Piazza Colombo.

VIA GALATA 30R ✦ TEL: 010 564332 ✦ WWW.PALATIFINI.IT
CLOSED SUNDAY ✦ OTHER LOCATION: VIA CESAREA 21/R,
010 564955 (SOUTH OF VIA XX SETTEMBRE)

Pasticceria Tagliafico

TAGLIAFICO IS ACROSS THE STREET FROM CONFETTERIA ROSSI, NEAR THE ENTRANCE TO THE *MERCATO orientale*, and has one of the city's most tempting displays of pastries. It was founded in 1923 and is still run by the energetic Tagliafico family. Both varieties of Genoese *pandolce* (*all'antica* and the classic variety) are good and never cloying, the etheral aniseed Lagaccio cookies are among the city's best, and the cakes, pastries and chocolates are all delicious and handmade using recipes handed down the generations. There's a small bar area where you can sip an espresso with your pastries.

VIA GALATA 31R ✦ TEL: 010 565714
OPEN 8AM *to* 8PM, CLOSED SUNDAY

UPPER GENOA

Includes: **Castelletto, Corso Firenze, Corso Magenta**

*I*N THE LATE 1800S, AS GENOA GREW, HUNDREDS OF SUMPTUOUS *PALAZZI* WERE BUILT ON the looping, panoramic avenues halfway up the hillsides, and this became the city's new upper-class district. The views from Castelletto are inspiring, and so too is the quality of several neighborhood food establishments.

COFFEE, ICE CREAM,
GOURMET FOODS, PASTRIES

De Regibus

*O*WNED AND OPERATED SINCE 1960 BY THE DE REGIBUS FAMILY, THIS CLASSIC BOURGEOIS PASTRY, chocolate and candy shop is known to insiders as one of Genoa's finest. Unsung, small but handsomely appointed, with black granite floors, and tempting displays, it's located about 250 yards west of the Castelletto esplanade. Everything is made in-house, and everything is exceptionally good, from the airy but flavorful aniseed *anicini* and *lagaccio* cookies, to the tender *amaretti del Sassello*, the classic white or chocolate *torrone*, and jellied quince *cotognata*, not to mention the jam tarts and sponge cakes. The delicious chocolates include a crispy, hazelnut-studded *croccantino*, and *ghiande* (milk-chocolate-coated almond paste, shaped like acorns). The meringues are ethereal and barely sweet, and come in a variety of shapes, colors and flavors — tongue-shaped *fragola* (strawberry) and *cacao* (cocoa), for instance, or chocolate-dusted *funghi* mushrooms.

CORSO FIRENZE 26-28R ✦ TEL: 010 251 2656 ✦ CLOSED MONDAY

Gelateria Guarino

THERE ARE TWO CELEBRATED ICE CREAMERIES ON THE PANORAMIC OUTCROP CALLED CASTELLETTO, once the site of a fortress perched over Genoa's *caruggi*, now a prestigious address where the city's old-money families lord it over town. Some Genoese swear by the Sicilian *gelateria* at the far end of the *spianata*, with its sweet, puffy, showy ice creams, while others plump for Guarino, which is also an excellent pastry shop and coffee bar. Guarino *gelati* are not showy, are made traditionally with top ingredients, and the *panera*—fresh coffee and whipped heavy cream—is remarkably good. All the *semifreddi* are outstanding. Buy a cone or *coppetta* and walk with it about a hundred yards southwest to the terrace overlooking the slate roofs of old Genoa, the port and sea.

VIA CROSA DI VERGAGNI 25R, SPIANATA CASTELLETTO

TEL: 010 251 0810 ✦ CLOSED MONDAY

Pasticceria Magenta

THE FUNICULAR FROM GENOA'S DOWNTOWN AREA STOPS ACROSS THE STREET FROM THIS OLD NEIGHborhood *caffè* and *pasticceria*, disgorging passengers into a nicely landscaped park, so the shop's clientele of well-healed Castelletto regulars is admixed with the occasional tourist. On a par with nearby De Regibus when it comes to classic cookies and cakes, Magenta also serves delicious breakfast pastries—airy jam- or almond-filled brioches—and a decent cup of coffee, supplied by the predictable Covim, and therefore best when transformed into a frothy cappuccino.

CORSO MAGENTA 21R ✦ TEL: 010 251 3289 ✦ CLOSED TUESDAY

Rosticceria Castelletto

A NEIGHBORHOOD INSTITUTION, ON THE CORNER OF THE ESPLANADE, FACING THE BUS STOP AND Corso Firenze, this corner delicatessen makes some of the best *cima alla genovese* and *torta pasqualina* in town. It also bakes excellent focaccia, and remarkably good *farinata* (afternoons only).

SPIANATA CASTELLETTO 75R ✦ TEL: 010 251 0304

CLOSED SUNDAY

Ravioli and Pansòti

....

THE GENOESE CLAIM TO HAVE INVENTED RAVIOLI. AS WITH MOST OF THE REGION'S cult foods, a handy old tale is told to "prove" Genoese geneology. In the 1100s a clan of cooks with a tavern in the Val Lemme near the town of Gavi Ligure proudly bore the name "Raviolus," and it was they who perfected the recipe: a square pasta envelope stuffed with meat, egg, cheese and herbs. Gavi was taken from Liguria and given to Piedmont in 1815. Ever since, the Piedmontese have also claimed ravioli as theirs. The story provides a diplomatic solution, probably reached in the nineteenth century, after Italian Unification. Defending ravioli against hostile attack are the Order of the Knights of Ravioli and Gavi wine, founded in 1973. Food historians waste their words reminding the knights that dishes similar to ravioli were popular among the Babylonians and Egyptians of old. Apicius, who was not Genoese or from Gavi, lists in his first-century BC *De re conquinaria* the ingredients for "fried envelopes [of pasta] stuffed with meat."

Never mind. The most imaginative Genoese etymology for *raviolo* comes from the 1841 *Casaccia* dictionary, or so claims Genoese poet Vito Elio Petrucci; few commentators have the book handy. According to Petrucci, quoting *Casaccia*, this wonderous food's name derives from the Greek *rabioles* in which "rha" is said to mean healthful herb, "bios" life and "leos" people. Ravioli therefore are not what we normally think of, but rather "herbs that give life to people." This might conceivably make sense for Genoa's *ravioli di magro*, which are filled with spinach or other greens, ricotta, egg and *parmigiano*, and usually sauced with tomato sauce, or herbs and melted butter or, occasionally, with pesto. It makes no sense when applied to classic Genoese meat-filled or fish-filled ravioli, both of which have been eaten on the Riviera — and in Gavi Ligure — for centuries.

Ligurians serve meat-filled ravioli on December 26th, the feast day of Saint Stephan. Back in the days of lean living, they were made at home from the leftovers of the Christmas beef stew, and dressed with the leftover sauce. Nowadays, ravioli are a favorite on Sundays, feast days and

special occasions, but few Ligurians make them at home or use leftovers to fill them, preferring to purchase them ready made at pasta *fresca* shops. Fish ravioli are filled with poached fish, dressed with herbs and olive oil, or sauced with fresh tomatoes or shellfish, and tend to be a warm-weather dish.

A variation on the theme of ravioli is *pansôti*, which are plump pasta purses filled with minced boiled chard or *preboggion* (field greens), and sauced with *salsa di noci*—crushed walnuts and cream. Cream has only become popular in recent decades on the Riviera. Older, better recipes for the sauce employ crushed walnuts, pine nuts, parsley and garlic, diluted with olive oil, which makes a kind of rustic pesto.

EASTERN GENOA

....

Includes: Albaro, Boccadasse, Borgo Pila-La Foce

*I*F YOU STEP OUT OF THE BRIGNOLE TRAIN STATION ON THE EASTERN EDGE OF CENTRAL Genoa, and walk toward the coast on the broad Viale delle Brigate Partigiane, or turn left on Corso Buenos Aires or another, parallel avenue, you'll enter a middle-class neighborhood of wide, grid-block streets lined by plane trees and monumental, late nineteenth-century *palazzi*. The name La Foce means "the mouth" and refers to the Bisagno River, which runs underneath Viale delle Brigate Partigiane and comes out near Genoa's fairgrounds and convention center. Borgo Pila is the part closest to Brignole and the church of Santa Zita. The local covered market is at 94A Via della Libertà, near the bus depot, about halfway to the sea, and is open 8am to 1:30pm weekdays and Saturdays.

Climb up to the perched neighborhood of Albaro, half a mile further east. Albaro is one of the city's wealthiest areas, and hidden among the villas, tennis clubs and luxury apartment

complexes are a handful of great food addresses. Boccadasse, on the seaside abutting Albaro's eastern end, is a charming fishing village within the city, with a remarkably good ice cream shop on an unexpected cove.

RESTAURANTS AND *FARINATA*

Antica Osteria della Foce

ABOUT A HUNDRED YARDS NORTH OF THE MODERN, STRIKINGLY GRACELESS CHURCH OF SAN Pietro alla Foce, which is on Via Cecchi, this corner eatery with big red-framed windows is famed for its *farinata* and simple, homey food, so much so that it's difficult to get a reservation. Locals line up for take-out *farinata* and savory tarts, and aspiring guests do the same in hopes of getting one of the ten tables in the airy, high-ceilinged dining room. The only way in without fail is to reserve far ahead, or request a 7pm dinner seating and promise to be gone by 8pm. The *osteria* and its *farinata*-maker have been here for decades; white-haired and laconic, *il maestro* cut his teeth, with his brother Edo, in Sori, and his presence has helped ensure success for the current owners. They are affable, talkative Monica Capurro, who waits on table, and her bespectacled husband Andrea Giachino, who boxes the take-out orders and keeps the till; they do what they can to accommodate you, but at times seem overwhelmed by the *osteria*'s popularity. In reality, though there are logs stacked high around the wood-burning oven, and paper placemats on red-and-white waxed tablecloths, this is less an *osteria* than it was in decades past. A hybrid *Torte e Farinata* joint and neo-*trattoria*, it's favored by an upscale Genoese clientele. The servings are generous, so take a half-order of *farinata* unless you plan to eat little else, and ask for it *ben cotta*—well done. The house style is on the soft side. Note: it's only served at dinnertime. The menu changes, and there are specials. In addition to the perennial pasta with good pesto or *pansôti* with very creamy walnut sauce, you might find delicious, large, plump housemade *cuori*, which are heart-shaped green *ravioloni* stuffed with puréed borage, and sauced with pine nuts and rosemary (and more cream than you'd expect to find in Genoa). There's a delicious *cima alla genovese*, and a *tortino* of anchovies and zucchini, squid stewed with peas, octopus and potatoes, or succulent sautéed swordfish with artichokes and zucchini. Of the desserts, several are housemade, including a luscious dark chocolate pie, and a hazelnut-and-chocolate molded confection with a compote of fresh mandarine oranges in the center. On the short but well-chosen wine list are several reliable wines from Bisson and La Felce, and a few bottlings you'll find nowhere else, including white Coronata Assûie and red Trei Paexi, both from up-and-coming winemaker Andrea Bruzzone in the Valpolcevera in Genoa's western outskirts.

VIA RUSPOLI 72R ✦ TEL: 010 553 3155 ✦ CLOSED SATURDAY
LUNCH *and* SUNDAY ✦ INEXPENSIVE *to* MODERATE

Farinata Santa Zita

SPARTAN, LONG AND NARROW, WITH IMMENSELY HIGH CEILINGS, WOODEN TABLES AND A BIG OVEN HALFWAY down one side, this neighborhood *farinata* joint also serves delicious savory tarts, *panissa*, special *farinate* with toppings, and *mesciua*, the mixed-bean soup of La Spezia, plus a small selection of Ligurian classics. It's a favorite among locals, hidden on a back street between the church of Santa Zita and Piazza Paolo da Noli in a totally untouristed part of town.

VIA SANTA ZITA 35R ✦ TEL: 010 588545
CLOSED SUNDAY *and* MONDAY ✦ INEXPENSIVE

Sola Enoteca Cucina & Vino

A GENOA INSTITUTION SINCE THE 1980S, THIS UPSCALE WINE BAR AND RESTAURANT ON THE corner of Via C. Finocchiaro Aprile, one block east of Viale delle Brigate Partigiane, has the look and feel of an English pub or steak house of old (there are bentwood chairs and green lampshades), but serves classic Ligurian cuisine — *trenette* with pesto, stewed octopus, savory tarts, *stoccafisso* with pine nuts and potatoes — matched to countless excellent wines, which you can try by the glass or bottle, and also buy to take with you. Pino Sola and his family know everything there is to know about Italian wine, and happily guide guests through the long list of wineries, including those of top Riviera winemakers such as De Battè, Bruna or Colle dei Bardellini. Sola also has a wine shop and tasting room on Piazza Colombo, downtown.

VIA BARABINO 120R ✦ TEL: 010 594513
CLOSED SUNDAY *and* AUGUST ✦ MODERATE *to* EXPENSIVE

Trattoria Vegia Arbà

WHEN THEY WERE VERY YOUNG, BACK IN 1980, ROBERTO SORIANO AND HIS SISTER MARINA took over this long-established neighborhood *trattoria* on a tree-lined square, and, flanked by the faithful Albina, nearly thirty years later, they're still working together. Marina cooks, Roberto runs the place and Albina does a little of each. The two small dining rooms are as sunny and bright as ever, the tablecloths yellow. Office workers and the millionaires who own the surrounding villas crowd in, as they always have. The only thing that's gone is the garden dining area, which in 2006 was sacrificed to the ubiquitous automobile. The *trattoria*'s name means "old Albaro" and is apt, for here you'll find the unchanging, deliciously simple cooking of this neighborhood, which until the postwar boom was practically the countryside. Start with *panissa fritta* or fried *cuculli* fritters, then try the minestrone or *trenette* with pesto or the *corzetti* with walnut sauce. There's excellent *cima alla genovese* and the increasingly hard-to-find *tomaxelle* veal rolls. Codfish lovers are well served, but so too is anyone who loves tripe. If you were wondering why the focaccia is so good, it's supplied by Al Forno di Albaro. The wine list is surprisingly long for a *trattoria*, with many regional bottlings, plus wines from the Veneto and Alto Adige.

PIAZZA LEOPARDI 16R ✦ TEL: 010 363324
CLOSED SUNDAY *and* MONDAY ✦ MODERATE

AMARETTI, COFFEE, FOCACCIA
AND PASTRIES, ICE CREAM

Amaretti Cavo

DIFFICULT TO SPOT, ON A BUSY THOROUGHFARE BETWEEN PIAZZA TOMMASEO AND THE ELEVATED train viaduct, this simple, old-fashioned, family-run cookie and pastry factory in the basement of an apartment building, down a rutted driveway, has been around for over a hundred years and makes extraordinarily delicious *amaretti di Voltaggio*, named for a village on the border of Liguria and Piedmont. Founder Attilio Cavo came from Voltaggio, and the family still operates an *amaretti* outlet there. Made with almonds, egg whites and sugar, Voltaggio *amaretti* are plumper, softer and slightly sweeter than most others found in Liguria. The scent of them baking fills surrounding streets. Buy a bag of *amaretti* and head for more scenic surroundings.

VIA MONTEVIDEO 43R ✦ TEL: 010 316733

WWW.CAVO.IT ✦ OPEN DAILY EXCEPT MONDAY 7:30AM *to* 12:30PM *and*, ON THURSDAY *and* FRIDAY, ALSO *from* 2:30PM *to* 6:30PM

Antico Biscottificio della Foce

NEAR THE EYESORE CHURCH OF SAN PIETRO ALLA FOCE, THE BEST THING ABOUT THIS SPARTAN OLD cookie factory is the scent—it fills Via Cecchi with the smell of baking *lagaccio*, aniseed, *canestrelli*, chocolate *baci di dama* and ladyfinger cookies, jam tarts and *pandolce*, all good, none outstanding. It's worth patronizing if you happen to be in the neighborhood, or lunching/dining at Antica Osteria della Foce, which is around the corner.

VIA CECCHI 43-45R ✦ TEL: 010 587261

CLOSED SUNDAY AFTERNOON *and* MONDAY MORNING

L'Aromatica

ON THE CORNER OF VIA DI TREBISONDA AND PIAZZA TOMMASEO, AT THE FOOT OF THE WINDING ROAD UP to Albaro, this boutique stuffed with artisanal pasta, spices, cookies, *pandolce*, olive oil and balsamic vinegar, sauces, spreads and creams, is actually the main retail outlet for L'Aromatica brand coffees, which are used in a fair number of *caffè* in Genoa and elsewhere. There are three pure-Arabica blends, all of them very good, on the dark, strong end of the spectrum, and a variety of others with Robusta blended in at 20 percent or more (most *caffè* use these, because they're cheaper and contain more caffeine). The roasting facility (not open to the public) is north of Staglieno cemetery inland from central Genoa at Molassana; the

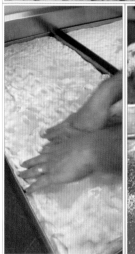

beautiful cake called *torta di rose*, which is fashioned from translucent layers of dough, with decorative pastry roses on top, and perfumed throughout with rose petal water.

VIA ALBARO 24R ✦ TEL: 010 363315 ✦ OPEN DAILY 5AM *to* 8PM

Latteria Bavari

OWNER ROBERTO MULAS USES COVIM'S TOP ARABICA BLEND—SMERALDO—TO MAKE GOOD, STRONG coffee and frothy cappuccino, at this unremarkable neighborhood bar with a handful of tables on the landscaped traffic circle that links La Foce and Albaro. The *gelati* are housemade and good, and the Amaretti Cavo factory is just up the street, making this is a fine spot to sip on something while savoring an *amaretto* and resting the feet.

PIAZZA TOMMASEO 38-40R ✦ TEL: 010 313532
OPEN 7:30AM *to* 7:30PM (LATER IN SUMMER)
CLOSED SUNDAY AFTERNOON

Pasticceria Svizzera

THE UBIQUITOUS LORD BYRON LIVED IN THE HANDSOME VILLA WHICH HOUSES THIS HISTORIC PASTRY shop, on the main road through Albaro. In business since the Swiss baker Vital Gaspero founded it over a hundred years ago, Pasticceria Svizzera is a Genoa institution, and though it's more celebrated for its catering than anything else nowadays, it's still one of the city's best places to savor excellent *pandolce* and other classics of the repertoire.

VIA ALBARO 9R ✦ TEL: 010 362 9278
WWW.PASTICCERIASVIZZERA.IT
CLOSED SUNDAY AFTERNOON *and* MONDAY

Torrefazione Caffè Ugo Romoli

FOUNDED IN 1924 AND STILL IN THE SAME FAMILY, THIS LOCAL COFFEE ROASTER HAS FOUR RETAIL outlets in Genoa, and a roasting plant inland (not open to the public). Romoli also roasts coffee for other clients, including Panarello, the famous bakery-coffee shop chain in Genoa, whose coffee is remarkably good. There's probably no other roaster in the region, and possibly no other in Italy, with more excellent mono-varietal Arabica coffees and blends, than Romoli. What's particularly nice about Romoli is, at the bar you can taste a single dose of anything they have, freshly ground for you. You can also mix and match beans. The bar blend, a secret recipe, is pure Arabica, from a variety of South and Central American countries, and is strong and flavorful. The mildest Arabica blend, "Dolce," has some South Indian Arabica mixed in, and is smooth and chocolatey. The boutique also sells candies and sweets and delicious *orzo*, toasted barley, a coffee substitute for those who can't drink coffee at night. Romoli will grind it for you fresh. Brew it like drip coffee, or *alla napoletana*. For a full list of Romoli locations, visit the website.

CORSO BUENOS AIRES 57/59R ✦ TEL: 010 562655
WWW.CAFFEROMOLI.IT ✦ CLOSED SUNDAY

Fabbrica cioccolato Zuccotti

ON A DEAD-END STREET BEHIND THE SOARING DOME OF THE CHURCH OF SANTA ZITA, THIS OLD CHOCOLATE factory with a faded, painted glass sign and atmosphere to match, turns out delicious, creamy, buttery filled chocolates in the French and Belgian style. There are usually over two dozen to choose from, and they're made fresh daily.

VIA DI SANTA ZITA 36R ✦ TEL: 010 580504 ✦ CLOSED SUNDAY

WESTERN GENOA

Includes: Arenzano, Mele, Prà

THE PROMONTORY PRÀ OCCUPIES WAS BLIGHTED IN THE 1960S AND '70S BY FREEWAYS, RAILways and low-cost housing projects. Since the 1990s, heavy industry, shipping, and fishing have decamped, and basil has become the area's economic mainstay. The Riviera accounts for 40 percent of Italy's basil production, which tops 1,100 tons per year, worth tens of millions of dollars wholesale. Close to a quarter of the Riviera's major growers are in Prà. Half of the region's DOP, highest quality basil is grown in or near Prà. Because it's considered superior, Prà's DOP basil retails at about twice the price of competitors'. Home cooks and high-end restaurants, not big industry, buy it. So can you, direct from a hothouse. Ironically, the neighborhood has only a few restaurants or *trattorie* serving great pesto. One of them is worth seeking out, even if it means a long, winding drive.

Abutting Mele perches on hills about four miles behind Prà and Voltri. The river valleys below are filled with basil hothouses and rusting former paper mills and industrial plants; the handsome hillsides are sculpted by farm terraces. North of Mele on the SS456 two-lane highway, which begins at the Voltri seaside train station, is the sprawling hamlet of Fado, home to **Osteria Enoteca Baccicin du Caru** (Via Fado 115, Tel: 010 631804, inexpensive to moderate, open for lunch daily, for dinner Friday and Saturday only or by reservation). The friendly, professional brother-and-sister team of Rosella and Gianni Bruzzone are the third generation to run this exceptionally pleasant roadside *trattoria*, which has been in business since 1890. The décor is simple but tasteful, done in yellow tones, with tiled floors, sturdy wooden tables and garland-pattern tablecloths. Rosella's cod fritters are perfection: light, crisp, never greasy or fishy. By advance request, Gianni makes the pesto in a big marble mortar, using two wooden pestles; the ingredients are excellent, and include basil from the Ratto hothouse (see below). The pesto dresses what might be the lightest, most flavorful homemade potato gnocchi anywhere (they're

made using 25 percent wheat flour and 75 percent mashed *quarantina* heirloom potatoes). The classic chard-and-meat filled ravioli with ground beef, mushroom sauce or pesto are outstanding; so too are the rustic, partly chestnut-flour *maltagliati* fresh pasta. Main courses range from delicious *cima* or roasts, to long-stewed rabbit, goat with white beans or roasted suckling pig with rosemary and garlic. The desserts—all housemade—include buttery, thick *canestrelli* cookies, *semifreddo* with *torroncino* and hot chocolate sauce, and moist almond-chocolate cake (ask for a small

taste of each). The wine list changes constantly, and features mostly Piedmontese or Lombard wines, plus a few Ligurian bottlings such as inky Ormeasco Superiore DOC from Fontanacota, or Colli di Luni Vermentino from La Colombaia. Note: this is among the most authentic and enjoyable of Ligurian *trattorie*, and the pesto is as good as pesto gets.

In scenic terms, Arenzano is another story. This tony outlying suburb is where many Genoese millionaires live, or moor their speedboats — at the marina. Inland about two miles from the train station, first following the Via Aurelia toward Cogoleto, then taking the second right turn where the Centro Artigianale is located, and following signs to **Agriturismo Argentea** (Via Val Lerone 50, Tel: 010 913 5367, www.agriturismoargentea.com, by reservation only, closed Sunday for dinner), you'll discover a handsome, family-run, upscale farmhouse B&B on an olive-dotted hillside. Argentea sells and serves delicious organic food. Affable husband-and-wife owners Giulianna Bellotti and Giovanni Molinari, she Piedmontese, he Ligurian, raise livestock and horses, and make delicious regional specialties (*torta pasqualina*, *torta di zucca*, *mandilli di saea*, rabbit Ligurian-style, *cima alla genovese*), following the seasons. In summer, the basil is homegrown; if you ask ahead, they'll make pesto for you using a mortar and pestle. The wine — Dolcetto DOC and Barbera red, Cortese white — is highly quaffable, though not Ligurian; it comes from Giulianna's sister's winery in Piedmont. Note that lunch is served on weekends only or by arrangement. If you're a hiker, you can follow the Alta Via dei Monti Liguri high-mountain, long-distance hiking path from the train station, through town and then across the highway and inland to the farm.

Genoese Pesto Mania and the Basil of Prà

....

WHAT'S PALE-GREEN, SMELLS LIGHTLY OF CITRUS AND MINT, AND DRIVES GENOESE mad with gluttonous desire? In two words, basil and pesto.

Untold millions of tiny Genovese sweet basil plants grow along the seaboard. But it's the hothouses of the western Genoese suburb of Prà that produce what most Italians and 99.9 percent of Ligurians claim to be the world's best commercially grown basil. Ask them what the very best basil of all is, and they'll point unabashedly to their own anemic-looking homegrown plants on shady windowsills or in leafy gardens. Ligurians disdain the herb when it's dark green and tough, the result of direct sun, which also gives it a mint-like flavor. The small, delicately scented, convex-leaf Genovese varieties of basil were developed here long ago and are nowadays grown almost exclusively in diffuse light under glass, the best of the best coming from Prà. The sheer quantity of plants—all harvested by hand—is overwhelming to contemplate. The rough total in each greenhouse ranges from 150,000 to 200,000 at any one time, and the yearly production from each averages 3 to 5.5 million plants.

In 1990, local boosters created Prà's Sagra del Pesto, a yearly festival featuring a religious procession, pasta feast, and sauce-making contest. When Pope John Paul II visited Genoa that same year, Prà's enterprising parish priest, Giorgio Parodi, brought him a bowl of pesto and prevailed upon His Holiness to bless the city with it, instead of holy water. "Not only did he," Parodi admitted a few years ago, "he also ate the pesto!" And loved it.

You can hardly exaggerate the significance of this peculiar blessing to Ligurians, whether practicing Catholics or not. Pesto is more than a culinary icon. Like pizza to Neapolitans, it's a cultural touchstone. Genoese are fervent regionalists, convinced their sauce is like no other and can't be reproduced elsewhere. To them, the guarantors of authenticity are sweet, light Ligurian DOP olive oil, plump Riviera pine nuts, fresh garlic, preferably from Vessalico, near Imperia, coarse sea salt from Cervia, a fifty-fifty blend of *pecorino romano fiore sardo* from Sardinia and excellent aged *parmigiano reggiano*, with the option, for those in the Recco area, of adding *prescinsêua*, the fresh cow's-milk cheese rarely encountered outside Liguria. Essential to the equation are the pale green color and mild, citrus flavor of tender shade-grown or hothouse Genovese basil.

Handmaking pesto in the traditional manner with a mortar is straightforward. What really counts is the quality of the ingredients, and the mortar—made of marble—and pestle—made of olive wood. Where a food processor chops or liquefies, mortar-pounding and grinding releases the herb's essential oils and produces the optimum tattered, crushed texture. For purists, pesto made without a mortar isn't pesto at all, it's a "basil milkshake." However, the number of Ligurians—particularly chefs at busy restaurants—who actually make pesto by hand is tiny.

Fresh pesto is at its best for only a few days and must be refrigerated, while to last more than a few months, bottled pesto must either be ultra heat treated or contain preservatives.

The bulk of Genovese basil seed is now produced by specialized Italian agro-industrial firms operating outside Liguria, notably in Cesena on the Adriatic coast. That seed is sown from Provence to California with varying results. Only a handful of Ligurian commercial growers produce their own heirloom seed; none is in Prà or even the Province of Genoa, and heirloom seed isn't generally considered better by growers. That invites the question: what makes Genovese basil grown in or near Genoa special or superior—if indeed it is? Simple, say partisan experts: the air, water, soil and microclimate. Prà's soil has a neutral pH, and its gently curving, south-facing promontory receives year-round, day-long sunshine plus salty Mediterranean breezes. It's hot by day, cool at night, so the basil plants rarely overheat; too much heat can cause oxidation. Perhaps most important, the area is blessed with abundant spring water from the mountains behind it. The combination is ideal for growing basil. The proof that Prà basil is indeed different and better is, if you remove Genovese seeds or seedlings from Prà and grow them elsewhere, they don't grow as well nor does the basil taste the same. Controlled experiments by an Italian government laboratory show that transplanted seeds and seedlings develop into plants with thick stems and tougher, darker leaves than those left in Prà. Most importantly to Ligurians, those wayward basil plants taste of mint, not basil. Despite these findings, the prestigious DOP label was awarded not only to growers in Prà but also to others growing excellent basil elsewhere on the Riviera.

RESTAURANTS SERVING EXCELLENT PESTO MADE WITH A MORTAR

La Brinca

VIA CAMPO DI NE 58, NE (GE) ✦ TEL: 0185 337480
MODERATE *to* EXPENSIVE

Ca' Peo

VIA DEI CADUTI 80, LEIVI (GE) ✦ TEL: 0185 319696
WWW.CAPEO.INFO ✦ VERY EXPENSIVE

Ostaja

VIA PIACENZA 54R, GENOA ✦ TEL: 010 835 8193
WWW.OSTAJA.IT ✦ INEXPENSIVE *to* MODERATE
Reserve your pesto ahead, and be prepared to pay extra, and the chef will make it with a mortar and pestle at:

Agriturismo Argentea

VIA VAL LERONE 50, ARENZANO (GE) ✦ TEL: 010 913 5367
WWW.AGRITURISMOARGENTEA.COM ✦ INEXPENSIVE

La Cucina di Nonna Nina

VIALE FRANCO MOLFINO 126, SAN ROCCO DI CAMOGLI (GE)
TEL: 0185 773835 ✦ WWW.NONNANINA.IT
MODERATE *to* EXPENSIVE

Osteria Enoteca Baccicin du Caru

VIA FADO 115, MELE (GE) ✦ TEL: 010 631804
INEXPENSIVE *to* MODERATE

Rosa

LARGO F. CASABONA 11, CAMOGLI (GE)
TEL: 0185 773411 ✦ EXPENSIVE

Zeffirino

VIA XX SETTEMBRE 20/7, GENOA
TEL: 010 5705939 ✦ VERY EXPENSIVE

*P*RÀ'S "ORDINE DEI CAVALIERI DELLA CONFRA-TERNITA DEL PESTO," CREATED IN 1992, IS a self-styled "brotherhood" of nutty pesto "knights" bent on promoting Prà and protecting its basil and pesto from industrial imitations (www.confraternitadelpesto. org). Similar aims motivate "PalatiFinì," a rival association of "refined palates"; it was also born in the 1990s. Palati-Fini created the International Mortar-made Pesto Championship (www.pestochampionship.it/). The contest is held each April in downtown Genoa at Palazzo Ducale, the magnificent frescoed seat of the former Genoese Republic. PalatiFini and other militants, such as local food expert Virgilio Pronzati, point out that under 20 percent of the pesto served worldwide comes from Liguria. The globe's biggest pesto facility is in Japan, and the number-one pesto-making country in quantitative terms is… Denmark, followed by Holland. Both organizations, spurred on by Virgilio Pronzati, continue to clamor for a Genoese Pesto DOP label, correctly pointing out that imitations often use inferior basil, cheese and pine nuts, not to mention low-quality oil and salt. So far, the European commission has demured, prompting PalatiFini to create its own label, with "pesto" written in gold on a black background, and the outline of a mortar, encircled in green.

The latest excogitations of basil and pesto fanatics are Pesto e dintorni, a pesto extravaganza with lectures, conferences, debates, pesto-making courses and more, held in October, also at Palazzo Ducale; and the putative Parco del Basilico, a "basil park" on Prà's coastal strip and inland areas, launched in 2007 and featuring basil-grower's hothouses and terraced plantations, pesto-maker's workshops, monuments, museums, restaurants and gift shops, all open to the public. So far the park is more virtual fledgling than anything else, though you can visit its handsome headquarters on the seafront in **Villa Doria Podestà** (Via Prà 63, Tel: 010 613 1908, www.parco-basilico.it, weekdays 8:30am to 12:30pm, look for the freeway overpass and palm tree) and, in theory, arrange to take a guided tour of hothouses.

RESTAURANTS SERVING EXCELLENT PESTO MADE WITH A FOOD PROCESSOR

Antica Osteria del Bai

VIA QUARTO 12, GENOA ✦ TEL: 010 387478
EXPENSIVE *to* VERY EXPENSIVE

Antica Osteria della Castagna

VIA ROMANA DELLA CASTAGNA, GENOA
TEL: 010 399 0265 ✦ EXPENSIVE

Garibaldi Cafè

VIA AI QUATTRO CANTI DI S. FRANCESCO 40R, GENOA
TEL: 010 247 0847 ✦ MODERATE

La Terrazza di Milly

PIAZZA LUIGI PITTO 4R, GENOA ✦ TEL: 010 391711
MODERATE *to* EXPENSIVE

Le Rune

VICO DOMOCULTA 14R, GENOA ✦ TEL: 010 594951
MODERATE *to* EXPENSIVE

Ristorante Da ö Vittorio

VIA ROMA 160, RECCO (GE) ✦ TEL: 0185 74029
EXPENSIVE *to* VERY EXPENSIVE

Ristorante Ferrando

VIA D. CARLI 110, SERRA RICCÒ (GE) ✦ TEL: 010 751925
MODERATE *to* EXPENSIVE

Ristorante-Focacceria Manuelina

VIA ROMA 278-296, RECCO (GE) ✦ TEL: 0185 74128
MODERATE *to* EXPENSIVE

Ruscin Antica Trattoria 1893

SALITA STELLA 198, GENOVA BAVARI
TEL: 010 3450391 ✦ MODERATE

Trattoria Bruxaboschi

VIA F. MIGNONE 8, GENOVA SAN DESIDERIO
TEL: 010 3450302 ✦ EXPENSIVE

SUBURBAN/OUTLYING GENOA

....

Includes: Nervi, Sant'Olcese, Staglieno, Torriglia

ERVI IS A WEALTHY RESORT SUBURB ON GENOA'S EASTERN EDGE. IT'S STUDDED WITH villas, parks and museums. The seaside promenade curls over boulders and cliffs, and in and out of coves. Perched on it, just below the Nervi train station, is the longtime local hangout, **Hotel Marinella** (Passeggiata Anita Garibaldi 18, Tel: 010 372 8343, www.hotelmarinella-nervi.com), which was built in the 1930s and looks like an old-fashioned ferry boat, with rounded ends and wrap-around windows. It serves a good cup of espresso, and very good housemade focaccia (plain, with herbs or minced white onions), focaccia *con formaggio*, grilled vegetables in olive oil, and a variety of tasty snacks. It's a fine place for refreshments or a light lunch.

La Bottega del Pesto (Via Aurelia 42R, Tel: 010 3291617, www.bottegadelpesto.com, closed Sunday afternoon) is on Nervi's main street, the ancient Roman Via Aurelia highway, at the eastern edge of town near the church of Sant'Ilario. Outside Prà and Mele, this family-owned hole-in-the-wall is among the most reliable producers of excellent pesto. Ezio, Elio and other members of the Rondini family have been making pesto for over thirty years. It (and creamy *salsa di noci* walnut sauce) is all they make, supplying local gourmets, a handful of restaurants, specialty food shops and bakeries. The ingredients are of the highest quality: basil from Prà, Domenico Ramoino's extra virgin Taggiasca oil, pine nuts from Liguria or Tuscany, and good-quality cheese. They also sell fresh and dry artisanal pasta, Ramoino brined and bottled Taggiasca olives and extra virgin olive oil, and stuffed sweet peppers in olive oil.

Sant'Olcese, a no-frills hill town perched about six miles as the crow flies inland from central Genoa, but twice that by car, is the home of the celebrated Salame di Sant'Olcese, eaten throughout the region. Light, tender and fresh, it's a delicious blend of pork and veal; other pure-pork salamis and small *salamini* are also made in Sant'Olcese. There are two long-established, equally excellent and equally famous family-owned salami-makers here, within shouting distance of each other.

Salumificio Cabella (Via Sant'Olcese 38, Tel. 010 709809, closed Wednesday afternoon and Sunday), is slightly north of the center of town, near Piazza Oxila, and makes its salami with garlic and wine; also delicious is *testa in cassetta* head cheese, and *mostardella*, a kind of sausage which can be eaten cooked or raw, and is served in thick slices. **Federico Parodi Salumificio** (Via Sant'Olcese 25 and 63, Tel: 010 709827, www. parodisantolcese.com, open daily) has a retail outlet facing the church on Piazza della Chiesa; its factory (visit on weekdays, by appointment) is farther down the same road. Parodi uses a wood-burning oven in the drying room, so the salami has a slightly smoked flavor; the business has been around since 1880, and is into its fourth generation.

STAGLIENO

Staglieno is the monumental cemetery (and neighborhood) due north of Genoa's Brignole train station. It used to be the city's main tourist attraction, and is well worth a visit. A little too close to the graveyard to be fashionable — 300 yards north of the main gate, on the west bank of the riverside drive — is the oddball, outstanding **Ostaja** (Via Piacenza 54R, Tel: 010 835 8193, www. ostaja.it, dinner only, closed Sunday and Monday, inexpensive to moderate), an insiders' address run by the husband-and-wife team of Paolo and Paola Vitiello, recent retirees (he from the merchant marine, she from an office job). Everything served is of the highest quality, from the Venturino olive oil on up. The exquisite *mandilli*, *picagge* and *pansôti* are handmade using a rolling pin and knife; the pesto is made fresh daily using a mortar and pestle; the walnut sauce is the real thing, containing no cream. The fish is wild, never farmed, and follows the catch; the air-dried cod with potatoes is excellent. There are also succulent veal stews and roasts. Desserts are good; they come from a reliable pastry shop. The short wine list is outstanding, with bottlings from Bisson, Bruzzone, Durin, Fontanacota and Ramò. The atmosphere and décor match: rustic wood paneling and unrendered stone walls, heavy wooden tables with paper placemats, and black-and-white photos of old Genoa. Clients are bona fide food lovers. Be warned: Friday nights feature accordion-and-organ music. Paolo tickles the ivories and segues from *Strangers in the Night* to Genoese hits of yesteryear.

TORRIGLIA

Torriglia, in a valley at about 2,500 feet above sea level, has an imposing ruined castle and mountain atmosphere. It lies inland northeast of Genoa over the coast range, a good hour's drive from the seaside (take highway 226 east from Busalla, or highway 45 northeast past Staglieno cemetery and through Bargagli). On the first Sunday in September there's a colorful local honey festival, with every type of honey and honey-related food imaginable. The chestnut festival is held in late October or early November and called La Castagnata (for info call 010 95029). Beyond being a summer retreat for working- and middle-class Genoese, with a stunning backdrop provided by the peaks of the Antola Regional Park, it's the homeland of *canestrelli di Torriglia*, the lifesaver or daisy-shaped cookies that are often dusted with powdered sugar. Several pastry shops and small factories make them (and *amaretti*, cakes and other treats). There's a local food festival dedicated to them, held mid May (call 010 944038 for info). Reliable sources are **Pasticceria Guano** (Piazza Cavour 2, Tel: 010 944290, closed Monday), a long-established cookie factory that's on the main square. **Antico Forno** (Piazza Gastaldi 15, Tel: 010 944081, closed Sunday) is more recent, but the *canestrelli* are excellent. Family-run and in a family home is friendly **La Torrigiana** (Via Canale 3, Tel: 010 942219, always open in summer, closed winter but open by appointment); look for the big cookie hanging outside. Like those of Antico Forno, their *canestrelli* have no preservatives, colorings or artificial flavorings.

Two good, old-fashioned restaurants in the center of town serve classic Ligurian food in a comfortable setting, and offer *canestrelli* and other Torriglia treats on their dessert menus. **Hotel della Posta 1906** (Via Matteotti 39, Tel: 010 944050, closed Monday, inexpensive to moderate) is slightly more upscale, has been around for over a century, and makes everything from pasta to dessert in-house. **Trattoria A Beccassa** (Via Roma 8, Tel: 010 943211, closed Monday, inexpensive to moderate) is also very good and has a terrace for fine-weather dining.

Easter Savory Tart

THE SUPREME EXPRESSION OF THE LIGURIAN SAVORY TART IS *TORTA PASQUALINA*, MADE primarily at Easter (Pasqua). The star ingredient is chard or artichoke hearts, sometimes both, and they are layered or mixed with *prescinsêua* fresh cow's milk cheese. Mysteriously, when the ingredients are mixed and not layered, the tart is usually called *torta cappuccina*. In theory, each layer is separated by a sheet of dough, and several spaces are made in the filling into each of which soft butter is spooned and an egg is cracked.

In a 1930 newspaper article, the scion of an old family, Giovanni Ansaldo, called his fellow Genoese an "endangered species," remarking that their imminent demise, at the hand of bureaucrats in Rome, was a shame because they had given the world two great things: America (thanks to native son Christopher Columbus) and *torta pasqualina*. Ansaldo's classic piece, often reproduced in cookbooks and essay collections, set forth the "Twenty-Four Beatitudes of Torta Pasqualina." According to these, the pious and the patient make the tart with either 24 angelic layers of dough (the number of beatitudes in the Roman Catholic church), or 33 (the age of Christ at Crucifixion). But in more than two decades on the Riviera, this correspondent has yet to counter *torta pasqualina* with more than six sheets of dough. Insiders know why there are six and not 33 sheets. Those willing to apply Jesuitical logic save work by using three top sheets and three bottom sheets: three and three, side by side, make 33.

Pandolce Christmas Cake

AIRY MILANESE *PANETTONE* IS POPULAR EVERY-WHERE IN NORTHERN ITALY AND ABROAD, WHILE Genoa's traditional Christmastide dessert has pretty much remained a local specialty, probably because the Genoese are famously retiring and unskilled at self-promotion, and, more practically, because *pandolce* is too labor-intensive and the ingredients too costly to allow industrial bakeries to make it profitably. *Pandolce* is called *pandoçe* in Genoese dialect, and it comes in two formats. Low, dome-shaped *pandolce all'antica* is misnamed, because the "normal" leavened variety is actually older. Both types are buttery, studded with candied fruit and perfumed with orange-flower water. The *all'antica* type is dense, lasts longer and is much richer than normal *pandolce*, which, like any leavened coffee cake, is best within two days of being baked. Until the postwar economic boom, *pandolce* was commonly made at home and often crowned with laurel leaves, a sign of regal distinction, probably linked to the arrival of the three kings of the Orient. The eldest family member — usually grandmother — gave it a ritual kiss before cutting and serving it, the first piece going to the youngest in the tribe. Nowadays, *pandolce* is made by many Ligurian bakeries, and the *all'antica* type is available year-round in some, particularly those in Camogli, Recco and Genoa.

CHAPTER 10

Greater Savona – Il Savonese

Province: **Savona.** *Includes:* **Albissola Marina,
Celle Ligure, Quiliano, Sassello, Savona, Stella.**

*T*HE SAVONESI, A POWERFUL MARITIME PEOPLE OF PRE-ROMAN DESCENT, WHO STRUGGLED FOR centuries against the Republic of Genoa but were finally subsumed by it, brought the art of making soap to Marseille. That, the theory goes, is where *savon de Marseille*, the pale-colored natural soap, got its name—from Savona. Strangely, the Savona area is not know for its soap, but rather for its wine, oil, cheese, *amaretti* cookies and fish—and more or less constant wind. Perhaps it was the wind that drew seafolk here in the first place: it's a fine place for sailing. The seaboard is smoothly contoured compared to the jagged eastern Riviera di Levante or Genoa, and the coastal strip is wider here than in most of the rest of the region, leaving room for agriculture. Greenhouses and fields of leaf vegetables, olive groves and fruit tree orchards extend into the mountainous interior, which is sprinkled with stony hamlets, cloaked with thick forests and boasts one of Liguria's tallest coastal mountains, Monte Beigua, almost 4,000 feet above sea level and a lovely regional parkland.

ALBISSOLA MARINA

*A*LBISSOLA IS DIVIDED INTO TWO SECTIONS, WITH THE SUPERIORE DISTRICT INLAND, AND the Marina on the seaside, as might be expected. This is where Ligurian ceramics have been made for the last 500 years, and you will find great quantities of them displayed wherever you go. The weekly open market is held on Tuesday in the center of town. **Ristorante La Familiare** (Piazza del Popolo 8, Tel: 019 489480, closed Monday, moderate to expensive) is what some call a "revival restaurant." Enter from the seaside promenade, or walk down narrow alleys like Via Colombo or Via Repetto in the center of old Albissola, and you come upon the small square where stands city hall and this remodeled, updated but old-style *trattoria*. La Familiare fills the ground floor of a village house (with a terrace for al fresco dining), but, apart from the recipes and the millennial setting, there's nothing "old" here. No little old cook rolls out the pasta in a cluttered kitchen. Rather, a young Ligurian named Giovanni, and a transplanted Sicilian, Pina, have endeavored to recreate a *trattoria* of the days before their birth, but with an open-plan kitchen you see into from the stylish dining room, which draws a mix of well-heeled locals and visitors. Though not served as it would be in a little old *trattoria*, the food is authentically good, starting with the octopus salad or classic stuffed vegetables, and delicious housemade ravioli with spinach and ricotta, all of them executed with a light touch. The classic main courses range from delicate stuffed squid or hearty *buridda* stew made with air-dried cod, to whole roasted fish or irresistible mixed small fry. If fish isn't your thing, there's usually classic Ligurian rabbit, stewed with pine nuts, olives and herbs. The house desserts are familiar—comfort food served with panache—and include fruit tarts, puddings and tiramisu. The wine list is long on regional offerings, but the house wines are very good, and you can get them by the carafe.

CELLE LIGURE

I F YOU HAPPEN TO BE DRIVING THROUGH ON THE VIA AURELIA, STOP BY **PESCHERIA NELLO** (Via Ghiglino 9, Tel: 019 990014, open 8am to 1pm and 4:30pm to 6pm, closed afternoons on Sunday, Monday and Thursday). Not far from this small resort town's main street, which leads to the seafront and Piazza Sisto IV, about 250 yards from the train station, Nello is a highly respected fish shop run by a former fisherman and his family, and makes excellent salted anchovies—*acciughe in barattolo*—in the old-fashioned way (whole, gutted but not skinned or de-finned), with local, fresh fish. There are many upscale fish restaurants in Celle Ligure, most of them designed to please tourists and vacationing Turinese or Milanese. Take your pick. The local open market is held on Friday.

QUILIANO

T HERE'S ONLY ONE REASON TO DRIVE INLAND FROM SAVONA OR VADO LIGURE (SITE OF AN electrical power generating facility, whose smokestacks are visible from miles around) and that's the wine. In Roman times the village was named Aquilianum, and while there's no proof that winegrowing has continued since the days of the Caesars, Quiliano does have a handful of very old vineyards. In the Middle Ages, the Marchesi del Carretto made white wine here, as a document from the 1200s attests. Buzzetto, a light-bodied white made with Lumassina grapes, is what the local wine is called, and it can be very pleasant, though rarely remarkable. The most interesting winemaker in the area, **Innocenzo Turco** (Via Bertone 7A, Quiliano (SV), Tel: 0198 87120), is best known for his Colline Savonesi Granaccia, the best of which comes from the Vignetto dei Cappuccini vineyard. The grape variety is Alicante, and was brought to Liguria centuries ago by Spanish occupiers; this powerful, ruby red wine, which reaches 13.5 to 14 percent alcohol, is pleasantly dry, with lots of red fruit, berries, even cherries in the nose, with a spicy, peppery taste that lingers on the tongue and palate. It's a might too close to California to be Ligurian.

SASSELLO

*J*NLAND ABOUT THIRTEEN MILES AS THE SEAGULL FLIES FROM SEASIDE COGOLETO (HOME OF historic pastry shop **Antica Pasticceria Lino Rossi**, Via Colombo 58, Tel: 010 918 3483), or Varazze and Albissola, Sassello is a characterful village typical of the *entroterra savonese*, a cross between Liguria and Piedmont, which is only a few miles further north. It is famed for its *amaretti*. In the nineteenth century, Sassello was a fashionable mountain resort, surrounded by chestnut forests, near the Monte Beigua, and that's when the main *amaretti* factories got going. Nowadays Monte Beigua is a regional nature preserve, and Sassello is a sleepy but charming place, with a nice church, and great food, including two places to eat, a century-old butcher shop, and an old flour mill powered by water. The easiest way to get to Sassello is to start at the Albissola Superiore train station and drive north on SP334, Strada Provinciale del Sassello, passing through Stella.

Upscale and ambitious, with a foot in both Piedmont and Liguria, **Pian del Sole** (Via Pianferioso 23, Tel: 019 724255, www.hotel-piandelsole.com, closed Monday in winter, moderate) is Sassello's comfortable, spacious gourmet restaurant-hotel, about a hundred yards from the center of town on the road to Acqui. It's owned and operated by passionate chef Ivano Ravera and his wife Carla Porta. Ivano and his assistants make everything from the three types of delicious bread to the pasta—ravioli stuffed with borage and dressed with wild herbs and olive oil, or with delicate wild asparagus, pappardelle with a rich, gamy pheasant-based sauce, or chestnut-flour *gnocchetti* sauced with melted Castelmagno cheese and crispy sautéed onions—and even do the smoking of fish and game—salmon, duck, pheasant—in the restaurant's kitchen, using juniper berries collected locally. In fall, there are local wild mushrooms cooked in many ways and which pop up in many dishes, from beef stews to pasta sauces. Chestnuts go into luscious desserts such as Monte Bianco or *budino di castagne*—both Piedmontese.

Trattoria Vittoria (Via G. Badano 8, Tel: 019 724138, closed Saturday and 25 days in January, inexpensive to moderate) has been around since the 1930s, a Sassello institution, on the highway near the old flour mill, and run for the last decade or so by Anna and Giuliana. Simplicity is everything, from the entrance—you step through the kitchen into the big dining room that wraps around a sturdy column—to the simple, housemade pasta—classic ricotta-and-spinach ravioli *alla genovese* with mushroom or meat sauce, gnocchi with pesto, tagliatelle with mushroom sauce. Also good and homey are the stuffed vegetables, roast veal or pork, and classic Ligurian rabbit with olives, pine nuts and potatoes. For dessert, *crostata* or crème caramel. The house wines are fine, but there's a good choice of bottles, too, from Ligurian wineries.

Founded in the early 1900s and still in the same family, **Macelleria-Salumeria Giacobbe** (Piazza Giacomo Rolla 7, Tel: 019 724118, closed afternoons on Sunday, Monday and Thursday) is in the center of town, at the crossroads of the main provincial highways. In addition to selling top-quality fresh meat of all kinds, which they raise and dry-hang themselves, they also make delicious boiled ham and pancetta coated with wild herbs, and an unusual, rich and exquisite *paté di lardo*, from their own salted lard. **Il Mulino di Sassello** (Via G. Badano 31, Tel: 019 724021, closed afternoons on Sunday and Thursday), a centuries-old watermill on the main provincial highway near the center of town, is still used for grinding flour, and supplies local restaurants, bakeries and residents. The equipment includes granite millstones driven by the water from a mossy mill race. The Assandri family of millers are into their fifth generation, and are proud to show visitors around, and demonstrate how flour is milled. Il Mulino also sells farm produce from local growers, including delicious apples from an orchard in nearby Piedmont, dry beans and other types of flour (chestnut, chickpea), plus olive oil and wine.

Sassello's biggest and best-known maker of *amaretti* is **Amaretti Virginia** (Località Prapiccin 6, Stada Provinciale per Acqui,

Tel: 019 724119, www.amarettivirginia.com, open 8am to 1pm and 2pm to 4pm weekdays, from 10am weekends), which is two miles out of town on the way to Acqui, and has been in constant operation since 1860. Visitors are welcome. Cookie lovers won't want to miss the experience for the scent alone.

Amaretti Giacobbe (Località Pian Ferioso 62, Strada Provinciale del Sassello, Tel: 019 724860, www.sassello.com) was founded in 1955 by local bakers Antonio and Gina Giacobbe, and was taken over by Gina's son and granddaughter in 1991, and is still family-run. Its classic, tender *amaretti*, made with bitter and sweet almonds, egg whites and sugar, are still the best, but you can also try more recent types made with natural flavors (apricot, chocolate, cherry, chestnut, citrus fruits, hazelnut, coffee

or rum). The Giacobbe's factory isn't open to the public; buy the *amaretti* at two *caffè* and a gourmet foods shop on Sassello's main square, Piazza Rolla. Named after Gina Giacobbe and owned by the family, **Bar Gina** (corner Via G. Badano/Piazza Rolla, Tel: 019 724280, closed Thursday), has all the *amaretti*, wrapped in the original style of wrapper that shows a little girl with the name "Giacobbe"; another village *caffè* (serving snacks), also on the square, **Bar-Tavola Calda Levey** (Piazza Rolla 2, Tel: 019 724057), sells the *amaretti* but in different wrapping; ditto the fine specialty foods and dry or pickled mushroom shop **Nonsolofunghi** (Piazza Rolla 11, Tel: 019 723 4277, winter hours vary widely) run by Alessandra Olivieri.

Mushrooms abound around Sassello, and the village's other fine mushroom specialist, **L'Artigiana del Fungo**, is a wholesaler who doesn't sell direct to the public (Tel: 019 720245 for info), but rather through yet another *caffè* on the main square, **Bar Jole** (Piazza Giacomo Rolla 9, Tel: 019 724136); ask the barman, Franco, about mushrooms or which *amaretti* he prefers and you'll learn a lot (he sells Amaretti Virginia).

SAVONA

A PORT CITY OF ABOUT 62,000 INHABITANTS, DUE WEST OF GENOA, HEMMED BY mountains and fronted by the sea, Savona has character. Like La Spezia, it's not the most scenic of Riviera cities, and its checkered past is writ large in the buildings and layout of town. Nonetheless, Savona boasts wonderful food, including homegrown *amaretti*, *chinotti* (candied bitter citrus), coffee and *farinata di grano* made with wheat flour; astonishingly helpful and friendly citizens; and a degree of authenticity not always found in more picturesque places. Currently in the throes of gentrification, Savona's historic downtown is experiencing a renaissance. Driving it in part are funds generated from hosting the giant Costa cruise ships that somehow manage to enter the small harbor.

Cycles of destruction and reconstruction are what this city is all about, starting with Savona's disastrous backing of the Carthagenians against ancient Rome. Still standing, near the port, are three of the many medieval towers that once studded the cityscape; others were topped; look carefully and you can see parts of them jutting from facades. Ghibelline Savona was Guelf Genoa's greatest Riviera rival, which is why Genoa attacked and subjegated it in 1153, 1170, 1202, 1227, 1241, 1255, 1317, 1332, 1397 and 1440. Savona guessed wrong again in 1527 and cut a deal with the French against its nemesis. The Genoese, led by Admiral Andrea Doria, responded in 1528 by filling Savona's harbor, dismantling its castle and slaughtering most of its people. Savona recovered in time to be targeted in the early 1940s by Nazis and Fascists — it was a Resistenza stronghold — and simultaneously damaged by RAF and USAF bombers. It was then rebuilt hastily by real estate speculators. Miraculously, the small port and surrounding alleyways are magical, and the tree-lined, nineteenth-century avenues behind them, such as Corso Italia, are handsome. The tourist information office is at Corso Italia 157R, Tel: 019 840 2321, www.inforiviera.it.

The weekly outdoor market is held on Monday. Savona's covered market faces the medieval towers and port, and is open daily from 7am to 1:20pm, and, additionally, on Friday and Saturday afternoons from 4:30pm to 7:30pm. On the second floor, you'll find not only the usual fruit-and-vegetable stands, but also a horse-meat butcher who sells donkey-meat jerky and donkey or horse meat salami; a dry goods and salt cod stand (**Da Gianni**); and a refreshment stand serving good locally roasted Minuto Caffè (**Minuto**'s coffee factory is on the outskirts of Savona, Via Nazionale Piemonte 3, Tel: 019 853540, www.minutocaffe.it). You can buy various good Arabica blends direct; take Corso Agostino Ricci along the western riverbank and follow your nose. Downstairs, on the market's ground floor, are the fish stands. Among them, **Grigiomar** (Mercato Ittico, Via P. Giuria 5-2, Tel: 019 821149, open 6am to 1pm daily except Monday) salts its own fresh, local anchovies, which are exceptional. When you step into the fish market from the street, Grigiomar is directly ahead, at the back.

RESTAURANTS AND *PANISSA* FRY SHOP

Bacco Osteria con Cucina

BEARDED AND ROTUND LIKE HIS HERO, BACCHUS, THE OWNER OF THIS LIVELY *OSTERIA* NEAR THE port, in Savona's medieval alleys, is Francesco Doberti, one of the city's more colorful characters. The long, narrow dining room is packed with small, stone-topped tables, where a mixed bag of locals and out-of-towners sit cheek-by-jowl under ship and airplane models dangling from the ceiling. Every inch of wall space is covered by a photo or painting, or a shelf with bottles and jars on it. Raucous and jocular, Doberti moves with surprising agility through the kitsch, delivering marinated or stuffed-and-fried anchovies, minestrone or gnocchi with pesto, tripe soup, codfish *buridda*, stuffed squid, breaded and fried brain, and a dozen other earthy, authentic Ligurian specialties. The desserts are all housemade, simple and tasty. The wine list includes many local producers of Lumassina and Vermentino, plus Pigato from a bit further afield, and the racier red wines being made these days on the Riviera di Ponente.

VIA QUARDA SUPERIORE 17/19R ✦ TEL: 019 8335350, WWW. OSTERIABACCO.IT. CLOSED SUNDAY. MODERATE *to* EXPENSIVE

Casa della Panizza

THE ONLY SURE WAY TO FIND THIS HOLE IN THE WALL, OUT OF WHICH COME DELICIOUS WRAPPERS full of freshly fried chickpea *panissa*, is to ask or follow a local. It's on an armspan-wide alleyway in the heart of Savona's medieval section; there's no number on the building or doorway. But, if you show up around lunch or dinner time, you'll see a line of Savonesi of every imaginable description. Join it and step into a grotto of good smells, where a lone woman of indeterminate age slices lumps of golden chickpea polenta into slivers that, when fried in vats of bubbling oil, look like the old-fashioned fries that come with fish and chips. Equipped with a six-inch wooden skewer, you eat them piping hot, out of a thick, yellowish rough paper cone, or a white *panino* sandwich. There's nothing simpler or more divine.

VICO DEI CREMA 4R ✦ NO TELEPHONE
OPEN MONDAY *through* SATURDAY 8AM *to* 2PM
and 3:30PM *to* 8PM, CLOSED SUNDAY

Osteria Cu de Beu

AT THE PORT'S WESTERN END, FRONTED BY FISHING BOATS AND YACHTS, THIS *OSTERIA*-HANGOUT RUN by Carlo Doberti, son of Bacco (see above), has three long marble-topped tables outside. In fine weather, perfect strangers become companions. In the echoing dining room, with black-and-white floors and bentwood chairs, Pilsner Urquell flows on tap. The *osteria* is often open 24/7. Imagine a sports bar and sailor's tavern back home, then add in the stuffed vegetables, fried or marinated anchovies, ravioli with meat sauce, *picagge* with pesto, squid in its own ink with tender peas, or, from the *entroterra*, a rich veal stew with potatoes and porcini. You might even find snails, with garlicky, herby sauce. The desserts are simple: tarts with pine nuts and pastry cream, or lemon, and *latte dolce*—custard. The wine list features local favorites, including Buzzetto di Quiliano.

CALATA SBARBARO 34 ✦ TEL: 019 821091
OPEN 7AM *to* 4PM *and* 6PM *to* 3AM DAILY EXCEPT SUNDAY,
24/7 IN HIGH SEASON ✦ INEXPENSIVE *to* MODERATE

Vino e Farinata—Osteria con Cucina

ON THE MAIN MEDIEVAL ALLEYWAY FROM SAVONA'S NINETEENTH-CENTURY VIA PALEOCAPA TO THE PORT, you come upon a small shopfront through whose bay window you glimpse a giant, roaring, wood-burning oven, flanked by the establishment's owner, Giorgio Del Grande, who alternately tosses in bundles of wood, or shoves pans and trays around with a long paddle. Inside, two lines of locals await from late morning onwards, one for the take-out *farinata*—which comes in the usual chickpea variety or the only-in-Savona wheat variety. The other line is for a table, because there's no telephone, and no email, and the only way to reserve here is to show up in person in the morning and stake your claim with Angelina or Bruna, Giorgio's sisters. Beyond this purgatorial entrance is a long, narrow dining room with simple wooden tables. Even further inside the vaulted cavern are two more dining rooms, these instead with nicely dressed tables. The food is simple: start with the delicious, thoroughly cooked, amazingly thin yet lusciously unctuous *farinata* (the wheat type is pale, almost white, and has the texture and flavor of old-fashioned fried bread). Also baked in the wood-burner, the stuffed sardines or anchovies (depending on that day's catch) are like tall finger-sandwiches with a *parmigiano*-bread-crumb-and-egg filling that's tinted green by parsley. The marinated anchovies are refreshingly lemony and sprinkled with marjoram or oregano. There's also *cima alla genovese*, pasta *con pesto*, *buridda*, fresh fish grilled or fried, and simple desserts like *crostata* or tiramisu, all housemade. The wines aren't particularly distinguished, but the house rosé goes with anything.

VIA PIA 15 ✦ NO TELEPHONE ✦ CLOSED SUNDAY *and* MONDAY

INEXPENSIVE *to* MODERATE

AMARETTI, CHINOTTI, COFFEE, GOURMET FOODS, ICE CREAM, OLIVE OIL, PASTRIES, WINE

Amaretti Astengo

FOUNDED IN 1878 AND INTO ITS FIFTH GENERATION, THE ASTENGO FAMILY PASTRY SHOP IS SAVONA'S oldest to continuously make excellent *amaretti di Savona*, which marry sweet and bitter almonds to sugar and egg-white—no flour. *Astengo amaretti* are totally natural, with no preservatives, and come individually wrapped in air-tight plastic wrappers. They're sweeter and crispier than some others in town, and are "the best" for those who favor those qualities. Handsome, the small corner pastry shop hasn't changed much in the last 130 years. Beside the *amaretti*, many other classic Riviera pastries, cakes (the *sacripantina* is exquisite), chocolates and cookies are sold, and are very good indeed.

CORNER OF VIA MONTENOTTE (#16R) *and* VIA ASTENGO

TEL: 019 820570 ✦ CLOSED MONDAY

Bar Besio

FOUNDED IN 1860 BUT REMODELED SINCE, THIS COFFEE AND PASTRY SHOP, DRY GOODS AND specialty food bou-tique is under the arcades of Savona's main square, facing the monument to the dead of the world wars. Unaffili-ated with the Besio *amaretti* factory, its main draw is not the coffee, pastries or even the atmosphere of yester-year, but rather the jars of candied *chinotti* and *chinotti*

jams (and other *chinotti* products) made by other members of the Besio family in a candying factory on the other side of town (Via Sant'Ambrogio, Tel: 019 860507, www.besio1860.it, by appointment only). *Chinotti* are green, the size of a quail's egg, and taste like the bitter oranges traditionally used by the English to make bitter orange marmalade. There appears to be more than one type of citrus identified as *chinotto*, however. *Citrus myrtifolia,* alias myrtle-leaved citrus fruit, is one. As suggested by the other, more widely accepted scientific name, however, *Citrus sinensis var. plumosus,* the plant originates in China, and was brought to the Savona area in the 1500s. Savona and nearby towns have been growing these unusual citrus fruits since the 1800s, and there are a dozen specialized farmers of them, but Besio is the only *chinotti* candier left in Savona. The taste? Bittersweet, zesty — delicious.

PIAZZA MAMELI 21R ✦ TEL: 019 827443 ✦ OPEN 7AM *to* 8PM DAILY

La Bottega del Caffè F.lli Pasqualini

THIS SMALL COFFEE SHOP ON ONE OF DOWNTOWN SAVONA'S MAIN, PORTICOED STREETS SELLS the excellent coffees made in Villanova d'Albenga by roaster Torrefazione F.lli Pasqualini. Knock back a strong, dark espresso at the bar, or buy ground coffee or beans to go.

VIA PALEOCAPA 149 ✦ TEL: 019 833 6383 ✦ CLOSED SUNDAY

Caffè Due Merli

FIVE ALLEYWAYS MEET IN THE HEART OF OLD SAVONA TO FORM THE TINY SQUARE WHERE CAFFÈ DUE Merli has its outdoor tables. The interior is the size of a broom closet, but luckily winters are mild in Savona, so you can sit outside, dressed warmly, any time of year, and admire the medieval *palazzi* arrayed on all sides, and the wonderful sculpted high-relief Mary Magdalene on a wall kitty corner. The coffee is a special mix of Arabicas made for Caffè Due Merli by La Genovese, a fine regional roaster based in Albenga, and it's potent but good. Each cup comes with a chocolate-covered hazelnut and a tiny glass of sparkling mineral water.

PIAZZA MADDALENA 1R ✦ TEL: 019 833 5010
OPEN DAILY 7:30AM *to* 9PM EXCEPT SUNDAY

Casa del Caffè — Caffè 3 Moretti

JUST WEST OF CORSO ITALIA IN THE NINETEENTH-CEN-TURY PART OF TOWN, NOT FAR FROM THE CATHEDRAL, this coffee roasting house opened in 1943, when political correctness wasn't an issue, so its owners may be forgiven for the name and logo, which remind those old enough to remember of Little Black Sambo. Affable, long-time coffee roaster Vincenzo Cosentino took over in 1999 and continues to do the buying and roasting of top-quality beans. Of his many coffee blends, the Arabica Super Dolce is remarkably mild and stands out for its excellence. 3 Moretti coffee is found in a handful of *caffè* in the Savonese, and is brewed right next door at Malaga Café, an otherwise undistinguished establishment. Be warned, though, that while Malaga's coffee is good, it isn't made with Cosentino's best, mildest blend, but rather a dark-roasted, potent blend which locals prefer. Casa del Caffè also sells candies, chocolates and cookies.

PIAZZA GIULIO II 14R ✦ TEL: 019 821993

CLOSED THURSDAY AFTERNOON

Oleificio Polla Nicolò

YOU MIGHT EASILY MISTAKE THIS OLIVE OIL SHOP FOR A FASHION BOUTIQUE, SO SPARKLING AND attractive are its displays. Luckily, the oils made since 1875 by the Polla family, now into its fourth generation at the helm, in the inland village of Toirano (behind Loano), are not just nicely packaged, they're also very good. The mill isn't normally open to the public, so this sales room is handy, and there's another in Loano, where the company's business offices are located. Polla grows most of its own olives near Toirano, but also buys in from the Imperia area. Taggiasca is the only variety used. The millstones are granite, but everything else is ultra modern, which isn't a bad thing. The DOP oils and special selections are fruity, flowery, low in acid and uniformly well made. Also sold are delicious condiments, olive patés, brined olives, bottled porcini, tomato sauce, artichoke spread, arugula pesto and classic basil pesto, honeys and more.

PIAZZA GIULIO II 16R ✦ TEL: 019 848 5454

WWW.OLIOPOLLA.IT

CLOSED TUESDAY AFTERNOON *and* THURSDAY

Pasticceria Besio

THE FOURTH AND FIFTH GENERATIONS OF THE BESIO-TORELLO FAMILY OWN AND RUN THIS HISTORIC cookie and *amaretti* factory, founded in 1902, and still in the same back-court workshop in the center of Savona's nineteenth-century district. Besio's award-winning *amaretti* are particularly excellent and flavorful, in part because they're lighter and more cakey than many, but also and primarily because, compared to the competition, they contain more sweet and bitter almonds — a

natural, fresh ingredients to turn out dozens of delicious flavors of seasonal fruit or cream-based ice creams. The pistachio and hazelnut are to die for—rich and creamy without being fatty or too sweet—and the fruit is true to the essence of the fresh, ripe peaches, apricots, strawberries and other local or exotic fruits used. Locals hang out at the milk bar, slugging down milkshakes made with Superfrutto ice creams, but there's nowhere to sit, and the place is often check-by-jowl with customers, so order a cone and walk with it toward the medieval alleyways of town, which are more attractive than Piazza Diaz.

PIAZZA DIAZ 17R ✦ TEL: 019 800567 ✦ OPEN 8:30AM *to* 1AM DAILY

STELLA

. . . .

NORTH OF ALBISSOLA SUPERIORE AND SOUTH OF SASSELLO IS STELLA, A VILLAGE near the Monte Beigua regional park, where Sardinian shepherd Pasquale Usai grazes his herd of 600 ewes, whose milk goes into delicious, award-winning cheeses Pasquale and his wife make and sell at their farm in Corona (**Usai Pasquale Coltivatore Diretto**, San Bernardo (SV), Località Corona 177, Tel: 019 703137). Affable, retiring Pasquale moved to Liguria when young, and has been making his Ligurian-Sardinian cheeses here since the 1970s. The fresh or aged *pecorino* is naturally perfumed by the wild herbs and grasses the ewes eat, and has a firm, perfectly porous consistency, like excellent Sardinian or Tuscan *pecorino*. Pasquale also makes luscious ricotta, and fresh *formagetta* cheeses, and sells direct from the farmstead. The biggest challenge is finding the place. From Albissola Superiore take the two-lane SP334 highway Strada Provinciale del Sassello north through Stella to SP32 and then west, heading toward San Bernardo. Once you get to the hamlet of Corona, look for the sign or ask for *il pastore* (the shepherd); if you reach San Bernardo you've gone too far. Usai's cheeses can be bought in many better cheese shops on the Riviera, including Parlacomemangi.com/Bottega dei Sestrieri in Rapallo.

Top Winemakers Riviera di Ponente, From Savona to France

....

Massimo Alessandri

FRAZIONE COSTA PARROCCHIA, RANZO (IM) ✦ TEL: 0182 53458

WWW.MASSIMOALESSANDRI.IT

Anfossi

VIA PACCINI 39, BASTIA D'ALBENGA (SV) ✦ TEL: 0182 20024

Aschero Laura

PIAZZA VITTORIO EMANUELE 7, PONTEDASSIO (IM)

TEL: 0183 293515

Bruna

FRAZIONE BORGO, VIA UMBERTO I 81, RANZO (IM)

TEL: 0183 318082, 0183 318928

Cascina delle Terre Rosse

VIA MANIE 3, FINALE LIGURE (SV) ✦ TEL: 019 698782

Colle dei Bardellini

LOCALITÀ BARDELLINI, VIA FONTANAROSA 12, IMPERIA (IM)

TEL: 0183 291370 ✦ WWW.COLLEDEIBARDELLINI.COM

Durin

VIA ROMA 202, ORTOVERO (SV) ✦ TEL: 0182 547007

Fèipu dei Massaretti

REGIONE MASSARETTI 7, BASTIA D'ALBENGA (SV)

TEL: 0182 20131

Foresti

VIA BRAIE 223, LOCALITÀ CAMPOROSSO MARE (IM)

TEL: 0184 292377 ✦ WWW.FORESTIWINE.IT

Le Petraie

VIA MAZZINI 9, PIEVE DI TECO (IM) ✦ TEL: 0183 36161

Lupi

VIA MAZZINI 9, PIEVE DI TECO (IM) ✦ TEL: 0183 36161

WWW.VINILUPI.IT

Ranise Agroalimentari

VIA NAZIONALE 30, IMPERIA ✦ TEL: 0183 767966

WWW.RANISE.IT

Azienda Agricola La Rocca di San Nicolao

VIA DANTE 10, FRAZIONE GAZZELLI, CHIUSANICO (IM)

TEL: 0183 52304 ✦ WWW.ROCCASANNICOLAO.IT

Le Rocche del Gatto

REGIONE RUATO 2, SALEA D'ALBENGA (SV) ✦ TEL: 0182 21175

WWW.LEROCCHEDELGATTO.IT

Azienda Agricola San Dalmazio

LOCALITÀ ARVEGLIO, ALBENGA (SV) ✦ TEL: 019 884820

Azienda Agricola Sommariva

REGIONE SIGNOLA 2, ALBENGA (SV) ✦ TEL: 0182 559222

Tenuta Giuncheo

LOCALITÀ GIUNCHEO, CAMPOROSSO (IM) ✦ TEL: 0184 288639

WWW.TENUTAGIUNCHEO.IT

Terre Bianche

LOCALITÀ ARCAGNA, DOLCEACQUA (IM) ✦ TEL: 0184 31426

WWW.TERREBIANCHE.COM

Turco Innocenzo

VIA BERTONE 7A, QUILIANO (SV) ✦ TEL: 0198 87120

La Vecchia Cantina

VIA CORTA 3, SALEA D'ALBENGA (SV) ✦ TEL: 0182 559881

Vio Claudio

FRAZIONE CROSA 16, VENDONE (SV) ✦ TEL: 0182 76338

Top Olive Oil Makers
of the Western Riviera di Ponente

· ·

Infosso A e C

VIA IV NOVEMBRE 96, CHIUSAVECCHIA (IM) ✦ TEL: 0183 52418

Azienda Agricola Giuseppe Cotta

VIA AMEGLIO 5, FRAZIONE PANTASINA, VASIA (IM)

TEL: 0183 282145 ✦ WWW.AGRICOTTA.COM

Azienda Agricola Valle Ostilia

VIA CASCIONE 20, VILLA FARALDI (IM) ✦ TEL: 347 882 6230

Baglietto e Secco

VIA ROMA 137, VILLANOVA D'ALBENGA (SV) ✦ TEL: 0182 582838

La Baita

FRAZIONE GAZZO, BORGHETTO D'ARROSCIA (IM)

TEL: 0183 31324 ✦ LABAITAGAZZO@KATAMAIL.COM

Benza Frantoiano

VIA DOLCEDO 180, IMPERIA ✦ TEL: 0183 280132

WWW.OLIOBENZA.IT

Cooperativa Olivicola di Arnasco

PIAZZA IV NOVEMBRE 8, ARNASCO (SV) ✦ TEL: 0182 761178
WWW.COOPOLIVICOLARNASCO.IT

Dino Abbo

VIA ROMA 11, LUCINASCO (IM) ✦ TEL: 0183 52411
WWW.DINOABBO.IT

Frantoio di Sant'Agata d'Oneglia

VIA SANT'AGATA/STRADA DEI FRANCESI 48,
SANT'AGATA D'ONEGLIA (IM) ✦ TEL: 0183 293472
WWW.FRANTOIOSANTAGATA.COM

Olio Roi

VIA ARGENTINA 1, BADALUCCO (IM) ✦ TEL: 0184 408004
WWW.OLIOROI.COM

Ranise Agroalimentari

VIA NAZIONALE 30, IMPERIA ✦ TEL: 0183 767966
WWW.RANISE.IT

CHAPTER 11

·····

Finale Ligure – Il Finalese

*Province: Savona. Includes: Calice Ligure,
Calizzano, Finale Ligure, Loano, Noli, Varigotti*

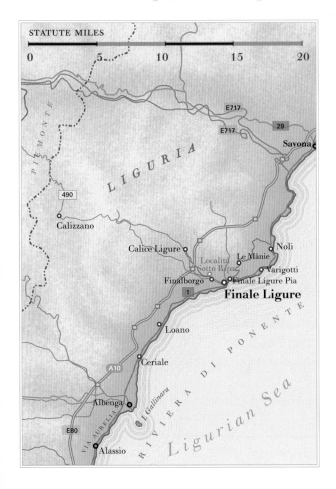

*T*HE ATTRACTIVE AREA FRAMING FINALE LIGURE AND FINALBORGO GOES BY THE NAME FINALESE, and includes a handful of charming seaside resorts, many perched villages, and a vast, sparsely populated hinterland terraced with olive and chestnut groves. One of the Riviera's main chestnut-producing villages, Calizzano, is here.

CALICE LIGURE

*O*NLY A FEW MILES INLAND FROM FINALE AND THE SEA, CALICE LIGURE FEELS REMOTE AND mountainous. It's not even halfway to Calizzano, the isolated mushroom capital of the Riviera di Ponente, on the old highway put through a century ago to give access to the sea to the Piedmontese. There are two reasons to detour here. First, the fabulous, handmade, old-fashioned ice creams of **Pastorino** (Via Vittorio Veneto 31, Tel: 019 65472, off-season hours vary widely). It's on the main road, where it does a dog leg. *Gelato*-lovers who recognize the real deal and not a pumped-up imitation will drive here from far and wide.

Second, Calice has two very good restaurants, one of them somewhat fussy and serving *nouvelle* versions of old recipes (Al Tre); the other likeable and about a hundred years old, and somewhat misleadingly called **Locanda Piemontese** (Piazza Massa 4, Tel: 019 65463, closed Monday dinner and Tuesday, always open in July and August, inexpensive to moderate). It's not really a *locanda* (a hotel or coaching inn), though it feels and looks like one, and is near the highway that brought prosperity to town. The food is more Ligurian than Piedmontese, witness the classic stuffed vegetables and *cappon magro*, or the housemade Genoese ravioli filled with meat and sauced with hearty meat-and-tomato sauce. You can get a nice mixed fry of fingerlings, or thick, luscious *buridda* fish stew, but truth be told, fish seems out of place, and the rabbit with pine nuts and olives is more satisfying. If you're visiting in fall—the best time for these parts—you might luck out and find fresh porcini or braised wild boar on the menu. The beef comes from Argentina, alas, and can be skipped. Try the housemade ice cream, or the *gobeletti* filled with apricot jam and served with creamy, warm *zabaione*. The wine list includes plenty of good Ligurian bottlings.

CALIZZANO

SURROUNDED BY CHESTNUT FORESTS ON THE SLOPES OF THE ALTA VAL BORMIDA INLAND FROM Finale Ligure half an hour by car, Calizzano is one of Liguria's prime centers for mushrooms (porcini, chanterelles and a local variety called *cicalotti* or *cicotti*), plus chestnuts and wild or cultivated berries (currants, elderberries, raspberries, bilberries and blueberries). Though far flung, it's worth the scenic drive up river valleys and terraced hillsides past Calice Ligure to get here, particularly in the late summer or fall, when fresh mushrooms, berries and chestnuts are at their best. The rest of the year, such produce is sold dried or pickled.

The Calizzano mushroom fair, on the streets of the village, dubbed Funghi in Piazza, is held the second Sunday in October. The chestnut fair, during which fresh, roasted and dried chestnuts, and chestnut flour, are sold, is called Festa d'Autunno, and is held the following Sunday. At both, autumnal food is served, and most shops are open nonstop, from early morning to late at night. There are many places to stock up on the local bounty. **Azienda Agricola Jole Buscaglia** (Via Matteotti 59/2, Tel: 338 176 2650, open Saturdays only, 7:30am to 8pm or by appointment) is owned and operated by Jole Buscaglia, whose primary business is growing vegetables, including potatoes, tomatoes, zucchini, chard and bell peppers, plus cranberry beans, cucumbers and pumpkins. Buscaglia uses only small quantities of organic pesticide, and prides himself on being "almost organic." Many of the vegetables he grows, as well as the wild mushrooms and chamomile he gathers, are available fresh or dried. Seasonally he grows strawberries, raspberries and bilberries. Though most of his clients are wholesalers, he does sell retail, usually by appointment.

As the name suggests, **La Bottega dei Funghi** (Via G.B. Pera 4, Tel: 019 79642, from June through December open Monday to Saturday, closed Sunday, open daily from January to May) sells mushrooms in every imaginable form. On the same street, **Perrone Tabò Maria** (Via G.B. Pera 51, Tel: 019 79637, open Monday to Saturday, closed Sunday; open daily in October) has mushrooms, conserves and local specialties. Upscale and celebrated among roving Italian gastronomes is **Santamaria & C.** (Via Sforza Gallo 12 and Via Trento e Trieste 1, Tel: 019 790 6065, www.santamaria-sv.it, from January to mid September open

Wednesday to Monday, closed Tuesdays; daily from mid September to Christmas), in the middle of Calizzano's medieval grid. White-collar employees until the late 1990s, owners Federico and Silvia Santamaria reinvented themselves as mushroom and berry hunter-gatherers. They sell their finds fresh, dried, preserved in olive oil, or in the form of jams, jellies and gelatins, including an unusual apple-and-rosemary savory jelly ideal for accompanying cheese. They also buy in fresh fruit of all kinds and transform it into jam and preserves, some made with little or no added sugar. Also sold are local, handmade salamis and cheeses.

Still in town, on the highway running around the medieval section north toward Murialdo, is **Bar-Gelateria Pinotto** (Piazza San Rocco 16, Tel: 019 79533, closed Wednesdays in winter, open daily in summer), an ice creamery owned by Giuseppe Riolfo and his family, famous for its chestnut ice cream, made from scratch and studded with luscious, chunky bits of chestnut. Ice creams are only made here from Palm Sunday (a week before Easter) to the end of October. Other delicious seasonal ice cream flavors, all from scratch, include wild berries and other local fruits.

FINALE LIGURE AND FINALBORGO

L IKE SEVERAL OTHER TOWNS OF ANCIENT ORIGIN, FINALE IS DIVIDED INTO SEVERAL seaside districts backed in their hinterland by a medieval fortified safe-haven. The center of Finale Ligure Marina is long, narrow and charming, spreading along the shoreline between two small rivers, the Porra (near the train station) and Sciusa. East of the Sciusa is Finale Ligure Pia. Follow the east bank inland half a mile and you'll find **Frantoio Artigianale Magnone** (Via Calvisio 156, Tel: 019 602190), which makes its own very good extra virgin olive oils and works as a miller for local growers; if you can't make it to the mill, pick up Magnone oils and olives at their boutique in Via Molinetti, between Via del Santuario and Piazza Toscana.

Up a corkscrew road to the northeast of Finale Ligure Pia, on Strada Panoramica delle Mànie, is Le Mànie, where **Cascina delle Terre Rosse** (Via Mànie 3, Tel: 019 698782), a top winery, makes excellent Riviera Ligure di Ponente DOC Vermentino, and a big, flowery Pigato called Apogeo (plus "Solitario," a blend of Barbera, Granaccia and Rossese). It also sells extra virgin olive oils and olives brined or packed in olive oil.

The Benedictine church and abbey near the mouth of the river at Finale Ligure Pia, inland a few hundred yards from the coast, is home to **Azienda Agricola Apiario Benedettino** (Via al Santuario 59, Tel: 019 601730). Led by head beekeeper Don Giovanni, the Benedictine brothers here make about a dozen types of excellent, cold-extracted, non-pasteurized *miele* and *melata*, and, in their two boutiques, sell scores of related products from co-ops and other religious orders, plus books on bees. They also make a dozen types of grappa and citrus or herbal liqueurs, on site, at Distilleria la Baita, plus cosmetics and health care products, elixirs and curative plant extracts. Shy but friendly Don Giovanni has been here since 1958, and, if asked, will teach you everything you ever wanted to know about the husbandry of bees and the secrets of honey. The shop is around the back of the abbey church; ring the bell, someone is always there. The upscale *erboristeria* (herbal cures boutique) flanks the church out front, and is closed on Sunday. And make sure to peek inside the splendid church and cloisters.

Though small, Finale Ligure is wealthy and well supplied. Piaggio, the motor manufacturer, is based on the western edge of town. However, most Finale restaurants cater to tourists or jet-setters. Authentic regional food is served inland, several miles away, on the road to Calizzano, at **Ca' del Moro** (Via per Melogno 34, Frazione Olle, Tel: 019 696001, closed Wednesday and February, moderate), a local, family-style hangout with an echoing dining room.

There are three very good specialty food shops in town. **Chiesa** (Via Pertica 13, Tel: 019 692516, closed afternoons on Sunday and Wednesday in winter), is on the main pedestrian road in the old part of town. Founded in 1913, and presided over since 1933

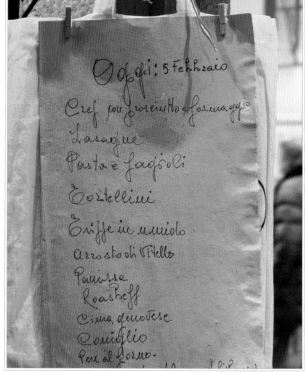

by *mater familias* Laura Chiesa, this wonderful delicatessen has everything from succulent seafood salad to gnocchi with pesto, roasts, rabbit with pine nuts and olives, and delicious puddings or pears poached in red wine, plus hams, salamis and cheeses by the score. Best of all, you can order anything in the shop and eat it for lunch at the **Chiesa** *tavola calda* restaurant around the corner, on Vico Gandolino (closed Sunday, inexpensive). Also old-fashioned and family-run, **La Familiare** (Piazza Vittorio Emanuele II 21, Tel: 019 692662, closed afternoons on Sunday, Monday and Thursday), on the main square, has excellent Ramoino olive oil and wines from Terre Rosse (and roast chickens and tasty take-out foods). On the main street running west from the square, **Terre di Mare** (Via Giuseppe Garibaldi 21, Tel: 019 692111, open daily) is an upscale dry goods boutique specializing in delicacies typical of the Mediterranean (the shop's name means "lands on the sea"). There are vegetables pickled and bottled in olive oil, extra virgin oils, anchovies, pestos and many other sauces and treats, plus *amaretti Virginia* cookies.

Across the street from Terre di Mare is historic **Caffè-Pasticceria Ferro** (Via Giuseppe Garibaldi 10, Tel: 019 692753, closed Tuesday), founded in 1872, but owned and operated since 2000 by boisterous, friendly Elena Casanova. The house specialties are divine *chifferi*, a corruption of *kipfel* (half moon in German); these tiny, crescent-shaped almond-paste pastries were invented in Vienna in 1683, to celebrate victory over the Ottoman Turks. *Chifferi* are covered with almond shavings and are to die for. Equally outstanding are the *amaretti soffiati* — puffy, ultra-light *amaretti* with orange zest and lemon juice. The coffee is excellent Pasqualini espresso. Take a table on the rear terrace, facing the magnificent cathedral. Not to be missed.

The best ice cream in town comes from **Gelateria Il Dattero** (Via Pertica 10, Tel: 348 582 3087, closed Monday and November and February), a few shopfronts west. Ice cream-maker Valter

Piazza apprenticed himself to cult *granita*/gelato masters at Bar dell'Amicizia, on the island of Lampedusa, near Sicily, and this explains his remarkable skill with Sicilian-style ices, sorbets and fruit ice creams; his frozen yogurts are outstanding, and the nut-flavored ice creams are made with the best-quality pastes (pistachios from Bronte, for example). Finale's own coffee roaster, since 1967, **Caffè Giovanacci** (Via Rossi 28, Tel: 019 692506, closed Monday), is in a handsome, vaulted shop across the street. The roasting facility is in the outskirts. The top Arabica blend is remarkably mild, and worth stocking up on.

Inland about one mile from the western end of Finale is castellated Finalborgo, a pleasant place to stroll and admire the architecture. Ice cream-lovers flock to **Bar Centrale** (Piazza Garibaldi 28, Tel: 019 691768, closed Tuesday), with tables on the stage-set main square. At friendly local hangout **Caffè del Borgo** (Via Nicotera 10, Tel: 349 159 3490, closed Wednesday), with tables on a shady side street, you can sip or buy freshly roasted Giovanacci coffee. If you missed the Benedictine Brothers in Finale Ligure Pia, buy local honeys and honey-based products of all kinds — soaps, candles, pollen, cosmetics, lotions — made by Antonino Savasta at **Apicoltura Burgum Mielizia** (Via Lancellotto 2, Tel: 019 689 8415, open weekends in winter, afternoons in summer, phone ahead). The shop is in a narrow alley between Piazza Porta Testa and the Romanesque church of Santa Caterina. Try the tree-heather honey, or *melata*, from the sap of a variety of forest and pastureland plants.

Locals favor **Trattoria Invexendu** (Piazza del Tribunale 1, Tel: 019 690475, open for lunch daily, dinner Thursday through

Saturday only, moderate), which, though redecorated in the 1990s, has been around for a century, has a sunny, glassed-in terrace on a handsome square, and a sunny yellow décor. Served are good regional dishes, including borage-stuffed ravioli and flavorful skewers of mutton (*rostelle*).

Half a mile north, following the river along Finalborgo's eastern walls, is pocketsized winery **Casanova** (Località Sotto Ripa 2, Tel: 019 690612, phone ahead), run by affable partners Giacomo Casanova and Franco Comelli, makers of award-winning Pigato, and fine Vermentino, Lumassina, Rossese and Granaccia. Look for the roadside chapel, pair of giant eucalyptus trees and, across the bridge, the trio of 150-year-old flame cypresses. Casanova's family has been in the wine trade since 1927; the winery was founded in 1983, and uses stainless steel, temperature-controlled tanks to make true-to-type wines. Total production is a mere 15,000 bottles.

The weekly open market at Finale Ligure Marina is held Thursday; at Finalborgo, Monday.

LOANO

N OT AMONG THE MOST ALLURING RIVIERA TOWNS, LOANO DOES HAVE ONE FINE OLIVE oil maker, and an excellent ice creamery, worth a stopover if you're driving through on the Via Aurelia. The weekly open market is held on Friday.

From Via Aurelia head down Via Trento e Trieste and Via Ramella to Piazza Massena, in the center of town. **Oleificio Polla Nicolò** (Via Ghilini 46, Tel: 019 668027, www.oliopolla. it, closed Thursday afternoon and Sunday), is a family-run olive oil mill based here, with an upscale sales room in Savona, and a mill inland at Toirano. The Loano shop sells the same bottled specialty foods as the showroom in Savona. Call to arrange a visit of the oil mill when it's in operation, from October to March.

On the seaside drag, in the center of Loano, is the award-winning **Gelateria Bar Gelmo** (Corso Roma 146, Tel: 019 668041). The fruit flavors are exceptional, the nut- or chocolate-based ones rich and well balanced. Equipped with a Gelmo cone, your stroll along Loano's seaside promenade will be all the more pleasant.

NOLI

....

NOLI IS AMONG THE MOST ATTRACTIVE RESORTS ON THE RIVIERA DI PONENTE, A kind of western Lerici. The setting is stunning: the rocky cape of Capo di Noli tumbles into the sea on the south end of town. Steep hills and cliff-faces back Noli, and the curving coast highway blissfully avoids the historic central area. There's no train line, either. Slinky medieval walls wrap the village, climbing the hillsides like caterpillars, and there are stone towers and hulking Romanesque churchs scattered around. On pocketsized squares, shady loggias with uneven arches add to the atmosphere.

The weekly outdoor market is held on Thursday morning; clothing and sundries are sold on Corso Italia, the seaside promenade, while most of the food stands are on Piazzale Battisti, the big parking lot north of the creek, near the bus station. The tourist office is also on the seaside promenade at Corso Italia 8, Tel: 019 749 9003, noli@inforiviera.it, www.inforiviera.it.

In addition to the usual tourist restaurants, of the classy, upscale places in town the best is **Pino** (Via Cavalieri di Malta 39, Tel: 019 749 0065, closed Tuesday lunch and Monday, expensive). It's located several hundred yards inland, on the main road between the creek and Via De Ferrari, and serves good, fresh fish and regional food, without indulging in unnecessary complication.

The most traditional food in town is found at studiously rustic, family-style **Ü Bucün du Preve** (Via Musso 16, Tel: 019 748241, closed Wednesday and January, moderate), located north of the Loggia della Repubblica, behind city hall. The pasta (*trofie* or lasagne with pesto, *taglierini* with seafood) is housemade, and the swordfish steak is sautéed with crushed anchovies and porcini — an old Riviera di Ponente recipe. There's also classic *stoccafisso* or rabbit stewed with pine nuts, herbs, olives and potatoes. The fresh-fruit or jam tarts, and other simple desserts, are also housemade. Wines range from the Ciliegiolo of the Levante, to local bottlings such as Pigato, Vermentino and Ormeasco.

Noli is famous for its fish, particularly its *cicciarelli*, a small bluefish that looks and tastes similar to an anchovy or sardine. They're often the main ingredient in local fish soup, or are flash-fried in olive oil, or pickled *allo scabecciu* in vinegar, usually with sage and rosemary. The best place to see them (or buy them bottled) is **Pescheria Cerisola Clelia** (Via Colombo 106, Tel: 019 748618, closed Thursday afternoon, Sunday morning and Monday), a fish shop on the main curving road that runs from Piazza Garibaldi to Piazza Morando and Piazza Ronco, and then north through the remaining medieval section of town. Also sold are anchovies in salt or olive oil.

The best pastries, single-serving jam tarts and cookies in Noli come from modish, French-inspired **Pasticceria La Crêpe** (Via Colombo 61, Tel: 019 748 5769, closed Wednesday, winter hours vary), which is on the same long, curving street as the fish shop. Focaccia, sandwiches and simple desserts are only part of the equation at aptly named **Nonsolopizza** (Corso Italia 26, Tel: 019 748 5195, off-season hours vary widely), which is on the seaside promenade. In fact the best things here are the ice creams and sorbets, all made from scratch, using ripe, fresh fruit and high-quality nut pastes.

VARIGOTTI

A FASHIONABLE AND HANDSOME RESORT STRUNG ALONG A STUNNING STRETCH OF uneven coast, with no train tracks to blight it, Varigotti is a few miles north of Finale Ligure or south of Noli on the scenic Via Aurelia. The weekly summertime outdoor market is held on Wednesday morning in Via degli Ulivi, the main road one up from the seaside. Unless you've reserved far ahead and plan to eat at the very expensive, international-style, Michelin-starred Muraglia-Conchiglia d'Oro, you're better off dining elsewhere.

Winemaker **Paolo Ruffino** (Via Strada Vecchia 19, Tel: 019 698522) has his vineyards and winery above Varigotti, on the pre-modern back road that loops up and over the hills to Noli. He's earning a reputation for excellent Colline Savonesi IGT wines, including an unusual blend he calls "Mataossu."

In the Pietra Grossa hills behind Finale Ligure, another Ruffino, this time **Domenico Ruffino** (Strada del Borriolo 9, Località Colle di Varigotti, Tel: 019 698044, cell 3484521161, domenicoruffino@hotmail.com) owns old olive groves at his farm, Pria Grossa. Head due north from Via Aurelia on Strada Vecchia for two blocks and turn left, driving uphill westwards. Domenico makes fine extra virgin oils from the rare olive variety Colombaia, which has an almond-like taste. Benedictine monks at Finale Ligure (or Varigotti) are thought to have perfected its cultivation over 1,000 years ago. Ruffino also brines and bottles his Colombaia olives, which are delicious.

CHAPTER 12

....

Albenga to Alassio

*Provinces: Imperia and Savona. Includes: Alassio,
Albenga, Bastia d'Albenga, Leca d'Albenga and
Salea d'Albenga, Vessalico, Villanova d'Albenga.*

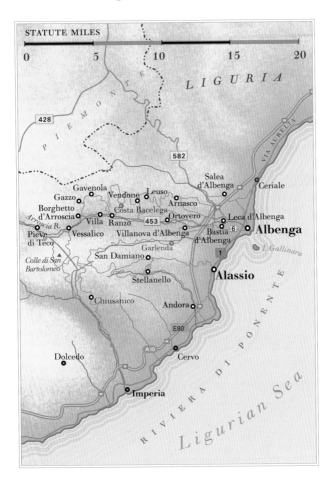

S UNNY, WITH SEVERAL WIDE RIVER VALLEYS BACKED BY ROUGH MOUNTAINS CLOAKED WITH chestnut trees, Albenga and its hinterland stretches across two provinces and has great food and wine. This is the homeland of Pigato, the only-in-Liguria white wine with a deep straw color, fruity, flowery and herby to the nose, smooth and rich on the palate. The olive oils, made primarily from Taggiasca olives, are excellent, and the heirloom garlic of Vessalico is renowned throughout the region.

"If a person wished to retire from his acquaintance, to live absolutely unknown and yet in the midst of physical enjoyments," wrote Thomas Jefferson in 1787 as he traveled on the western Riviera di Ponente, "it should be in some of the little villages of this coast, where air, water and earth concur to offer what each has most precious." Even more so than his fellow Americans, the English took Jefferson's advice. Throughout the nineteenth century they colonized this stretch of coast to such an extent that they (and smaller colonies of other foreigners, Russians in particular) outnumbered local residents until the beginning of World War One. The English had their own hotels, churches, villas, botanical gardens (such as celebrated Villa Hanbury), restaurants, even hairdressers. English understatement in dress and manners is still the rule in Alassio, a peculiar enclave.

ALASSIO

N OWHERE MORE THAN IN ALASSIO DO YOU HEAR ECHOES OF THE AREA'S "COLONIAL" past. Nowadays the bulk of visitors comes from Turin and Milan, but the style is still international, and upscale. Officially called Via XX Settembre, but known to locals as Il Budello, meaning the gut or intestine, this medieval main alleyway is hemmed by venerable buildings. However, most of central Alassio was rebuilt in the late 1800s, and is elegant, airy and green. The seaside promenade deserves particular admiration, because it's free of blight. There you'll find a handful of fashionable restaurants and *caffè*, such as **Caffè Mozart**, where beautiful people admire the view, each other and themselves.

Alassio's international character means that, while the food is good, it's less faithful to regional roots than elsewhere in Liguria. But there is one neo-*trattoria* serving local specialties, one place to taste local wines, plus several remarkable, historical pastry makers and coffee-and-tea salons. Lovers of sweets will not want to miss the *baci di Alassio*, which are not chocolate kisses in the normal sense but rather walnut-shaped sandwich cookies made with chocolate and powdered almonds, with a filling of creamy chocolate or hazelnut-and-chocolate cream, depending on who makes them. Another specialty, *pan del Marinaio* or *pan del Pescatore* (the same thing) is none other than *pandolce alla genovese* in the low, dense *all'antica* version, full of raisins and candied fruit.

The weekly outdoor market is held on Saturday morning on Via Gastaldi, near the municipal swimming pool. The tourist office is at Via Mazzini 68 (Tel: 0182 647027, www.inforiviera.it), near the train station and small public garden. Get a map from them before wandering into the alleys near the beach.

TRATTORIA

Osteria dei Matetti

STEP OUT OF THE TRAIN STATION AND TURN LEFT, HEADING EAST ON VIA DANIELE HANBURY; NEAR the gardens of Piazza Stalla you'll find this stylish neo-*trattoria*, opened less than a decade ago. Many B&W photos of kids in school uniforms hang on the walls. A blackboard lists what's on offer that day. Luckily the food isn't anything you'd get in a school cafeteria. The wood-burning oven is used for making good, thoroughly cooked *farinata* in fall and winter, and savory tarts year-round, but this isn't an old *Torte e Farinata* joint with colorful, roughneck characters. The pesto is light and delicious, and goes into the minestrone, or tops the local variety of green spinach lasagne, called *gasse*. Meat dishes are few, but the meat-and-tomato sauce that comes with the classic Genoese ravioli is very good, and the long-stewed rabbit with olives and pine nuts is excellent. Fish dishes depend on the catch; expect to find stuffed, baked anchovies or sardines, octopus stewed with tomatoes or squid filled with pine nuts, breadcrumbs, herbs and *parmigiano*. The housemade *crostata* jam tarts are delicious—buttery and crusty without being too sweet. Stick to the local wines.

VIA DANIELE HANBURY 132 ✦ TEL: 0182 646680
CLOSED MONDAY *from* SEPTEMBER *through* JUNE; IN JULY *and*
AUGUST OPEN DAILY FOR DINNER ONLY ✦ MODERATE

COFFEE, ICE CREAM, PASTRIES, WINE

La Bottega del Caffè Pasqualini

O N THE MAIN ALLEYWAY IN THE HEART OF OLD ALAS-
SIO, THIS NARROW LITTLE COFFEE HOUSE SELLS THE
excellent coffees of Torrefazione Pasqualini, whose factory
is in Villanova d'Albenga. You can also buy Pasqualini coffees at
the company's outlets in Savona, Porto Maurizio and San Remo.

VIA XX SETTEMBRE 53 ✦ TEL: 0182 660187 ✦ CLOSED MONDAY

A Cuvea Gelateria

O N THE SAME SMALL SQUARE AS ITS ARCH RIVAL
BALZOLA, THIS ICE CREAMERY, WITH ITS OWN *CAFFÈ*
and snack food place facing it, has the best fruit ice
creams in town.

PIAZZA MATTEOTTI 3 ✦ TEL: 0182 660060
OPEN 9AM *to* 11:30PM DAILY *from* MARCH *through* OCTOBER,
CLOSED NOVEMBER *and* TUESDAYS IN WINTER

Antico Caffè, Pasticceria Balzola

J N A POCKETSIZED SQUARE FLANKED BY VIA XX SET-
TEMBRE, ONE ROW INLAND FROM THE BEACH, THIS
historic pastry shop, *caffè* and, formerly, musical variety
theater, has been in constant operation and run by the same family since it opened in 1900. Affable and irrepressible, Pasquale
Balzola Jr., now a man of mature years, still bubbles with the
enthusiasm of his parents and grandfather, the founder of the
dynasty. Balzola no longer hosts music and theater performances
in the square, which is filled with its tables much of the year,
but compensates with a new ice creamery and focaccia emporium
(**Alter Ego**, Via XX Settembre 5), within a few shopfronts of the
original. Close your eyes and imagine a salon on the Titanic, as
rendered by Hollywood or CineCittà circa 1930, then add a pinch
of Disneyland, and you'll begin to form a picture of the interior
of this unique shop. The chandeliers are in the style of Murano,
and so, too, is the tearoom beyond the bar area. It might be on
Piazza San Marco, in Venice, or at least a film set of same. Balzola

is famous for its *baci di Alassio*, made in huge quantities and shipped all over Italy (and the world). They're delicious, but so, too, are the *amaretti dei nonni*, Balzola's patented version of soft, almond-flavored meringues. The classic Sacher—chocolate and jam in layers—vies for your attention with an elaborate *torta tartufata*—a chocolate truffle cake wearing a coif of dark-chocolate kisses and a milk-chocolate ribbon sprinkled with powdered sugar. The ice creams Balzola churns out appear to have been inflated under high pressure, which isn't far off the mark; to call them handmade or artisanal would not be precise. They make quite a show when mixed and matched in the countless, extravagantly complicated *coppe* which vacationers gobble here—kiwis and mixed berries and ice cream of several flavors in the Coppa Esotica, for instance, or *baci* and meringues and other cookies and whipped cream and chocolate in the Coppa Bacio. An experience not to be missed.

PIAZZA MATTEOTTI 26 ✦ TEL: 0182 640209

WWW.BALZOLA.NET ✦ CLOSED MONDAY *and* NOVEMBER

Café Pasticceria San Lorenzo

ALSO ON A SMALL SQUARE FLANKING IL BUDELLO, THE MAIN ALLEYWAY OF OLD ALASSIO, ABOUT A hundred yards west of Balzola, this long-established pastry shop and *caffè* (they spell it in the French fashion) is the great rival. Its *baci di alassio* are good, but what brings in the locals and vacationers are the many other classic pastries — Italian, Austrian and French-inspired — and the setting. The café wraps around the pastry shop, occupying an entire block, and extends onto Alassio's gorgeous seaside promenade. So while the kisses might be even better elsewhere, classy San Lorenzo has its charms.

VIA VITTORIO VENETO 69 ✦ TEL: 0182 642500
CLOSED WEDNESDAY IN WINTER

Cappa Pasticceria

EVERYONE IN ALASSIO KNOWS THAT MILD-MANNERED ADELINDA ZULIAN OF CAPPA, A SMALL, MODEST pastry shop on the western end of the medieval alleyway that runs across town, makes the best, the most flavorful, luscious, chocolatey *baci di Alassio* anywhere, period. Her rivals may be bigger, with nice outdoor terraces, and are certainly more famous, but their size and fame are probably why they can't compete with this dedicated sole artisan, whose other creations (such as *cappelli di prete* tri-cornered shortbread pastries filled with dark, flavorful almond paste, or almond-covered chocolates with a creamy peanutty core) are also exquisite. Buy a bag of kisses and other chocolates and pastries, and take them with you.

VIA XX SETTEMBRE 138 ✦ TEL: 0182 642962
CLOSED SUNDAY AFTERNOON *and* TUESDAY

Enoteca Wine e Spirit Carpe Diem

THE PRETENTIOUS NAME, AND THE SCULPTED SLATE PLAQUE NEXT TO THE DOOR, SPEAK MUCH about the style of this glitzy wine boutique, filled with spotlit crates of premium wines from Italy, France and elsewhere. If you don't mind the investment, it's a good place to do wine tasting by the glass, because the selection of Riviera bottlings is excellent. Take a seat in one of the comfortable leather armchairs and try the best from Feìpu dei Massaretti, Alessandri Massimo, Laura Aschero, Maria Donata Bianchi and others.

VIA XX SETTEMBRE 17 ✦ TEL: 0182 470025
OPEN DAILY (UNTIL MIDNIGHT IN SUMMER)

Terre di Mare

*A*S IT HEADS WEST, THE BUDELLO DOWN THE MIDDLE OF TOWN CHANGES NAME FROM VIA XX SETTEMBRE to Via Vittorio Veneto, and this is where you'll find Terre di Mare, an upscale boutique selling a wide selection of vegetables and olives bottled in olive oil, pesto and other sauces, bottled anchovies, extra virgin oils, jams, honeys, cookies and more. They have another shop, in Finale Ligure.

VIA VITTORIO VENETO 84 ✦ TEL: 0182 640349 ✦ OPEN DAILY

ALBENGA

*B*OOSTERS INSIST THAT THIS PRE-ROMAN TOWN ON THE CENTA RIVER HALFWAY BETWEEN Savona and Imperia is nicknamed "the San Gimignano of the Riviera." Apart from the fact that it once had fifty medieval towers in its handsome, wall-girded midst, and a bloody, checkered past populated by Guelfs and Ghibellines,

The Garlic of Vessalico

O THERWISE UNREMARKABLE, THE VILLAGE OF VESSALICO, IN THE ALTA VALLE ARROSCIA, inland from Albenga, is known among Ligurians for its delicately piquant, pink-skinned heirloom garlic. Pesto purists will go out of their way to purchase fresh *aglio di Vessalico* to make the perfect sauce. The yearly Fiera dell'Aglio Vessalico, which started in 1760, is held the first week of July. Garlic enthusiasts from far and wide brave the heat and besiege the stands. Prices are high, because demand is great and supply limited. The garlic is grown exclusively on steep terraces near Vessalico totaling a mere seventeen-and-a-half acres. On average, only 72,000 heads are harvested a year. They are sold by the braid, each braid made up of twenty-four heads. Braiding helps keep the garlic fresh. Before dawn, the plants are uprooted, stalks and all, and woven together while the tops are still tender and green. They're stored in shady areas, where the plants continue to "live" in their braided state. Locals claim this is why the garlic cloves remain firm and juicy for as long as ten months. Information on the garlic festival is available at Tel: 0183 793245 or 0183 767428, www.cciaa-imperia.com.

If you miss the garlic festival but want to try *aglio di Vessalico*, you can buy it nearby in the perched village of Gavenola at **Alimentari Rovere** (Strada Mezzacosta 2, Tel: 0183 31144) or in Genoa at **Le Gramole Olioteca** (Via dei Macelli di Soziglia 69R, Tel: 010 209 1668, www.legramole.com).

For a traditional *trattoria* experience in the center of the village, try **Da Maria** (Piazza Manfredi 66, Tel: 0183 31057, closed Monday, very inexpensive). Everything is housemade, from the savory tarts and surprisingly authentic *cima alla genovese* and focaccia *con formaggio* in the style of Recco, to the meat or spinach-filled ravioli with meat sauce or pesto, and the *pansôti* with walnut sauce. In fall and winter there's wild boar stew; the rabbit, raised in the village, is slow-cooked with wine, pine nuts, olives and herbs. The jam tart is perfection, but so too is the tiramisu or pudding. The house wines are quaffable local Pigato or Dolcetto.

the comparison doesn't stand scrutiny. For one thing, unlike San Gimignano, Albenga is as flat as a *testarolo*. Founded by the Ingauni—Ligurian Celts—it was developed by the Romans, but is pure Ligurian. It feels like two places in one, a boisterous beach resort for the working and lower middle classes, and a charming citadel isolated from the beach community by the usual mix of stately nineteenth-century villas and banal postwar apartment buildings. Fields of artichokes—the celebrated, spiky *spinosi di Albenga*—spread across the river valley, amid hothouses, where basil and prized vegetables grow. Don't let the homeliness of Albenga's outskirts dissuade you from exploring the citadel, rebuilt in the 1300s after being destroyed by the rival Genoese. It's where you'll find most of the great food and wine Albenga has

to offer. Vineyards and olive groves stipple nearby hills. There's a long-established olive oil maker in town, Sommariva, who also makes delicious conserves, among them the local variation on *macheto*—anchovies, olive paste and capers. The local coffee roaster, La Genovese, is excellent. And the produce is peerless.

Albenga's big, sprawling flea market-style clothing and food market, on the eastern outskirts of town, is held from 7am to 4pm on Wednesday, and fills Via Dalmazia and parts of Viale Liguria, Via Gorizia and Via Patrioti. The organic food market (and crafts market) is held in Piazza San Michele, and other squares and alleys in the center of the medieval section of town, every second Saturday of the month. Get a map from the local tourist office, in a gazebo on Piazza del Popolo (Tel: 0182 558444, www.inforiviera.it).

TRATTORIA AND *FARINATA*

Hosteria Sutta Ca'

*I*N AN ALLEYWAY ON THE NORTHWEST SIDE OF THE MEDIEVAL PART OF TOWN, THIS SIMPLE LITTLE *trattoria* does all the right things, serving high-quality local specialties in a pleasant (predominantly yellow-and-white) interior, in what was a convent, with friendly but not overbearing or rushed service. The prices seem impossibly low in these days of funny money. Just one example: the house olive oil is an excellent extra virgin from Ramoino. Menu items are recited by the waiter, and change daily according to the market. You might find housemade *pansôti* topped with walnut sauce or dressed simply with fresh marjoram, olive oil and pine nuts, or green-and-yellow housemade *tagliolini* with pesto, tomatoes and olives, or perhaps minestrone *alla genovese*, or polenta with porcini and leeks, followed by light, flavorful steamed *baccalà* with steamed vegetables, translucent slices of *vitello tonnato* or a nice piece of grilled meat or fish. The desserts are housemade, too, and feature luscious tiramisu, or *crostata* with sour cherry jam and cracked hazelnuts on top. Local wines include Pigato Ravera, and very good Rossese and Ormeasco Sciac-trà di Pornassio, both by Lupi. The excellent house coffee is locally roasted by La Genovese, and there's even a coffee-tasting menu, featuring the roaster's top mono-varietals. You can taste them and also buy vacuum-packed cans to take home.

VICOLO ROLANDI RICCI 10 ✦ TEL: 0182 53198
CLOSED THURSDAY NIGHT *and* SUNDAY
INEXPENSIVE *to* MODERATE

Puppo Farinata e...

*O*N A NARROW BACK ALLEY ON THE NORTHERN SIDE OF THE MEDIEVAL CITY, THIS POPULAR *FARINATA* eatery is run by two charming young women, Elena and Marta, who stoke the twin wood-burners and whisk the scorching-hot *farinata* out to hungry locals seated under the vaults at marble-topped wooden tables, or lined up for take out. Also served are simple but tasty Ligurian specialties — savory tarts and baked stuffed vegetables, and more. But the *farinata* is the thing — crispy on top, unctuous and irresistible.

VIA TORLARO 20 ✦ TEL: 0182 51853 ✦ WWW.DAPUPPO.IT
CLOSED SUNDAY LUNCHTIME *and* MONDAY YEARROUND;
from MID JUNE *to* MID SEPTEMBER OPEN EVENINGS ONLY

ANCHOVIES, CHEESES, COFFEE,
GOURMET CONSERVES, ICE CREAM,
OLIVE OIL, PASTA *FRESCA*, PASTRIES

A Bütega du Caffè

THIS SMALL COFFEE-GROCERY-SWEETS-AND-DRY GOODS SHOP IN THE CENTER OF MEDIEVAL ALBENGA is a good place to stock up on everything from dried porcini to chestnut flour, local dry beans to the coffees of La Genovese, which you can buy by weight and have ground fresh.

PIAZZA SAN FRANCESCO 45 ✦ TEL: 0182 51313 ✦ CLOSED SUNDAY

Baxin

A NARROW LITTLE PASTRY SHOP IN A CENTURIES-OLD BUILDING ON THE MAIN SQUARE OF MEDIEVAL Albenga, Baxin (pronounced bah-sheen) is a Riviera institution, around since 1826, and is the home of the lightweight Baxin biscuit, made with no fat, just flour, sugar, lemon juice, honey, fennel seeds, milk and baking soda. The Bria family have owned and operated Baxin since 1933 and are into their third generation. They continue to make huge quantities of Baxin, but also churn out half a dozen other cookie types, including *baci della strega* (walnut-shaped sandwich cookies made with powdered chocolate and almonds, lemon juice and eggs, and filled with white chocolate cream), *baci di Alassio* (similar, but with hazelnut cream), plus crispy *ossa da mordere* ("bones of the dead") pine nut cookies, and panfrutto, a local version of *pandolce alla genovese*, with lots of raisins and pine nuts.

PIAZZA IV NOVEMBRE 1 ✦ TEL: 0182 52923
WWW.BAXIN.IT ✦ CLOSED SUNDAY *and* MONDAY

Casa del Gelato

STEP OUT OF THE TRAIN STATION, HEAD WEST ONE BLOCK AND WALK UP THE MAIN DRAG LEADING TO Piazza del Popolo and the medieval section of town. You'll see Casa del Gelato on the west side of the street. Take a cone and wander off — the location and premises aren't special. The ice cream is. The finest local seasonal fruit, plus high-quality hazelnuts from Piedmont and fresh-brewed La Genovese coffee, go into the flavorful, soft yet well-balanced *gelati* made here.

VIA MARTIRI DELLA LIBERTÀ 108 ✦ TEL: 0182 540914
OPEN DAILY IN SUMMER, IN WINTER ON FRIDAY,
SATURDAY *and* SUNDAY ONLY

Da Claudio e Adele — Formaggi e Salumi

HIDDEN DOWN A SHORT, NARROW BACK ALLEY IN THE HEART OF MEDIEVAL ALBENGA, THIS SIMPLE ham-and-cheese shop is the best place in town to pick up picnic supplies, including the few local cheeses made in the hills near Albenga by shepherd Aldo Lomanto. They include *brusso*, *giuncata* and ricotta. You'll also find delicious *pecorino di fossa*, not to mention prosciutto *crudo*, *culatello di Zibello*, *bottarga*, *mosciamme*, artisanal dry pasta and other delicacies.

VIA PALESTRO 6 ✦ TEL: 0182 51475 ✦ CLOSED SUNDAY

Enoteca Ingaunia DOC

WHAT APPEARS TO BE A HUMBLE FRUIT-AND-VEGETABLE AND GROCERY SHOP IN THE CENTER of old Albenga, with stands on tiny Piazza delle Erbe, turns out to have the area's best selection of local olive oils (Ramoino, Galleano, Roi, Dino Abbo, Delizie del Ponente) and wines (Poggio dei Gorleri, Maria Donata Bianchi, Lupi, Massaretti, Colle dei Bardellini, Bruna), not to mention dried porcini, and artisanal dry pasta from Pastificio Fiore (in Carasco, near Chiavari, on the eastern Riviera). In short, this is a remarkable little shop run by an enthusiastic food lover and his aged mother.

VIA G.M. ODDO 12/PIAZZA DELLE ERBE 7 ✦ TEL: 0182 554953.
CLOSED SUNDAY *and* MONDAY, OPEN DAILY IN SUMMER.

Gelateria Festival des Glaces

DON'T LET THE FRENCH NAME PUT YOU OFF. ON THE WEST SIDE OF THE TRAIN STATION, ON A MODERN, tree-lined avenue leading to the beach, this big ice cream shop run by dynamic Laura and Mirco is where vacationers and some locals go in summer to sit out at shaded tables and enjoy elaborate ice cream creations. The menu features dozens of them, mostly classics, and many made with fresh fruit — your best bet. Of the nut-based *gelati*, the hazelnut is luscious, the pistachio very good though quite sweet, and the *croccante pinolo*, with chunky toasted pine nuts, the best of all.

VIALE ITALIA 47 ✦ TEL: 0182 542997
OFF-SEASON HOURS VARY WIDELY

Pastificio Fontana

FOUNDED IN 1954 AND NOW INTO ITS SECOND GENERATION, THIS SPARTAN PASTA *FRESCA* SHOP, ON a narrow, short, back alley in the heart of old Albenga, makes all the local and Genoese pastas, from eight-shaped *corzetti* in the style of the Val Polcevera, to the *trofie* of Recco and Sori. The walnut sauce is done in the old-fashioned way, with walnuts, *parmigiano*, garlic, marjoram, extra virgin olive oil and no cream. Affable pasta-maker Domenico Fontana buys only the best ingredients, including basil from Prà, which goes into his delicious pesto. One sauce you'll find nowhere else is Il Ragu del Contadino, a savory blend of anchovies, capers, black olives, sun-dried tomatoes and pickled artichokes that's lovely on pasta or *crostini*.

VIA PALESTRO 24 ✦ TEL: 0182 50597
CLOSED SUNDAY AFTERNOON *and* MONDAY

La Genovese Caffè e Dintorni

THE ORIGINAL LA GENOVESE COFFEE ROASTING FACTORY WAS HERE, ON A SIDE STREET ABOUT halfway between the train station and the medieval part of town. You can see one of the old roasters displayed in the shop window. The coffee is now produced at a modern plant on the outskirts of town (in Regione Bottino) and the premises have been remodeled into an upscale gourmet food boutique. Along-side the many fine blends or mono-varietal coffees (from Jamaican Blue Mountain, Brasilian Santos Flor, Kenya AA Washed, to Guatemalan Antigua), you'll find gifts, candies, *pandolce*, bottled sauces and more.

VIA VITTORIO VENETO 16 ✦ TEL: 0182 50452
WWW.LAGENOVESE.IT ✦ CLOSED SUNDAY

Pasticceria Grana

ALSO ON VIA PALESTRO, NEAR ALBENGA'S BEST PASTA *FRESCA* AND HAM-AND-CHEESE SHOPS, IN the heart of old Albenga, this pastry shop, founded in 1952, has been run for the last decade by pastry chef Roberto Vanzini. Out front, Miriam Vanzini will tempt you with all the specialties, which range from *cannoncini*—tiny puff-pastry tubes bursting with fresh pastry cream—to *gobeletti* shortbread "goblets" filled with apricot jam, *amaretti*, *pandolce* (classic or with chocolate chips), Baxin dry cookies with fennel and aniseed, and, of course, *baci di Albenga*, the local, walnut-shaped chocolate-and-hazelnut sandwich cookies with chocolate cream inside, similar to *baci di Alassio*.

VIA PALESTRO 7 ✦ TEL: 0182 50875 ✦ CLOSED MONDAY

Pescheria Pinto Porta Molino

THE BEST LOCAL FISH SHOP, IN THE OLD PART OF ALBENGA, NEAR THE PORTA MOLINO CITY GATE, Pinto salts and bottles its own local anchovies, which are particularly delicious and delicate.

VIA MEDAGLIE D'ORO 2 ✦ TEL: 0182 559208 ✦ OPEN MORNINGS ONLY, DAILY, *and* SATURDAY AFTERNOON, CLOSED SUNDAY

Antico Frantoio Sommariva

BUILT INTO ALBENGA'S MEDIEVAL WALLS, ON THE NORTH SIDE OF TOWN, THIS LABYRINTHINE OLIVE oil and specialty foods shop, which was founded over a century ago, includes a "museum" of olive oil making. Sommariva's mill was here for decades (it's now on the outskirts of town), and the crusher and much other hard-driven equipment is still on site, though rearranged for didactic or display purposes. Watch your head as you twist and turn down passageways, ducking through yard-thick walls, amid antique implements of stone and olive wood. Children love it. In a back room full of items crafted from olive wood, Sommariva holds tastings of its oils, which range from *nuovo mosto* (a cold-pressed extra virgin that's unfiltered, and some of which is certified organic) to a filtered extra virgin, or a pure Taggiasca extra virgin, right down to a standard *olio di oliva* suitable for bottling pickled vegetables and the like. The Sommariva family are into their fourth generation, with Agostino now at the helm. Perhaps even more appealing than the oils are the bottled olives (in brine or extra virgin olive oil) and organic pesto (made with DOP basil grown by Sommariva, DOP *parmigiano* and DOP *pecorino romano*, among the best bottled pestos available), wild arugula sauce, bottled baby artichokes and sun-dried tomatoes. The Caviale del Centa is a flavorful paste made of Taggiasca olives, anchovies from the Centa River estuary and capers, which echoes the *macheto* anchovy paste of times gone by, and is exquisite as a topping for *crostini*. There are many other delicious sauces, creams and pesto variations made and sold here, plus one item you will find nowhere else: Jerusalem artichokes bottled in extra virgin olive oil.

VIA G. MAMELI 7 ✦ TEL: 0182 541143
WWW.OLIOSOMMARIVA.IT ✦ CLOSED SUNDAY

BASTIA D'ALBENGA, LECA D'ALBENGA

BASTIA AND LECA ARE SUBURB-HAMLETS IN THE ORBIT OF ALBENGA, ON LOW HILLSIDES. THIS IS olive oil and wine country, but also boasts a pair of fine cheesemakers. **I Formaggi del Boschetto** (Regione Boschetto, Bastia d'Albenga, Tel: 0182 20687, call ahead to make sure someone is around), owned by Sicilian shepherd Aldo Lomanto, produces over a dozen typical Ligurian or Sicilian-style seasonal cheeses with ewe's or goat's milk (plus one, a *toma*, made with a blend of both and cow's milk). In summer, Lomanto transfers his herd of nearly 1,500 head to high pastures near France, so you're unlikely to find him making cheese at the farmstead. When he has enough cheese on hand to supply stores, you can find his curds at Da Claudio e Adele in Albenga.

Cow's milk cheeses from **Azienda Agricola Fratelli Benedetti** (Regione Murassi 2, Leca d'Albenga, Tel: 0182 21445, call ahead) range from ricotta and *bruss* to *toma*. Here, too, the herd is rounded up in summer and transported to Alpine pastures in Piedmont, so unless you drive to the isolated cheese-making facility Benedetti uses in Upega, near Cuneo, you can only buy these cheeses in Liguria from November through May.

Anfossi Azienda Agraria (Via Paccini 39, Bastia d'Albenga, Tel: 0182 20024) makes not only excellent wines and extra virgin olive oils, but also prepares and packs paté d'olive olive spread, *crema al crescione* (watercress spread), very good pesto, and baby *carciofini* artichokes in extra virgin oil. Anfossi is half a mile off the SP582 highway, near the autostrada.

Three other top wineries, the first in Bastia, the other two in Salea, are: **Fèipu dei Massaretti** (Regione Massaretti 7, Tel: 0182 20131); **Le Rocche del Gatto** (Regione Ruato 2, Tel: 0182 21175, www.lerocchedelgatto.it); **La Vecchia Cantina** (Via Corta 3, Tel: 0182 559881). See page 340, An Olive Oil-and-Wine Route: Albenga to Andora, for more.

VILLANOVA D'ALBENGA

A SUBURB OF ALBENGA NEAR THE TOWN'S AIRPORT, THERE ARE TWO REASONS TO follow highway SP6 to Villanova. First, to buy coffee from the roasting facility of **Torrefazione F.lli Pasqualini** (Via Roma 167, Tel: 0182 582591, closed Saturday afternoon and Sunday). They don't serve coffee here, but you can pick up vacuum packs of the top blend, Arabica Gold, with which you'll make a strong, dark coffee with chocolate overtones. Also on sale are *torrone*, *panettone*, jams, honeys, chocolates, olive oils, olives packed in brine or in oil, bottled sauces of all kinds, toasted barley (coffee substitute) and more. If the beans are being roasted when you visit, ask to watch. Pasqualini is happy to let you see how they work.

The second reason to visit is to buy olive oil from **Baglietto e Secco** (Via Roma 137, Tel: 0182 582838, by appointment), down the same main street; they make excellent DOP extra virgin oils.

AN OLIVE OIL-AND-WINE ROUTE:

ALBENGA TO ANDORA

Because of the scattered locations of olive oil makers, wineries, food producers, shops and restaurants in the area, the best way to discover them is to budget a day, rent a car and take the road trip inland. The distances are relatively short, but roads are narrow with many curves. Expect to spend one whole day for a round-trip tour.

S TART IN THE HINTERLAND OF ALBENGA, IN THE PROVINCE OF SAVONA. WEND YOUR WAY THROUGH vineyards and olive groves inland as far as Borghetto d'Arroscia or Vessalico, edging the Province of Imperia, and then drive back to the coast via Ortovero and Villanova d'Albenga. From there, head southwest to Stellanello and Andora. Because most of the properties listed below are small and family run, the opening hours vary widely. It's wise to phone ahead. There are dozens of oil mills and wineries in the area. This is a select list. For a complete listing of wineries visit www.

enotecapubblica.it; for certified DOP oil makers, visit www.consorziodoprivieraligure.it.

Drive inland from Albenga (or Ceriale) into the flatlands — dotted with hothouses full of flowers and live plants — to Salea d'Albenga, where winery **La Vecchia Cantina** (Via Corta 3, Salea d'Albenga (SV), Tel: 0182 559881), owned by Umberto Calleri, makes excellent Riviera Ligure di Ponente DOC Vermentino, and mellow, honey-sweet Passito di Pigato, a dessert wine. Also in Salea, another top winery, **Le Rocche del Gatto** (Regione Ruato 2, Salea d'Albenga (SV), Tel: 0182 21175 and 335 522 3547, www.lerocchedelgatto.it, open daily, Sunday by appointment), owned by Fausto De Andreis and Chiara Crosa di Vergagni, makes a big, flowery Pigato called Spigàu Crociata, plus an interesting Ormeasco red called Macajolo, which has more body than most. Still in Salea, though in another district of this sprawling farm area, is another Calleri, this time **Marcello Calleri** (Regione Fratti 2, Salea d'Albenga (SV), Tel: 0182 20085), whose up-and-coming winery makes very good Vermentino and Pigato.

Due south a few miles, in similar farm scenery, Bastia and Leca d'Albenga have more than their share of great oil and wine makers, and two fine cheesemakers — **I Formaggi del Boschetto** (Regione Boschetto, Bastia d'Albenga, Tel: 0182 20687) and **Azienda Agricola Fratelli Benedetti** (Regione Murassi 2, Leca d'Albenga, Tel: 0182 21445). (See Bastia/Leca d'Albenga entries for details; page 339.)

Anfossi Azienda Agraria (Via Paccini 39, Bastia d'Albenga (SV), Tel: 0182 20024), based in a historic fortified farmhouse, where Mario Anfossi and his partner Paolo Grossi make excellent Rossese and Pigato, and remarkable extra virgin olive oils (plus olive or watercress spread, pesto, and exquisite local vegetables packed in extra virgin oil). Winery **Fèipu dei Massaretti** (Regione Massaretti 7, Bastia d'Albenga (SV), Tel: 0182 20131) makes premium wines, including one of the region's top-ten Riviera Ligure di Ponente DOC Pigatos. Nearby, Giobatta Vio turns out very good organic wines at **Bio Vio** (Via Crociata 24, Bastia d'Albenga (SV), Tel: 0182 20776). Run by Caterina Zorelli and her family, **Azienda Agricola e Agriturismo Il Nostro Oliveto** (Via Becchignoli 51, Bastia d'Albenga (SV), Tel: 348 245 1655, www.ilnostroliveto.it), a micro-operation with olive groves in Bastia, makes good extra virgin olive oils, and offers lodging at a farmhouse B&B. **Frantoio Marco** (Via Piemonte 152, Leca d'Albenga, Tel: 0182 20055, frantoio.marco@tin.it), a small operation run by Eugenio Marco, makes DOP oils from both Arnasca

Top Wineries for Riviera Ligure di Ponente DOC Pigato

· · · · · · · · · · · · · · · · · · · ·

GENETIC SCIENCE PROVES THAT PIGATO IS A CLOSE RELATIVE OF VERMENTINO, BUT OVER the centuries has developed its own character—bigger, fatter, sun- and heat-loving. Pigato grapes thrive and mature fully, becoming speckled, only on the western Riviera di Ponente and its inland territories.

Massimo Alessandri

The winery's best wines: Vigne Veggie, Costa de Vigne

FRAZIONE COSTA PARROCCHIA, RANZO (IM) ✦ TEL: 0182 53458 WWW.MASSIMOALESSANDRI.IT

Bruna

The winery's best wines: Baccan, Le Russeghine

FRAZIONE BORGO, VIA UMBERTO I 81, RANZO (IM) TEL: 0183 318082, 0183 318928

La Vecchia Cantina

VIA CORTA 3, SALEA D'ALBENGA (SV) ✦ TEL: 0182 559881

Claudio Vio

FRAZIONE CROSA 16, VENDONE (SV) ✦ TEL: 0182 76338

Durin

VIA ROMA 202, ORTOVERO (SV) ✦ TEL: 0182 547007

AA.DURIN@LIBERO.IT

Feipu dei Massaretti

REGIONE MASSARETTI 7, BASTIA D'ALBENGA (SV)

TEL: 0182 20131

Lupi

The winery's best wine: Le Petraie

VIA MAZZINI 9, PIEVE DI TECO (IM)

TEL: 0183 36161 ✦ WWW.VINILUPI.IT

Azienda Agricola San Dalmazio

LOCALITÀ ARVEGLIO, ALBENGA (SV) ✦ TEL: 019 884820

Azienda Agricola Sommariva

REGIONE SIGNOLA 2, ALBENGA (SV) ✦ TEL: 0182 559222

Azienda Agricola La Rocca di San Nicolao

The winery's best wine: Vigna di Proxi

VIA DANTE 10, FRAZIONE GAZZELLI, CHIUSANICO (IM)

TEL: 0183 52304 ✦ WWW.ROCCASANNICOLAO.IT

Top Wineries for DOC Vermentino

....

Azienda Vitivinicola La Baia del Sole

The winery's best: Colli di Luni DOC Vermentino Sarticola

VIA FORLINO 3, ORTONOVO (SP) ✦ TEL: 0187 661821

Bisson

The winery's best: Golfo del Tigullio DOC Vermentino

CORSO GIANNELLI 28, CHIAVARI, (GE) ✦ TEL: 0185 314462

WWW.BISSONVINI.IT

Cascina delle Terre Rosse

*The winery's best: Riviera Ligure di Ponente DOC
Vermentino*

VIA MANIE 3, FINALE LIGURE (SV) ✦ TEL: 019 698782

Lunae Bosoni

*The winery's best: Colli di Luni DOC Vermentino Etichetta
Nera*

LOCALITÀ LUNI, VIA BOZZI 63, ORTONOVO (SP)

TEL: 0187 669222 ✦ WWW.CANTINELUNAE.COM

Claudio Vio

*The winery's best:
Riviera Ligure di Ponente DOC Vermentino*

FRAZIONE CROSA 16, VENDONE (SV) ✦ TEL: 0182 76338

Lupi

*The winery's best: Riviera Ligure di Ponente DOC
Vermentino Le Serre*

VIA MAZZINI 9, PIEVE DI TECO (IM)

TEL: 0183 36161 ✦ WWW.VINILUPI.IT

Ottaviano Lambruschi

The winery's best:
Colli di Luni DOC Vermentino Costa Marina

VIA OLMARELLO 28, CASTELNUOVO MAGRA (SP)
TEL: 0187 674261 ✦ WWW.OTTAVIANOLAMBRUSCHI.COM

Azienda Agricola La Rocca di San Nicolao

The winery's best: Riviera Ligure
di Ponente DOC Vermentino Vigna di Proxi

VIA DANTE 10, FRAZIONE GAZZELLI, CHIUSANICO (IM)
TEL: 0183 52304 ✦ WWW.ROCCASANNICOLAO.IT

Santa Caterina

The winery's best: Colli di Luni DOC
Vermentino Poggi Alti

VIA SANTA CATERINA 6, SARZANA (SP) ✦ TEL: 0187 629429

Tenuta Giuncheo

The winery's best: Riviera Ligure
di Ponente DOC Vermentino Eclis

LOCALITÀ GIUNCHEO, CAMPOROSSO (IM)
TEL: 0184 288639 ✦ WWW.TENUTAGIUNCHEO.IT

La Vecchia Cantina

The winery's best: Riviera Ligure di
Ponente DOC Vermentino

VIA CORTA 3, SALEA D'ALBENGA (SV) ✦ TEL: 0182 559881

and Taggiasca olives, which he handpicks and mills himself.

Still in the hinterland of Albenga, at **Azienda Agricola San Dalmazio** (Località Arveglio, Tel: 019 884820), you can experience another of the region's top-ten Riviera Ligure di Ponente DOC Pigatos. Though **Azienda Agricola Sommariva** has its olive oil and wine boutique (and museum) in the center of historic Albenga, its vineyards, winery and olive oil mill are outside of town (Regione Signola 2, Tel: 0182 559222). Not only does Sommariva produce great organic olive oils, pesto and other sauces, it also makes a very fine Riviera Ligure di Ponente DOC Pigato.

Moving inland due west from Albenga, on the roller-coaster ridge road above the eastern side of the Arroscia River Valley, you come to Arnasco, site of the **Cooperativa Olivicola di Arnasco** (Piazza IV Novembre 8, Tel: 0182/761178, www.coopolivicolarnasco.it). The local olive variety here is known as Arnasca or, more commonly, Pignola, because it has a nutty flavor reminiscent of pine nuts—*pinoli*. The taste is believed by many to derive from the proximity of the olive trees to pine groves, but there's room for skepticism, since Pignola are found in other areas of Liguria with no pine trees. Arnasca olives are even smaller, and plumper, than Taggiasca olives, and they produce a very pleasant, slightly bittersweet oil. While at the cooperative, which was founded in 1984 and now has about 200 members, take at look at the "museum" of olive trees and rural living (Museo dell'Olivo e della Civiltà Contadina).

A few miles inland from Arnasco at Vendone, at about 1,000 feet above sea level, two top olive oil makers grow Arnasca and Taggiasca olives and make remarkable extra virgin products. **Claudio Vio** (Frazione Crosa 16, Tel: 0182 76338) is primarily a winemaker, and his Riviera Ligure di Ponente DOC Pigato is rightly considered among the region's best: it has all the classic qualities of a round, supple Pigato without excess fat. His oils, made from hand-picked olives, are excellent; he sells out quickly. In another outlying area of Vendone, **Azienda Agricola Bronda Renzo** (Località Cantone 18, Tel: 0182 76253), now into its seventh generation, grows Taggiasca and Arnasca trees on ten sloping acres. Bronda has its own olive oil mill, and makes astonishingly good organic oils, plus delicious *paté d'olive* and mushrooms packed in Bronda's excellent oils. If you're hungry, stop for a simple meal of Ligurian classics—housemade ravioli and other pasta, long-cooked rabbit with pine nuts, olives and herbs—at **Trattoria L'Alpino** (Via Ponzoni 89, Frazione Leuso, Tel: 0182 76435, closed Monday, inexpensive).

If you continue to drive west you'll enter the Province of Imperia. Head south by southwest on looping narrow roads through the hamlet of Costa Bacelega and then southwest toward Highway SP 453, which is in the valley bottom, on the north side of the Aroscia River. There you will find the village of Ranzo. The municipal area of Ranzo comprises many outlying hamlets with similar and confusing names. The roads are very narrow and twist like corkscrews. Happily, Ranzo also has half a dozen wineries, four of which are outstanding. The first one that you'll encounter as you enter the village from the hillside is owned and operated by one of Liguria's leading winemakers, **Riccardo Bruna** (Frazione Borgo, Via Umberto I 81, Tel: 0183 318082). Among the most complex and delightful Pigato wines—period— are Bruna's Baccan, made with extremely ripe grapes from very old grapevines and redolent of herbs and spices and fruit; and Le Russeghine, slightly less muscular, but nuanced, and full of peachy, jasmine scents and flavors. A few hundred yards away in the village are two other fine wineries. One is on the same road as Bruna. **A Maccia** (Frazione Borgo, Via Umberto I 54, Tel: 0183 318003, www.amaccia.it) has been around since 1850, in the same family, and makes very good Pigato and Rossese, plus delicious extra virgin Taggiasca oils, following traditional methods handed down the generations. The wines and oils are organic, full of flavor, with no messing around. Another very talented Ranzo winemaker whose winery is nearby in the village is **Fiorenzo Guidi** (Via Parocchia 4, Tel: 0183 318076, www.guidifiorenzo.it). Guidi is particularly friendly and, with his family, makes classic DOC Riviera Ligure di Ponente Pigato. The fourth winemaker in the village is **Massimo Alessandri** (Frazione Costa Parrocchia, Tel: 0182 53458, www.massimoalessandri.it). His big, yet flowery and elegant Pigatos routinely win prestigious awards. Vigne Veggie is made from very old grapevines while Costa de Vigne is a classic, elegant Pigato. The red, from Granaccia and Syrah grapes, and called Ligustico, is aged for a year or more in new oak casks and, though well made, has little to do with Liguria, despite the name.

The road corkscrews up and around to perched Gavenola, home of classic *amaretti*, olive-oil perfumed dry biscuits and salt-free bread, all of which, plus mushrooms, oils and wines, and Vessalico garlic, are sold by the local grocery store, located behind the church, **Alimentari Rovere** (Strada Mezzacosta 2, Tel: 0183 31144, closed afternoons on Sunday and Wednesday). It's presided over by friendly Eliane Ferrari and her husband.

Also in the village, below the grocery on the main road, is a good bakery, **Panificio Cacciò** (Via Provinciale, Tel: 0183 31255, closed afternoons on weekends), where Flavio and Giancarlo bake all the local breads and treats. An authentic, casual, local *trattoria* with *cucina casalinga*, where the cook and owner Marilena makes everything, from the classic greens-and-ricotta or meat-filled ravioli with meat sauce (and other fresh pasta and delicious pesto) to the free-range boiled or stuffed hen (order it ahead), is located on the main road (highway SP78) as you enter the village from the east, and called **Bar Ristorante Da Marilena** (Borgo Villa 59, Tel: 0183 31054, closed Monday, inexpensive).

Just below the handsome hamlet of Gazzo, on the road to Borghetto d'Arroscia, is **La Baita** (Borgo Gazzo 19, Borghetto d'Arroscia (IM), Tel: 0183 31083, www.labaitagazzo.it, open only Fridays and weekends for lunch and dinner, daily in August), a farm, oil mill and restaurant (moderate to expensive). In operation since the 1880s and still part-owned by its founders, the restaurant serves seasonal produce, much of which comes from the family farm and olive groves nearby, at an altitude of nearly 2,000 feet (and therefore largely free of Mediterranean fruit fly infestation). Now in the hands of Marco Ferrari, the restaurant has gone upscale, in the process losing its endearing simplicity. Soups with porcini and other local wild mushrooms — formerly the house specialty — are still good, and the ravioli stuffed with field greens are housemade. Many excellent local cheeses are served, French-style, from a platter. Desserts revolve around the citrus fruit available from groves in the valley below; the sorbets are delicious and the olive oil ice cream surprising, to say the least. Happily the wine list is long, with over 200 wines, including most of the best Liguria has to offer. La Baita's oil maker Mirella Lapicirella grows exclusively Taggiasca trees, and makes outstanding oils that are light, flowery and beautifully balanced. The best are DOP Riviera dei Fiori; the other oil, called Agazan, is equally excellent. Also sold are brined olives, olive paté and bottled or dry mushrooms.

The main two-lane provincial highway, SP453, runs through Borghetto d'Arroscia, in the valley bottom. Follow it along the river back toward the coast, stopping at Ortovero, where you'll find two wineries. Family-run, friendly **Durin** (Via Roma 202, Tel: 0182 547007, aa.durin@libero.it, always open but phone ahead), one of Liguria's leading wineries, is at its best when it sticks to tradition. It grows and bottles excellent Riviera Ligure di Ponente DOC Pigato; look for the single-vineyard Vigna Braie,

which is fruity and plump. The Riviera Ligure di Ponente Rossese DOC is a well-balanced classic, while the Colline Savonesi
IGT Granaccia possesses the big, blackberry and red fruit nose
and flavor of New World wines. Likewise I Matti (meaning "the
crazies"), an unusual and also non-Ligurian marriage of Granaccia, Sangiovese and Barbera, with similar blockbuster qualities.
A very different, journeyman winery is **Cooperativa Viticoltori
Ingauni** (Via Roma 3, Tel: 0182547127), on the other end of the
same, main street through town.

Head southwest toward the Albenga airport at Villanova
d'Albenga, where under-rated olive oil maker **Baglietto e Secco**
(Via Roma 137, Tel: 0182 582838), on the main highway, produces
excellent extra virgin oils. Down the road, stop at **Torrefazione
F.lli Pasqualini** (Via Roma 167, Tel: 0182 582591) to buy freshly
roasted coffees (plus candies *panettone*, jams, honeys, chocolates,
and other specialty foods).

The Stellanello area inland from Andora is covered with
olive trees and has many good oil makers. To reach it, from Villanova d'Albenga, take looping, scenic, roller-coaster back roads
via Garlenda to San Damiano, Frazione di Stellanello, home to
one of the region's leading and longest-established makers of
organic Taggiasca olive oils, **Azienda Agricola San Damiano**
(Località Caio di San Damiano 12, Stellanello (SV), Tel: 0182
668101). Francesca Barnato and her family have owned olive
groves here for over 300 years, and now have about 3,200 Taggiasca trees spread over about twenty-five hilly acres. Their oils
are light and fruity, and often golden in hue. They still mill the
olives with traditional millstones.

Close by is **Frantoio da olive Rossi Simone** (Frazione San
Damiano, Pilone, Tel: 0182 668085, cell 338 127 5544), while
a bit further afield are **Frantoio Artigianale Mantello Mauro**
(Frazione Albareto 19, Stellanello (SV) Tel: 0182 668318, cell 338
154 3897) and **Frantoio da olive Bestoso Domenico** (Frazione
Borgonuovo 28, Stellanello (SV), Tel: 0182 668031).

Drive toward the coast and Andora. In coastal hills nearby,
the most promising new winery is **Cascina Praiè** (Località
Colla Micheri, Andora, Tel: 019 602377). Since the beginning
of this century, winemakers Massimo and Anna Maria Vigli-
etti have been producing nearly organic, very good whites,
including Vermentino Le Cicale and Pigato Il Canneto, plus
other ambitious red blends less true to the soil and traditions
of Liguria. The Province of Imperia starts at Cervo, just
southwest of Andora.

CHAPTER 13

Greater Imperia– L'Imperiese

Province: Imperia. Includes: Borgomaro, Cervo, Chiusanico, Diano Castello, Diano Marina, Diano San Pietro, Dolcedo, Imperia, Lucinasco-Sarola, Imperia-Oneglia, Imperia-Porto Maurizio, Pieve di Teco, Pontedassio, Pornassio, San Bartolomeo al Mare

MPERIA? THERE IS NO THERE, THERE. "IMPE-RIA," AN INVENTED NAME, IS THE RESULT OF a 1923 administrative fusion of the small seaside towns of Oneglia and Porto Maurizio (and a handful of adjacent villages and hamlets) on either side of the Impero River. The municipality also gave its name to the vast Province of Imperia, which, on its eastern end, starts between the coastal towns of Andora and Cervo, running west from there to France, and inland to Piedmont. The coastline is uniformly built up, a tangle of postwar speculation, while the hinterland is handsome and sparsely populated, with a profusion of olive groves, vineyards, farms, orchards and flower-growing concerns spread among hillside and valley villages. Greater Imperia—the coastline and *entroterra* on either side of Oneglia and Porto Maurizio—boasts some of the Riviera's top olive oil makers.

CERVO-SAN BARTOLOMEO AL MARE-VILLA FARALDI

HE PROVINCE OF IMPERIA STARTS NEARBY, BETWEEN MARINA DI ANDORA AND CAPO CERVO. Stacked by the sea on a laid-back hill, wrapped by ruined walls and spiked with a crumbled castle, Cervo is a gorgeous operetta set, with alleyways that burrow and climb to the spectacular Baroque church of San Giovanni Battista. Cervo Alta, the upper section of town, is the fief of San Giorgio, the cult restaurant. Since the late 1950s, the same mother-and-son team have been wowing diners with personalized variations on local and not-so-local foods—with an emphasis on fish and sea-food—in increasingly luxurious, stone-paved surroundings, and with ever more saffron, sesame seed, mustard and French-style raspberry coulis in the mix. Happily, Caterina and Alessandro now also own a more accessible though very tony olive oil and specialty foods shop, serving tasty snacks and wines by the bottle or glass, in a grotto underneath the restaurant. It's called **Il Sangiorgino** (Via A. Volta 19, Cervo Alta, Tel: 0183 400175, www.ristorantesangiorgio.net), and has a vast range of fine extra virgin DOP oils, bottlings from top wineries, and the inevitable "kisses" of Cervo, which are much the same as the *baci* of half a dozen other seaside towns, and just as delicious.

Due west of Cervo but joined by the hip to it, San Bartolomeo al Mare has more to offer inland than on its beaches. One fine pastry and cake shop is on the main coast highway, **Pasticceria Racca** (Via Aurelia 88, Tel: 0183 400863). Its owner trained at Stratta, the famous Turinese chocolatier. Try the excellent pine nut-studded *pinolata* and the candied fruit, and then head inland, due north, following the riverbed and signs to Villa Faraldi. About half a mile beyond the fork in the road to Frazione Chiappa, you'll find the mill and retail shop of **Frantoio Elena Luigi** (Borgo Richieri 8, Chiappa/San Bartolomeo al Mare, Tel: 0183 400470, elenaluigisnc@libero.it, closed Sunday). This small olive oil concern with a mix of traditional and high-tech equipment is run by three sisters and their father, who produce lovely, sweet, pure Taggiasca olive oils, plus very good pesto using DOP basil; artichoke or walnut spread; pitted olives with herbs; olive paté; salted or oil-packed anchovies; and stuffed *peperoncini* chili peppers.

Return to the riverbed and continue north toward Villa Faraldi, stopping at Frazione Riva, where oil maker **Gocce d'Olio** (Via Lepanto 2, Villa Faraldi, Tel: 0183 41118, www.goccedolio. com) uses both high-tech continuous presses and traditional millstones to make a variety of very fine extra virgin olive oils, exclusively with Taggiasca olives it grows above the coastal strip west of the mill.

Continue toward Villa Faraldi on Via Cascione for two small firms making classic DOP Riviera dei Fiori oils. At #8 you'll find **Azienda Agricola Varaldo Elena** (Tel: 0183 41018, simoneelena@libero.it), and at #20 **Azienda Agricola Valle Ostilia** (Tel: 347 882 6230, www.valleostilia.it, info@valleostilia.it), which also sells excellent pickled vegetables, including Albenga artichokes, bottled in its own extra virgin oil, as well as brined olives and coarsely mashed olive paste, similar to that used by bakers to make *pan di polpa* olive bread. Valle Ostilia also has a boutique in San Bartolomeo al Mare (Via Viali 16, Tel: 0183 403973).

DIANO ARENTINO- DIANO CASTELLO-DIANO GORLERI-DIANO MARINA- DIANO SAN PIETRO

A FEW MILES EAST OF IMPERIA ARE SEVERAL villages and hamlets whose names begin with "Diano." Diano Marina, on the coast, is a beach resort; the others are in the hinterland behind, scattered across hills and through valleys cloaked with olive trees and stippled with grapevines—and holiday homes.

Starting in the hamlet of Borello in the Diano Arentino municipal district, the area farthest inland from the coast, is **Frantoio U Vescu** (Via Virgili 4, Tel: 0183 43120, by appointment only), maker of very good extra virgin oils, though no longer a member of the DOP consortium. This is pretty much a one-man operation, with owner Bruno Trucco aided by his wife (who has a full time job). Trucco has 800 Taggiasca trees and makes classic oils using old-fashioned methods and machinery. They're riper, softer and sunnier than many, and have been awarded honorable mentions in several contests.

Premium winery **Maria Donata Bianchi** is on the main street in the center of oval, medieval Diano Castello (Via delle Torri 16, Tel: 0183 498233, by appointment). The firm's vineyards are scattered around Diano Arentino. By Ligurian standards this is a fair-sized operation, producing about 40,000 bottles per year all told. The Vermentino and Pigato are very well made, balanced and fully fleshed without fat. Less traditional, "La Mattana" is a blend of Syrah and Granaccia, and will please those who like New World-style wines. The company also makes very good olive oils.

On the southern edge of the village, on highway SP36 (the main, two-lane road), is small olive oil maker **Pierandrea Costa** (Strada San Pietro 5, Tel: 0183 429171, mlucia67@libero.it, by appointment only). His oils are also made from Taggiasca olives, and are very good.

Il Colle degli Ulivi (Località Sant'Angelo 40, Diano Marina, Tel: 0183 405583, info@ilcolledegliulivi.com, www.colledegliulivi.com, open daily but phone ahead) is on a hillside overlooking the coast and Marina area. Though the company was founded in the 1950s, many of the Taggiasca olive trees are over a hundred years old. Family run, and into its third generation, everyone from Adelmo and his wife Marisa, to their children Claudia, Paola and Luca, are involved in growing, picking and packing olives (and artichokes, tomatoes, fava beans, basil and other produce from their own fields and greenhouses) and making excellent DOP and other oils. The *mosto* is classic: unfiltered and slightly cloudy but sweet and delicious, and slighter riper than some. With the second-choice extra virgin oils the family makes flavored chili and lemon oils, which are unusual but useful in cooking. Two products you'll find here and nowhere else are *piccantizzia*, a concoction of sun-dried tomatoes softened by boiling in vinegar and wine, with crushed anchovies, olive paste, capers, extra virgin olive oil and spices; *Bruxia beck* instead are *peperoncini* chilis in extra virgin oil with vinegar and salt. There's classic Genoese pesto and pesto made without garlic. Though it's worth driving up for a visit, the family also keeps a boutique in the center of Diano Marina (Via San Francesco d'Assisi 7, Tel: 339 121 0419).

If you have a hard time finding information about **Poggio dei Gorleri** (Via San Leonardo, Frazione Gorleri, Tel: 0183 495207, 334 346 9441, www.poggiodeigorleri.com, by appointment weekdays), that may be because the winery used to be called Montali e Temesio. Giampiero Merano and his sons Davide and Matteo took it over, with veteran Fabrizio Ciufoli making the wines. Surrounded by umbrella pines and vineyards, with views over the coast directly below, this is an upscale, up-and-coming operation with New World moxy. Luckily, new oak barrels aren't part of the picture. The pure Vermentino and Pigato, made in stainless steel tanks, are nonetheless big (13 percent alcohol), fruit-forward wines with fancy labels and Latin names. "Cycnus" has peachy, almost over-ripe flavors that are enhanced by complexity and a nice Ligurian bittersweet finish. Aprìcus has more fruit and flowers than many other Ligurian whites, while the easy-to-drink Vigna Sorì preserves more of the light freshness associated with the region.

Saguato Stefano Frantoio Olive Olio (Via Saguato 1-5, Diano San Pietro, Tel: 0183 49280, www.anticofrantoiosaguato.it) has been around since 1915, when grandfather Stefano Saguato bought and remodeled a sixteenth-century fortress-millhouse. Grandson Stefano Saguato and family make very good DOP and other Taggiasca oils blended together from three distinct groves. While there's plenty of old oil milling machinery on display, nowadays the mill has relatively modern equipment. Also made in-house are brined olives, olive paté, sun-dried tomatoes packed in olive oil and pesto. Located just southwest of Diano San Pietro, the easiest way to reach the mill from the main coast highway is to take Via Mimose inland (in just a few miles it changes name to Via Campodonico, Via Goachino Rossini, Via Case Sparse and Corso Luigia Saguato).

Also in the sprawling San Pietro area, **Venturino Bartolomeo** (Via Molini 1, Diano San Pietro, Tel: 0183 429505, info@frantoioventurino.com, www.frantoioventurino.com) is another family-run firm, established in 1945, with about 1,500 of its own Taggiasca trees in nearby groves (it also buys Taggiasca olives from other local growers). The top oils are DOP Riviera dei Fiori, and are typical of the area, with more gold in the color, and ripeness in the taste, than are found in most other districts of Liguria. The house's second oil, Valli della Taggiasca, is very similar to the DOP, and also low in acid (under 0.5 percent), with a tiny amount of non-Taggiasca oil in it. Venturino's milling equipment is old fashioned, with big granite millstones. Also sold are tiny artichokes, sun-dried tomatoes, eggplants, mushrooms and porcini packed in oil, plus pesto and arugula sauce.

IMPERIA-ONEGLIA

THE BIRTHPLACE OF ADMIRAL ANDREA DORIA, THE GENOESE REPUBLIC'S GREATEST NAVAL hero, and once the port of the Kingdom of Savoy, Oneglia is a small but prosperous town on the east side of the Impero River, relatively free of eat-and-run tourism. Surrounded by industrial plants, including the Agnese pasta factory, its

Everything You Ever Wanted to Know about Olives, Oil and the Mediterranean

. . . .

CLEVER MARKETING AND SINCERE PASSION FOR CRAFT OCCASIONALLY GO TOGETHER. Here's an example. In the early 1990s, at the height of the Mediterranean Diet craze, one of Oneglia's big, old olive oil producers, Fratelli Carli, created the Museo dell'Olio in landscaped grounds abutting their factory. This private museum is still among the best sources anywhere for accessible, hands-on, down-to-earth information about the 6,000-year-plus history of olives and olive oil and the way they have shaped Mediterranean culture, from North Africa to the Middle East, Greece to Italy, Spain and Portugal. Outside the museum are a pair of 1,000-year-old olive trees with thick, gnarled trunks, and a set of conical old millstones. Inside are eighteen spotlit, stone-paved rooms with videos and displays ranging from ancient oil lamps to Roman oil amphorae in a vertically sectioned ship, to reconstructed olive mills from centuries past, and precious silver or glass oil recipients, not to mention photos of old Oneglia, and lots of handsome Olio Carli tin cans, from the company's founding in 1911 onward. There's also a museum *caffè* and shop, where you can buy olive-related gifts, cards, Carli oils and more. The ultra-modern factory next door is open for tours. If you visit during harvest season, you can see how the Carli mill produces perfectly good extra virgin, very good DOP Riviera dei Fiori and work-a-day refined olive oils. The operation has the merit of being transparent. From the Oneglia train station, head northeast on the main road, Via Garessio, to #11, Tel: 0183 7080 or 295762, www.oliocarli.it. Open daily except Sunday 9am to 12:30pm and 3pm to 6:30pm, free admission.

outskirts are less than attractive. Happily the older parts of town between the train station and the sea are handsome and make for pleasant strolling. The main square is Piazza Dante. Under its soaring arcades are several great places for coffee, pastries and ice cream. The town's main street, leading east off Piazza Dante, is Via Bonfante. It's also arcaded. On either side spread atmospheric medieval alleyways lined with hole-in-the-wall shops. Surprisingly, Oneglia has three artisanal coffee roasters and one rather large one, but is above all the gateway to the province's great olive oil country. The names of olive oil dynasties are writ large: there's an Isnardi shopping gallery, for instance, and a Via Ardoino, both in the center of town. The seaside portico, Calata Cuneo, fronting the working port, is charming, painted pink then white then yellow. Under it are restaurants and *caffè*, plus a celebrated fish shop with excellent, traditional salted anchovies. The wholesale fish market, a colorful scrimmage, is also held here, when the boats come in with the catch (anchovies in the morning, most other fish in the afternoon). The weekly open market is held on Saturday morning in Piazza Maresca, behind the church of San Giovanni, and is one of the Riviera's biggest and most authentic. Fronting it on the western end is the Andrea Doria covered market, which is open weekday and Saturday mornings.

The restaurant scene is typical of the coast, with upmarket, modish restaurants serving *cucina creativa* and fish, and little else of interest. The most regionally true (and popular) place to eat is **Beppa** (Calata Cuneo 44/ Via Doria Andrea 24, Tel: 0183 294286, closed Tuesday, expensive). It has been in the same family since the 1950s, with a handsome, vaulted interior, views out from the port-side arcade, and high-quality, fresh ingredients (the olive oil on your nicely napped table is extra virgin from Ardoino, the fish is delivered direct from the boats moored out front).

ANCHOVIES, COFFEE, ICE CREAM, OLIVE OIL, PASTRIES, WINE

Caffè Piccardo

MARIA TERESA AND CARLA PICCARDO ARE THE THIRD GENERATION TO OWN AND OPERATE THIS landmark *caffè*, pastry shop and ice creamery on the main square; Piedmontese chef *pasticcere* Patrizio Ghio makes the delicious pastries. A grandfather clock ticks behind the cash register. Well-healed locals gather to lunch on daily specials, sip

tea, chat and watch each other in big, beveled mirrors. There are also tables outside under the arcades, and a second set of beveled mirrors to go with them. Take a seat in the spacious salon and savor classic miniature jam tarts, brioches, *torrone* with almonds and honey, *pandolce all'antica* (here called *pan du Sciabeccu*), plus specialties such as *stroscia*, a round of shortbread flavored with white vermouth, lemon zest and olive oil; *pinolata*, with pine nuts and almond paste; *gobeloni*, which look like upside-down cupcakes, filled with apple bits and apple jam; and *baci di Imperia* chocolate sandwich cookies. The coffee is supplied by Covim, which makes for a good cappuccino. It also goes into the coffee ice cream. Along with the other thirty or so flavors available in high season (half that in winter), it's remarkably good. There's nothing showy or sugary about the *gelati*. A frozen delight you'll find nowhere else in the region: old-fashioned ice cream bars, called Pinguini, made with the same molds the founder bought a hundred years ago. The Pinguini come in *crema* (vanilla cream), *crema e banana* and *gianduja*, and are hand-dipped in melted chocolate.

PIAZZA DANTE 1-2 ✦ TEL: 0183 293696

OPEN DAILY 6:30AM *to* 8:30PM

Enoteca Lupi

O N THE MAIN PEDESTRIAN ALLEYWAY NORTHEAST AND PARALLEL TO VIA BONFANTE, THIS CAVERNOUS, labyrinthine old wine shop is the lair of opinionated, extroverted Angelo Lupi and his family, the same family of winemakers as Tommaso Lupi in nearby Pieve di Teco. As you'd expect, among the thousands of Italian wines sold here you'll find the best of the Riviera. Typically, on offer are ten each of Pigato and Vermentino, and eight each of Ormeasco and Rossese, but the mix might change according to the owner's judgments, formed by regular closed-session tastings with a group of six close collaborators. You'll also find Lupi's own wines, naturally, including Riviera Ligure di Ponente DOC Vermentino Le Serre, which is particularly excellent. Many fine extra virgin olive oils from the area are also sold, as well as the full line of oils and olive-based products from Frantoio Sant'Agata di Oneglia di Mela C. & C. The Lupis are diamonds in the rough; don't be put off if they seem challenging in their approach. If you happen to come in when bottles are open and tastings are going on, it's just possible you'll be asked to join in, free of charge and with utmost informality.

VIA V. MONTI 13 ✦ TEL: 0183 291610

CLOSED SUNDAY *and* THE SECOND HALF OF AUGUST

Pescheria Delmonte "U Balincio"

IN THE DELMONTE FAMILY FOR THREE GENERA-TIONS, AND, SINCE 1960, WITH GIOVANNI, ALIAS U Balincio, at the helm, this spotlessly clean fishmonger's shop is at the far eastern end of the arcaded seafront, where the palm trees begin. The fish is always fresh, sometimes still alive, and the ancho-vies are salted in the old-fashioned way, meaning the heads are removed with a tug, which also pulls out most of the guts, and the fish, with bones, fins and skin still attached, are lay-ered with coarse sea salt and macerated in brine, weighed down with a stone, for two months, until ready to eat.

CALATA G.B. CUNEO 77 ✦ TEL: 0183 292738

CLOSED WEDNESDAY AFTERNOON *and* SUNDAY

Torrefazione Caffè Brasil

ON A SHORT STREET TO THE EAST OF THE TOWN CEN-TER, ABOUT 300 YARDS FROM THE TRAIN STATION, this corner *caffè* and coffee roasting establishment is a longtime favorite among locals, who gather here to read the newspaper or play cards. Since the 1960s, the Berio family have been buying fine Arabica and good Robusta beans and toast-ing them several times a week in small batches. You can smell the scent for blocks around. Of the eight blends, the bar blend,

Brasil, is the best. It's dark roasted and strong, and makes flavorful *cappuccini*. Also sold are cookies and candies.

VIA DON ABBO 7-9 ✦ TEL: 0183 294967
CLOSED SATURDAY AFTERNOON *and* SUNDAY

Tuttogelato

THIS IS ONEGLIA'S "OTHER" ICE CREAMERY, IN THE CHIC SHOPPING CENTER THAT BEARS THE NAME of an oil dynasty based in nearby Pontedassio. The end of the Roman Empire? For those tired of the humdrum, fuddy duddy flavors, there are surprising delights in store, such as chunky, pungent *gorgonzola*-and-*porcino* gelato, mussel or shrimp ice cream, red wine-flavored gelato and, of course, given the address, the inevitable Taggiasca olive ice cream. The owners teach at the hotel-and-restaurant trade school, and feel it necessary to introduce novelty into the mix. Luckily, for the retrograde ice cream lover, the less trendy flavors, including many from fresh fruit or freshly brewed coffee, are delicious.

GALLERIA ISNARDI 4 ✦ TEL: 0183 299040 ✦ CLOSED TUESDAY

OLIVE OIL MAKERS IN OR NEAR IMPERIA-ONEGLIA

Olio Carli

See olive museum sidebar page 357.

Ranise Azienda Agroalimentari

ROBERTO RANISE MAKES OUTSTANDING EXTRA VIRGIN DOP OLIVE OILS FROM TAGGIASCA OLIVES GROWN at the family groves in Lecchiore, near Dolcedo, a medieval hill village inland from Oneglia; here the Ranise family run a pleasant B&B (Tel: 0183 280048). The headquarters and sales room are on Via Nazionale, the main highway that runs north from the Oneglia train station toward the autostrada. Ranise doesn't own an olive oil mill, but has worked with a local *frantoio* for decades. The crushing is done traditionally with granite millstones; the rest of the extraction, settling and bottling process is ultra-modern. Ranise was among the first oil makers to be awarded DOP Riviera dei Fiori status, and his oils are delicate and flowery, with a slight almond *amaretto* aftertaste. Ranise also makes remarkable pesto, olive pastes and several flavored oils (with herbs or lemon), and sells brined Taggiasca olives.

VIA NAZIONALE 30 ✦ TEL: 0183 767966, WWW.RANISE.IT. OPEN WEEKDAY MORNINGS *and* AFTERNOONS STARTING 3PM, *and* BY APPOINTMENT

Frantoio di Sant'Agata di Oneglia di Mela C. & C.

WITH ITS MILL AND HEADQUARTERS DUE NORTH OF ONEGLIA SEVERAL MILES, NEAR THE autostrada, Impero River and municipal hospital, and most of its olive groves at about 1,000 feet above sea level on terraces above and around the mill, this family-run olive-growing and oil-making concern (not affiliated with the giant Santagata olive oil company of Genoa and Chiavari) uses ultra-modern, two-phase, eco-friendly continuous presses to produce what are among the Riviera di Ponente's finest extra virgin olive oils. Pure-Taggiasca Cru Primo Fiore from the Campagne Martine Fascei grove at 1,600 feet above sea level, has less than 0.3 percent acid, a golden hue and pine nut-and-flowers flavors; the "Buon Frutto" is also very good, though slightly less subtle, made with a mix of Taggiasca and other varieties. The olives are handpicked and milled within twenty-four hours. Antonio Mela's family have been in the olive oil business in the area since 1827, though the operation as currently organized was founded in 1987. The family also makes olive oils flavored with fresh lemon, chili pepper, basil and black truffle (with a chunk of truffle in it), plus a wide range of excellent olive-based products, from the ubiquitous brined olives and olive paté, to grilled vegetables packed in oil, pesto or tomato sauce for pasta, and vegetable spreads, which are sold at better gourmet food shops everywhere in the region, and locally by Enoteca Lupi, in the center of Oneglia.

VIA DEI FRANCESI 48, FRAZIONE SANT'AGATA DI ONEGLIA TEL: 0183 293472 ✦ WWW.FRANTOIOSANTAGATA.COM RETAIL SALES WEEKDAYS 9AM *to* 5:30PM

IMPERIA-PORTO MAURIZIO

....

*I*MPERIA-PORTO MAURIZIO IS ABOUT TWO MILES WEST OF ONEGLIA, PAST THE AGNESE PASTA factory and Jolly coffee roasting plant, across the Impero River. Skirt the waterfront wasteland (being converted into sports facilities and bike lanes). Perched on a spur, Porto Maurizio spills down to the sea. The port area, called Borgo Marina, now bereft of fishing boats, is filled with sleek yachts. Porto Maurizio is named for the saint who lived and died nearby, and the vast church dedicated to him, perched near the top of the hill, has the biggest cupola in Liguria. But the town is much older than Maurizio; it was founded by the Romans, thrived as a pirate stronghold and medieval city state, and came into the orbit of Genoa about 800 years ago. The seaside is handsome, with a land-scaped promenade. The twisting alleyways and small squares, perched loggias and breathtaking staircases, are long on atmosphere. However, Porto Maurizio is somewhat short on gastronomy, with the usual glitz or snack food and not much between. Beyond the beauty, it's worth stopping here for the olive oil, olive paté, sauces, sun-dried tomatoes, pickled vegetables, jams and honeys at **Azienda Agricola La Giara** (Via Scarincio 62, Borgo Marina, Tel: 333 312 4989, www.la-giara.it, closed Sunday afternoon and Monday). La Giara's olive groves and farm are on the Monte Grazie, inland, but they sell their wares from a tiny boutique on the main seaside road near the port.

If you visit Porto Maurizio in the evening, and you love pizza and chaos, **L'Oasi** (Piazza Sant'Antonio 15, Borgo Marina, Tel: 0183 666892, dinner only starting at 7:30pm, closed Monday, inexpensive) is a cult pizzeria on the main square of Borgo Marina, about 150 yards west of La Giara. The waiters do not take your food order, unless you opt for the good, housemade *pappardelle* with *ragu*; they simply offer to the first comers the pizzas that have just been pulled from the oven. Take a seat at a table inside or, preferably, outside on the square, and when the pizza you desire appears, claim it. There are dozens of types of pizza, some classic and excellent, others overly ambitious or perfumed with truffle oil. If the experience seems too stressful to contemplate, across the square you'll find a charming, barrel-vaulted, modish restaurant called **Hostaria del Pellegrino** (Via Sant'Antonio 7, Tel: 0183 667028, closed Monday, Tuesday lunch out of season, dinner only in July/August, expensive), which fancies itself an *osteria*, and serves very good seafood and a handful of updated Ligurian dishes.

Up top, on the palm-tree-lined, slate-paved Via XX Settembre, between Via Cascione and Piazza Roma, **Bar Breakfast** (Via XX Settembre 43, Tel: 0183 64614, closed Sunday) brews and sells excellent Torrefazione Pasqualini coffees. Closer to Piazza Roma, **Pasticceria Gelateria da Maurizio e Charlie** (Via XX Settembre 53/55, Tel: 0183 62482, closed holiday afternoons), a friendly, neighborhood pastry shop and ice creamery, makes delicious, classic Ligurian sweets, including big *gobeletti* with apricot jam and fresh apple bits, and unshowy but luscious ice creams from scratch. The best place to buy a picnic is **Salumeria Re** (Via Cascione 9, Tel: 0183 61657, closed Sundays September through June), on the main road in the upper part of town; the pickled and bottled delicacies are very good, as are the hams and cheeses.

OLIVE OIL MAKERS IN THE IMMEDIATE SURROUNDINGS OF IMPERIA-PORTO MAURIZIO

Scores of olive growers and oil mills are scattered around Imperia. The following ones are within a few miles of the coast, and may be reached by car in a matter of minutes. Northwest and inland of Porto Maurizio, on the way to Caramagna and Dolcedo on the Strada Colla, you'll find **Benza Frantoiano Olio Extravergine** (Via Dolcedo 180, Caramagna (IM), Tel: 0183 280132, www.oliobenza.it). Benza is one of the region's premier olive oil makers. Nearly 4,000 Taggiasca olive trees owned by the Benza family, in the business since the mid-1800s, fill groves around Dolcedo, Lecchiore and even further inland at Prelà. The company uses state-of-the-art milling equipment (and mills for other growers, such as Valle Ostilia of Villa Faraldi) to make three remarkable extra virgin olive oils: Primuruggiu, the cream of the crop, with a name that evokes the old-fashioned milling techniques no longer used here; it's sweet but spicy, complex and nutty. Dulcedo is a classic DOP Riviera dei Fiori oil, with all the fruity, flowery, pine nut scents and flavors you'd expect; and Buonolio is as close as you'll find nowadays to an old-fashioned "peasant oil," made with fully ripe olives, and therefore fattier and less flowery than those pressed from slightly immature olives. Benza also makes outstanding brined olives, olive paté and vegetables packed in oil. The mill is open to visitors and is near highway SP39, on a narrow drive that branches off Via Dolcedo.

Also in the Dolcedo municipal area, west of the village on Via Santa Brigida/highway SP42, is **Azienda Agricola Giordano Valerio** (Via Bellissimi 12, Costa Carnara, Tel: 339 819 1076, www.giordanovalerio.it), family-owned growers of Taggiasca olives, and makers of very good DOP extra virgin oils, bottled olives, pickled vegetables, sauces and other specialty foods. **Frantoio Ghiglione Giuseppe** (Via Ciancergo 23, Tel: 0183 280043, www.frantoioghiglione.it, open weekdays, Saturday morning and by appointment), a friendly family of Taggiasca olive growers and makers of very good extra virgin oils (some of them organic) since 1920, are equipped with both traditional and modern, continuous presses. The mill and boutique are in the center of atmospheric Dolcedo, above Via Garibaldi and Via Mameli. The family's trees grow at about 1,300 feet above sea level, and the olives are handpicked and milled within twenty-four hours, meaning they can be left to ripen fully, producing golden-hued, soft, sweet oils; they also buy high-quality Taggiasca olives from their neighbors. You can taste the oils (and the olive paste, pitted olives, pesto, sun-dried tomatoes or eggplants in oil and more) at the mill.

For a simple, home-cooked meal near Dolcedo, with local specialties, made from scratch from produce grown on the farm, including the quaffable Vermentino white wine or *uva nera* red (of mixed grape varieties), and very good olive oil, try casual **Agriturismo Ca' da Ninna** (Via Uliveto 8, Frazione Costa Carnara, Tel: 0183 280279, cell 347 088 6776, by reservation only three days ahead; open weekdays for dinner, Sundays for lunch, or by arrangement for parties of eight people minimum; inexpensive). The farmhouse is less than two miles north of the Ghiglione mill, toward the mountains. Follow signs to Costa Carnara. Ninna's *farinata*, *cima*, and *frittata di verdura* are very good; everything follows the seasons, including the ravioli stuffed with chard and ground veal, and sauced with meat and tomatoes, walnuts or pesto.

From Dolcedo, head due north on the winding back road toward Prelà and look for the hamlet of Molini di Prelà, drive through and follow the road to Pantasina, where you'll find **La Mola** (Via Pantasina 10, Località Molini di Prelà, Tel: 0183 282418, www.oliomola.com). This olive grower and oil maker is also an upscale farmhouse B&B, with a swimming pool and views galore. When it comes to methodology, however, everything is old-fashioned, from the way the olives are handpicked and selected by grandpa Pietro Ghiglione, aided by his wife

Marilena and sons Gianfranco and Vincenzo, to the old-fashioned millstones and presses. The family's oils are usually sold by mail order, but you can also buy direct.

Also in Pantasina, just beyond the main square, is the store and oil mill of **Azienda Agricola Giuseppe Cotta Agriturismo Il Roccolo** (Via Ameglio 5, Frazione Pantasina, Vasia (IM), Tel: 0183 282145, 333 798 1164, www.agricotta.com, open 9am to 12:30pm and 2:30pm to 7:30pm daily and by appointment). This small, multi-generational, family-run farm is also a B&B. Monica and Giuseppe Cotta have about 1,500 Taggiasca trees on gorgeous, terraced hillsides, and make about 6,000 liters of sweet, flowery, golden-hued, excellent, certified organic extra virgin oils in the traditional, old-fashioned way. The millstones are granite, the press is hydraulic. The oil is merely centrefuged, not filtered. The top of the line oils, available only in exceptional years, are Inprimis (early harvest) and Dulcis (mature olives), and both are worth going out of your way to find. You can always stay — the B&B is comfortable, cozy and nicely appointed, set amid nearby lavender fields, with spectacular views out to sea. Also sold are the family's lavender and lavender essence, and delicious bottled brined olives, pitted olives in olive oil and olive paté, plus very good pesto.

Due west of Porto Maurizio from the Via Aurelia seaside highway, go inland on two-lane highway SP96; it twists and turns up past the autostrada toward Civezza; before reaching Civezza, you'll find Piazza della Torre in Poggi and **Saglietto Olio Agriturismo** (Via Carli 21, Poggi (IM), Tel: 0183 651308 www.saglietto.it), a multi-generational oil maker and, recently, luxury farmstead B&B with five lovely lodgings. Enrico and Tiziana Saglietto make a golden-hued, soft, sweet but full-bodied and mature 100 percent Taggiasca extra virgin oil that's cold-pressed using traditional methods and bottled without being filtered. The family also makes about 2,500 bottles a year of nice, traditional Vermentino.

AN OLIVE OIL-AND-WINE (AND GOURMET FOODS) ROUTE:

IMPERIA PROVINCE AND ITS EXTENDED HINTERLAND

....

Note: Because of the scattered locations of olive oil makers, wineries, food producers, shops and restaurants in the area, the best way to discover them is to budget a day or two, rent a car and take the road trip inland. The distances are relatively short, but roads are narrow with many curves. Expect to spend at least one whole day for a round-trip tour.

THE VALLEY OF THE IMPERO RIVER DIRECTLY BEHIND IMPERIA LEADS TO SCORES OF VALLEY or perched villages and towns and then into dramatic mountain scenery. Following it over a mountain pass you enter the upper Valley of the Arroscia River and, to the west, the mountains bordering France. Because most of the wineries and olive oil concerns listed below are small and family run, the opening hours vary widely. It's wise to phone ahead. There are dozens of oil mills and wineries in the area. This is a select list. For a complete listing of wineries visit www.enotecapubblica.it; for certified DOP oil makers, visit www.consorziodoprivieraligure.it.

Start in the Impero River Valley on busy highway SP28, heading due north for about five miles to industrious Pontedassio, a town that spreads primarily along the eastern side of the valley bottom. Named for a long-gone bridge (*ponte*) with wooden planks (*assi*), this is where the Agnesi dynasty of pasta makers got its start, at a watermill on the Impero River near the wooden bridge.

Nowadays, Pontedassio is best known among food lovers as the headquarters of olive oil kingpin **Pietro Isnardi** (Via Torino 156, Tel: 0183 7981, info@olioardoino.it, www.olioardoino.it), a big, high-end company which also owns **Olio Ardoino**. They're on the main highway, here called Via Torino. Isnardi/Ardoino are marketing and packaging masters, and have adopted handsome foil wrapping and ancient Roman-sounding names to promote their oils. They include Vallaurea, Drupa Aureus, Fructus Aureus and Oleum Mundum (made with pitted Taggiasca olives). The most complex and satisfying of them are the *mosti*, Vallaurea and Fructus. The company mix includes DOP Riviera dei Fiori and other extra virgin oils made with olives from outside Liguria.

On the town's main square is medium-sized winery **Laura Aschero** (Piazza Vittorio Emanuele 7, Tel: 0183 293515 and 710307, by appointment), among the first, in the 1980s, to make full-fleshed, powerful Pigato and Vermentino, and still very good. The Aschero vineyards are close to Diano Arentino and Diano Castello, over the hill to the east. Also near town is less well-known winemaker **Giacomo Alberti** (Via Nazionale, Regione Aribaga, Tel: 0183 779003, info@lattealberti.it, by appointment), whose Riviera Ligure di Ponente DOC Vermentino is very good, with all the hallmarks of regional typicity.

Drive north from Pontedassio about three miles to Sarola, on the west side of the valley, near where Strada Colle di Nava disappears into a tunnel. Here **Domenico Ramoino** (Via XX Settembre, Tel: 0183 52646) makes excellent pure Taggiasca olive oils. The top of the line is Anchisa, also the name of an olive grove, where the olives are handpicked at the ideal degree of ripeness and rushed to the mill, yielding very sweet, delicate, flavorful oils.

Go back to the river valley and cross it, driving uphill to the hamlet of Gazzelli and its central Piazza Belmonte, then down to Via Dante, where two oil makers are based. **Gian Battista Fasolo** (Via Dante 4, Tel: 0183 52703) is a family-run firm into its third generation. The excellent, classic DOP olive oils are made from organic Taggiasca olives grown in groves at from 800 to 1,700 feet above sea level, and relatively free of fruit fly damage; they're milled with old millstones, and the oils are of the most traditional kind. Also sold are brined olives and *pasta d'olive* spread. On the same road, find well-known wine and oil maker **Azienda Agricola La Rocca di San Nicolao** (Via Dante 10, Tel: 0183 52304, www.roccasannicolao.it). The winery's vineyards and olive trees are also at the upper limit; stressed to survive, they produce remarkable grapes and Taggiasca olives. Both the Riviera Ligure di Ponente DOC Vermentino and Pigato Vigna di Proxi, named for a vineyard, are well balanced, round and satisfying. The DOC Riviera dei Fiori extra virgin oils are true to type.

Farther along the same twisting road is Chiusanico. From Gazzelli, either drive to Chiusanico and back to the main highway looping north via perched Torria, and backtrack south a few miles, or turn around, go back to the highway and head north to Chiusavecchia, where many oil makers are based. The husband-and-wife team at tiny **Azienda Agricola Damiano** (Via IV Novembre 69, Tel: 0183 52717) owns groves of Taggiasca trees on hillsides nearby, and are often difficult to reach. Keep trying.

Though not organic growers, they apply as few treatments as possible against the fruit fly. The oils are very good, and the *polpa di olive* (coarse olive paté), and pitted Taggiasca olives packed in olive oil or brined whole olives, are excellent. Damiano sells direct, at itinerant outdoor markets or by mail order.

On the same road in Chiusavecchia is bigger, better-known **Olio Anfosso** (Via IV Novembre 99, Tel: 0183 52418, anfosso@ olioanfosso.it, www.olioanfosso.it), a reliable producer of fine oils. Drive west from Chiusavecchia up the two-lane road and into the center of the village of Lucinasco, where one of the Riviera's top artisanal oil makers is found. **Azienda Agricola Agriturismo Dinoabbo** (Via Roma 2BIS, Tel: 0183 52411 or 0183 52811, www.dinoabbo.it), makes pure-Taggiasca, old-fashioned, stone-milled oils from the olives handpicked from about 6,500 trees on surrounding hills. Abbo calls the first run off, made under light pressure, Oiu de s'ciappa. It's expensive and sells out fast. Like other upscale producers with a marketing sense, Abbo wraps his bottles in eye-catching tin foil. The mill is now also a pleasant, nicely furnished farmhouse B&B (with views of olive groves and the sea) and serves simple, delicious meals featuring fresh local ingredients.

Head west from Lucinasco on the back road to the scattered hamlet of Ville San Sebastiano (part of Borgomaro) and **Azienda Agricola Il Frantoio** (Via Pellegrino 20, Tel: 0183 6146, info@ ilfrantoio.it, www.frantoio.it), a small oil mill making good extra virgin oils; it's located on the west side of the municipal area. Nearby, two other reputable olive oil makers, **Paolo Pellegrino** (Strada Ville San Pietro, Borgomaro, 0183 54004) and **Alberto Marvaldi** (Via Candeasco 9, Tel: 0183 54016) produce classic DOP Riviera dei Fiori extra virgin oils. It's worth stopping at the bakery and cake shop **Panificio Gandolfo Bruna** (Via P. Merano 43, Tel: 0183 54057), in the center of the village, for the local specialty, *biscotti di Borgomaro*, made with aniseed and mint, plus good *pandolce* and focaccia.

Back down in the Impero River Valley, follow the main highway north through a tunnel (or up and over the olive tree line at Colle di San Bartolomeo, enjoying the expansive views) and then down to medieval, riverside Pieve di Teco in the Valle Arroscia, where the olives and vineyards again thrive. (Before entering Pieve di Teco, if you'd like to visit Vessalico, Liguria's garlic capital, drive due east for about three miles on highway SP453; see 330 for details).

Azienda Lupi (Via Mazzini 9, Pieve di Teco, Tel: 0183 36161, www.vinilupi.it) is the highly rated, long-established family winery of medium size — big by Ligurian standards, producing about 130,000 bottles a year — which maintains a well-stocked wine shop in downtown Oneglia. Winemaker Tommaso Lupi's Riviera Ligure di Ponente DOC Vermentino Le Serre and Pigato Le Petraie are remarkable classics of their kind. Lupi's Ormeasco Superiore Le Braje is a particularly well-made red of medium body.

On Pieve di Teco's handsome main street, which is flanked by porticoes and archways, **Panificio Pasticceria Pignone Giorgio & C.** (Via Mario Ponzoni 50, Tel: 0183 36351) bakes delicious *amaretti*, *pinolata* (here a luscious pine nut-studded cake), and one of the specialties of town, the *biscotto fagoccio*, which is made with ground hazelnuts and is light and airy. Another fine bakery, which makes the large, rustic loaf known as *pagnotta pievese*, is **Panetteria Fratelli Ferrari** (Via Piave 79, Tel: 0183 36271, closed Wednesday). The focaccia is spiked with fresh basil (in summer), or olives and oregano, tiny *pomodorini* tomatoes or walnuts.

Continue north on the twisting highway (or skip ahead by taking the narrow back road that branches left and west to Mendatica) to the hamlet of Acquetico and the up-and-coming Ormeasco winemaker **Colle Sereno** (Piazza San Giacomo 1, Tel: 0183 36167, 339 771 1140). A few miles north are the terraced vineyards of fortified mountain town Pornassio. Three reputable wineries making very good, light Ormeasco di Pornassio red and the sweet Passito version of the same, and/or Ormeasco Sciac-tra rosé, are based here: **Azienda Agricola Lorenzo Ramò** (Via Sant'Antonio 9, Tel: 0183 33097), a multi-generational firm now run by Gianpaolo and Marino Ramò; on the road leading to the perched castle is small, family-run **Azienda Vitivinicola-Agri-cola Eredi Ing. Guglierame** (Via Castello 10, Tel: 0183 33037). You'll find **Cantina Case Rosse** (Via Nazionale 31, Tel: 0183 33024) in the hamlet of Case Rosse, amid chestnut groves, as you drive west from Pornassio on an even twistier back road toward the atmospheric, stacked medieval village of Cosio d'Arroscia.

In Cosio, near the main square, beekeeper **Apicoltura Dino Gastaldi** (Via San Rocco 8, Tel: 0183 327714, phone any time) makes delicious, pure mountain honeys and *melata* from a variety of plants, including rhododendron. The honey shop is at Via Don Bosco 20, but call Gastaldi at home and ask him to come to the store. Cheesemaker **Marco Favero** (Via Cavour 1, Tel:

0183 327848, from 11am daily) makes delicious local cow's milk cheeses; he's away with his herd, or at the cheese factory, early in the morning but by late morning is usually around, and is always available in the afternoon.

If you're hungry, before heading west to Cosio d'Arroscia, detour north from Case Rosse on the main highway SS28 toward the Colle di Nava mountain pass and **Albergo Ristorante Lorenzina** (Via Nazionale 65, Case di Nava, Tel: 0183 325044, www.albergolorenzina.com), perched at about 3,000 feet above sea level. This comfortable place has been in the same family since 1926 (and is into its third generation). It's designed for big summer crowds, and has a huge dining room with white walls and wooden tables draped with white cloths. Old fashioned but upscale, you'll find all the regional specialties plus boar and venison, porcini done in half a dozen ways, a good selection of local cheeses, and housemade desserts featuring local ingredients such as *semifreddo di amaretti*, creamy whipped cream pudding with nougat and hot honey, or wild berries. The wine list is long on local bottlings, from Bruna, Ramò, Case Rosse and many others.

Several miles west of Case Rosse through chestnut groves is Mendatica, a medieval mountain town built in the 1200s as a way-station for tax collectors and stopover for shepherds. It has many handsome fountains carved from stone. As the crow flies, the French border is about five miles away. Between Mendatica, the Maritime Alps and France at Frazione San Bernardo you'll find **Agriturismo Il Castagno** (Via San Bernardo 39, Tel: 0183 328718, il.castagno@libero.it, www.ilcastagnosrl.it), which produces and packages olives and olive oil, cheeses and other typical Ligurian and local mountain products.

The Mediterranean may be twenty miles south, but you're in Alpine territory. In late fall, winter or early spring, check the snow reports and road conditions before driving over Passo Garlenda to Triora and back to the coast, either via the Valle Argentina or Pigna, Isolabona and Dolceacqua.

CHAPTER 14:

·····································

San Remo to Ventimiglia and the border with France

Province: **Imperia.** *Includes:* Apricale, Arma di Taggia, Castel Vittorio, Badalucco, Baiardo, Bordighera, Dolceacqua, Isolabona, Mulini di Triora, Perinaldo, Pigna, San Remo, Soldano, Triora, Valle Argentina, Ventimiglia.

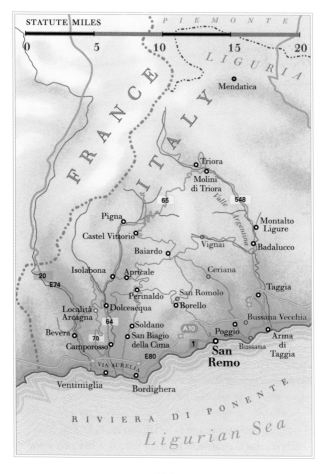

*T*HE CONTRAST OF SUN-WASHED, SOPHISTICATED COAST AND RURAL HINTERLAND IS PARTICULARLY striking in the far west of the region. This landscape of stone and scrub forged the wiry prose of Italy's great twentieth-century writer, Italo Calvino, who grew up in the San Remo area. Calvino witnessed the way modern industry, tourism and commercial flower-growing were killing off the farming life of his ancestors. Like his fictional characters, he was troubled by the "palm trees, casinos, hotels, villas" of the rich, and fled. From the alleys of old San Remo he climbed through the geometrical glasshouses of carnations engulfing the old terraced farmsteads, and then further up through stands of pine trees to the safety of the chestnut forests. That is what many locals and visitors continue to do to find the rural heart of the region, and its most authentic food.

BORDIGHERA

*C*ONSIDER FOLLOWING CALVINO OR CLAUDE MONET, WHO LEFT THE PROMENADES OF FASHIONABLE, beautiful Bordighera to wander into the Sasso Valley behind the city, where he was "dazzled" by the "diabolical colors" of almond and peach trees set amid groves of palms, lemons and olives. Like Alassio, Bordighera is elegant, orderly and distinctly international in atmosphere and tastes. It's home to several Michelin-starred restaurants. Bordighera's best coffee (made by Piedmontese roaster Caffè Vergnano) is served at stylish **La Casa del Caffè** (Corso Italia 15A/17, Tel: 0184 261624, closed Wednesday), which has a pleasant outdoor terrace, and is located on the west side of town, about a hundred yards north of the Via Aurelia (called Via Vittorio Emanuele II here). This being Bordighera, you can also have a cup of tea, or sip wine by the glass and snack on delicious sandwiches, light lunches, salads and treats. The ice creams are made in-house and are very good, especially the fresh fruit flavors.

SAN REMO

....

THE WESTERN RIVIERA'S OLDEST RESORT TOWN, PALM-LINED SAN REMO BEGAN ATTRACTING genteel travelers in the mid 1800s, and its Hôtel de Londres was the prototype of many grand hotels. To it and the San Remo casino, built around 1900, came German emperors and poets; English kings, botanists, butterfly hunters and Victorian lady watercolorists; and Russian Tsarinas, their courts and sycophants. The casino still draws an international clientele, though these days the Russians are more likely to be oligarchs with laundry to do. Since the end of World War II, San Remo has morphed from old money to new, with an overlay of Las Vegas. The glitz and glam surrounding the annual Festival di San Remo pop song extravaganza (in late February) adds to the feel.

Divided into three, San Remo's nineteenth-century villas, hotels, tree-lined promenades, fashionable restaurants and shopping streets lie along the coast, which is relatively flat. Behind them are the charming, narrow alleyways of the Piano neighborhood, centered on the cathedral, but founded in ancient Roman times. Above Piano is San Remo's medieval aery, the Pigna (pinecone). This tangle of alleys and pocketsized squares, whose buttressed buildings are held up by scaffolding, is struggling to gentrify itself. Many residents from below avoid it and describe it as unsafe, especially at night, because of its immigrant population. They cite as typical the transformation of former 400-year-

old Pigna eatery, Hosteria della Costa, into La Casbah. However, casual, unprejudiced visitors are more likely to find the Pigna more touristy than dangerous.

San Remo has an excellent municipal covered market, in an eyesore of a building in Piazza degli Eroi Sanremesi, northeast of the cathedral and Via Palazzo (formerly the Roman road, now the town's most atmospheric shopping street). The market is closed weekday afternoons (and Sunday from October through April). Here you'll find everything from baked goods (including rustic bread from Triora and savory *canestrelli* from Taggia) to oil, wine and a wide selection of fruits and vegetables from local truck farms (Coltivatori Diretti—on the market's northern end). At stands eleven and five, enthusiastic Maura Ragazzoni displays the celebrated white beans of Badalucco, Ceriana, Conio and Pigna, plus dry porcini or sun-dried tomatoes, candied or dry fruit, and good extra virgin olive oils.

The dining scene is a challenge; an American fast food restaurant has opened on the main square, Piazza Colombo, with another on a pedestrianized street nearby. Eat-and-run tourism parallels the modish bars, clubs and restaurants catering to the casino and festival crowd. Kitsch throwback **Cantine Sanremesi** (Via Palazzo 7, Tel: 0184 572063, open daily until 9pm except Monday, inexpensive to moderate) serves *sardenaira*, San Remo's answer

to focaccia or pizza, plus anchovies, *baccalà* and decent *farinata*, in a cellar with cheek-by-jowl seating. Less touristy places for *sardenaira*, savory tarts and very good chickpea *farinata* are **Tavernetta** (Via Palazzo 129, Tel: 0184 507293, closed Sunday), at the eastern end of Via Palazzo since 1950; and **Maggiorino** (Via Roma 183, Tel: 0184 504338, open 7:30am to 2:30pm and 4:30pm to 7pm, closed Sunday and holidays, inexpensive), on the western end of

San Remo's main automobile thoroughfare.

The most authentic place to dine is upscale **Nuovo Piccolo Mondo** (Via Piave 7, Tel: 0184 509 9012, closed Monday night and Sunday, moderate to expensive), on an alleyway between Corso Matteotti and Via Roma in the center of the seaside section of town. It calls itself an *antica trattoria* but is a handsome, small, vaulted restaurant with old prints on the white walls, starched tablecloths, and a solicitous staff used to English-speaking customers. Happily, the grilled, roasted or stewed fish and squid are fresh and skillfully prepared, and the *cima alla genovese*, boiled octopus and potatoes, and even the classic tripe, are surprisingly true to type. The desserts are simple and housemade. The wine list, though short, includes some of the Riviera's best.

For a snack and a glass of wine—there are usually half a dozen good Ligurian bottlings available daily—**Ristorante Enoteca Ostricheria Bacchus** (Via Roma 65, Tel: 0184 530990, open daily 10am to 9pm, inexpensive to moderate) is a fallback. Forget the imported oysters and stick to simple savory tarts, salami and cheese, stuffed vegetables and the like. Bacchus is also a wine shop. A better stocked and infinitely more stylish wine shop, inconveniently located on a back road north of Piazza Colombo, is **Enoteca Marone** (Via San Francesco 61, Tel: 0184 506916, closed Monday morning and Sunday). It carries thousands of bottlings, including those of Liguria's top wineries; also sold are local specialty foods (olive oil, brined olives, pesto).

Two outstanding stores sell specialty canned, bottled and dry foods from the region and elsewhere. Wonderfully old-fashioned and upscale **Salumeria Crespi** (Via Palazzo 84, Tel: 0184 507688, closed Sunday) is on the corner of Via Mameli, halfway down Via Palazzo, and stocks everything from bottled anchovies to dried mushrooms and *biscotti di Pontedassio* (lightly sweet toasts with olive oil, butter and sugar, for dipping in milk), to excel-

lent bottled pesto, pastas and *canestrelli di Taggia*. On the main street two down from Via Palazzo parallel to the sea is **Sciolè Mirella** (Via Roma 125, Tel: 0184 533399, msciole@libero.it, closed Sunday). This appealing corner shop has been here since the late 1950s. The current owner has freshened up displays and sells very good cheeses (including local *toma* from the *entroterra*), air-dried or salt cod, organic produce, beans from Badalucco and other *entroterra* villages, and a wide range of honeys, sauces, spreads, anchovies in oil and pesto with or without garlic (which, however, contains cashews, and is rather strong and herbal tasting). There are usually about ten each of fine local wines and extra virgin olive oils.

More recent and glamorous, a few shopfronts from the Ariston theater in the center of San Remo, is **Opera Magé i Sapori**

della Terra Taggiasca (Via Cavour 21, Tel: 0184 574235, info@ operamage.com, www.operamage.com, closed Sunday), which also has a boutique in Arma di Taggia. In this outlet you'll find fine house-branded DOP olive oils, honeys, dry pasta such as *corzetti*, and sauces, including tomato-and-porcini sauce and pesto (made with Prà basil, *parmigiano* and extra virgin olive oil).

Buy down-to-earth picnic supplies, take-out dishes such as savory tarts, and ham and cheese, at **Salumeria Bellini** (Via Corradi 54, Tel: 0184 573208, closed Sunday) near the corner of Via Pietro Calvi, a hundred yards west of the western end of Via Palazzo.

For sweets, including *baci di San Remo* (big, mandarine-sized chocolate kisses with chocolate filling), head to adorable timewarp **Pasticceria Primavera** (Via Palazzo 51, Tel: 0184 507487, closed Sunday afternoon and Monday). This small pastry shop halfway down Via Palazzo, unchanged by the Rambaldi family since 1950, makes its kisses daily, and they're remarkably rich, tender and flavorful, with a hint of rum in the filling. **Pasticceria San Romolo** (Via Carli 6, Tel: 0184 531565, closed Monday afternoon and Sunday) is further west several hundred yards, toward the casino, between Corso Matteotti and Via Roma, and is an equally venerable operation, with canvas marquees on the street. Locals and Festival types line up several deep to buy the house specialty, *romoletti*, a *baci*-like sandwich cookie with powered hazelnut in

the flour, and chocolate cream filling. Buy *pane di Triora* or *canestelli di Taggia* at spartan neighborhood bakery **Panetteria Bellerio Rolando** (Corso Garibaldi 118, no telephone, closed Wednesday afternoon and Sunday).

For coffee (or tea) and a snack or light lunch, your best bet is not on the seaside but rather at **Caffè Ducale** (Via Matteotti 145, Tel: 0184 1955202, open daily 7am to 11pm), which is a block from the Ariston theater, where the Festival di San Remo is held. This multi-level, modish bar, restaurant and *caffè* frequented by beautiful people serves Illy coffee, has perfectly decent food, two dozen teas, and a wine bar with many fine Riviera wines by the glass. Across the street is rival **Bar Pasticceria Festival** (Via Matteotti 196, Tel: 0184 504355, open daily 7am to 1am), a less glitzy, family-run *caffè* that has been here for over fifty years and has very good housemade pastries, and the best ice cream in town. In summer, the road is pedestrian only, and Festival has tables outside, from which you can watch the glamour crowd. If you get a take-out *coppetta*, it won't be the usual paper cup, but rather a colorful, fancy plastic dish. The *semifreddi* are particularly delicious, especially the coffee flavor, from freshly brewed Lavazza.

San Remo's friendly, long-established coffee roaster is **Torrefazione Elena** (Via Fiume 36, Tel: 0184 505502, closed Saturday afternoon), in business in the same spot, between the Garibaldi traffic circle and the seaside, on the east side of town, since 1863. Every morning, small batches of very good beans are roasted with an antique, wood-fueled machine. Various blends are sold; the top-two pure Arabicas ("bar" and "bar extra") are very good. No coffee is served here, but you can taste the bar blend at half a dozen places in town: Nazionale, Sabrina, Rex, Metro and Pasticcera Très Bon.

Another source for excellent freshly roasted coffee is **La Bottega del Caffè Pasqualini** (Via de Benedetti 23, Tel: 0184 502209, closed Sunday), which is between the market and San Siro cathedral.

Colorful winemaker and olive oil maker **Luigi Calvini** (Strada Solaro 76, Tel: 0184 660242, www.luigicalvini.com, always open but phone ahead if possible), whose family winery, boutique and artisanal oil mill are perched above the western edge of town, within neighing distance of the San Remo equestrian and tennis clubs, makes good classic olive oils and Riviera di Ponente DOC wines (Pigato and Rossese), plus several unusual table wines you'll find nowhere else. Armean is made with Rossese and Moscatello, is light in flavor and body, with a pale red hue, and goes with just about everything; Brigantino is a quaffable light white, low in alcohol, made from Garganico, Moscato and Vermentino grapes, and equally easy to drink with everything from seafood to pesto. The family's vineyards and olive trees are near Ceriana, at about 1,300 feet above sea level, and therefore the olives are little damaged by fruit fly rot.

VENTIMIGLIA

N OCTOPUS OF ROADS, HIGHWAYS AND TRAIN TRACKS, BOUNDED TO THE WEST BY A riverbed, Ventimiglia is a soulful place that seems out of place on the border of France's prosperous, orderly Côte d'Azur. Urban planners appear to have been absent when Ventimiglia grew from a fishing village into a city. In the postwar period, as prosperty lured inhabitants down to the seaside, the medieval heights of old Ventimiglia were allowed to deteriorate. In recent decades, they've become a bedroom community for itinerant street hawkers from Africa and Eastern Europe. Efforts to revitalize Ventimiglia are underway. In 2005 the ancient Roman theater of Albinitimilium reopened, and is now a venue for opera and concerts.

The best thing about Ventimiglia is the Friday flea and food market, which runs for about a mile and a half along the seaside, and is open from before dawn to well after dusk (officially, 9am to sunset). Among the thousands of stands you'll find old and new clothing, jewelry, antiques real and fake and food items of all kinds. The fruit, vegetable and flower market is housed in a ramshackle, open-ended structure that would be equally at home in Naples or on the southern shores of the Mediterranean.

It's therefore all the more surprising that two of Liguria's most prestigious and expensive, French-influenced, international-style restaurants officially belong to Ventimiglia, though, granted, they're in the gorgeous western suburbs of Grimaldi Inferiore and Ponte San Ludovico. In town, for a good, casual Ligurian *trattoria* meal based around grilled fish and classic dishes — *pansôti* with walnut sauce, tagliatelle with pesto (made, in summer, with homegrown basil), mixed small fry, jam tarts, tiramisu, crème caramel and *panna cotta* — head about 300 yards west of the station toward the mouth of the Roya River on the road flanking the public park and you'll come upon **Chez Lino** (Via Milite Ignoto 1C, Tel: 0184 351412, www.ristorantelino.it, info@ristorantelino.it, closed Sunday, inexpensive to moderate). Friendly Elio De Marco has owned and run it with panache since 1969. The wine list includes many fine whites and reds from the Riviera di Ponente.

Honey lovers won't want to miss meeting passionate, border-crossing beekeeper and honey-maker extraordinaire **Marco Ballestra** (Via Girolamo Rossi 5, Tel: 0184 351672, www.mielepolline.

The Rock Villages of the Western Riviera

THE DESIGNATION "RIVIERA" LEAVES OUT THE PLEATED, MOUNTAINOUS INTERIOR— *l'entroterra*—covering nine-tenths of Liguria's territory. This vertical landscape abounds in unsung valleys, mountain parklands and perched villages. Most inland Ligurian villages are between 1,000 and 1,600 years old. As the Roman Empire collapsed and the invasions of the Middle Ages began, coast-dwellers fled to the mountains. The best-known *entroterra* villages are on the region's western edge near France. They're set against the backdrop of the Maritime Alps, at up to 3,000 feet above sea level. Hewn from the mountainsides and blending in with them are Perinaldo, Apricale and Baiardo, dubbed "Rock Villages" by English travelers of the 1700s. They cling to peaks only a few miles inland from San Remo and Bordighera, but ten times that by coiling road. It's worth the effort to visit them because they're a feast for the eyes, nose and stomach.

Once off the coast, there are no casinos or fancy marinas. Tourism is increasingly important to the local economy, but this is still a farm area, with abundant produce, wine and food. From valley floor to mountaintop, terraces tier the slopes like staircases. In valley bottoms grow vegetables and citrus fruit. Above them start the olive groves and vineyards. Farther up the slopes are fruit tree orchards, yellow mimosa plantations and caterpillar-like hothouses that snake along for hundreds of yards, filled with flowering plants. Dolceacqua, footing the Rock Villages in the Nervia Valley, is where Rossese DOC wines come from. This delightful light red is little known outside Liguria. Other attractive villages in the vicinity include Castel Vittorio, Ceriana, Badalucco, Perinaldo, Pigna, Triora and Mulini di Triora; Bussana and Bussana Vecchia are closer to the coast.

The dishes popular in this border region are distinctive, and there is great emphasis laid on antipasti and local white beans. A meal might begin with translucent slices of raw artichokes drizzled with olive oil, followed by grilled eggplant slices, and three types of fritters fried in olive oil: baby artichokes, streaky *pancetta* or *formaggio di malga* cow's milk cheese from high Apennine pastures. The antipasti continue with thin slices of savory tart (made with minced field greens or squash) and zucchini stuffed with a meatless egg, cheese and bread filling. Less common, you might be served succulent *barbagiuai*, which are rustic ravioli filled with puréed pumpkin and white beans, and spicy, fermented *brusso* cheese. For the sumptuous pasta course, there are fettuccine with wild mushrooms from Apennine woods. Mouthwatering second courses include hearty polenta and pork sausages, rabbit sautéed with pine nuts and herbs, or *crava e faxeu*, goat sautéed with onions, white beans and crushed chili pepper flakes. Other local baked goods and sweets include *pane di Triora*, a rustic country bread baked and sold atop chestnut leaves; *michetta* mini-brioches often shaped into a knot and similar to croissants in texture and flavor; focaccia *verde*, a savory tart of chard and olives, usually found in Dolceacqua; and *pansarola di Apricale*, a lightly sweet deep-fried strip of dough scattered with sugar.

it, closed Sunday and Monday), whose honey boutique is near the gas station, seaside park and mouth of the Roya River on the west side of town. Margherita, Marco's mother, runs the boutique while Marco, who started mastering the art of beekeeping at age sixteen back in 1978, is busy with his buzzing charges and honey pots, mostly over the border in France (where he makes the honey and related products at Miellerie de la Roya, Rue Pasteur 34, Breil sur Roya/Alpes Maritimes/France, Tel: 33 493 04 4620, open Saturday 10am to 12:30pm and 4:30pm to 7pm, and Sunday morning). His hives are in hills above the Valle Roya and Valle Nervia linking Liguria to France; in summer he moves them to higher, cooler ground in Piedmont. Marco makes over a dozen types of delicious honey—from powerful fir, rosemary, tree heather and chestnut honeys, to sweeter acacia honey or mild linden and mixed wild flower *millefiori* honey; sometimes the bees come home with arbutus (strawberry tree) or even raspberry pollen and those honeys are rare, slightly bitter yet exquisite. Marco also makes dried fruit in honey, spice bread with honey, *torrone* nougat with honey, and creamy spreads of hazelnut and honey, pistachio and honey or hazelnut, chocolate and honey. This is one of the only places on the Riviera where you can get fresh, untreated pollen.

In the center of town, near the train station, locals head to **Panetteria Dallorto Paolo** (Via Stazione 1, Tel: 0184 351036, closed Sunday) for by-the-slice pizza, *sardenaira*, flavorful savory tarts to snack on and delicious bread rolls. More upscale and also in central Ventimiglia, on the main street two in and parallel to the seaside, is **La Boutique del Pane Mondino** (Via Roma 38, Tel: 0184 351361, closed Wednesday afternoon and Sunday), which makes very good, classic Genoese focaccia, specialty breads of all kinds, good chickpea *farinata* with extra virgin olive oil, and chocolatey, spiced *castagnole* sweets.

The best place for a good cup of coffee and a snack or light lunch is clean, modern **Caffè Paris** (Via della Repubblica 2, Tel: 0184 358050, open daily 7am to 7pm except Monday), which is near the public park and riverside on the western end of town.

In this same area you'll find **Frantoio Gaziello** (Via San Secondo 14, Tel: 0184 351456, info@oliogaziello.com www.oliogaziello.com, closed Sunday and holidays). This family-owned, century-old mill makes very good, classic extra virgin oils—with flavors of pine nuts, herbs and artichokes—from its own handpicked Taggiasca and other olives. Dulcifructo is golden hued and particularly sweet, made from ripe olives picked late in the season, whereas *mosto* is tangy and spicy. Gaziello is equipped with continuous presses. The mill and shop next door to it are about 300 yards due west of the train station, between Via Cavour and Via San Secondo, in downtown Ventimiglia.

The valleys behind Ventimiglia are full of olive oil mills and winemakers. In the city's immediate vicinity there are two. From Ventimiglia's seaside, either go up highway SS20 from the coast and turn west at the confluence of the Bevera River, cross the railroad tracks, pass the Bevera train station and take the curving two-lane road west up the Bevera Valley about 300 yards, or take Via Gallardi all the way from the Via Aurelia (called Corso Francia here), the seaside highway at the western edge of town, and follow the Roya River upstream. In the municipal area of the village of Bevera you'll find **Abbo Srl Azienda Olearia** (Via Maneira 2, Bevera, Tel: 0184 211012, info@olioabbo.it, www. olioabbo.it, by appointment). This highly respected oil making family is now into its fourth generation. Back in 1893 Secondo Abbo founded the firm. He was killed in World War II during an Allied bombing raid. His grandson Gianpaolo Abbo, and Gianpaolo's son Giovanni and French wife Annie, and their daughter Isabella, now make the sweet, light, golden-hued DOP Riviera dei Fiori oils. The Abbo family has its own olive groves, but also buys from local growers. All oils are made with state-of-the-art equipment; some are certified fair trade and/or organic.

AN OLIVE OIL-AND-WINE (AND GOURMET FOODS) ROUTE:

THE HINTERLAND OF TAGGIA, SAN REMO, BORDIGHERA AND VENTIMIGLIA

....

Note: Because of the scattered locations of olive oil makers, wineries, food producers, shops and restaurants in the area, the best way to discover them is to budget several days, rent a car and take the road trip inland. The distances are relatively short, but roads are narrow with many curves.

EXPECT TO SPEND A TWO FULL DAYS AND ONE NIGHT ON A ROUND-TRIP TOUR; YOU WILL WANT to overnight halfway (in Apricale, Triora, Pigna or Castel Vittorio, for instance) and finish your visit the following day.

Behind Taggia, San Remo, Bordighera and Ventimiglia, and the many nearby Riviera dei Fiori seaside resorts, rise hundreds of hothouses glinting in the year-round sun. Through the white-washed glazing you catch glimpses of roses, peonies, lemon and orange trees, lillies, orchids, hydrangeas, jasmine, bouganvillea and a thousand other flowering or green plants grown here and shipped around the world to nurseries and florists' shops. In spring, poppies grown for their seeds fill the landscape with a kaleidoscope of colors. Among the staggered terraces escapees from the hot houses thrive in the open air, a permanent, free-form flower show. Inland, the greenhouses are likely to be filled not only by houseplants and flowers, but also by vegetables and herbs. As far as can be seen, the hills are clothed in vines and olive trees. To explore the *entroterra*, pick a river valley and head up it. The Valle Argentina is behind Taggia; the Armea River flows just east of San Remo; the Sasso, Vallebona, Vallecrosia and Nervia valleys are directly behind or west of Bordighera. Once inland, roads on ridges and hillsides link the main towns and villages.

Because most of the properties listed below are small and family run, the opening hours vary widely. It's wise to phone ahead. There are dozens of oil mills and wineries in the area. This is a select list. For a complete listing of wineries visit www.enotecapubblica.it; for certified DOP oil makers, visit www.consorziodoprivieraligure.it.

Start at Arma di Taggia, a block and a half off of the Via Aurelia coast highway and only a hundred yards or so from the sea, at specialty food boutique **Opera Magé i Sapori della Terra Taggiasca** (Via Boselli, Tel: 0184 504113, info@operamage.com, www.operamage.com, closed Sunday), which also has a boutique in San Remo near the Ariston theater. They sell a wide variety of good house-branded DOP oils (from hand-picked Taggiasca olives that are milled within forty-eight hours of picking), honeys, dry pasta such as *corzetti*, and sauces, including tomato-and-porcini sauce and pesto (made with Prà basil, *parmigiano* and extra virgin olive oil).

Also in Arma di Taggia is family-owned oil maker **Oleificio G. Boeri** (Via Stazione 40, Tel: 0184 43460, www.olioboeri.it), founded in 1881, with a retail boutique just south of the main traffic circle (on Via Aurelia) west of the Argentina River. The extra virgin oils from Taggiasca olives are very good, made using a combination of old granite millstones and modern extraction technology. The mill is inland in Badalucco at Via C. Colombo 94.

Head inland on highway SP548 due north up the Valle Argentina. **Casa Olearia Taggiasca** (Regione Prati e Pescine, Argine Sinistro, Tel: 0184 486044, www.CasaOleariaTaggiasca. it) is on the east bank, across from the highway. This ultra-modern, ambitious, expanding supplier to top-end restaurants and food boutiques sells to Hediard in Paris, Peck in Milano and Bergdorf Goodman in New York, and works with Alain Ducasse in product development. You'll find dozens of sauces, pickled vegetables and good DOP extra virgin olive oils here, made with state-of-the-art, continuous presses.

Get back on SP548 and continue north a few miles following signs toward Triora and Badalucco. About one mile before reaching the village of Badalucco, at the crossroads marked Bivio Vignai, you'll see a giant snail shell sign advertising the restaurant **Vecchio Frantoio** (SP548/Bivio Vignai, Badalucco, Tel: 0184 408024, closed Tuesday, the second half of January and the first ten days in July, moderate to expensive). The restaurant occupies a former watermill from the 1880s. Those who like millstones and timbers will enjoy the décor. Family run, the menu is regional and features tasty gnocchetti, ravioli stuffed with field greens and dressed with wild herbs and butter or olive oil, stewed rabbit with olives, pine nuts and capers, and the comforting local obsession, *branda cuiun* (mashed salt cod and potatoes, with olive oil, lemon juice and vinegar). In season, you'll find venison or boar with polenta, and succulent snails stewed for four hours with rosemary, thyme, bay and chili. The desserts are housemade and simple but satisfying (chocolate pudding with *amaretti*, or vanilla pudding with whipped cream and local acacia honey). Stick to local bottlings.

Keep driving north toward Badalucco. In under two miles you'll see the sign in the valley bottom telling you that you're entering the village, whose historic center is on the hillside ahead. Before driving uphill into Badalucco, you'll see the retail boutique and mill of award-winning **Olio Roi** (Via Argentina 1, Badalucco, Tel: 0184 408004, www.olioroi.com; mill visits from October to March). The current scion, and third generation of this oil-making dynasty, founded in 1900, is Franco Boeri. Boeri selects the best olives by hand and mills them immediately after picking. Olio Roi still uses granite millstones, in conjunction, however, with continuous presses. Some of the oils are organic. Boeri's Carte Noir extra virgin is exceptional; it merely drips out of the crushed, piled olives, with no pressure applied. Only 4,000 numbered bottles are made per year. The other 100 percent Taggiasca oils are classics in their genre. Also sold are olive oil soaps, olive-inspired ceramics and accessories, cosmetics, preserved fruit, vegetables packed in extra virgin oil, pesto, pesto *rosso* (made with tomatoes) and *salsa verde*. No preservatives are used.

Drive uphill into the village. Badalucco is celebrated for its dry white beans, which go into stews, often made with kid or mature goat. On the main road through the village, SP548, where it curves, on the north end, is **Frantoio Giobatta Panizzi** (Via G.B. Boeri 50, Tel: 0184 408097, open daily), a food shop and olive oil maker. The mill has been around for centuries; the private "olive oil museum" is a fledgling, however. Here you can buy the white beans of Badalucco, plus dry or salted cod, salted anchovies, brined olives, vegetables bottled in olive oil and housemade sauces including the piquant *salsa bersagliera* (oregano, salted anchovies and pinenuts). The extra virgin oils from 100-percent Taggiasca olives grown on the family's 700 or so trees (or bought from local growers) are good.

Return to the Valle Argentina and continue to handsome, medieval Molini di Triora, once filled with working watermills for grinding grain, chestnuts or olives. Parallel to the main highway and one block west of it is family-run **Trattoria Giovanna** (Via Nuova 54, Tel: 0184 94026, closed Monday and from late October to December, moderate), an old-fashioned place with waiters in penguin suits. In fall, the menu revolves around porcini, prepared in every imaginable way — porcini salads, breaded and fried porcini, grilled porcini and porcini risotto. The housemade ravioli are called *bombolotti* and are filled with field greens and dressed with butter and sage. In fall and winter, you'll find boar and game, stewed or roasted. For dessert, don't miss the pie made with wild berries. There's a good selection of local wines.

In the center of the village is **Hotel-Ristorante Santo Spirito** (Piazza Roma 23, Tel: 0184 94019, www.ristorantesantospirito. com/, closed Wednesday and 20 days in February, moderate). This simple though comfortable establishment, with pine half-panelling, white walls adorned by copper pots, and white cloths on the tables, has been in the same clan since 1897. The Zucchetto family uses the founders' recipes. Produce from the family farm is transformed into delicacies such as snail paté, or delicate snails stuffed into crêpe-like *crespelle* pasta and dressed with wild mushrooms, ravioli stuffed with nettle tops and chard and dressed with herbs and butter, stewed chickpeas and chard *zemin*, wild mushrooms cooked in many ways, sautéed local trout, simple roast kid with wild herbs, long-stewed, spiced, succulent boar, venison with black currant sauce, hare with hazelnuts and partridge with grapes. The wine list is good, with many regional bottlings.

Next door is the family's outlet for its farm produce and specialty foods, **La Bottega di Angelamaria** (Piazza Roma 26, Tel: 0184 94021), run by Angelamaria Zucchetto. Here you can buy chestnut and chickpea flour, local honeys and fruit gelatins, cheeses, liqueurs (including one made with wild plums), home-grown basil and wild or cultivated berries.

Far above, reached by a corkscrew road, is Triora (www. comune.triora.im.it), an enchanting, and much-visited hamlet famous for its association past and present with "witches" — le Streghe di Triora. You will hear about little else, and see enough witch kitsch to last a lifetime. Luckily, the teetering stone village is among the region's most captivating, and the views of green, forested or terraced hills mesmerizing.

A long-time local favorite for serious lunches, celebrations and the like is the hotel-restaurant **Colomba d'Oro** (Corso Italia 66, Tel: 0184 94051, www.colombadoro.it, closed Tuesday and in winter, moderate). A cloister where breakfast is served to hotel guests is part of the ensemble. The menu features traditional savory tarts, the *sardenaira* of San Remo, ravioli stuffed with field greens and dressed with butter, herbs and fresh tomatoes, Badalucco bean soup with crispy bacon, and simple, divine roast lamb spiked with garlic and wild herbs. There's a good wine list, with many local wineries represented. The restaurant is cozy, with fireplaces, old wooden furniture, half-paneling and brass and copper pots; the fine-weather terrace offers close-up views of the village, and see-forever panoramas.

On the same street is the celebrated specialty food maker and boutique **La Strega di Triora** (Corso Italia 50, Tel: 0184 94278, www.lastregaditriora.it, open 9:30am to 7pm daily in July and August, closed Tuesday the rest of the year). For over twenty years, Augusto Borelli and Luana Bertol have been doing what most country stores did quietly once upon a time: sell high-quality local produce, and make the housemade, genuine delicacies of the region, from egg to apple. On the shelves or in the sparkling display cases of this upscale operation are difficult-to-find cheeses (including pungent, tangy *bruzzo*), salamis from all over Italy, fresh or preserved fruit jams made the old-fashioned way in copper pots (try the dry chestnut or fig jams), pasta sauces with fresh homegrown basil and beefsteak tomatoes, and dried, pickled or fresh mushrooms (including hard-to-find *cicotti*—*Tricholoma Portentosum*—alias *cicalotti*) packed in good extra virgin olive oil. The family's own Taggiasca extra virgin olive oil is light and flowery. The house chocolate is of course called *baci della Strega*, and come in two types, milk chocolate "for her" and bittersweet "for him;" the filling is made with hazelnuts from Piedmont, which is only a few miles north. The *cubaite* wafer cookies, made in fall and winter, come in a beautiful gift box. There's much more on offer, including five types of local white or spotted beans.

Also on the main road, unsung purist **Angiolino Asplanato** (Corso Italia 37, Tel: 0184 94290, closed Wednesday) bakes delicious, fragrant round loaves of *pane di Triora*, and that's it—no pastries or any other distractions.

Either return to the coast the way you came, or drive southwest on the two-lane, chase-your-tail highway to Pigna. Here, on the main road (highway SP64), just outside the twisting alleyways of this atmospheric, stacked medieval aery, is **Alimentari La Posta** (Via San Rocco 58-60, Tel: 0184 241666, closed Monday), a grocery selling local vegetables packed in olive oil, local beans (*fagioli di Pigna*), a good selection of cheeses, honeys and more. **Forno Papalia** (Corso de Sonnaz 94, no telephone, closed Sunday), on the looping road that goes from the highway around the village's medieval core, bakes wonderful breads, including rustic, mixed-grain *pane nero* (black bread), and a few simple treats.

On the same road, **Azienda Agricola Allavena Maria Giovanna** (Corso de Sonnaz 118, Tel: 0184 241394) is a husband-and-wife grower of white Pigna beans and maker of pure Taggiasca extra virgin olive oil, produced in the traditional manner (it's milled at the co-op).

In the bull's eye of the village, another small, family-run operation, **Azienda Agricola Allavena Massimo** (Via Carriera Piana 76, Tel: 0184 241513, cell 338 581 7258, massimo.allavena@libero.it), also grows Pigna beans and Taggiasca olive trees and makes good, organic extra virgin olive oil.

A few miles due south as the crow flies, but many times that by a tortuous, climbing road, is the hamlet of Madonna Assunta, part of Castel Vittorio, a mountain resort community. A hotel-restaurant of the health spa variety located here is **Ristorante Hotel Terme** (Località Madonna Assunta, Tel: 0184 241046, closed Tuesday dinner and Wednesday, and from Epiphany to mid February, moderate). The well-spaced tables are dressed with white cloths. Big windows let in lots of sunlight, and the requisite copper pots adorn the walls. The cooking is homey, with Signora Gloria in the kitchen. Her starters include plump *pansôti* filled with field greens and sauced with crushed walnuts; simple, succulent roast lamb; rabbit with olives and pine nuts cooked with Rossese wine; and classic, long-stewed goat or lamb with white beans. There's a good selection of regional and local wines.

In Castel Vittorio proper are three good *trattorie*, all serving local dishes, including *turtun* — vegetable-filled savory tart — at reasonable prices. **Osteria del Portico** (Via Umberto I 6, Tel: 0184 241352, closed Monday, inexpensive to moderate), on the main road heading south out of town, is an authentic, simple spot where owner-cook Mara Allavena makes delicious savory tarts with chard or potatoes, rabbit, snails and *stoccafisso*. **Busciun** (Piazza del Busciun, Tel: 0184 241073, closed Tuesday, inexpensive to moderate), is a local hangout, with sidewalk tables on the square, serving mushrooms, rabbit, snails and savory tarts, all housemade, often using the owners' own produce, and it's the only place in the village open Mondays. A notch up the scale, with nice views from the glassed-in dining room, and a handful of Genoese dishes in the mix, is **Hotel-Ristorante Italia** (Via Umberto I 56, Tel: 0184 241089, closed Monday and January, moderate).

If you still haven't purchased white beans and oil, grower **Giovanni Maltini** (Via Roma, 7, Tel: 0184 241005) makes a nice extra virgin with his Taggiasca olives.

Southeast of Castel Vittorio about six miles and perched at nearly 3,000 feet above sea level is Baiardo, a moody place in disconcertingly beautiful scenery. An earthquake in 1887 devastated the village. It has been repaired and gentrified. A Romanesque porch fronts the ruined church at the village's highest point, built in the Middle Ages atop a pagan temple. From the belvedere behind, you see the Alpine border with France, and can trace many of the roads you've traveled so far.

From Baiardo, you have three options: either return to the coast through Ceriana to Poggio, or skirt the east side of Monte Bignone to San Romolo, and from there descend steeply to San Remo, or continue southwest from Baiardo to Apricale (recommended).

On a back road due north of Apricale, accessed via the main highway from Baiardo to Foa, **Biofattoria Azienda Agricola Gamba Patrizio** (Località Foa, Apricale, 0184 208351, cell 339 126 2157, patrizio.gamba@tin.it, www.biolivataggiasca.com) is where idealistic Patrizio Gamba makes organic oils from century-old Taggiasca trees, on what is meant to be a didactic farm for school kids. The oils are feather light and fruity, and uncontaminated. Gamba also makes brined olives and olive paté.

Compact, stippled with *campanili* and splayed across a sloping ridge, Apricale was established in the Bronze Age. Its Latin name (Apricus) means "sunwashed," and, as you discover in summer, is apt. Some buildings are ninth century, though documents only go back to 1016. Apricale is the site of summertime theater, with costumed medieval and Renaissance events. Self-styled artists have applied contemporary murals to many walls.

Thanks to a lively tourist trade, there's little risk of going hungry. **Trattoria A Ciassa** (Piazza Vittorio Emanuele II 2, Tel: 0184 208588, dinner only, closed Wednesday, inexpensive to moderate) is where Caterina Paoli makes homey food, from flash-fried squash flowers to stuffed vegetables, borage-filled ravioli with porcini sauce to rabbit-stewed with pine nuts, olives and Rossese wine, or *cima alla genovese*. The *zabaglione* and *crostata* are very good; the local dessert in Apricale is *pansarole* (tatters of lightly sweetened dough fried in olive oil and sprinkled with powdered sugar); they're often paired with sweet wine, or, as here, with a dollop of *zabaglione*.

Humble, and with surprisingly good food, is local hangout **Trattoria-Pizzeria-Bar La Lucertola** (Via Roma 48, Tel: 0184 209003, closed Mondays in winter, inexpensive to moderate). On offer are many local classics, including ravioli, mushrooms, rabbit and boar. Upscale, with a slightly self-important feel but good food and gorgeous views is **La Capanna da Bacì** (Via Genova 10, Tel: 0184 208137, www.locanarugi.it/baci.html, closed Monday for dinner and Tuesday, moderate to expensive). There are oversized wine glasses on the tables, and beautiful people from the coast mix it up with tony (often foreign) visitors. Ask for a table on the semi-enclosed terrace, and watch the procession of appetizers arrive, from pickle-sized salamis via vegetable fritters oozing tangy *stracchino* cheese, to savory tarts of field greens, and classic stuffed zucchini. The rabbit-filled ravioli sauced with stewed rabbit are delicious, so too are the *branda cuiun* and roast leg of lamb, or long-stewed wild boar. The wine list features many good regional wines, and is especially strong on Rossese di Dolceacqua, which is grown on terraces directly below. Another fashionable, upscale neo-*trattoria* with similar fare, served with even more studious refinement, is **Apricale da Delio** (Piazza Vittorio Veneto 9, Tel: 0184 208008, www.ristoranteapricale.it, closed Monday and Tuesday and the second half of November, expensive to very expensive).

In the tangled center of Apricale, **Danila Pisano** (Via Martiri Della Libertà 64, Tel: 0184 208551, cell 339 195 8000) makes very good, organic, pure Taggiasca olive oil; her groves are nearby, and you can visit them by appointment. To purchase her oils, and the very pleasant, classic, organic Rossese di Dolceacqua she also makes, visit her winery in Soldano (Via San Martino 20, same cell #, also by appointment). It's in the center of the village, near the pharmacy and parking lot.

Beer is not a Riviera specialty. However, an entertainingly self-conscious micro-brewery has set up in Apricale, **Piccolo Birrificio** (Via IV Novembre 20, Tel: 0184 209022, www.piccolobirrificio. com, off-season hours vary). It's located on a curve in the main road west to Isolabona. Pablo Neruda's musings on apples, the moon and nudity are quoted as inspiration. Most of the beers are made seasonally, and will appeal to those who like sweets and spices.

From Apricale, either drive west to Isolabona and from there to Dolceacqua and the coast via the Nervia River Valley (recommended); or drive due south to Perinaldo and Soldano, following the Vallecrosia to the coast between Bordighera and Comporosso Mare.

On the highway about halfway between Apricale and Isolabona, in a modern building, find **Cantine del Rossese – Gajaudo** (Strada Provinciale 7B, Tel: 0184 208095, info@cantinagajaudo. com, www.cantinagajaudo.com), reputable makers of Rossese di Dolceacqua and Vermentino. The standard non-reserve wines are truer to type and less oaky than the big, New World-style wines for which Gajaudo is known. Also sold are good extra virgin olive oil from Taggiasca olives, and brined olives, spreads and sauces.

If you enjoy eating at home, in this case someone else's home, about a mile north of the medieval center of Isolabona, near the junction with the road from Apricale, is **Agriturismo La Molinella** (Via Roma 60, Tel: 0184 208163, lamolinella@tiscali-net.it, www.lamolinella.it). This simple B&B serves homey, local classic dishes and is open for Saturday dinner and Sunday lunch year round, by reservation only.

Practically next door is oil maker **Paolo Cassini** (Via Roma 62, Tel: 0184 208159, cassini.p@tiscalinet.it, www.oliocassini.it), whose light, fragrant, herby and flowery S'ciappau Gran Cru extra virgin run off oil, made without pressure, from Taggiasca olives, won a gold medal at the Los Angeles County fair in 2006. The family has been making oil here since 1962; Paolo is the third generation, having taken over from his grandparents and parents. His other oils, cold pressed using modern, continuous presses, are also remarkably good. A purist and perfectionist, Cassini and his family hand pick the olives from the 665 trees they own — they have counted them — and mill them immediately. Cassini is no longer in the DOP olive oil consortium, having judged its rules too lax. He also mills olives for other local olive growers. The brined Taggiasca olives he sells are of particularly high quality.

Downstream about two miles, atmospheric, rough-and-tumble Dolceacqua spreads up both sides of the Nervia River Valley. An elegant humpback stone bridge from the fifteenth century flies over the river; from high above the eastern side of the valley, the partly destroyed, gape-eyed castle of the Doria clan frowns down on a tangle of sloping alleyways built from 1000 to 1200 AD. Dolceacqua was a wealthy Doria stronghold for centuries, and is bigger and more populous than most other inland villages of the district. Nowadays this is largely due to its leading role in wine- and olive oil-making. It gave its name to the red wine, Rossese di Dolceacqua.

Traditional, local fare is the specialty of simple, homey *trattoria*-pizzeria **La Rampa** (Via Berberis 5, Tel: 0184 206198, closed Monday and in December, inexpensive to moderate), in a clearing among the tangled medieval alleys, with a pleasant outdoor terrace. Cook Anna Maria Garoscio makes many Dolceacqua classics, savory tarts and stuffed, baked vegetables, pizzas of all kinds and *farinata*, and very good *trenette* with pesto. The rabbit with pine nuts, olives and herbs, and the grilled meats, are equally tasty, as are the desserts (*crostata*, tiramisu, ice cream), all of them house-made. Many local and regional bottlings are available.

Right nearby, on the sloping west side of the valley, **Raffo Francesca Alimentari** (Salita S. Sebastiano 8, Tel: 0184 206044) makes delicious *michette* croissants and *crocette* (the same, but cross shaped) and other baked goods, and sells local wines and olive oils. For a savory snack or pastry, try **Alimentari Panetteria Garoscio Cinzia e Silvia** (Piazza Garibaldi 8, Tel: 0184 204007, closed Wednesday afternoon and Sunday), a grocery and bakery near the river, that makes fragrant, delicious pizzas, good classic focaccia, the local *torta verde* and pizza *verde* and savory tarts, plus *michette*, *crocette* and *torta taconata*, which is a jam tart with fresh slices of apple mixed in.

Enoteca Re (Via Patrioti Martiri 21, Tel: 0184 205051, enotecare@libero.it, www.enotecaredolceacqua.it, closed Monday and November 1 to mid December) is one of the best-stocked wine shops in the region, with over 2,000 different bottlings from wineries around the world.

Highly regarded, multi-generational wine and olive oil maker **Terre Bianche** (Località Arcagna, Tel: 0184 31426, www.terre-bianche.com, closed in November) is perched above and to the west of Dolceacqua at Arcagna and reached by coiling highway SP70 on the west side of the valley. Larger than many estates, with thirty-five acres of vineyards and olive or fruit trees, Terre Bianche was founded in 1870. The Arcagna area is among the best for growing Rossese, and the first vineyard of the variety was planted here. The firm began making Pigato and Vermentino much later. Since the 1990s Terre Bianche has also been growing organic fruits, vegetables and herbs, which it uses primarily to supply its upscale, *agriturismo* (a farmstead B&B serving food). Winemakers Franco Làconi and Filippo Rondelli are adepts of new oak, and have not shied away from experimentation. Their Arcana Bianco is a successful if blowsy blend of Vermentino and Pigato, which underscores the close genetic affinity of the grape varieties. The standard Rossese di Dolceacqua is truest to type; the single-vineyard Bricco Arcagna is bigger, with New World characteristics. The recently invented Arcana Rosso blends Cabernet into Rossese and also has a New World, fruit-forward bigness which pleases certain palates. Guests at the handsome, luxurious Terre Bianche B&B have the privilege of savoring the house wines and food, and wandering through the panoramic grounds, vineyards and olive groves.

Back in the Nervia River Valley, drive toward the coast. About five miles south of Dolceacqua is Camporosso, a sizable medieval village with many churches and atmospheric alleyways, long important as the burial site of the Doria clan. It sits in the valley bottom along the river, fronted by a seaside community, Camporosso Mare, and hemmed by hills and perched hamlets. One of them, Località Giuncheo, at about 700 feet above sea level, is where you'll find small, traditional Taggiasca olive grower and oil maker **Roberto Rota** (Tel: 0184 288702, cell 333 719 6943, r.u.s.02@tiscali.it). His trees are on the hills in Giuncheo and in abutting Località Pesservin, and his extra virgin oils are light, sweet and fruity. The top of the line Crudum is better than it sounds, and is the run-off, made with little or no pressure, of freshly crushed olives.

In the same neighborhood, **Tenuta Giuncheo** (Tel: 0184 288639, www.tenutagiuncheo.it) is an ambitious maker of fine wines, some traditional and true to type, others noticeably oaked and high in ripe fruit and alcohol. The winery's muscular Vermentino Eclis is barrel-aged for a year, and then bottle-aged for another eight months before being marketed. Vermentino Le Palme is also oaked; the standard Vermentino DOC Riviera Ligure di Ponente is made and aged in stainless steel, and is more subtle and less alcoholic than either. The classic Rossese di Dolceacqua DOC commonly reaches a bruising 14 percent alcohol, and is sunny and rich even though it is also made and aged in stainless steel. Even more New World or French in style is oaky, inky Vigneto Pian del Vescovo, also a Rossese, and bound to please those used to modern Tuscan or Californian wines.

Lower down and closer to the sea is fair-sized, reliable winery **Foresti** (Via Braie 223, Località Camporosso Mare, Tel: 0184 292377, www.forestiwine.it, open daily from 8am to 7pm, call ahead if possible). Owner Marco Foresti will gladly show you around if he has time, and give you a taste of one of his four wines, Rossese, Rossese Superiore, Pigato and Vermentino. All are very good, largely traditional and true to type, well balanced and professionally made.

If instead of going to Dolceacqua you chose to drive direct from Apricale to perched Perinaldo, another castle-crowned village, at 1,800 feet above the Vallecrosia, pause for a look at the view, which embraces the Mediterranean and Alps. Perinaldo's native son Gian Domenico Cassini was born in the castle in 1625, became the world's most renowned astronomer (in Paris), and gave his name to the Cassini NASA spacecraft. Nowadays Perinaldo is largely inhabited by Germans, Dutch and French, who have restored village houses top to bottom (and taken over what was long the best restaurant in town). **Alimentari L'Anfora** (Via Maraldi 17, Tel: 0184 672499, closed Wednesday), is the local grocery store; in addition to picnic supplies, it sells good extra virgin oils from the Camporosso and Vallecrosia area, plus local brined olives, olive patés and vegetables under oil.

From Perinaldo drive due south on the curlicue highway to Soldano. At 800 feet above sea level, the village is not as high as Perinaldo but still boasts sweeping views over vineyards, olive groves, flower-filled greenhouses and the sea. On the north side of town you'll find a medieval gateway and maze of alleyways. Below them, on the main road south, near the newsstand, is **Azienda Vitivinicola Tenuta Anfosso** (Corso Verbone 31 and 175, Tel: 0184 289906, cell 338 311 6590, tenutanfosso@libero.it, www. tenutanfosso.com, boutique closed Sunday). Look for the barrel on the side of the road. Long known for its excellent pure-Taggiasca extra virgin olive oil, the Anfosso family also makes award-winning Rossese di Dolceacqua red, an intriguing Rossese Bianco (a rare local variety of this normally red grape), grappa, brined olives, and vegetables packed in excellent oil. Among the many specialty items sold in the boutique, the pesto (which is actually prepared for them by a local artisan) contains their powerful, homegrown basil. In 2002 Alessandro Anfosso and his wife Marisa Perrotti became the fourth generation to run the firm, which was founded in 1888 by Giacomo Anfosso. Some of his original vines, it's claimed, in the Poggio Pini vineyard, are still alive. These very old vines, and others planted in more recent decades, produce the grapes that go into Anfosso's brawny Rossese di Dolceacqua DOC Superiore (which is actually made by winemaker Walter Bonetti). Most of the winery's other vineyards are below, in San Biagio della Cima (Località Lovaira).

Another multi-generational, excellent, family-run winery on the same street in Soldano is **Enzo Guglielmi** (Corso Verbone 143, Tel: 0184 289042, www.enzoguglielmi.com), in business since the mid-1800s. In the 1960s, Enzo switched from making the bulk wine of his forefathers to high-quality bottled wines and has perfected them over the last forty years. Like the Anfosso family, Enzo also has a vineyard at Poggio Pini, with southwest exposure, and this is where his best grapes are grown on old vines. With them he makes classic Rossese di Dolceacqua DOC and Superiore, the latter a bruiser, with at least 14 percent alcohol; it evokes ripe red fruit and strawberry jam, and keeps for three years or more.

Also in Soldano, near the pharmacy, is the winery of organic oil-and-wine maker **Danila Pisano** (see 395 for details).

Down the ridge road a few more miles is San Biagio della Cima, poised above Verbone Creek in Vallecrosia. Who knows whether the ancient Romans of Villa Martis, which lies under the village, made wine. One fine, modern winery here is **Azienda Agricola Maccario Dringenberg** (Via Torre 3, Tel. 0184 289947, cell 333 206 3294, by appointment). Local winemaker Giovanna Maccario and her non-native husband make big Rossese di Dolceacqua Superiore, and the rare Rossese Bianco, a soft, quaffable white. ⚓

FOOD AND WINE GLOSSARY

LIGURIANS ARE FOOD REGIONALISTS. THEY ALTERNATE BETWEEN USING standard Italian and local dialect names for foodstuffs and dishes. The following glossary lists regional favorites you're likely to encounter on your travels. It is not exhaustive: Liguria boasts scores of indigenous sweets, cheeses and fish or meat preparations, sauces and cooking techniques, some of which are found only in a single village or valley.

Where one exists, the standard Italian name (with plural form, where helpful) is followed by the dialect name, and an English translation or explanation. Where there is no standard Italian name, only the dialect and English translation or explanation is given. Similarly, if there is no dialect name, only the Italian and English are given. Note that many foods have more than one name in standard Italian and dialect, and there are many sub-regional variations in the dozens of Ligurian dialects found from La Spezia to Ventimiglia. A recent study by the compilers of *Il Bugiardino*, an almanac, found twenty variations in about thirty miles for the word "olive."

....

Abboccato: Wine that is slightly sweet.

Acciuga (pl. acciughe)—anciòe, anciuga—anchovy: The scientific name of the Mediterranean anchovy is *Engraulis encrasicholus*. It is very different from the Atlantic sprat (*Clupea harengus*) or a similar Mediterranean fish, the true sardine or pilchard (*Sardinia pilchardus*). Filled with a classic Ligurian *ripieno* and baked or fried, anchovies are called *anciòe pinn-e* or *acciughe ripiene*. Baked anchovy-and-potato casserole is *torta di acciughe*. Fresh, raw, fileted anchovies marinated in lemon juice and olive oil are *acciughe sotto limone* or *acciughe marinate*. Anchovies cured and packed in salt are *acciughe sotto sale*.

Agliata—aggiadda, aggiàa, ajé: A powerful sauce of crushed garlic, salt, white bread, vinegar or white wine, and, optionally, pine nuts, it is especially popular on the extreme western end of the Riviera di Ponente, near France. *Pesto d'aglio*, a garlic pesto, is similar, but has no bread, vinegar or wine, using crushed pine nuts, cream and *parmigiano* instead to create an unctuous consistency.

Amabile: Semi-sweet wine.

Asciutto: Dry wine. When applied to dry pasta, the term is *pastasciutta*.

Baccalà: Salt cod. In Liguria, air-dried cod is called *stocca-fisso*.

Baciocca: Savory potato and bacon tart, baked on terracotta or iron disks, or stones, in the fireplace, a specialty of inland areas of the eastern Riviera di Levante.

Barbagiuai: Plump, rustic ravioli stuffed with puréed pumpkin and white beans, and spicy, fermented *brusso* cheese, and sometimes cooked on hot stones. Served only inland on the region's border with France.

Bianchetto (pl. bianchetti)—gianchetu (pl. giancheti)—whitebait or spawn: Three varieties of fish are called *bianchetti* (the plural is nearly always used). *Bianchetti da galla* are newborn, translucent, inch-long anchovies or sardines. Anyone with qualms about depleting fish stocks can guiltlessly enjoy a similar tiny fish called *bianchetti da fondo*, which grow to only an inch or so as adults. See also *rossetti*, another species of edible minnow. The best way to prepare *bianchetti* or *rossetti* is to dunk them in boiling water and serve them immediately with a squeeze of lemon. They are equally exquisite flash-fried in olive oil.

Biscotti del Lagaccio: Genoese aniseed or fennel-seed flavored cookies that are feather light, porous and semi-sweet, and look like transversal slices of baked sponge. In Sarzana they go by the name *biscotti della salute* (healthful cookies). Another, related aniseed cookie is made in Taggia, on the western Riviera di Ponente, and called *biscotti di Taggia* or *bescheutti da Quaeixima*, because originally served during Lent (*Quaresima*).

Bieta, bietola. Chard: Beta vulgaris—the original, short, thin-stemmed Italian chard—grows wild and is also widely cultivated on the Riviera, and goes into savory tarts, stews and soups (such as *zemin di ceci*) and filled pasta.

Bottarga—bottariga, buttariga—air-dried gray mullet or tuna roe: The roe is usually scraped over seafood pasta dishes the way *parmigiano* is scraped over other sauces, though sometimes it is crumbled into seafood salads. It is also served in the form of shavings, drizzled with olive oil and sprinkled with lemon juice. Mullet *bottarga* is more flavorful than tuna *bottarga*, and considerably more expensive.

Brandacujon, Branda Cuiun: Similar to French *brandade*, though less homogenous, this flavorful mashed mixture of boiled air-dried cod, garlic, parsley, pine nuts and potatoes is a favorite of the western Riviera di Ponente.

Brusso, bruss, bruzzo: Ewe's milk ricotta which is salted, mixed with liqueur, herbs, seasonings, hot chili pepper or black pepper, and aged for widely varying periods, until it is pungent. *Brusso* is a specialty of the valleys and hilltop villages on the extreme western edge of Liguria, bordering France.

Buccellato: A lifesaver-shaped lightly sweet dessert cake, flavored with orange-flower water or lemon juice, and studded with pine nuts and raisins, made in the La Spezia area.

Buridda: A thick, flavorful fish stew, made with fresh fish or squid, sometimes mixed with salt cod or air-dried cod and dried mushrooms, usually porcini. It is most popular on the western Riviera di Ponente.

Cagliata, quagliata—prescinsêua, prescinsöa—farmstead or cottage cheese: Fresh cow's milk cheese, similar to cottage cheese though less lumpy, used widely in savory tarts and, in the Recco-to-Chiavari area, mixed into pesto.

Canestrelli: Lifesaver-shaped cookie (sweet version) or pretzel-like *aperitivo* cracker (savory version, made in Taggia, on the western Riviera di Ponente). Liguria is the homeland of *canestrelli*; many villages make variations on the theme, and add their village name to the term, as in *canestrelli di Torriglia* (or Rovegno, in the Alta Val Trebbia); both look like a daisy with the center removed.

Capponmagro—cappunmagru: A delicious if enormously complicated Ligurian seafood-and-vegetable salad, typical of the nineteenth century. The classic recipe calls for one large lobster, a whole fresh fish, twenty-four each of prawns, shrimp and oysters, eight boiled eggs, six salted anchovies, plenty of olives and mushrooms in oil, capers, garlic, parsley, pine nuts, bread crumbs, beets, green beans, goat's beard salsify, artichokes and sea biscuits, plus various vegetable garnishes. A green parsley sauce goes on top. *Capponmagro* is now served at weddings and banquets, but can sometimes be purchased from delicatessens.

Capponata—cappponnadda—sea-biscuit salad: Served on the eastern Riviera di Levante and usually made with ripe plum tomatoes, garlic, spring onions, bell peppers, black olives, olive oil and crumbled sea biscuits, with salted anchovy filets and canned or air-dried tuna (and, optionally, mozzarella). It once contained true *mosciamme*—air-dried porpoise or dolphin. See *condiggion* for a related salad served on the western Riviera di Ponente.

Carciofo (pl. carciofi)—articiocca—artichoke: Ligurian artichokes come primarily from the Albenga area on the western Riviera di Ponente, and are spiny (*spinosi*), small and flavorful.

Carne all'uccelletto—carne a l'öxelletto: Lean veal, thinly sliced and then finger-shredded, sautéed with garlic, laurel leaves and white wine.

Castagnaccio. Chestnut-flour tart: See *panella.*

Chinotto: Sometimes called myrtle-leaved citrus fruit, from its common Latin name *Citrus myrtifolia*, *chinotto* is a kumquat-sized bitter orange that grows on the Riviera and, in the form of *chinotto* syrup, is used to flavor drinks and *apertivi*. (Another widely accepted scientific name, however, *Citrus sinensis var. plumosus*, suggests a Chinese origin.) The fruit is also brined, boiled and candied and served in *chinotto* syrup. It is popular on the western Riviera di Ponente. Visit www.chinotto.com and www.besio1860.it for details.

Ciàppa: An olive-oil based sea biscuit about five or six inches in diameter, made in the Taggia area of the western Riviera di Ponente. *Ciàppa* also refers to slabs of slate, small, flat river rocks or stones found on beaches which, when heated in a fire, are used for cooking meat, fish and crepe-like pastas or savory tarts.

Cicciarello, cicerello, lussetto: This tiny bluefish, similar to a young anchovy or sardine, is found only on the coast of the western Riviera di Ponente. Its scientific name is *Gymnammodites cicerellus*. Sometimes added to fish soup, or flash-fried in olive oil, it is also commonly pickled *allo scabecciu* (see *scabeccio*).

Cima di vitello—çimma pinn-a—stuffed shoulder or breast of veal: The veal is stuffed until taut with a mixture of ground veal, offal, brains and organs rarely described or eaten in America, to which are added fresh peas and artichoke hearts, pine nuts, herbs, eggs and grated cheese. Bound together, *cima* is boiled and then pressed and chilled, a process requiring several hours. Few Ligurians make the dish at home, leaving the task to specialist butchers, delicatessen owners and caterers, who sell it sliced thin. It is eaten cold or at room temperature, an excellent picnic food, often served on Easter Monday.

Nowadays offal is rarely included among the ingredients.

Ciuppin'—Fish (and/or squid) soup: This thick soup or thin stew is made with rockfish and squid, with minced onion, garlic, parsley, hot chili pepper and white wine, and served in bowls on top of sea-biscuits. The closest non-Ligurian equivalent is *cioppino*, from Livorno (the ancestor of San Francisco's *cioppino*).

Condiggion, condion, condijun: A salad made with sea-biscuits and various other vegetable and piscine ingredients, similar to Ligurian *capponadda*, but containing large quantities of sliced cucumber and air-dried mullet roe. Served on the western Riviera di Ponente.

Coniglio—coniggio—rabbit: As popular as poultry, rabbit is usually fricaséed with herbs, pine nuts, olives, white wine, chicken broth and olive oil and called *coniglio alla ligure*. The same dish is called *coniggio a-a carlonn-a* on the eastern Riviera di Levante and *coniggio a-a sanremasca* in the San Remo area.

Corzetti—corxetti, croseti: Medallion-shaped, flat, fresh or dry pasta impressed with a wooden stamp, or flattened with the palm of the hand, and served with mushroom-and-tomato sauce, pesto or meat sauce, popular in the Chiavari area of the eastern Riviera di Levante. *Corzetti avvantaggiati* are made with whole wheat and bran mixed into the flour, and shaped like butterflies, a specialty of the Taggia area on the western Riviera di Ponente.

Corzetti della Val Polcevera: Tiny, homemade pasta twists shaped like an eight and made with soft bread flour, a specialty of the Val Polcevera behind Genoa. The pasta is made ahead and allowed to dry before being cooked. It is dressed with meat or mushroom sauce.

Cozze: Mussels. See *muscoli*.

Cubàite, cuppette: Unusual wafer cookie with crisp outer shells and creamy or honey-infused filling, often of crushed hazelnuts, walnuts or almonds, and candied citrus fruit, typical of the valleys and hilltowns of the Ligurian-French border area of the western Riviera di Ponente.

Dolce (pl. dolci)—döçe—sweet: Sweet wine and sweets (desserts).

Farinata—fainâ—chickpea-flour savory tart: Crustless and thin, *farinata* is oven-baked in large copper pans or iron trays; it can be seasoned with rosemary. Occasionally, *bianchetti* are added to the batter. *Farinata* can refer to savory tarts made with wheat or other flours (such as *faîna de Sanna* or *farinata di Savona*), but this is rare. *Farinata di zucca* is not *farinata* but rather a savory, crustless pumpkin tart, made in the western Genoese suburb of Sestri Ponente.

Fazzino, lisone, lisotto: A potato pancake made in the Valle Bormida, a valley behind the western Riviera di Ponente, and sometimes dressed with a rustic sauce made with onions or leeks and oil or lard.

Focaccia—fugassa—Ligurian flatbread: Olive oil is incorporated into the dough and also drizzled on top with partially dissolved sea salt. This pockmarked bread is about half an inch thick, crispy outside and tender inside. It is sometimes seasoned with sage or rosemary, or topped with sautéed white onions. When crushed olives or olive "skins" are added to the dough, the bread is called focaccia *con polpa d'olive* or *con pellette d'olive*. Focaccia *con formaggio* is wholly different, a thin, pale savory tart the diameter of a truck tire. The top and bottom crusts are made with translucent, olive oil-based dough, similar to focaccia or pizza dough but without yeast. Sandwiched between them is mild *stracchino* cow's milk cheese. Focaccia (or *torta*) *verde* is a crustless savory tart made with chard and olives, a specialty of the Dolceacqua area near the border with France. *Focaccine di mais* are cornmeal pancakes cooked on terracotta or iron disks, or slabs of slate, in a fireplace, or baked, and are found inland from the Tuscan border to Genoa.

Focaccia dolce sarzanese—fugassa döçe: Round leavened Christmastide lightly sweet dessert loaf from the Sarzana area on the Tuscan border, similar to *pandolce* but studded mostly with nuts.

Formaggetta: A fresh cow's milk cheese, usually cylindrical in shape, made in many Ligurian mountain and some seaside communities. On the western Riviera di Ponente, the milk used is often from ewes or even goats, and can optionally be mixed with cow's milk.

Fritelle—frisceu—fritters: Usually vegetable, cod or whitebait fritters, flash-fried in olive oil.

Frizzante: Slightly sparkling, bubbly, effervescent. Refers to wine and mineral water.

Funghi—funzi—mushrooms: Usually wild mushrooms, including porcini and *ovuli* (*amanita cesarea*). *Funghi secchi* are dry mushrooms. *Funghi sotto'olio* are preserved in olive oil. The popular inland dish, *funzi e patatte into tiàn,* a casserole of thick-sliced potatoes and mushrooms, is served in the autumn.

Giuncata—zuncò: Fresh ewe's milk cheese about an inch thick, made in the Savona area.

Gobeletti, cobeletti: Plump apricot jam-filled short-crust mini-pastries, shaped vaguely like goblets without stems, hence the name. Originally from Albenga, they're still made primarily on the western Riviera di Ponente, though many villages lay claim to them.

Lattuga (pl. lattughe)—leitughe—lettuce: **Leitughe pinn-e** (*lattughe ripiene*, also called *frati*) are lettuce leaves stuffed with a classic *ripieno* and simmered in white wine or broth.

Maccheroni di Natale—maccaroìn in broddo—large Christmastide macaroni: Usually cooked in a broth made from chicken, beef and pork and served with sausage meat.

Mandilli de saea/seia: Literally, silk handkerchiefs, aka large, rectangular lasagna-like pasta, typical of the eastern Riviera di Levante and Genoa. They are cooked individually, in the usual boiling, salted water, and dressed with pesto.

Marò: This dip of puréed fresh fava beans, garlic, oil and mint leaves is spread on bread or dry biscuits, and is a specialty of the western Riviera di Ponente.

Melata: Honey, made not from pollen but rather from tree sap or the sticky juices excreted by certain plants.

Mesciua, mesc-ciùa: Hearty soup of chickpeas, white beans and hulled wheat (*farro*), eaten in and around La Spezia.

Michetta: Mini-brioches usually in the shape of a knot, similar to croissants in texture and flavor, made in the Val Nervia on the border with France, and in the so-called Rock Villages above the river valley. Note, Ligurian *michetta* is unrelated to the Lombard bread roll of the same name.

Minestrone: Hearty vegetable soup with carrots, onions, zucchini, leeks, potatoes and just about any other available vegetable. When pesto is stirred in, it become *minestrone alla genovese* (for inexplicable reasons, in this case the pesto does not contain pine nuts and sometimes does not contain cheese).

Mosciamme—musciamme—air-dried porpoise, dolphin or tuna: Now exclusively made with tuna, because fishing porpoise and dolphin is illegal, this tender fish jerky is usually eaten as an antipasto or added to seafood salads.

Mosso: Slightly effervescent. Refers to wine.

inland from Genoa.

Salsa—sarza—sauce: A *salsa* is always raw; cooked sauces are called *sugo* or *tocco*.

Salsa di pinoli: A mild, white, pine nut pesto from Genoa made without basil or garlic. The ingredients are crushed pine nuts, oil, soft white bread, *prescinsêua* and salt.

Sanguinaccio: Blood sausage. What differentiates Liguria's version from all others, making it particularly delicious, is the addition of milk, ground pepper and crushed pine nuts to the pig's blood and ligaments that are boiled to make the sausage meat.

Sardenaira: A rustic pizza topped with anchovies or sardines, tomatoes, onions and black olives, and served along the western Riviera di Ponente. Also called *pissadella*, *pissaladiera*, *pissalandrea*.

Sbìra, sbirra: This Genoese tripe soup gets its flavor from bay leaves, and is now rarely found on menus.

Scabeccio, scabecciu: Fried mullet, *zerli* or *cicciarelli* pickled in vinegar, with sage and rosemary. In other regions of Italy, the technique is known as *in carpione*.

Scorzanera: Black "goat's beard" salsify, a long root vegetable with a slightly bitter flavor, usually braised or deep-fried and inexplicably popular on the Riviera.

Secco: Dry. Refers to wine, salami, cheese and other products.

Sott'oli, sottoli: Literally "under oil," meaning mushrooms or other vegetables and, occasionally, fish or cheese, preserved in olive oil. (*Sott'aceti* are foods pickled in vinegar).

Spongata, spungata: A puff-pastry pie stuffed with jam, dried fruits and nuts, made in the Sarzana area of the eastern Riviera di Levante.

Spumante: Sparkling wine.

Stecchi: Short wooden skewers threaded with veal, brains and other offal, dipped in a batter of *parmigiano*, breadcrumbs and herbs such as sage, and deep fried. They can also be made with goat meat or kid, mutton or lamb, and sometimes go by the name *rostelle* (in Bestagno, in the Province of Imperia, there's a Sagra delle rostelle, a local festival, where goat-meat skewers are served).

Stoccafisso—stocchefisce—air-dried cod: This cod is not salted; in Liguria, salt cod is *baccalà*, which, in other regions of Italy (and the Mediterranean) can mean either salt or air-dried cod. The two most popular ways to prepare air-dried cod are *stocchefisce accomodòu*, where the cod is stewed with potatoes, carrots, celery, onions, garlic, parsley, white wine, pine nuts, olive oil, olives, tomato sauce and dried porcini, or *in tocchetto*, with tomato sauce and dried mushrooms.

Testa in cassetta, soppressata: Headcheese. Made with the cheeks and other fleshly parts of the pig's head, plus the cartilage and fat.

Testarolo (pl. testaroli)—tèstarol, testaroi, testaieu: An ancient pancake of pasta cooked on thick terracotta plates or cast-iron disks in the fireplace. Often it is cooled, snipped into squares and cooked again in just-boiled (not boiling) water. *Testaroli* are usually dressed with olive oil and grated cheese or pesto. A specialty of the Lunigiana district bordering Tuscany, they're also found in *entroterra* valleys elsewhere along the Riviera and in northern Tuscany. A similar, crêpe-like pasta is the *panigaccio, panigazzo (panigacci, panigazzi)*, which is often wider and thinner than a *testarolo*, and not boiled. It's eaten at room temperature like a wrap, filled with cheese or cold cuts, or daubed with olive oil or pesto.

Tomaxelle. Veal rolls: These rolls of flattened veal are usually stuffed with ground beef, mushrooms, pine nuts, breadcrumbs, egg, grated *parmigiano*, marjoram and olive oil.

Torta pasqualina—torta pasquâlinn-a—Eastertide savory tart: This many-layered savory tart is filled with chard or artichokes, ricotta or *prescinsêua* cheese and cream, *parmigiano* and marjoram.

Torta salata: Savory tart, usually filled with vegetables. Favorites are artichokes, chard and squash. In the Lunigiana and the Sarzana and La Spezia areas, such tarts are sometimes called *stirpada, scherpada* or *scarpazza*. On the border with France, they're often called *torta verde*.

Trenette: Flat, dry ribbon pasta, like flattened spaghetti, similar to linguine. Usually sauced with pesto.

Trofie, troffie, trofiette: Delicate pasta twists, often described as looking like curled wood shavings, about one inch to one-and-one-half inches long, made without egg, and sauced with pesto, a specialty of the Recco and Sori area of the eastern Riviera di Levante. *Trofiette* are shorter than *trofie*.

Tocco—toccu, tûccu—cooked sauce: Made primarily with meat, tomatoes and/or mushrooms. The classic Ligurian meat sauce is of beef, onion, carrots, celery, olive oil, red wine, tomato concentrate, broth and dried porcini.

Zemin: Chickpea-and-chard stew, with garlic and a pinch of chili, often served with crumbled sea-biscuits, typical of the eastern Riviera di Levante.

Zeraria: A kind of headcheese made with pork and beef, boiled with black pepper, lemon juice and bay leaves, and found only in the western Riviera di Ponente, in and near the hilltop village of Ceriana.

Zerro (pl. zerri), zerli, zerla, partigia: Tiny bluefish (*Spicara smaris*) similar to *cicciarelli* and prepared in the same way, in soups, fried or pickled in vinegar. *Zerli* abound in the neighborhood of Noli, on the western Riviera di Ponente.

INDEX OF PLACE NAMES

. . . . ,

A

. . . .

Acquetico *372*

Alassio *324*

Albenga *329*

Albissola Marina *288*

Albissola Superiore *288*

Allegrezze *126*

Andora *349*

Apricale *394*

Arcagna *397*

Arenzano *271*

Arma di Taggia *388*

B

. . . .

Badalucco *389*

Baiardo *393*

Bastia d'Albenga *339, 341*

Bevera *387*

Beverino *116*

Bocca di Magra *58*

Bolano *78*

Bordighera *376*

Borghetto d'Arroscia *348*

Borgomaro *371*

Borgonovo Ligure *124*

Borzonasca *126*

C

. . . .

Calice Ligure *310*

Calizzano *311*

Camogli *170*

Campomorone *217*

Camporosso *397*

Capreno *214*

Carasco *132*

Case di Nava *373*

Case Rosse *372*

Castel Vittorio *393*

Castelnuovo Magra *59*

Castiglione Chiavarese *134*

Celle Ligure *289*

Cembrano *118*

Cervo *352*

Chiavari *135*

Chiusanico *370*

Chiusavecchia *370*

Cinque Terre (Riomaggiore,
   Manarola, Corniglia,
   Vernazza, and Monterosso) *84*

Conscenti di Né *152*

Corniglia *93*

Corona *303*

Cosio d'Arroscia *372*

D

. . . .

Diano Arentino *354*

Diano Castello *354*

Diano Gorleri *354*

Diano Marina *354*

Diano San Pietro *354*

Dolceacqua *396*

Dolcedo *366*

F

. . . .

Fado *270*

Finalborgo *313*

Finale Ligure *313*

G

. . . .

Gavenola *330, 347*

Gazzelli *370*

Gazzo *348*

Genoa *220*

I

Imperia *365*
Imperia-Oneglia *356*
Isolabona *395*
Isoverde *217*

L

La Spezia *97*
Lavagna *147*
Leca d'Albenga *339, 341*
Lerici *66*
Levanto *104*
Loano *319*
Lucinasco *371*
Luni *63*

M

Madonna Assunta *392*
Maissana *117*
Manarola *92*
Mele *270*
Molini di Triora *390*
Montemarcello *69*
Monterosso *39, 94*
Monterosso-Beo *94*

N

Né *152*
Nervi *281*
Nicola di Ortonovo *70*
Noli *320*

O

Ortonovo *63*
Ortovero *348*

P

Paggi *133*
Pantasina *367*
Perinaldo *398*

Pieve di Teco *372*
Pigna *392*
Poggi *368*
Pontedassio *369*
Pornassio *372*
Portofino *181*
Porto Maurizio *365*
Portovenere *108*
Prà *269*
Punta Chiappa *172, 179*

Q

Quiliano *289*

R

Ranzo *347*
Rapallo *183*
Recco *189*
Rezzoaglio *126*
Riomaggiore *87*
Rocco d'Aveto *129*
Rochetta Vara *116*
Ruta di Camogli *195*

S

Salea d'Albenga *341*
San Bartolomeo al Mare *352*
San Biagio della Cima *399*
San Massimo di Rapallo *203*
San Pietro Vara *118*
San Remo *377*
San Rocco di Camogli *195*
Sant'Olcese *281*
Santa Giulia *150*
Santa Margherita Ligure *204*
Santa Maria *116*
Santo Stefano d'Aveto *127*
Sarola *370*

Sarzana *72*
Sassello *290*
Savona *293*
Sesta Godano *117*
Sestri Levante *159*
Soldano *395, 398*
Sori *211*
Staglieno *282*
Stella *303*
Stellanello *349*

T

Tavarone *117*
Toirano *299*
Torriglia *283*
Torza *118*
Triora *391*

U

Uscio *216*

V

Val di Vara *116*
Varese Ligure *119*
Varigotti *321*
Vendone *346*
Ventimiglia *383*
Vernazza *94*
Vessalico *330*
Villa Faraldi *352*
Villanova d'Albenga *340, 349*
Vincinella *78*
Volastra *89*

Z

Zerli *155*

INDEX OF VENUES

A

A Bütega du Caffè, Albenga *334*

A Cantina de Mananan, Corniglia *93*

A Cuvea Gelateria, Alassio *326*

A Maccia, Borgo/Ranzo *347*

Ä Posa-a, Portovenere *110*

Abbo Srl Azienda Olearia, Bevera *387*

Agriturismo Argentea, Arenzano *271, 274*

Agriturismo Ca' da Ninna, Costa Carnara/Dolcedo *367*

Agriturismo Il Castagno, San Bernardo/Mendatica *373*

Agriturismo La Bicocca, Rapallo *188*

Agriturismo La Molinella, Isolabona *395*

Agriturismo-Azienda Agricola Roberto Noceti, Carasco/Paggi *133*

Al Boschetto, Sori *214*

Al Forno di Albaro, Genoa *266*

Albergo Ristorante Lorenzina, Case di Nava *373*

Alberto Marvaldi, Borgomaro *371*

Alimentari Andrea de Vincenzi, Varese Ligure *120*

Alimentari L'Anfora, Perinaldo *398*

Alimentari La Posta, Pigna *392*

Alimentari Panetteria Garoscio Cinzia e Silvia, Dolceacqua *396*

Alimentari Rovere, Gavenola *330, 347*

Alter Ego, Alassio *326*

Amaretti Astengo, Savona *297*

Amaretti Cavo, Genoa *263*

Amaretti Giacobbe, Sassello *292*

Amaretti Virginia, Sassello *291*

Amici, Varese Ligure *119*

Andrea Bruzzone, Genova-Bolzaneto *52*

Anfossi Azienda Agraria, Bastia d'Albenga *304, 339, 341*

Anfosso A e C, Chiusavecchia *306*

Angiolino Asplanato, Triora *392*

Antica Drogheria Ferrea, Genoa *228*

Antica Drogheria M. Torielli, Genoa *229*

Antica Osteria da Caran, La Spezia *98*

Antica Osteria del Bai, Genoa *276*

Antica Osteria della Castagna, Genoa *276*

Antica Osteria del Caruggio, Portovenere *110*

Antica Osteria della Foce, Genoa *261*

Antica Osteria di Vico Palla, Genoa *221*

Antica Pasticceria Lino Rossi, Sassello *290*

Antica Salumeria Elena e Mirco, Moliceiara/ Castelnuovo Magra *61*

Antica Sciamadda, Genoa *222*

Antica Trattoria Centro, Levanto *105*

Antica Trattoria dei Mosto, Né *152*

Antica Trattoria delle Rose, Sori *214*

Antica Trattoria Rocchin, Borzonasca *126*

Antica Trattoria Sà Pesta, Genoa *223*

Antica Tripperia la Casana, Genoa *230*

Antico Biscottificio della Foce, Genoa *264*

Antico Caffè , Pasticceria Balzola, Alassio *326*

Antico Forno, Torriglia *283*

Antico Frantoio Sommariva, Albenga *338*

Antico Salumificio Castiglione, Castiglione Chiavarese *134*

Apicoltura Burgum Mielizia, Finalborgo *318*

Apicoltura Dino Gastaldi, Cosio d'Arroscia *372*

Apicoltura Ribaditi, Santa Maria/Calice al Cornoviglio *116*

Apricale da Delio, Apricale *394*

Arcobaleno Gelateria, Lerici *68*

Armando—Pasticceria/ Gelateria, La Spezia *101*

Armanino, Genoa *231*

Aschero Laura, Pontedassio *304*

Attilio Noceti, Paggi/ Carasco *37, 133*

Azienda Agricola Agriturismo Dinoabbo, Lucinasco *371*

Azienda Agricola Allavena
Maria Giovanna, Pigna *392*

Azienda Agricola Allavena
Massimo, Pigna *392*

Azienda Agricola Apiario
Benedettino, Finale
Ligure Pia *314*

Azienda Agricola Bronda Renzo,
Cantone/Vendone *346*

Azienda Agricola Damiano,
Chiusavecchia *370*

Azienda Agricola e Agriturismo
Il Nostro Oliveto, Bastia
d'Albenga *341*

Azienda Agricola Fratelli
Benedetti, Leca
d'Albenga *339, 341*

Azienda Agricola
Giacomelli, Palvotrisia/
Castelnuovo Magra *64*

Azienda Agricola Giordano
Valerio, Dolcedo *367*

Azienda Agricola Giuseppe
Cotta, Pantasina/
Vasia *306, 368*

Azienda Agricola Il Frantoio,
Ville San Sebastiano/
Borgomaro *371*

Azienda Agricola Il Monticello,
Bradia-Sarzana *55, 76, 79*

Azienda Agricola Jole
Buscaglia, Calizzano *38, 312*

Azienda Agricola La Giara,
Imperia-Porto Maurizio *365*

Azienda Agricola La Pietra
del Focolare, Ortonovo *66*

Azienda Agricola La Rocca
di San Nicolao, Gazzelli/
Chiusanico *305, 343, 345, 370*

Azienda Agricola Le
Rattatuie, Cembrano *118*

Azienda Agricola Lorenzo
Ramò, Pornassio *372*

Azienda Agricola Maccario
Dringenberg, San Biagio
della Cima *399*

Azienda Agricola Mooretti,
Allegrezze/Santo
Stefano d'Aveto *127*

Azienda Agricola Orseggi, Santa
Giulia di Lavagna *77, 150*

Azienda Agricola Rùe
de Zerli, Né *155*

Azienda Agricola Sacco, Prà *279*

Azienda Agricola San Dalmazio,
Arveglio/Albenga *305, 343, 346*

Azienda Agricola San
Damiano, Stellanello *349*

Azienda Agricola Santa
Catarina, Sarzana *77*

Azienda Agricola Sommariva,
Albenga *305, 343, 346*

Azienda Agricola Valle Ostilia,
Villa Faraldi *306, 353*

Azienda Agricola Varaldo
Elena, Villa Faraldi *353*

Azienda Lupi, Pieve di Teco *372*

Azienda Vitivinicola Tenuta
Anfosso, Soldano *399*

Azienda Vitivinicola-Agricola
Eredi Ing. Guglierame,
Pornassio *372*

Azienda Vitivinicola La Baia
del Sole, Ortonovo *54, 344*

B

Bacco Osteria con
Cucina, Savona *294*

Baglietto e Secco, Villanova
d'Albenga *306, 340, 349*

Baj Pasticceria, Rapallo *185*

Bajeicò, Portovenere *110*

Balletin Pescheria,
Sestri Levante *161*

Bar Besio, Savona *297*

Bar Breakfast, Imperia-
Porto Maurizio *366*

Bar Centrale, Finalborgo *318*

Bar Centrale, Riomaggiore *90*

Bar Colombo, Santa
Margherita Ligure *206*

Bar Crovetto, Sori *213*

Bar Gelateria Davide,
Chiavari *141*

Bar Gelateria Lamia,
Portovenere *110*

Bar-Gelateria Pinotto,
Calizzano *38, 313*

Bar Gelateria Verdi, Chiavari *144*

Bar Gina, Sassello *292*

Bar Jole, Sassello *293*

Bar Pasticceria Festival,
San Remo *382*

Bar Pippi, San Rocco
di Camogli, *199*

Bar Ristorante Da Marilena,
Gavenola *348*

Bar Vittoria, Santa
Margherita Ligure *211*

Bardi, Santa Margherita
Ligure *205*

Bar-Ristorante dell'Amore,
Riomaggiore *88*

Bar-Tavola Calda Levey,
Sassello *292*

Baxin, Albenga *334*

Bellavista, La Spezia *98*

Benza Frantoiano Olio
Extravergine, Dolcedo,
Imperia *306, 366*

Beppa, Imperia-Oneglia *359*

Bio Vio, Bastia d'Albenga *341*

Biofattoria Azienda
Agricola Gamba Patrizio,
Foa/Apricale *395*

Bisson, Chiavari *52, 54, 344*

Boasi Caffè Torrefazione,
Genoa *231*

Boasi Caffè, Genoa *248*

Bonanni Fellegara,
Riomaggiore *97*

Bonanni—Antiche Bottiglierie
Genovesi, Genoa *248*

Bontà Nascoste, Lerici *67*

Bottega dello Stoccafisso,
Genoa *231*

Bruciamonti, Genoa *249*

Bruna, Borgo/Ranzo *304, 342*

Buffa—Fabbrica Cioccolato,
Confetteria, Genoa *249*

Bugliani Panifico
Pizzeria, Sarzana *76*

Buranco, Monterosso *97*

Busciun, Castel Vittorio *393*

C

Cà Bianca di Francesco
Bruzzo, Chiavari *77, 146*

Ca' del Moro, Finale
Ligure/Olle *314*

Ca' di Gòsita, Gòsita/Né *155*

Ca' Du Luasso, Lavagna *148*

Ca' Peo, Leivi *274*

Café Pasticceria San
Lorenzo, Alassio *328*

Caffè Bocchia, Chiavari *139* /
Rapallo *185* / Recco *194*
/ Lavagna *149* / Sestri
Levante *162*

Caffè Defilla, Chiavari *135, 141*

Caffè Costituzionale, Sarzana *74*

Caffè degli Specchi, Genoa *224*

Caffè Ducale, San Remo *381*

Caffè Due Merli, Savona *298*

Caffè Gelateria Balilla,
Genoa *247*

Caffè Le Clarisse, Levanto *105*

Caffè Paris, Ventimiglia *386*

Caffè Pasticceria Mangini, Genoa *253*

Caffè Piccardo, Imperia-Oneglia *359*

Caffè del Borgo, Finalborgo *318*

Caffè Giovanacci, Finale Ligure *318*

Caffè-Pasticceria Ferro, Finale Ligure *317*

Canevello—Salumeria Sottoripa, Genoa *233*

Cantina Case Rosse, Case Rosse *372*

Cantina Cooperativa Agricoltura Cinque Terre, Groppo/Riomaggiore *54, 91*

Cantin-a du Púsu, Rapallo *186*

Cantine d'Italia, Rapallo *186*

Cantine del Rossese-Gajaudo, Isolabona *395*

Cantine Lunae Bosoni, Palvotrisia/Castelnuovo Magra *65*

Cantine Sanremesi, San Remo *378*

Cappa Pasticceria, Alassio *328*

Casa del Caffè, Bordighera *376*

Casa del Caffè—Caffè 3 Moretti, Savona *299*

Casa del Cioccolato, Genoa *234*

Casa del Gelato, Albenga *335*

Casa della Panizza, Savona *295*

Casa Olearia Taggiasca, Prati e Pescine/Arma di Taggia *389*

Casanova, Finalborgo/Sotto Ripa *319*

Cascina delle Terre Rosse, Finale Ligure *304, 313, 344*

Cascina Praiè, Colla Micheri/Andora *349*

Caseificio Val d'Aveto, Rezzoaglio *126*

Centro Salagione di Monterosso, Monterosso *39*

Chez Lino, Ventimiglia *383*

Chicco Caffè , Genoa *250*

Chiesa, Finale Ligure *314, 317*

Choco Emotion, Camogli *176*

Ciak Wine & Food, Monterosso *96*

Cioccolateria Dolce… più Dolce, La Spezia *102*

Claretta Panificio Grissinificio, Genoa *234*

Claudio Vio, Vendone *342, 344, 346*

Colle dei Bardellini, Bardellini/Imperia *304*

Colle del Telegrafo, Riomaggiore *89*

Colle Sereno, Acquetico *372*

Colomba d'Oro, Triora *391*

Confetteria Rossi, Genoa *255*

Conte Picedi Benettini, Baccano di Arcola *79*

Cooperativa Agricola Lavagnina, Lavagna *151*

Cooperativa Casearia Val di Vara, Varese Ligure *118*

Cooperativa Olivicola di Arnasco, Arnasco *307, 346*

Cooperativa Pescatori, Camogli *176*

Cooperativa Viticoltori Ingauni, Ortovero *349*

Coopertiva San Pietro Vara, Varese Ligure *120*

Copello Pasticceria, Chiavari *140*

Cremeria Ciarapìca, Genoa *265*

Cremeria Colombo, Genoa *250*

Creuza de Mà di M. Peirano
e C., Arenzano *279*

D

Da Claudio e Adele—Formaggi
e Salumi, Albenga *335*

Da Fiorella Ristorante-Bar,
Nicola di Ortonovo *71*

Da Gianni, Savona *294*

Da Lino, Recco' *189*

Da Maria, Vessalico *330*

Da Nicco, Ruta di Camogli *197*

Da Ö Pescôu, Lavagna *149*

Da ö Vittorio, Recco *189*

Da Rina, Genoa *224*

Da Silvio, Sarzana *74*

Danielli, Genoa *250*

Danila Pisano, Apricale *395, 399*

De Regibus, Genoa *256*

Diego Panetta, Serra Riccò *279*

Dino Abbo, Lucinasco *306*

Do Spadin, Camogli/
Punta Chiappa *172*

Dolci Delizie, Uscio *216*

Domenico Barisone Cooperativa
Viticoltori Coronata,
Genova-Coronata *52*

Domenico Ramoino, Sarola *370*

Domenico Ruffino, Varigotti *321*

Drogheria Giovanni Ameri,
Chiavari *37, 139*

Durin, Ortovero *52, 304, 343, 348*

E

Edo Bar, Sori *213*

El Portico, Portofino *182*

Enoteca Baroni, Lerici *68*

Enoteca Bisson, Chiavari *145*

Enoteca Ciak, Monterosso *95*

Enoteca Coop Vallata di
Levanto, Levanto *106*

Enoteca Il Mulino del Cibus,
Molicciara/Castelnuovo
Magra and Sarzana *76*

Enoteca Ingaunia DOC,
Albenga *335*

Enoteca Internazionale,
Monterosso *96*

Enoteca La Nicchia, Levanto *107*

Enoteca Lupi, Imperia-
Oneglia *361*

Enoteca Marone, San Remo *380*

Enoteca Pubblica,
Castelnuovo Magra *59*

Enoteca Re, Dolceacqua *396*

Enoteca Sola, Genoa *251*

Enoteca Sotto l'Arco, Vernazza *94*

Enoteca Susto, Genoa *235*

Enoteca Vinum, Levanto *106*

Enoteca Wine e Spirit Carpe
Diem, Alassio *328*

Enzo Guglielmi, Soldano *52, 399*

EVO Oleo Granoteca, Genoa *251*

F

Fabbrica cioccolato
Zuccotti, Genoa *269*

Farinata Santa Zita, Genoa *262*

Farinata, Genoa *246*

Federico Parodi Salumificio,
Sant'Olcese/Genoa *282*

Fèipu dei Massaretti, Bastia
d'Albenga *304, 339, 341, 343*

Fiordiponti, Santa
  Margherita Ligure *206*

Fiorella d'Amore, Genoa *246*

Fiorenzo Guidi, Ranzo *347*

Foresti, Camporosso
  Mare *304, 398*

Forlini e Cappellini, Manarola *92*

Forno Papalia, Pigna *392*

Francesco Ratto, Prà *277*

Franco Casoni, Chiavari *146*

Frantoio Artigianale Magnone,
  Finale Ligure Pia *313*

Frantoio Artigianale
  Mantello Mauro, Albareto/
  Stellanello *349*

Frantoio Bo, Sestri
  Levante *77, 166*

Frantoio da olive Bestoso
  Domenico, Borgonuovo/
  Stellanello *349*

Frantoio da olive Rossi Simone,
  San Damiano/Stellanello *349*

Frantoio di Sant'Agata
  d'Oneglia, Sant'Agata
  d'Oneglia *306, 364*

Frantoio Elena Luigi, Chiappa/
  San Bartolomeo al Mare *353*

Frantoio Gaziello,
  Ventimiglia *386*

Frantoio Ghiglione
  Giuseppe, Dolcedo *367*

Frantoio Giobatta Panizzi,
  Badalucco *390*

Frantoio Marco, Leca
  d'Albenga *341*

Frantoio U Vescu, Borello/
  Diano Arentino *354*

Fratelli Carli, Imperia-
  Oneglia *357*

Fratelli Centenaro, Genoa *252*

Fratelli Klainguti Bar
  Pasticceria, Genoa *235*

G

Garibaldi Cafè, Genoa *276*

Gelateria Amedeo, Genoa *265*

Gelateria Artigiana Costa
  Giulio, Genoa *265*

Gelateria Baciollo, Sestri
  Levante *161*

Gelateria Bar Gelmo, Loano *319*

Gelateria Cavassa, Recco *195*

Gelateria Festival des
  Glaces, Albenga *336*

Gelateria Frigidarium,
  Rapallo *187*

Gelateria GROM, Genoa *252*

Gelateria Guarino, Genoa *257*

Gelateria Il Dattero,
  Finale Ligure *317*

Gelateria Il Porticciolo,
  Levanto *106*

Gelateria K2, Sestri Levante *163*

Gelateria Profumo, Genoa *238*

Gelateria Zico, Corniglia *93*

Gemmi Pasticceria Bar
  Confetteria, Sarzana *75*

Gerolamo Pernigotti—
  Gamalero, Genoa *253*

Giacomo Alberti,
  Pontedassio *370*

Gian Battista Fasolo,
  Gazzelli/Chiusanico *370*

Giovanni Maltini, Castel
  Vittorio *393*

Girarosto da Paolo,
  Bradia/Sarzana *73*

Gli Ulivi, Riomaggiore *89*

Gocce d'Olio, Villa Faraldi *353*

Gran Caffè Tritone Gelateria,
  Sestri Levante *165*

Granbazzar, La Spezia *103*

Granite/Gelati, Sori *213*

Grigiomar, Savona *294*

H

Hostaria del Pellegrino,
Imperia-Porto Maurizio *365*

Hostaria della Luna Piena,
Santo Stefano d'Aveto *128*

Hosteria Sutta Ca', Albenga *333*

Hotel della Posta 1906,
Torriglia *283*

Hotel Marinella, Nervi/
Genoa *281*

Hotel-Ristorante Italia,
Castel Vittorio *393*

Hotel-Ristorante Santo Spirito,
Molini di Triora *390*

I

I Formaggi del Boschetto,
Bastia d'Albenga *339, 341*

I Maestri del Pesto,
Mele/Genoa *280*

I Pescatori, Lerici *67*

Il Ciliegio, Beo/Monterosso *95*

Il Colle degli Ulivi,
Sant'Angelo/Diano
Marina *354*

Il Forno di Germano,
Varese Ligure *120*

Il Giardino dei Semplici,
Chiavari *151*

Il Laboratorio del Pesto,
Levanto *107*

Il Mattarello Pazzo, Bolano *78*

Il Minatore, Né *154*

Il Monticello, Bradia/
Sarzana *55, 76, 79*

Il Mulino del Cibus, Molicciara/
Castelnuovo Magra *64*

Il Mulino di Sassello *291*

Il Pesto di Prà di Bruzzone e
Ferrari, Prà/Genoa *280*

Il Pesto Più di Prà di
Rebuffo Fassone Ramella,
Prà/Genoa *280*

Il Portico, Chiavari *138*

Il Ristoro dei Grimaldi,
Genoa *226*

Il San Lorenzo, Santa
Margherita Ligure *205*

Il Sangiorgino, Cervo *352*

Il Sottobosco, Tiglieto *196*

Innocenzo Turco, Quiliano *290*

L

L'Aromatica, Genoa *264*

L'Artigiana del Fungo,
Sassello *292*

L'Artigiano del Cioccolato,
La Spezia *101*

L'Isola delle cose buone,
La Spezia *102*

L'Oasi, Imperia-Porto
Maurizio *365*

La Baia del Sole, Luni *66*

La Baita, Gazzo/Borghetto
d'Arroscia *306, 348*

La Bimare Torrefazione,
Sestri Levante *161*

La Bottega dei Funghi,
Calizzano *312*

La Bottega dei Piaceri,
Camogli *176*

La Bottega dei Sestieri,
Rapallo *185*

La Bottega del Caffè
Pasqualini, Alassio *326*

La Bottega del Caffè
Pasqualini, San Remo *382*

La Bottega del Caffè F.lli
Pasqualini, Savona *298*

La Bottega del Formaggio, Chiavari *139*

La Bottega del Pesto, Nervi, Genoa *281*

La Bottega di Angelamaria, Molini di Triora *391*

La Bottega di Mastro Antonucci, Camogli *175*

La Boutique del Pane Mondino, Ventimiglia *386*

La Brinca, Né *153, 274*

La Cantina del Polpo, Sestri Levante *160*

La Cantina di Colombo, Genoa *227*

La Cantina Levantese di S. Lagaxio, Levanto *52, 105*

La Capanna da Bacì, Apricale *394*

La Casa del Caffè , Bordighera *376*

La Casetta, Avegno *216*

La Colombiera, Castelnuovo Magra *54, 66*

La Cucina di Nonna Nina, San Rocco di Camogli *196, 274*

La Familiare, Finale Ligure *317*

La Felce di Marcesini Andrea, Ortonovo *66*

La Focacceria, Recco *193*

La Genovese Caffè e Dintorni, Albenga *336*

La Mola, Molini di Prelà *367*

La Palma, Santa Margherita Ligure *204*

La Paranza, Santa Margherita Ligure *205*

La Pia Centenaria, La Spezia *100*

La Pietra del Focolare, Ortonovo *55*

La Pizzaccia, Portovenere *110*

La Polenza di Lorenzo Casté, Corniglia *55, 93*

La Polenza di Maria Rita Rezzano, Vernazza *94*

La Rampa, Dolceacqua *396*

La Strega di Triora, Triora *391*

La Taverna di Colombo, Genoa *226*

La Terrazza di Milly, Genoa *276*

La Torrigiana, Torriglia *283*

La Vecchia Cantina, Salea d'Albenga *305, 339, 341, 342, 345*

La Veranda, Tavarone *117*

Latteria Bavari, Genoa *268*

Laura Aschero, Pontedassio *370*

Le Cantine Squarciafico, Genoa *224*

Le Due Lune, Sarzana *75*

Le Gramole Olioteca, Genoa *234, 330*

Le Petraie, Pieve di Teco *304*

Le Rocche del Gatto, Salea d'Albenga *305, 339, 341*

Le Rune, Genoa *276*

Locanda della Marchesa, Nicola di Ortonovo *70*

Locanda Piemontese, Calice Ligure *311*

Lucchi e Guastalli, Vincinella *77, 78*

Luchin, Chiavari *136*

Luciano Capellini, Volastra/ Riomaggiore *54, 91*

Luigi Calvini, San Remo *382*

Lunae Bosoni, Ortonovo *55, 344*

Lupi, Pieve di Teco *305, 343, 344*

M

Maccia, Ranzo *347*

Macelleria Angelo Torrazza, Campomorone/Gazzolo *217*

Macelleria Paolucci, San Rocco di Camogli *198*

Macelleria-Salumeria Giacobbe, Sassello *291*

Maggiorino, San Remo *378*

Magnani Salumi e Formaggi, Ortonovo *63*

Manuelina, Recco *189, 193*

Marcellino Pane e Vino, Montemarcello *70*

Marcello Calleri, Salea d'Albenga *341*

Marco Ballestra, Ventimiglia *383*

Marco Favero, Cosio d'Arroscia *372*

Maria Donata Bianchi, Diano Castello *354*

Mario Ferrando, Prà/Genoa *279*

Mario Mattoli, Chiavari *134*

Massimo Alessandri, Costa Parrocchia/Ranzo *304, 342, 347*

Massimo Solari, Chiavari *77, 133*

Maura Ragazzoni, San Remo (covered market) *378*

Mazzini-Graglia Salumeria Rosticceria, Rapallo *187*

Migone Enoteca, Genoa *238*

Minuto Caffè, Savona *294*

Molinari & Pasini—M&P, Riomaggiore *97*

Monna Bianca, Lavagna *150*

N

Natale Sassarini, Monterosso *97*

Non Solo Vino, Riomaggiore *90*

Nonsolofunghi, Sassello *292*

Nonsolopizza, Noli *321*

Nuovo Piccolo Mondo, San Remo *379*

O

Ö Bansin, Rapallo *184*

Ö Caratello, Lavagna *150*

Oleificio G. Boeri, Arma di Taggia *388*

Oleificio Polla Nicolò, Loano *319* and Savona *299*

Olio Anfosso, Chiusavecchia *371*

Olio Ardoino, Pontedassio *369*

Olio Carli, Imperia-Orneglia *357*

Olio Roi, Montalto Ligure/ Badalucco *307, 389*

Ombre Rosse, Genoa *225*

Opera Magé, Arma di Taggia/ San Remo *380, 388*

Ostaja San Vincenzo, Genoa *246*

Ostaja, Staglieno/Genoa *274, 282*

Osteria all'Inferno, La Spezia *99*

Osteria Cu de Beu, Savona *295*

Osteria dei Matetti, Alassio *325*

Osteria del Portico, Castel Vittorio *393*

Osteria Du Chicchinettu, Varese Ligure *120*

Osteria Enoteca Baccicin du Caru, Mele/Genoa *270, 274*

Osteria Tabacchi Da Drin, Capreno/Sori *214*

Ottaviano Lambruschi, Palvotrisia/Castelnuovo Magra *55, 65, 345*

P

Panarello, Genoa *254*

Panetteria Bellerio Rolando, San Remo *381*

Panetteria Dallorto Paolo, Ventimiglia *386*

Panetteria Fratelli Ferrari, Pieve di Teco *372*

Panificio Battalini & Ginocchio, San Pietro Vara *118*

Panificio Cacciò, Gavenola *348*

Panificio Cudì dei Fratelli Lorenzini, Ortonovo *63*

Panificio Fiore, Genoa *239*

Panificio Gandolfo Bruna, Borgomaro *371*

Panificio Lippi, Ruta di Camogli *200*

Panificio Maccarini, San Rocco di Camogli *200*

Panificio Pasticceria Fratelli Terarolli, Luni *63*

Panificio Pasticceria Pignone Giorgio & C., Pieve di Teco *372*

Panificio Patrone, Genoa *239*

Panificio Rizzoli Marcello, La Spezia *103*

Panificio Rocco Rizzo, Camogli *178*

Panificio Rosy, Riomaggiore *90*

Panificio Tosi, Sestri Levante *164*

Panificio Tumioli, Genoa *239*

Panificio-Pasticceria Moltedo, Recco *190*

Panifico Sanguineti, Né *158*

Paolo Calcagno, Celle Ligure *279*

Paolo Cassini, Isolabona *395*

Paolo Pellegrino, Borgomaro *371*

Paolo Ruffino, Varigotti *321*

Parmiggiani Fratelli, Varese Ligure *120*

Party House Enoteca con Cucina, La Spezia *100*

Pasta Fresca Dasso, Rapallo *187*

Pasta Fresca Franzi, Lerici *69, 280*

Pasticceria Alimentari Chiesa, Santo Stefano d'Aveto *129*

Pasticceria Bar Budicin, Ruta di Camogli *197*

Pasticceria Bar Riviera, Recco *195*

Pasticceria Besio, Savona *300*

Pasticceria Bianchi, Levanto *107*

Pasticceria Caffetteria Monteverde, Lavagna *149*

Pasticceria Gelateria da Maurizio e Charlie, Imperia-Porto Maurizio *366*

Pasticceria Grana, Albenga *337*

Pasticceria Guano, Torriglia *283*

Pasticceria La Crêpe, Noli *321*

Pasticceria Laura, Monterosso *96*

Pasticceria Magenta, Genoa *257*

Pasticceria Poldo, Pontedecimo/Genoa *280*

Pasticceria Primavera, San Remo *381*

Pasticceria Profumo, Genoa *240*

Pasticceria Racca, San Bartolomeo al Mare *353*

Pasticceria Revello, Camogli *177*

Pasticceria Rossignotti, Sestri Levante *163*

Pasticceria San Romolo, San Remo *381*

Pasticceria Svizzera, Genoa *268*

Pasticceria Tagliafico, Genoa *255*

Pasticceria Valeria, Savona *301*

Pastificio Artigianale Fiore, Graveglia/Carasco *132*

Pastificio Fontana, Albenga *336*

Pastificio Novella, Sori *213*

Pastificio Prato, Chiavari *144*

Pastificio Santa Rita, Né *157*

Pastorino, Calice Ligure *311*

Perrone Tabò Maria, Calizzano *312*

Pescheria Cerisola Clelia, Noli *320*

Pescheria Delmonte "U Balincio", Imperia-Oneglia *362*

Pescheria Nello, Celle Ligure *289*

Pescheria Pinto Porta Molino, Albenga *338*

Pestarino, Santa Margherita Ligure *206*

Pian del Sole, Sassello *290*

Piccolo Birrificio, Apricale *395*

Pierandrea Costa, Diano Castello *354*

Pietro Isnardi, Pontedassio *369*

Pinamonti, Santa Margherita Ligure *210*

Pino Gino, Missano/Castiglione Chiavarese *55, 77, 134*

Pino, Noli *320*

Pinotto, Calizzano *38*

Poggio dei Gorleri, Diano Marina *355*

Polpo Mario, Sestri Levante *160*

Prà Basilico e Pesto, Prà/Genoa *280*

Primula, Camogli *177*

Puny, Portofino *182*

Puppo Farinata e…, Albenga *333*

R

Raffo Francesca Alimentari, Dolceacqua *396*

Ranise Azienda Agroalimentari, Imperia *305, 307, 363*

Riccardo Bruna, Ranzo *347*

Riccardo Gaggero, Mele/Genoa *279*

Ripa Del Sole, Riomaggiore *87*

Ristorante Capannina Ciccio, Bocca di Magra *58*

Ristorante Da Angelo, Recco *189, 193*

Ristorante Da ö Vittorio, Recco *276*

Ristorante del Mulino Da Drin, Punta Chiappa/Camogli *172*

Ristorante Enoteca Ostricheria Bacchus, San Remo *379*

Ristorante Ferrando, Serra Riccò/Genoa *276*

Ristorante Hotel Terme, Madonna Assunta/Castel Vittorio *392*

Ristorante La Familiare, Albissola Marina *288*

Ristorante Lorenzina, Case di Nava *373*

Ristorante Nestin, Frazione Canepa/Sori *215*

Ristorante-Bar Monesteroli, Riomaggiore *89*

Ristorante-Bar Santuario di Montenero, Riomaggiore *89*

Ristorante-Focacceria Manuelina, Recco *276*

Ristorante La Margherita, Sesta Godano *117*

Roberto Casotti, Prà/Genoa *279*

Roberto Rota, Giuncheo/Camporosso *397*

Romanengo fu Stefano,
Genoa *241*

Romeo Viganotti di Alessandro
Boccardo, Genoa *243*

Roncagliolo e Simonetti,
Rapallo *188*

Rosa, Camogli *172, 274*

Rosticceria Castelletto,
Genoa *257*

Rùe de Zerli, Zerli/Né *155*

Ruffino, Varigotti *52*

Ruscin Antica Trattoria
1893, Genoa Bavari *276*

S

Saglietto Olio Agriturismo,
Poggi *368*

Saguato Stefano Frantoio Olive
Olio, Diano San Pietro *355*

Salsamenteria Antica,
Savona *302*

Salumeria Bellini, San Remo *381*

Salumeria Crespi, San Remo *380*

Salumeria Re, Imperia-
Porto Maurizio *366*

Salumificio Cabella,
Sant'Olcese/Genoa *282*

San Matteo Osteria, Genoa *238*

Santa Caterina, Sarzana
55, 77, 345

Santamaria & C.,
Calizzano *38, 312*

Santuario Nostra Signora di
Soviore, Monterosso *95*

Scandelin, Sori *211*

Sciolè Mirella, San Remo *380*

Seghezzo, Santa Margherita
Ligure *210*

Serafina Artigiana
Alimentari, Genoa *243*

Sola Enoteca Cucina &
Vino, Genoa *262*

Stampetta-Panificio
Pasticceria, La Spezia *103*

Superfrutto Gelateria,
Savona *302*

T

Taverna del Capitano,
Vernazza *94*

Taverna del Gallo Nero,
Varese Ligure *119*

Tavernetta, San Remo *378*

Tenuta Giuncheo,
Camporosso *305, 345, 397*

Terre Bianche, Arcagna/
Dolceacqua *305, 397*

Terre di Mare, Finale
Ligure/Alassio *317, 329*

Torrefazione Caffè Brasil,
Imperia-Oneglia *362*

Torrefazione Caffè
Pagliettini, Rapallo *188*

Torrefazione Caffè Ugo
Romoli, Genoa *268*

Torrefazione Elena,
San Remo *382*

Torrefazione F.lli Pasqualini,
San Remo/Villanova
d'Albenga *340, 349*

Tossini, Recco *192*

Trattoria A Beccassa,
Torriglia *283*

Trattoria A Ciassa, Apricale *394*

Trattoria Armanda,
Castelnuovo Magra *60*

Trattoria Bruxaboschi, Genoa
San Desiderio *276*

Trattoria Cavour, Levanto *104*

Trattoria Cornua, Cornua/
Lumarzo *216*

Trattoria Da Ugo, Genoa *228*

Trattoria dai Pironcelli, Montemarcello *70*

Trattoria della Raibetta, Genoa *227*

Trattoria Gianni Franzi, Vernazza *94*

Trattoria Giovanna, Molini di Triora *390*

Trattoria Invexendu, Finalborgo *318*

Trattoria Iolanda, Campomorone/ Isoverde *217, 277*

Trattoria L'Alpino, Frazione Leuso/Ranzo *346*

Trattoria La Rocca, Rocca/ Santo Stefano d'Aveto *129*

Trattoria Luigina, Genoa Granarolo *277*

Trattoria Marchin, Borgonovo Ligure *124*

Trattoria Picchetto, San Pietro Vara *118*

Trattoria Rina, Genoa *277*

Trattoria Settembrin, Carasco/Graveglia *132*

Trattoria Vëgia Arbâ, Genoa *263*

Trattoria Vittoria, Sassello *291*

Trattoria-Pizzeria-Bar La Lucertola, Apricale *394*

Turco Innocenzo, Quiliano *305*

Tuttogelato, Imperia- Oneglia *363*

U

Ü Bucün du Preve, Noli *320*

Ü Fainottö—Da Franco, Recco *192*

Ü Giancu, San Massimo di Rapallo *203*

Usai Pasquale Coltivatore Diretto, Corona/Stella *303*

V

Vecchio Frantoio, Vignai/ Badalucco *389*

Vedova Romanengo, Genoa *243*

Venturino Bartolomeo, Diano San Pietro *356*

Vineria, Santa Margherita Ligure *210*

Vini Liquori e Funghi Pareti Biagio, Santo Stefano d'Aveto *128*

Vino e Farinata—Osteria con Cucina, Savona *296*

Vio Claudio, Vendone *305*

W

Walter De Battè, Riomaggiore *52, 54, 92*

Z

Zeffirino, Genoa *274*

INDEX OF VENUES

BY TYPE

RESTAURANTS,
TRATTORIE,
OSTERIE, CAFFÈ
SERVING MEALS,
TORTE E FARINATA,
AGRITURISMO

A

A Cantina de Mananan,
Corniglia *93*

Agriturismo Argentea,
Arenzano *271, 274*

Agriturismo Ca' da Ninna,
Costa Carnara/Dolcedo *367*

Agriturismo La Molinella,
Isolabona *395*

Agriturismo-Azienda
Agricola Roberto Noceti,
Carasco/Paggi *133*

Al Boschetto, Sori *214*

Albergo Ristorante Lorenzina,
Case di Nava *373*

Amici, Varese Ligure *119*

Antica Osteria da Caran,
La Spezia *98*

Antica Osteria del
Bai, Genoa *276*

Antica Osteria della
Castagna, Genoa *276*

Antica Osteria del Caruggio,
Portovenere *110*

Antica Osteria della
Foce, Genoa *261*

Antica Osteria di Vico
Palla, Genoa *221*

Antica Sciamadda, Genoa *222*

Antica Trattoria Centro,
Levanto *105*

Antica Trattoria dei
Mosto, Né *152*

Antica Trattoria delle
Rose, Sori *214*

Antica Trattoria Rocchin,
Borzonasca *126*

Antica Trattoria Sà
Pesta, Genoa *223*

Apricale da Delio, Apricale *394*

B

Bacco Osteria con
Cucina, Savona *294*

Bar-Ristorante dell'Amore,
Riomaggiore *88*

Bellavista, La Spezia *98*

Beppa, Imperia-Oneglia *359*

Bontà Nascoste, Lerici *67*

Bar-Ristorante Da Marilena,
Gavenola *348*

Busciun, Castel Vittorio *393*

C

Ca' del Moro, Finale
Ligure/Olle *314*

Ca' di Gòsita, Gòsita/Né *155*

Ca' Du Luasso, Lavagna *148*

Ca' Peo, Leivi *274*

Caffè Defilla, Chiavari *135, 141*

Caffè degli Specchi, Genoa *224*

Cantine Sanremesi,
San Remo *378*

Casa della Panizza, Savona *295*

Chez Lino, Ventimiglia *383*

Chiesa, Finale Ligure *317*

Ciak Wine & Food,
Monterosso *96*

Colle del Telegrafo,
Riomaggiore *89*

Colomba d'Oro, Triora *391*

D

Da Fiorella Ristorante-Bar,
Nicola di Ortonovo *71*

Da Lino, Recco *189*

Da Maria, Vessalico *330*

Da Ö Pescôu, Lavagna *149*

Da ö Vittorio, Recco *189*

Da Rina, Genoa *224*

Da Silvio, Sarzana *74*

Do Spadin, Camogli/
Punta Chiappa *172*

E

Edo Bar, Sori *213*

El Portico, Portofino *182*

F

Farinata Santa Zita, Genoa *262*

Farinata, Genoa *246*

G

Garibaldi Cafè, Genoa *276*

Girarosto da Paolo,
Bradia/Sarzana *73*

Gli Ulivi, Riomaggiore *89*

H

Hostaria del Pellegrino,
Imperia-Porto Maurizio *365*

Hostaria della Luna Piena,
Santo Stefano d'Aveto *128*

Hosteria Sutta Ca', Albenga *333*

Hotel della Posta 1906,
Torriglia *283*

Hotel Marinella, Nervi/
Genoa *281*

Hotel-Ristorante Italia,
Castel Vittorio *393*

Hotel-Ristorante Santo Spirito,
Molini di Triora *390*

I

I Pescatori, Lerici *67*

Il Ciliegio, Beo/Monterosso *95*

Il Minatore, Né *154*

Il Mulino del Cibus, Molicciara/
Castelnuovo Magra *64*

Il Portico, Chiavari *138*

Il Ristoro dei Grimaldi,
Genoa *226*

Il San Lorenzo, Santa
Margherita Ligure *205*

L

L'Oasi, Imperia-Porto
Maurizio *365*

La Baita, Borghetto
d'Arroscia *348*

La Brinca, Né *153, 274*

La Cantina del Polpo,
Sestri Levante *160*

La Cantina di Colombo,
Genoa *227*

La Capanna da Bacì,
Apricale *394*

La Casetta, Avegno *216*

La Cucina di Nonna Nina, San
Rocco di Camogli *196, 274*

La Focacceria, Recco *193*

La Palma, Santa Margherita
Ligure *204*

La Paranza, Santa
  Margherita Ligure *205*

La Pia Centenaria, La Spezia *100*

La Pizzaccia, Portovenere *110*

La Rampa, Dolceacqua *396*

La Taverna di Colombo,
  Genoa *226*

La Terrazza di Milly, Genoa *276*

La Veranda, Tavarone *117*

Le Cantine Squarciafico,
  Genoa *224*

Le Rune, Genoa *276*

Locanda della Marchesa,
  Nicola di Ortonovo *70*

Locanda Piemontese,
  Calice Ligure *311*

Luchin, Chiavari *136*

M

Maggiorino, San Remo *378*

Manuelina, Recco *189,193*

Marcellino Pane e Vino,
  Montemarcello *70*

N

Nuovo Piccolo Mondo,
  San Remo *379*

O

Ö Bansin, Rapallo *184*

Ombre Rosse, Genoa *225*

Ostaja San Vincenzo, Genoa *246*

Ostaja, Staglieno/Genoa *274, 282*

Osteria all'Inferno, La Spezia *99*

Osteria Cu de Beu, Savona *295*

Osteria dei Matetti, Alassio *325*

Osteria del Portico,
  Castel Vittorio *393*

Osteria Du Chicchinettu,
  Varese Ligure *120*

Osteria Enoteca Baccicin du
  Caru, Mele/Genoa *270, 274*

Osteria Tabacchi Da Drin,
  Capreno/Sori *214*

P

Party House Enoteca con
  Cucina, La Spezia *100*

Pian del Sole, Sassello *290*

Pino, Noli *320*

Polpo Mario, Sestri Levante *160*

Puny, Portofino *182*

Puppo Farinata e…, Albenga *333*

R

Ripa Del Sole, Riomaggiore *87*

Ristorante Capannina Ciccio,
  Bocca di Magra *58*

Ristorante Da Angelo,
  Recco *189, 193*

Ristorante Da ö Vittorio,
  Recco *276*

Ristorante del Mulino Da Drin,
  Punta Chiappa/Camogli *172*

Ristorante Enoteca Ostricheria
  Bacchus, San Remo *379*

Ristorante Ferrando, Serra
  Riccò/Genoa *276*

Ristorante Hotel Terme,
  Madonna Assunta/
  Castel Vittorio *392*

Ristorante La Familiare,
  Albissola Marina *288*

Ristorante Lorenzina,
  Case di Nava *373*

Ristorante Nestin, Frazione
  Canepa/Sori *215*

Ristorante-Bar Monesteroli,
  Riomaggiore *89*

Ristorante-Bar Santuario di Montenero, Riomaggiore *89*

Ristorante-Focacceria Manuelina, Recco *276*

Ristorante La Margherita, Sesta Godano *117*

Rosa, Camogli *172, 274*

Ruscin Antica Trattoria 1893, Genoa Bavari *276*

S

San Matteo Osteria, Genoa *238*

Santuario Nostra Signora di Soviore, Monterosso *95*

Scandelin, Sori *211*

Sola Enoteca Cucina & Vino, Genoa *262*

T

Taverna del Capitano, Vernazza *94*

Taverna del Gallo Nero, Varese Ligure *119*

Tavernetta, San Remo *378*

Trattoria A Beccassa, Torriglia *283*

Trattoria A Ciassa, Aprícale *394*

Trattoria Armanda, Castelnuovo Magra *60*

Trattoria Bruxaboschi, Genoa San Desiderio *276*

Trattoria Cavour, Levanto *104*

Trattoria Cornua, Cornua/ Lumarzo *216*

Trattoria Da Ugo, Genoa *228*

Trattoria dai Pironcelli, Montemarcello *70*

Trattoria della Raibetta, Genoa *227*

Trattoria Gianni Franzi, Vernazza *94*

Trattoria Giovanna, Molini di Triora *390*

Trattoria Invexendu, Finalborgo *318*

Trattoria Iolanda, Campomorone/ Isoverde *217, 277*

Trattoria L'Alpino, Frazione Leuso/Ranzo *346*

Trattoria La Rocca, Rocca/ Santo Stefano d'Aveto *129*

Trattoria Luigina, Genoa Granarolo *277*

Trattoria Marchin, Borgonovo Ligure *124*

Trattoria Picchetto, San Pietro Vara *118*

Trattoria Rina, Genoa *277*

Trattoria Settembrin, Carasco/Graveglia *132*

Trattoria Vëgia Arbâ, Genoa *263*

Trattoria Vittoria, Sassello *291*

Trattoria-Pizzeria-Bar La Lucertola, Apricale *394*

U

Ü Bucün du Preve, Noli *320*

Ü Fainottö—Da Franco, Recco *192*

Ü Giancu, San Massimo di Rapallo *203*

V

Vecchio Frantoio, Vignai/ Badalucco *389*

Vino e Farinata—Osteria con Cucina, Savona *296*

Z

Zeffirino, Genoa *274*

GOURMET FOOD

Bakeries, caffè (coffee roasters and coffee shops), delicatessens, ice cream, pastry, chocolate and candy shops, and shops making or selling salted anchovies, cheese, dry goods, olive oils, pasta fresh or dry, salami and cured meats, beer and cookware.

A

A Bütega du Caffè, Albenga *334*

A Cuvea Gelateria, Alassio *326*

Ä Posa-a, Portovenere *110*

Agriturismo Il Castagno, San Bernardo/Mendatica *373*

Al Forno di Albaro, Genoa *266*

Alimentari Andrea de Vincenzi, Varese Ligure *120*

Alimentari L'Anfora, Perinaldo *398*

Alimentari La Posta, Pigna *392*

Alimentari Panetteria Garoscio Cinzia e Silvia, Dolceacqua *396*

Alimentari Rovere, Gavenola *330, 347*

Alter Ego, Alassio *326*

Amaretti Astengo, Savona *297*

Amaretti Cavo, Genoa *263*

Amaretti Giacobbe, Sassello *292*

Amaretti Virginia, Sassello *291*

Anfossi Azienda Agraria, Bastia d'Albenga *339, 341*

Angiolino Asplanato, Triora *392*

Antica Drogheria Ferrea, Genoa *228*

Antica Drogheria M. Torielli, Genoa *229*

Antica Pasticceria Lino Rossi, Sassello *290*

Antica Salumeria Elena e Mirco, Molicciara/ Castelnuovo Magra *61*

Antica Tripperia la Casana, Genoa *230*

Antico Biscottificio della Foce, Genoa *264*

Antico Caffè, Pasticceria Balzola, Alassio *326*

Antico Forno, Torriglia *283*

Antico Frantoio Sommariva, Albenga *338*

Antico Salumificio Castiglione, Castiglione Chiavarese *134*

Apicoltura Burgum Mielizia, Finalborgo *318*

Apicoltura Dino Gastaldi, Cosio d'Arroscia *372*

Apicoltura Ribaditi, Santa Maria/Calice al Cornoviglio *116*

Arcobaleno Gelateria, Lerici *68*

Armando—Pasticceria/ Gelateria, La Spezia *101*

Armanino, Genoa *231*

Attilio Noceti, Paggi/ Carasco *37, 133*

Azienda Agricola Apiario Benedettino, Finale Ligure Pia *314*

Azienda Agricola Fratelli Benedetti, Leca d'Albenga *339, 341*

Azienda Agricola Jole Buscaglia, Calizzano *38, 312*

Azienda Agricola La Giara, Imperia-Porto Maurizio *365*

Azienda Agricola Le Rattatuie, Cembrano *118*

Azienda Agricola Mooretti, Allegrezze/Santo Stefano d'Aveto *127*

Azienda Agricola Sacco, Prà *279*

B

Baj Pasticceria, Rapallo *185*

Bajeicò, Portovenere *110*

Balletin Pescheria,
Sestri Levante *161*

Bar Besio, Savona *297*

Bar Breakfast, Imperia-
Porto Maurizio *366*

Bar Centrale, Finalborgo *318*

Bar Centrale, Riomaggiore *90*

Bar Colombo, Santa
Margherita Ligure *206*

Bar Crovetto, Sori *213*

Bar Gelateria Davide,
Chiavari *141*

Bar Gelateria Lamia,
Portovenere *110*

Bar Gelateria Verdi, Chiavari *144*

Bar Gina, Sassello *292*

Bar Jole, Sassello *293*

Bar Pasticceria Festival,
San Remo *382*

Bar Pippi, San Rocco
di Camogli, *199*

Bar Vittoria, Santa
Margherita Ligure *211*

Bardi, Santa Margherita
Ligure *205*

Bar-Tavola Calda Levey,
Sassello *292*

Baxin, Albenga *334*

Boasi Caffè Torrefazione,
Genoa *231*

Boasi Caffè , Genoa *248*

Bottega dello Stoccafisso,
Genoa *231*

Bruciamonti, Genoa *249*

Buffa—Fabbrica Cioccolato,
Confetteria, Genoa *249*

Bugliani Panificio
Pizzeria, Sarzana *76*

C

Café Pasticceria San
Lorenzo, Alassio *328*

Caffè Bocchia, Chiavari *139* /
Rapallo *185* / Recco *194*
/ Lavagna *149* / Sestri
Levante *162*

Caffè Costituzionale, Sarzana *74*

Caffè Ducale, San Remo *381*

Caffè Due Merli, Savona *298*

Caffè Gelateria Balilla,
Genoa *247*

Caffè Le Clarisse, Levanto *105*

Caffè Paris, Ventimiglia *386*

Caffè Pasticceria Mangini,
Genoa *253*

Caffè Piccardo, Imperia-
Oneglia *359*

Caffè del Borgo, Finalborgo *318*

Caffè Giovanacci, Finale
Ligure *318*

Caffè-Pasticceria Ferro,
Finale Ligure *317*

Canevello — Salumeria
Sottoripa, Genoa *233*

Cappa Pasticceria, Alassio *328*

Casa del Caffè, Bordighera *376*

Casa del Caffè — Caffè 3
Moretti, Savona *299*

Casa del Cioccolato, Genoa *234*

Casa del Gelato, Albenga *335*

Caseificio Val d'Aveto,
Rezzoaglio *126*

Centro Salagione di
Monterosso, Monterosso *39*

Chicco Caffè , Genoa *250*

Chiesa, Finale Ligure *314, 317*

Choco Emotion, Camogli *176*

Ciak Wine & Food, Monterosso *96*

Cioccolateria Dolce… più Dolce, La Spezia *102*

Claretta Panificio Grissinificio, Genoa *234*

Confetteria Rossi, Genoa *255*

Cooperativa Casearia Val di Vara, Varese Ligure *118*

Cooperativa Pescatori, Camoglì *176*

Coopertiva San Pietro Vara, Varese Ligure *120*

Copello Pasticceria, Chiavari *140*

Cremeria Ciarapìca, Genoa *265*

Cremeria Colombo, Genoa *250*

Creuza de Mà di M. Peirano e C., Arenzano *279*

D

Da Claudio e Adele—Formaggi e Salumi, Albenga *335*

Da Gianni, Savona *294*

Da Nicco, Ruta di Camogli *197*

Danielli, Genoa *250*

De Regibus, Genoa *256*

Diego Panetta, Serra Riccò *279*

Dolci Delizie, Uscio *216*

Drogheria Giovanni Ameri, Chiavari *37, 139*

E

Enoteca Ingaunia DOC, Albenga *335*

EVO Oleo Granoteca, Genoa *251*

F

Fabbrica cioccolato Zuccotti, Genoa *269*

Federico Parodi Salumificio, Sant'Olcese/Genoa *282*

Fiordiponti, Santa Margherita Ligure *206*

Fiorella d'Amore, Genoa *246*

Forno Papalia, Pigna *392*

Francesco Ratto, Prà *277*

Franco Casoni, Chiavari *146*

Fratelli Centanaro, Genoa *252*

Fratelli Klainguti Bar Pasticceria, Genoa *235*

G

Gelateria Amedeo, Genoa *265*

Gelateria Artigiana Costa Giulio, Genoa *265*

Gelateria Baciollo, Sestri Levante *161*

Gelateria Bar Gelmo, Loano *319*

Gelateria Cavassa, Recco *195*

Gelateria Festival des Glaces, Albenga *336*

Gelateria Frigidarium, Rapallo *187*

Gelateria GROM, Genoa *252*

Gelateria Guarino, Genoa *257*

Gelateria Il Dattero, Finale Ligure *317*

Gelateria Il Porticciolo, Levanto *106*

Gelateria K2, Sestri Levante *163*

Gelateria Profumo, Genoa *238*

Gelateria Zico, Corniglia *93*

Gemmi Pasticceria Bar Confetteria, Sarzana *75*

Gerolamo Pernigotti— Gamalero, Genoa *253*

Gran Caffè Tritone Gelateria, Sestri Levante *165*

Granbazzar, La Spezia *103*

Granite/Gelati, Sori *213*

Grigiomar, Savona *294*

I

I Formaggi del Boschetto,
Bastia d'Albenga *339, 341*

I Maestri del Pesto,
Mele/Genoa *280*

Il Forno di Germano,
Varese Ligure *120*

Il Giardino dei Semplici,
Chiavari *151*

Il Laboratorio del Pesto,
Levanto *107*

Il Mattarello Pazzo, Bolano *78*

Il Mulino di Sassello,
Sassello *291*

Il Pesto di Prà di Bruzzone e
Ferrari, Prà/Genoa *280*

Il Pesto Più di Prà di
Rebuffo Fassone Ramella,
Prà/Genoa *280*

Il Sangiorgino, Cervo *352*

Il Sottobosco, Tiglieto *196*

L

L'Aromatica, Genoa *264*

L'Artigiana del Fungo,
Sassello *292*

L'Artigiano del Cioccolato,
La Spezia *101*

L'Isola delle cose buone,
La Spezia *102*

La Bimare Torrefazione,
Sestri Levante *161*

La Bottega dei Funghi,
Calizzano *312*

La Bottega dei Piaceri,
Camogli *176*

La Bottega dei Sestieri,
Rapallo *185*

La Bottega del Caffè F.lli
Pasqualini, Savona *298*

La Bottega del Caffè
Pasqualini, Alassio *326*

La Bottega del Formaggio,
Chiavari *139*

La Bottega del Pesto,
Nervi, Genoa *281*

La Bottega di Angelamaria,
Molini di Triora *391*

La Bottega di Mastro
Antonucci, Camogli *175*

La Boutique del Pane
Mondino, Ventimiglia *386*

La Cantina Levantese di S.
Lagaxio, Levanto *52, 105*

La Casa del Caffè ,
Bordighera *376*

La Familiare, Finale Ligure *317*

La Genovese Caffè e
Dintorni, Albenga *336*

La Strega di Triora, Triora *391*

La Torrigiana, Torriglia *283*

Latteria Bavari, Genoa *268*

Le Due Lune, Sarzana *75*

Le Gramole Olioteca,
Genoa *234, 330*

M

Macelleria Angelo Torrazza,
Campomorone/Gazzolo *217*

Macelleria Paolucci, San
Rocco di Camogli *198*

Macelleria-Salumeria
Giacobbe, Sassello *291*

Magnani Salumi e
Formaggi, Ortonovo *63*

Marco Ballestra, Ventimiglia *383*

Marco Favero, Cosio
d'Arroscia *372*

Mario Ferrando, Prà/Genoa *279*

Mario Mattoli, Chiavari *134*

Maura Ragazzoni, San Remo
(covered market) *378*

Mazzini-Graglia Salumeria
Rosticceria, Rapallo *187*

Minuto Caffè, Savona *294*

Moretti, Savona *299*

N

Non Solo Vino, Riomaggiore *90*

Nonsolofunghi, Sassello *292*

Nonsolopizza, Noli *321*

O

Opera Magé, Arma di Taggia/
San Remo *380, 388*

P

Panarello, Genoa *254*

Panetteria Bellerio Rolando,
San Remo *381*

Panetteria Dallorto Paolo,
Ventimiglia *386*

Panetteria Fratelli Ferrari,
Pieve di Teco *372*

Panificio Battalini & Ginocchio,
San Pietro Vara *118*

Panificio Cacciò, Gavenola *348*

Panificio Cudì dei Fratelli
Lorenzini, Ortonovo *63*

Panificio Fiore, Genoa *239*

Panificio Gandolfo Bruna,
Borgomaro *371*

Panificio Lippi, Ruta
di Camogli *200*

Panificio Maccarini, San
Rocco di Camogli *200*

Panificio Pasticceria Fratelli
Terarolli, Luni *63*

Panificio Pasticceria
Pignone Giorgio & C.,
Pieve di Teco *372*

Panificio Patrone, Genoa *239*

Panificio Rizzoli Marcello,
La Spezia *103*

Panificio Rocco Rizzo,
Camogli *178*

Panificio Rosy, Riomaggiore *90*

Panificio Tosi, Sestri
Levante *164*

Panificio Tumioli, Genoa *239*

Panificio-Pasticceria
Moltedo, Recco *190*

Panifico Sanguineti, Né *158*

Paolo Calcagno, Celle Ligure *279*

Parmiggiani Fratelli,
Varese Ligure *120*

Pasta Fresca Dasso, Rapallo *187*

Pasta Fresca Franzi,
Lerici *69, 280*

Pasticceria Alimentari Chiesa,
Santo Stefano d'Aveto *129*

Pasticceria Bar Budicin,
Ruta di Camogli *197*

Pasticceria Bar Riviera,
Recco *195*

Pasticceria Besio, Savona *300*

Pasticceria Bianchi, Levanto *107*

Pasticceria Caffetteria
Monteverde, Lavagna *149*

Pasticceria Gelateria da
Maurizio e Charlie,
Imperia-Porto Maurizio *366*

Pasticceria Grana, Albenga *337*

Pasticceria Guano, Torriglia *283*

Pasticceria La Crêpe, Noli *321*

Pasticceria Laura, Monterosso *96*

Pasticceria Magenta, Genoa *257*

Pasticceria Poldo,
Pontedecimo/Genoa *280*

Pasticceria Primavera,
San Remo *381*

Pasticceria Profumo, Genoa *240*

Pasticceria Racca, San
Bartolomeo al Mare *353*

Pasticceria Revello, Camogli *177*

Pasticceria Rossignotti,
Sestri Levante *163*

Pasticceria San Romolo,
San Remo *381*

Pasticceria Svizzera, Genoa *268*

Pasticceria Tagliafico, Genoa *255*

Pasticceria Valeria, Savona *301*

Pastificio Artigianale Fiore,
Graveglia/Carasco *132*

Pastificio Fontana, Albenga *336*

Pastificio Novella, Sori *213*

Pastificio Prato, Chiavari *144*

Pastificio Santa Rita, Né *157*

Pastorino, Calice Ligure *311*

Perrone Tabò Maria,
Calizzano *312*

Pescheria Cerisola
Clelia, Noli *320*

Pescheria Delmonte "U
Balincio", Imperia-
Oneglia *362*

Pescheria Nello, Celle
Ligure *289*

Pescheria Pinto Porta
Molino, Albenga *338*

Pestarino, Santa Margherita
Ligure *206*

Piccolo Birrificio, Apricale *395*

Pinamonti, Santa
Margherita Ligure *210*

Pinotto, Calizzano *38, 313*

Prà Basilico e Pesto,
Prà/Genoa *280*

Primula, Camogli *177*

R

Raffo Francesca Alimentari,
Dolceacqua *396*

Riccardo Gaggero,
Mele/Genoa *279*

Roberto Casotti, Prà/Genoa *279*

Romanengo fu Stefano,
Genoa *241*

Romeo Viganotti di Alessandro
Boccardo, Genoa *243*

Roncagliolo e Simonetti,
Rapallo *188*

Rosticceria Castelletto,
Genoa *257*

S

Salsamenteria Antica,
Savona *302*

Salumeria Bellini, San Remo *381*

Salumeria Crespi, San Remo *380*

Salumeria Re, Imperia-
Porto Maurizio *366*

Salumificio Cabella,
Sant'Olcese/Genoa *282*

Santamaria & C.,
Calizzano *38, 312*

Sciolè Mirella, San Remo *380*

Seghezzo, Santa Margherita
Ligure *210*

Serafina Artigiana
Alimentari, Genoa *243*

Stampetta-Panificio
Pasticceria, La Spezia *103*

Superfrutto Gelateria,
Savona *302*

T

Terre di Mare, Finale
Ligure/Alassio *317, 329*

Torrefazione Caffè Brasil,
Imperia-Oneglia *362*

Torrefazione Caffè
Pagliettini, Rapallo *188*

Torrefazione Caffè Ugo
Romoli, Genoa *268*

Torrefazione Elena,
San Remo *382*

Torrefazione F.lli Pasqualini,
San Remo/Villanova
d'Albenga *340, 349*

Tossini, Recco *192*

Tuttogelato, Imperia-
Oneglia *363*

U

Ü Fainottö—Da Franco,
Recco *192*

Usai Pasquale Coltivatore
Diretto, Corona/Stella *303*

V

Vedova Romanengo, Genoa *243*

Vini Liquori e Funghi
Pareti Biagio, Santo
Stefano d'Aveto *128*

OLIVE OIL MAKERS

A

A Maccia, Borgo/Ranzo *347*

Abbo Srl Azienda Olearia,
Bevera *387*

Agriturismo La Bicocca,
Rapallo *188*

Alberto Marvaldi,
Borgomaro *371*

Anfossi Azienda Agraria,
Bastia d'Albenga *339*

Anfosso A e C, Chiusavecchia *306*

Azienda Agricola Agriturismo
Dinoabbo, Lucinasco *371*

Azienda Agricola Allavena
Maria Giovanna, Pigna *392*

Azienda Agricola Allavena
Massimo, Pigna *392*

Azienda Agricola Bronda Renzo,
Cantone/Vendone *346*

Azienda Agricola Damiano,
Chiusavecchia *370*

Azienda Agricola e Agriturismo
Il Nostro Oliveto, Bastia
d'Albenga *341*

Azienda Agricola Giordano
Valerio, Dolcedo *367*

Azienda Agricola Giuseppe
Cotta, Pantasina/
Vasia *306, 368*

Azienda Agricola Il Frantoio,
Ville San Sebastiano/
Borgomaro *371*

Azienda Agricola La Giara,
Imperia-Porto Maurizio *365*

Azienda Agricola La Pietra
del Focolare, Ortonovo *66*

Azienda Agricola La Rocca
di San Nicolao, Gazzelli/
Chiusanico *370*

Azienda Agricola Orseggi, Santa
Giulia di Lavagna *77, 150*

Azienda Agricola San
Damiano, Stellanello *349*

Azienda Agricola Valle Ostilia,
Villa Faraldi *306, 353*

Azienda Agricola Varaldo
Elena, Villa Faraldi *353*

B

Baglietto e Secco, Villanova
d'Albenga *306, 340, 349*

Benza Frantoiano Olio
Extravergine, Dolcedo,
Imperia *306, 366*

Biofattoria Azienda
Agricola Gamba Patrizio,
Foa/Apricale *395*

C

Cà Bianca di Francesco Bruzzo, Chiavari *77, 146*

Casa Olearia Taggiasca, Prati e Pescine/Arma di Taggia *389*

Cooperativa Agricola Lavagnina, Lavagna *151*

Cooperativa Olivicola di Arnasco, Arnasco *306, 346*

D

Danila Pisano, Apricale *395, 399*

Dino Abbo, Lucinasco *307*

Domenico Ramoino, Sarola *370*

Domenico Ruffino, Varigotti *321*

F

Frantoio Artigianale Magnone, Finale Ligure Pia *313*

Frantoio Artigianale Mantello Mauro, Albareto/ Stellanello *349*

Frantoio Bo, Sestri Levante *77, 166*

Frantoio da olive Bestoso Domenico, Borgonuovo/ Stellanello *349*

Frantoio da olive Rossi Simone, San Damiano/Stellanello *349*

Frantoio di Sant'Agata d'Oneglia, Sant'Agata d'Oneglia *307, 364*

Frantoio Elena Luigi, Chiappa/ San Bartolomeo al Mare *353*

Frantoio Gaziello, Ventimiglia *386*

Frantoio Ghiglione Giuseppe, Dolcedo *367*

Frantoio Giobatta Panizzi, Badalucco *390*

Frantoio Marco, Leca d'Albenga *341*

Frantoio U Vescu, Borello/ Diano Arentino *354*

Fratelli Carli, Imperia-Oneglia *357*

G

Gian Battista Fasolo, Gazzelli/Chiusanico *370*

Giovanni Maltini, Castel Vittorio *393*

Gocce d'Olio, Villa Faraldi *353*

I

Il Colle degli Ulivi, Sant'Angelo/Diano Marina *354*

L

La Baita, Gazzo/Borghetto d'Arroscia *306*

La Mola, Molini di Prelà *367*

Lucchi e Guastalli, Vincinella *77, 78*

M

Massimo Solari, Chiavari *77, 133*

O

Oleificio G. Boeri, Arma di Taggia *388*

Oleificio Polla Nicolò, Loano *319* and Savona *299*

Olio Anfosso, Chiusavecchia *371*

Olio Ardoino, Pontedassio *369*

Olio Carli, Imperia-Orneglia *357*

Olio Roi, Montalto Ligure/ Badalucco *307, 389*

P

Paolo Cassini, Isolabona *395*

Paolo Pellegrino, Borgomaro *371*

Pierandrea Costa, Diano Castello *354*

Pietro Isnardi, Pontedassio *369*

Pino Gino, Missano/Castiglione Chiavarese *55, 77, 134*

R

Ranise Azienda Agroalimentari, Imperia *305, 307, 363*

Roberto Rota, Giuncheo/ Camporosso *397*

Rùe de Zerli, Zerli/Né *155*

S

Saglietto Olio Agriturismo, Poggi *368*

Saguato Stefano Frantoio Olive Olio, Diano San Pietro *355*

V

Venturino Bartolomeo, Diano San Pietro *356*

WINERIES AND WINE SHOPS

A

Andrea Bruzzone, Genova-Bolzaneto *52*

Anfossi, Bastia d'Albenga *304*

Aschero Laura, Pontedassio *304*

Azienda Agricola Giacomelli, Palvotrisia/ Castelnuovo Magra *64*

Azienda Agricola Il Monticello, Bradia-Sarzana *55, 76, 79*

Azienda Agricola La Pietra del Focolare, Ortonovo *66*

Azienda Agricola La Rocca di San Nicolao, Gazzelli/ Chiusanico *305, 343, 345*

Azienda Agricola Lorenzo Ramò, Pornassio *372*

Azienda Agricola Maccario Dringenberg, San Biagio della Cima *399*

Azienda Agricola San Dalmazio, Arveglio/Albenga *305, 343, 346*

Azienda Agricola Santa Catarina, Sarzana *77*

Azienda Agricola Sommariva, Albenga *305, 343, 346*

Azienda Lupi, Pieve di Teco *372*

Azienda Vitivinicola Tenuta Anfosso, Soldano *399*

Azienda Vitivinicola-Agricola Eredi Ing. Guglierame, Pornassio *372*

Azienda Vitivinicola La Baia del Sole, Ortonovo *54, 344*

B

Bio Vio, Bastia d'Albenga *341*

Bisson, Chiavari *52, 54, 344*

Bonanni Fellegara, Riomaggiore *97*

Bonanni—Antiche Bottiglierie Genovesi, Genoa *248*

Bruna, Borgo/Ranzo *304, 342*

Buranco, Monterosso *97*

C

Cantina Case Rosse, Case Rosse *372*

Cantina Cooperativa Agricoltura Cinque Terre, Groppo/ Riomaggiore *54, 91*

Cantin-a du Púsu, Rapallo *186*

Cantine d'Italia, Rapallo *186*

Cantine del Rossese-Gajaudo, Isolabona *395*

Cantine Lunae Bosoni, Palvotrisia/Castelnuovo Magra *65*

Casanova, Finalborgo/ Sotto Ripa *319*

Cascina delle Terre Rosse, Finale Ligure *304, 313, 344*

Cascina Praiè, Colla Micheri/Andora *349*

Claudio Vio, Vendone *342, 344, 346*

Colle dei Bardellini, Bardellini/Imperia *304*

Colle Sereno, Acquetico *372*

Conte Picedi Benettini, Baccano di Arcola *79*

Cooperativa Viticoltori Ingauni, Ortovero *349*

D

Danila Pisano, Soldano *395*

Domenico Barisone Cooperativa Viticoltori Coronata, Genova-Coronata *52*

Domenico Ruffino, Varigotti *321*

Durin, Ortovero *52, 304, 343, 348*

E

Enoteca Baroni, Lerici *68*

Enoteca Bisson, Chiavari *145*

Enoteca Ciak, Monterosso *95*

Enoteca Coop Vallata di Levanto, Levanto *106*

Enoteca Il Mulino del Cibus, Molicciara/Castelnuovo Magra and Sarzana *76*

Enoteca Ingaunia DOC, Albenga *335*

Enoteca Internazionale, Monterosso *96*

Enoteca La Nicchia, Levanto *107*

Enoteca Lupi, Imperia-Oneglia *361*

Enoteca Marone, San Remo *380*

Enoteca Pubblica, Castelnuovo Magra *59*

Enoteca Re, Dolceacqua *396*

Enoteca Sola, Genoa *251*

Enoteca Sotto l'Arco, Vernazza *94*

Enoteca Susto, Genoa *235*

Enoteca Vinum, Levanto *106*

Enoteca Wine e Spirit Carpe Diem, Alassio *328*

Enzo Guglielmi, Soldano *52, 399*

F

Fèipu dei Massaretti, Bastia d'Albenga *304, 339, 341, 343*

Fiorenzo Guidi, Ranzo *347*

Foresti, Camporosso Mare *304, 398*

Forlini e Cappellini, Manarola *92*

G

Giacomo Alberti, Pontedassio *370*

I

Il Monticello, Bradia/ Sarzana *55, 76, 79*

Innocenzo Turco, Quiliano *290*

L

La Baia del Sole, Luni *66*

La Cantina Levantese di S. Lagaxio, Levanto *52, 105*

La Colombiera, Castelnuovo
Magra *54, 66*

La Felce di Marcesini
Andrea, Ortonovo *66*

La Pietra del Focolare,
Ortonovo *55*

La Polenza di Lorenzo
Casté, Corniglia *55, 93*

La Polenza di Maria Rita
Rezzano, Vernazza *94*

La Vecchia Cantina,
Salea d'Albenga *305,
339, 341, 342, 345*

Laura Aschero, Pontedassio *370*

Le Due Lune, Sarzana *75*

Le Petraie, Pieve di Teco *304*

Le Rocche del Gatto, Salea
d'Albenga *305, 339, 341*

Luciano Capellini, Volastra/
Riomaggiore *54, 91*

Luigi Calvini, San Remo *382*

Lunae Bosoni, Ortonovo *55, 344*

Lupi, Pieve di Teco *305, 343, 344*

M

Maccia, Ranzo *347*

Marcello Calleri, Salea
d'Albenga *341*

Maria Donata Bianchi,
Diano Castello *354*

Massimo Alessandri, Costa
Parrocchia/Ranzo *304, 342, 347*

Migone Enoteca, Genoa *238*

Molinari & Pasini—M&P,
Riomaggiore *97*

Monna Bianca, Lavagna *150*

N

Natale Sassarini, Monterosso *97*

Non Solo Vino, Riomaggiore *90*

O

Ö Caratello, Lavagna *150*

Ottaviano Lambruschi,
Palvotrisia/Castelnuovo
Magra *55, 65, 345*

P

Paolo Ruffino, Varigotti *321*

Pino Gino, Missano/Castiglione
Chiavarese *55, 134*

Poggio dei Gorleri,
Diano Marina *355*

R

Riccardo Bruna, Ranzo *347*

Ruffino, Varigotti *52*

S

Santa Caterina, Sarzana
55, 77, 345

Santamaria & C.,
Calizzzano *38, 312*

T

Tenuta Giuncheo,
Camporosso *305, 345, 397*

Terre Bianche, Arcagna/
Dolceacqua *305, 397*

Turco Innocenzo, Quiliano *305*

V

Vineria, Santa Margherita
Ligure *210*

Vini Liquori e Funghi
Pareti Biagio, Santo
Stefano d'Aveto *128*

Vio Claudio, Vendone *305*

W

Walter De Battè,
  Riomaggiore *52, 54, 92*

ABOUT THE AUTHOR

....

David Downie is an American author and journalist who divides his time between France and Italy. For the last 20 years he has been writing about European food, culture and travel for magazines and newspapers worldwide. His books include *Enchanted Liguria: A Celebration of the Culture, Lifestyle and Food of the Italian Riviera*; *Cooking the Roman Way: Authentic Recipes from the Home Cooks and Trattorias of Rome*; *The Irreverent Guide to Amsterdam*; and *Paris, Paris: Journey into the City of Light*. His political thriller, *Paris City of Night*, will be published in fall 2008. *Hit the Road Jacques: A Skepitcal Pilgrimage Across Burgundy* is due out in spring 2009, as is Downie's second Terroir Guide, this one to Rome. Please visit David Downie's website at www.davidddownie.com.

ABOUT THE PHOTOGRAPHER

....

Alison Harris has worked throughout the world shooting photos for travel books, cookbooks, advertising campaigns, book covers, and magazine stories. Her latest books, *Markets of Paris*, *The Pâtisseries of Paris*, and *Chic Shopping Paris*, are published by The Little Bookroom.